W9-AAT-119

Building Web Applications with UML

Second Edition

Jim Conallen

Addison-Wesley

Boston • San Francisco • New York • Toronto • Montreal
London • Munich • Paris • Madrid
Capetown • Sydney • Tokyo • Singapore • Mexico City

Many of the designations used by manufacturers and sellers to distinguish their products are claimed as trademarks. Where those designations appear in this book, and Addison-Wesley was aware of a trademark claim, the designations have been printed with initial capital letters or in all capitals.

The author and publisher have taken care in the preparation of this book, but make no expressed or implied warranty of any kind and assume no responsibility for errors or omissions. No liability is assumed for incidental or consequential damages in connection with or arising out of the use of the information or programs contained herein.

The publisher offers discounts on this book when ordered in quantity for bulk purchases and special sales. For more information, please contact:

U.S. Corporate and Government Sales
(800) 382-3419
corpsales@pearsontechgroup.com

For sales outside of the United States, please contact:

International Sales
(317) 581-3793
international@pearsontechgroup.com
Visit Addison-Wesley on the Web: *www.awprofessional.com*

Library of Congress Cataloging-in-Publication Data

Conallen, Jim.
    Building Web applications with UML / Jim Conallen. — 2nd ed.
        p.   cm. — (The Addison-Wesley object-technology series)
    Includes bibliographical references and index.
    ISBN 0-201-73038-3 (alk. paper)
    1. Web site development. 2. Application software—Development. 3. UML (Computer science)   I. Title. II. Series.

TK5105.888.C654 2002
005.7'2--dc21   2002074575

Copyright © 2003 by Pearson Education, Inc.

All rights reserved. No part of this publication may be reproduced, stored in a retrieval system, or transmitted, in any form, or by any means, electronic, mechanical, photocopying, recording, or otherwise, without the prior consent of the publisher. Printed in the United States of America. Published simultaneously in Canada.

For information on obtaining permission for use of material from this work, please submit a written request to:

Pearson Education, Inc.
Rights and Contracts Department
75 Arlington Street, Suite 300
Boston, MA 02116
Fax: (617) 848-7047

ISBN 0-201-73038-3
Text printed on recycled paper
1 2 3 4 5 6 7 8 9 10—MA—0605040302
First printing, September 2002

To the memory of my father,
James Conallen, Jr.

Contents

Appendices

Foreword

In a recent interview of James Gosling, the primary author of Java, James discusses the challenges of developing complex software-intensive systems, noting that "when you have very large pieces of software, most of the tools look at the individual lines of code as text. It is often extremely powerful to look not at individual pieces of code but at a system as a whole." The interview goes on to explain that "instead of editing code in the form of text, as it is typically done, Gosling is working on a way to allow code to be edited as a visual model."[1]

The entire history of software engineering is marked by the rise in levels of abstraction, as is manifest in our programming languages, our platforms, and our methods. Abstraction is important, because this is the primary mechanism whereby humans grapple with complexity. The graphical modeling of software is simply another advance in abstraction, enabling developers to visualize, specify, construct, document, and reason about their systems.

The visual modeling of Web-centric systems is precisely the contribution that Jim Conallen has made to the industry. I first became exposed to Jim's work in 1998 when he presented an early paper on the topic. By that time, the unification efforts that ultimately led to the Unified Modeling Language (UML) were well under way, and it was an explicit goal on our part to be able to model Web-centric systems. We had the essential elements necessary to model such systems, but Jim brought to the table an exact way to do so, building on the UML's extensibility mechanisms.

It's been a delight to watch Jim's work grow and mature over the years. The combination of injecting his approach into a commercial modeling tool and Jim's personal involvement with a variety of interesting Web-centric systems has led us all to discover

---

1. Berger, M., "JavaOne: Gosling Hits 'Jackpot' with Futuristic Tools." *InfoWorld,* March 20, 2002.

things we did not know we did not know. That, plus the ascendance of platforms such as J2EE, have made Jim's modeling work even more relevant.

As such, I'm delighted to have the opportunity to introduce the second edition of Jim's book, *Building Web Applications with UML*. The world of Web development has changed in subtle ways since the first edition, primarily marked by our better understanding of what a sound Web-centric architecture looks like and the development process that leads us to that architecture. Both of these changes are reflected in this new edition: Jim addresses the most current developments in J2EE as well as work on the Rational Unified Process that is specifically targeted to the Web.

It has been a pleasure to work with Jim directly the past few years. He is a skilled modeler and architect, and has that rare combination of being an articulate geek, one who really groks the technology but can also communicate what he knows in an approachable fashion.

I think you'll really like this edition; I certainly did.

Grady Booch
Chief Scientist
Rational Software Corporation

Preface

The first edition of this book hit the streets late in 1999. For the most part, it was based on my experiences in developing Active Server Page–based applications for the retail and healthcare industries. I was an independent consultant then, but shortly before finishing the book I joined Rational Software Corporation. Working for Rational has given me the opportunity to visit and to work with many organizations that are in the process of building Web-centric applications. And I've seen everything, from well-managed teams producing top-quality software to chaotic teams desperately seeking the right guidance to a few others that still seem to be in denial.

In the two years since the publication of the first edition, I've also seen the rise of the J2EE platform, and have to say that since then most of my Web application development experience has been with J2EE architectures. As a result, most of the material in this second edition is oriented toward the Java environment. This doesn't mean that .NET developers, or even Cold Fusion and PHP developers, can't build applications with the guidance in this book. You can. It's just that the majority of the examples in the design and implementation chapters, and in the reference applications, are written for JavaServer Page–based applications.

The ideas in this book and in the previous edition are all the result of a desire to combine my object-oriented skills and the area of Web application development. I had little problem applying use case analysis, and it wasn't until I started creating analysis and design models that I realized things were going to get difficult. When creating a Web application, my conceptual focus was always on the Web page; and my idea of a model kept revolving around the concept of a site map. I knew that the navigation paths throughout the system were incredibly important to understanding the application and that any system model would have to include them.

My earliest attempts at modeling Web applications started with Rumbaugh's OMT (Object Modeling Technique), and later when UML (Unified Modeling Language) version 0.8 was publicly released, I began to apply it. I knew that for any modeling technique to be useful it needed to capture both the relevant semantics of Web-specific elements (e.g., Web pages and hyperlinks) and their relation to the back-end elements of the system (e.g., middle-tier objects and databases). At the time, I found both OMT and UML inadequate to express the things I thought were important in a Web application.

Being a somewhat successful object practitioner and engineer, I jumped to the conclusion that a whole new development methodology and notation was needed. After all, if the existing methods and notation didn't have what I needed, then the obvious solution was to invent one. This, of course, is a trap into which many of us in the software industry fall. In my free time, I started to draft new graphical and semantic ways to represent Web application architectures. Proud of my work, I began showing it to two of my colleagues—Joe Befumo and Gerald Ruldolph, both experienced object practitioners. Their immediate reaction was, Why? I tried to explain the issues involved with Web application development and the need for visually expressing their designs. Still, everyone I spoke with continued to think that developing a new method and notation was overkill.

I started to rethink what I was doing. I wasn't stuck up enough to think that I was right and everyone else was wrong; I had more homework to do. I reexamined my original needs: to express Web application designs at the appropriate level of abstraction and detail, and most important, as a part of the rest of the system's design. Because UML was taking the industry by storm, I realized that anything I did would have to work with UML.

So I went back to UML; this time it was in version 0.91, and a new concept was included—stereotypes. At first I was clueless as to what a stereotype was. The UML specification is not the easiest reading, after all. It was long and difficult, but I knew that any success in the area of modeling Web applications had to come from this direction. Eventually, I started to understand what was meant by stereotyping and the other extension mechanisms: tagged values and constraints. I was finally starting to see a light at the end of the tunnel.

I now had a mechanism with which I could introduce new semantics into the UML grammar, without disturbing the existing semantics. I always knew the key was to provide a consistent and coherent way to model Web-specific elements at the right level of abstraction with the models of the rest of the system. The UML extension mechanism provided me with the framework to do so.

The next step was to start defining the extension by creating stereotypes, tagged values, and constraints. The ability to use custom icons in diagrams with stereotyped elements went a long way to ease my concern for intuitive diagrams. Also Rational Rose, my visual modeling tool of choice, had just introduced a way to use your own stereotypes in Rose models. I quickly created a set of icons for Web-page abstractions. I tried to make them consistent, mostly rectangular with the stereotype indication in the upper left corner. I used filled-in dog ears to represent pages and unfilled dog ears to denote components. Icons without dog ears typically represented contained classes, which cannot be requested directly by a Web browser. The icon for Web-page components is pretty much a copy of the icon used by the three amigos in their *Unified Modeling Language User Guide.*[1]

Looking back, I remember spending less than a day drawing the icons; I didn't spend much time on it then, since I always believed that eventually someone with a little more experience would design some meaningful icons. In the four years since then, the icons have essentially remained the same; however, a more compact version is now available as a "decoration." This edition of the book also includes examples of how I hand draw many of the icons, just to show that it is possible to model Web systems on cocktail napkins. (Really, I do a fair amount of modeling and thinking about these things at conferences.)

As the extension evolved, and as a lot of the details and inconsistencies were getting corrected, I always kept an eye out for code-generation possibilities. In my mind, the modeling technique could be validated if it was possible (in theory only) to unambiguously generate and reverse-engineer code. I even prototyped some Rose scripts that did limited forward-engineering. From that point, things proceeded at a tremendous rate. I published a white paper on the Internet and presented the topic at the 1998 Rational Users' Conference in Orlando. Grady Booch took an interest in the work and encouraged me. Addison-Wesley asked if I was interested in expanding the topic into a book. If I had only known how difficult it was going to be to write, I'm not sure that I would have agreed. I followed the original white paper with a stream of other articles for both online and print publications and started to get a regular stream of e-mail comments on the extension.

Since the publication of the first edition of this book, Rational Rose has included automation for the Web modeling that was introduced in that book. I have had the opportunity to work with some top-notch engineers throughout that process—namely, Tommy Fannon and Simon Johnston—and have a greater appreciation for what goes on under the scenes of UML round-trip engineering functionality. With their insights and the input of many others, both in and out of Rational, I believe this new edition of the book and the Web-modeling profile are even more robust and applicable to the Web-centric architectures in use today.

Who Should Read This Book?

This book is meant to introduce architects and designers of client/server systems to the issues and techniques of developing for the Web. It will give the project manager an understanding of the technologies and issues related to developing Web applications. Because this book builds on existing object-oriented (OO) methodologies and techniques, it does not attempt to introduce them. It is expected that the reader has some familiarity with OO principles and concepts and with UML in particular. It is also expected that the reader is familiar with at least one Web application architecture or environment.

---

1. Grady Booch, James Rumbaugh, and Ivar Jacobson, *The Unified Modeling Language User Guide* (Reading, MA: Addison-Wesley, 1998).

For the client/server architect, this book serves as a guide to the technologies and issues of Web applications. The systems architect needs to make decisions about which technologies are appropriate to serve business needs, as expressed by the requirements and use cases. Chapter 7 defines three major client-tier architectural patterns that can help categorize a Web application's architecture. By examining these patterns and their advantages and disadvantages, the architect can make decisions that will define the technological bounds of the application. As with any engineering discipline, the architect must consider the tradeoffs for each technology to be employed in the application architecture. With a solid understanding of the technologies available, and their consequences, an appropriate combination can be put together to best meet the needs of the business problem.

For the analyst and designer, this book introduces an extension to UML that is suitable for expressing Web application design. This extension's key goals are to

- model the appropriate artifacts (e.g., Web pages, page relationships, navigation routes, client-side scripts, server-side page generation).
- model at the appropriate level of abstraction and detail.
- enable the Web-specific elements of the model to interact with the rest of the system's elements.

The analyst/designer should be able to express the execution of the system's business logic in terms of UML models. The idea is to have one unified model of a system's business logic. In the model some of the business logic is executed by traditional server-side objects and components (e.g., middle-tier components, transaction processing monitors, databases) and some of it by Web elements (e.g., browsers, client-side scripts).

For the project manager, this book discusses the potential problems and issues of developing Web applications. It also serves as a guide to the development team members' responsibilities, activities, and roles. In addition to the analyst/designer and the architect, other roles in the development process are discussed. The project manager, being responsible for the overall health of a project, needs a clear understanding of all the roles and responsibilities of the people involved with the process.

This edition of *Building Web Applications with UML* contains significantly more examples and diagrams. Responding to input from readers, I realized that they too can learn more and faster from well-constructed examples than from lengthy prose. To complement the book, I've provided two reference applications—a J2EE version of the Glossary application, which was described in the first edition, and a sample e-retail application. The e-retail application, however, contains only the client and presentation tiers because this is the focus of this book's modeling efforts.

It was my original intention to update the original ASP-based Glossary application for .NET. Because of the delayed release of the .NET tools and environment, however, I was unable to develop the application such that it properly leveraged all that the .NET environment has to offer.

Organization of This Book

This book is divided into thirteen chapters and five appendices. Conceptually it is also divided into two major parts. Chapters 1 through 5 are essentially an introduction to modeling Web application technologies and concepts. They provide the foundation on which the second part of the book is based. These chapters can be skipped by those intimately familiar with Web application architectures; however, at least a cursory reading is still suggested.

Chapter 2, Web Application Basics, is an introduction to the very basic Web application architecture. This chapter defines the term *Web application* and thereby its scope and focus. The chapter also defines the principal communication mechanisms and languages. Web application–enabling technologies are discussed. These are the infrastructures that transform simple Web sites (Web systems) into business logic execution systems.

Most of the complexities of designing Web applications are encountered when the client performs some of the business logic in the system. The technologies for allowing this are described in Chapter 3, Dynamic Clients. In this chapter, common Web technologies, such as JavaScript, applets, and ActiveX controls, are discussed. The Document Object Model (DOM) is introduced as the main object interface to client-side resources.

The basic Web application architecture, as described by the technologies in Chapters 2 and 3, are capable of delivering very useful Web applications and are especially useful for public Internet applications such as retail storefronts. For some applications, these basic ingredients are insufficient to deliver the sophisticated level of functionality required. The limiting factors are often the fundamental technologies of HTTP and HTML themselves. Web applications can be extended to encompass and use other communication and formatting technologies in addition to HTTP and HTML. In Chapter 4, Beyond HTTP and HTML, the most common of these technologies are reviewed and discussed.

The final chapter of the first part is Chapter 5, Security. No matter how nonthreatening or uninteresting an application may be, if it is on the Internet, then security is a concern. Even for intranet applications, security should be a concern. Securing a Web application is in many ways much harder than a traditional client/server application. By their very nature, Web servers are open to requests to any node on the network. The trick to making an application secure is in understanding the nature of security risks. Unfortunately, no one product or service that you can buy can guarantee a secure application. Security needs to be designed in an application, and it needs to be continually maintained in that application. New security holes in off-the-shelf software are being discovered all the time. Eventually, one of them will represent a risk to your application. By designing your system with this in mind, managing the next security risk that pops up will be easier.

The second part of this book is devoted to the process of building Web applications. It begins with Chapter 6, The Process, which reviews the entire process of developing OO systems. A sample Web application-development process is introduced.

This process is not a complete process but does provide enough detail to establish the context in which the models and artifacts of the process can be understood.

Chapter 7, Defining the Architecture, discusses the activities of defining the architecture of a Web application. Even though this activity usually follows a nearly complete examination of the requirements and use cases of the system, it is discussed earlier to help create the mind-set of developing Web applications. Because the process used here is iterative and incremental, when defining and elaborating the system's use cases, use case specifiers will have in the back of their minds a Web system architecture. In theory, this shouldn't be the case; in practice, however, and in an incremental and iterative process, it is not necessarily wrong to place use cases in the context of a specific architecture.

Chapter 8, Requirements and Use Cases, reviews the process of gathering a system's requirements and defining the system's use cases. All sorts of requirements can be gathered to help specify a particular system. One of the most useful techniques for gathering functional requirements is with use cases. *Use cases* provide a structured way to gather and express the functional requirements of a system; and they describe the interaction between a user of the system (called an actor) and the system. Use cases are textual documents that describe, in the language of the domain, what the system should do without specifying how it should do it. The *hows* are expressed in Chapters 9 and 10.

Chapter 9, The User Experience, introduces a new model to the development process—the User Experience (UX) model. The *UX model* describes the architecturally significant elements of the user interface. The creation of the UX model allows you to separate look-and-feel issues and engineering issues. In this chapter, the UX model is described as a contract between the user experience team that is responsible for designing and building the look and feel and the engineering team that is responsible for implementing the required business logic and functionality. The UX model is introduced at this point because, in many of the organizations I've visited, the activities of fleshing out user-experience artifacts happen shortly after the first set of requirements has been created, which is about the time analysts start modeling the solution.

About the same time user experience is being investigated, the analysis team is analyzing the use cases and requirements specifications of the system and starting to express them in terms of objects. This is the topic of Chapter 10, Analysis. *Analysis* is the activity of transforming the requirements of a system into a design that can be realized in software. An analysis model, which contains classes and class collaborations that exhibit the behavior of the system, is created, as defined by the use cases.

Chapter 11, Design, and Chapter 12, Advanced Design, discuss how to transform the analysis model into something that maps directly into system components (actual delivered modules). Chapter 11 is where the bulk of the Web Application Extension (WAE) for UML is introduced. Once the design model is completed, it can be mapped directly into executable code.

This book's final chapter, Chapter 13, Implementation, discusses the creation of code from the UML model. Because this edition of the book comes with several reference applications, and a detailed description of the WAE's code mappings (Appendix A), this chapter just introduces a few examples of implementing WAE designs.

The appendices are a big part of this edition. Appendix A, a summary of the WAE profile for UML, is a quick and detailed reference of the UML profile introduced in this book. The remaining appendices are realistic examples of applications in this book that have been modeled with the WAE profile. Appendix B contains the key UML diagrams of a typical online retail store. This application was developed in part from two architectural patterns, Controlled Controllers and Master Template, which are described in Appendices C and D, respectively. Appendix E contains the second reference application—a simple online glossary. The glossary application, which manages a set of definitions for a software development team, demonstrates the use and modeling of complex JavaScript objects. The source code can be downloaded from *www.wae-uml.org*, the Web site I've set up to support this book.

Acknowledgments

As with most books, the content, words, and ideas that you read represent only a fraction of the actual work that went into publishing it. The fine people who work for and at Addison-Wesley—in particular Joan Flaherty, Evelyn Pyle, Rob Mauhar, Dianne Wood, Marilyn Rash, and Paul Becker—deserve a lot of the credit for the success of this edition. I am impressed with their ability to understand some of the technical subtleties and to catch the odd technical mistake in the early drafts that had made it past my eyes on several occasions. I am quite proud of Joan's work, and when talking with other authors, rave about her skill and patience. Marilyn and Paul too have demonstrated a remarkable amount of patience and understanding that I am sure has gone far beyond their job descriptions. Not every author has the fortune of such a fine support team.

Additional thanks go to the people who have provided technical reviews of the material in this and previous versions. In particular, Grant Larsen, Simon Johnston, Dave Tropeano, and Kelli Houston of Rational Software offered detailed insights and comments that have greatly improved this book.

Finally, I need to thank my wife, Brenda, for her patience and understanding. Writing a book takes a lot of time and this edition, like the first, was mostly completed in the evening hours after a full day of work or on the weekends. Brenda's willingness to mind the children (Eion, Sean, and Evan) while I toiled away writing this book is a sacrifice and a gift that only a parent can truly understand.

Part One

Overview of Modeling and Web-Related Technologies

Chapter 1

Introduction

What This Book Is About

Simply put, this book is about building model-driven Web applications. It is not a book on how to use a particular tool, a step-by-step recipe, or new methodology. It is simply a guide for the project manager, architect, analyst/designer, and implementer of Web applications—anyone who wants to build robust, scalable, and feature-rich Web applications using the proven object-oriented techniques that traditional client/server applications have been built with for years now. This book builds on the techniques of object-oriented application development rather than defining its own. I say model-driven because the models are the fundamental driving factor in the evolution of the system's development artifacts.

Most of the ideas expressed in this book are not original, and for good reason. Many of the concepts and methods described in this book have developed and evolved over years of practice in multiple domains. These object-oriented practices have enabled projects to be delivered on time and on budget and, most important, have made them predictable. For the most part, the object-oriented principles described in this book are based on the collective works of Grady Booch, Jim Rumbaugh, and Ivar Jacobson, who are also known as the "three amigos."

The amigos are the principal creators of the Unified Modeling Language (UML), a notation for visually expressing the models of software-intensive systems. For many, UML also represents a method, although technically this is incorrect. UML is just a language but like any language expresses things with certain biases. In particular, UML expresses system models and designs in an object-oriented fashion, even though it is being used to express system types as varied as generic business organizational structures and processes to real-time embedded system designs.

The term UML is included in this book's title because it is at the heart of all the discussions of building Web applications in this book. Most of the original work in this text is in the Web Application Extension for UML (WAE). In it, the UML notation is extended with additional semantics and constraints to permit the modeling of Web-specific architectural elements as a part of the system's model. A major theme in this book is that it is critical to model *all* of a system's business logic, regardless of where or how it is being implemented in the system. For Web applications, this means that in our UML models, we need to capture the execution of business logic in Web pages, in client-side scripts, and in Web components. By having a single central model of all the business logic in a system, we are better able to understand it and eventually to elaborate on it in future releases of the system.

The first edition of this book was for the most part written before I joined Rational Software Corporation. At the time, I was an independent consultant specializing in Web applications. The ideas expressed in the first edition of the book were not, of course, supported by any vendor's tool. Rational Rose was and is my modeling tool of choice; with its extensibility interface, I managed to get some specialized icons in the tool and even create some scripts that would forward engineer ASP components from class diagrams. I am proud to say that since then, the Rose development team has included round-trip engineering of both ASP and JSP components.

Full support of the WAE specification is not, however, in the current version of the product; nor will it ever be. Some things simply are not appropriate for round-trip engineering. They may not be suitable for automation, but they are still important to model since the real goal of modeling is understanding and comprehension, not automation. This book lays out the entire specification with some recommendations on what is important and what is not. But in the end, it will be up to you and your team to decide how much detail you'll need in your models.

Because this is a book about building model-driven Web applications, it focuses on three key topics. Modeling, process, and Web architectures are discussed in the remainder of this chapter.

Role of Modeling

We model to understand complex things. Software today is more complex than ever. As a result, we model software. Our models describe what we want to build, what we are building, and what we have built. Models are used throughout the development life cycle and are key artifacts. Models often connect different types of artifacts—use case specifications to database tables—and provide a chain of responsibility and traceability.

These models are simplifications of reality. Models exist at various levels of abstraction. A level of abstraction indicates how far removed from the reality a model is. High levels of abstraction represent the most simplified models.[1] Low levels of

---

1. PowerPoint slides and your favorite clip art represent the highest levels of abstraction a system can have.

abstraction have close and near 1:1 correspondence with the things they are modeling. An exact 1:1 correspondence is no longer a model but rather a transformation of something in one form to another.

The real value of a model is not in what it contains but rather what is hidden. Class diagrams in a UML model, for example, do not include the individual statements of each class operation. These details are hidden in the model and are available only in the source code.[2] Class diagrams further hide things by not exposing all a class's operations, attributes, and associations. The choice of elements to suppress in a diagram is determined by its goal. Each class diagram is created for a reason: to communicate or to explain something. Details that don't help in communicating or explaining don't belong in the diagram. So most diagrams contain classes that have only the relevant details exposed.

Many models are involved in the development process. Each model has its viewpoint. In fact, part of a model's definition[3] is that it is a semantically complete view of a system. Each model is at a different level of abstraction. Because they model the same system, the mappings between the models of the same system are of immense importance. The mappings establish chains of traceability and dependency that help us connect the various and sometimes confusing artifacts of the development process. A user profile screen definition can be traced to the JSP code that implements it, and the state change behavior of a purchase order can be traced to a use case specification that defined it—all done through the various UML models of the system.

In addition to understanding, modeling has other benefits. It is a communication mechanism, allowing one group to communicate to another in a common language. Modeling encourages us to break the problem into manageable pieces. Because of its object-oriented roots, UML modeling in particular encourages us to think of things in terms of objects and to encapsulate properties and behaviors in objectlike concepts. Modeling with computer-aided software engineering (CASE) tools can help us generate source code and components directly from the models.

Before we go on, I need to make one point very clear. The role of modeling is not to produce code through automation or to produce documentation through reverse engineering. These are simply handy by-products of modeling software systems with CASE tools. All too often, we become obsessed with a particular tool's ability to round-trip engineer code and models, and we often miss the whole point of modeling. Automated round-trip engineering will make it easier to connect the abstractions in the model to source code artifacts, but it will not be able to construct a diagram that communicates a point. It won't be able to selectively hide or expose key properties that make understanding easier. Most reverse-engineering tools can reverse engineer only a source code structure. The few tools that attempt to reverse engineer behavioral

---

2. I consider source code itself a model, with the choice of variable names and comments the prime source of added value.

3. See James Rumbaugh, Ivar Jacobson, and Grady Booch, *The Unified Modeling Language Reference Manual* (Boston, MA: Addison-Wesley, 1998).

diagrams usually end up with diagrams so large and complex that they aren't even worth printing.

The real value in models and modeling is the ability to look at a simplification of a system through a particular viewpoint where the system becomes easier to understand. If the models are as complex as what is being modeled, there is little point in modeling.

Role of Process

The process provides a framework and a context to understand things in. Models make it easier to understand complex things, but because multiple models are made for any given system, exactly how and when they are created is just as important as the models themselves.

This book describes in some detail the process of creating Web applications, but it is not meant to be a complete process handbook. The process of developing software is such a large topic that the vast majority of the material in it would have very little Web application–specific material. Instead of creating a complete process manual for Web application development, I decided to create a book that introduces the basics of the process, just enough to set the context for the Web application–specific discussions.[4] In this way, you can identify and understand the important aspects of Web application development without its being tied too closely to a specific software development process. This separation of Web application development material from the process makes it easier for those with specialized and customized development processes to use the material in this book.

Influences of Architecture

Architecture influences just about everything in the process of developing software. Architecture gives us the rules and regulations by which we must construct the software and, to some degree, how we even think about the problem. In the early days of computing, we thought of our problems in terms of batch processing. The business problem had to be thought of in terms of assembling a lot of information, formatting it appropriately, and then submitting it to the system for processing. Today, we have interactive systems that can prompt us, walk us through the collection of data, and process that data at much greater speeds than ever before.

The Web has given us a new variation on the standard client/server system. With the proliferation of networks and HTML browsers as standard software,[5] it is now

---

4. For a book that details the process specifically for J2EE enterprise applications, see Peter Eeles, Kelli Houston, and Wojek Kozaczynski, *Building J2EE Applications with the Rational Unified Process* (Boston, MA: Addison-Wesley, 2002).

5. Even my phone is capable of browsing Web pages over the Internet.

possible to deliver and to deploy a system to users almost anywhere. There are limitations, however, to Web architectures. Their fundamental paradigm of interaction is stimulus/response. The server doesn't control the client directly, and as a general rule, all interaction with the system must be initiated by the client. When this is not the desired behavior, additional elements must be added to the architecture, and the result is a more complex, sometimes brittle system.

Web architectures are evolving. In the first edition of this book, most of my experience was with applications based on Microsoft's Active Server Pages (ASP) and the first version of JavaServer Pages. Because these technologies were relatively new, the systems they were used in had relatively simple architectures. The mappings between components and Web pages were simple, and the types of functionality found in the pages' scripts were straightforward. There were drawbacks to these simple architectures. They had a tendency to evolve into difficult-to-maintain monsters.

Today, more and more teams are adopting Web-centric architectures. Collectively, the industry is gaining more and more experience with Web systems. More and more technologies are being applied to Web architectures. The use of patterns and common mechanisms is gaining momentum.[6] All these factors are resulting in Web systems with relatively complex architectures as the norm.

In the first edition of this book, the Web Application Extension for UML (WAE) profile was introduced and was suitable for the majority of Web architectures in use at the time. When the first version of the Java Pet Store came out, I used it as a tool for understanding J2EE systems. At first, I had a lot of difficulty making the connections between the documentation supplied by the Blueprints book[7] and the source code. At the time, unfortunately it did not come with UML models,[8] which would have bridged the gap between the high-level text and the source. So I set about creating a UML model of the application. Along the way, I discovered a number of new architectural elements that made it difficult to model with the current version of the WAE. What was well suited to modeling the relatively simple applications of many Active Server Page–based Web applications was unsuited for the relatively complex architectural elements I found in the Java Pet Store.

It wasn't as though the Java Pet Store introduced anything new that couldn't be done with any other Web development platform.[9] It's just that this application used so much of the J2EE API (application programming interface) set and created a well thought-out and robust architecture that it exposed many limitations of the first version of the

---

6. In my opinion, patterns and reusable assets are where the future of software development in general is heading.

7. Mark Johnson, Inderjeet Singh, and Beth Stearns, *Designing Enterprise Applications with the J2EE™ Platform, Second Edition* (Boston, MA: Addison-Wesley, 2002).

8. The current release of the Pet Store example does come with a very simple UML model; however, the version I have is little more than a summary of the key Java classes in the application and not a rich model as prescribed by this book.

9. I'm sure that the marketing folk at Sun Microsystems would argue this point, however.

WAE. The results of that effort have in part contributed to the WAE's evolution into this second version (WAE2-UML).

As a companion resource to this book, I have created a WAE-UML portal on the Internet at www.wae-uml.org. It's my intention to maintain this portal as a resource to those interested in the details of Web modeling and who are looking for additional examples or discussions related to the topic. For the time being, this Web site is hosted by a spare computer I keep in my closet. If for any reason the traffic and activity increase significantly, I'll find a suitable host.

This book, the Web site, reference applications, and models are all intended to help development teams understand the issues involved in building Web-centric applications. The information in this book is presented at varying levels of detail. It is not expected that every reader will use or be interested in every chapter; rather, the entirety of this text is intended for the team as a whole. This book is meant to be a companion to other fine application development books, that address specific aspects of the development process or technology. The reference applications and models are the most detailed source of information applied to a specific example and a great resource for those of us who learn best by example. The Web site is an attempt to keep this information as current as possible, to actively engage practitioners, and to elicit real-world experiences so that the entire community of Web application developers, especially modelers, will be successful in developing applications that work well.

Chapter 2

Web Application Basics

Web applications evolved from Web sites or Web systems. The first Web sites, created by Tim Berners-Lee while at CERN (the European Laboratory for Particle Physics), formed a distributed hypermedia system that enabled researchers to have access to documents and information published by fellow researchers, directly from their computers. Documents were accessed and viewed with a piece of software called a browser, a software application that runs on a client computer. With a browser, the user can request documents from other computers on the network and render those documents on the user's display. To view a document, the user must start the browser and enter the name of the document and the name of the host computer where it can be found. The browser sends a request for the document to the host computer. The request is handled by a software application called a Web server, an application usually run as a service, or daemon, that monitors network activity on a special port, usually port 80. The browser sends a specially formatted request for a document (Web page) to the Web server through this network port. The Web server receives the request, locates the document on its local file system, and sends it back to the browser; see Figure 2-1.

This Web system is a hypermedia system because the resources in the system are linked to one another. The term Web comes from looking at the system as a set of nodes with interconnecting links. From one viewpoint, it looks like a spider's web. The links provide a means to navigate the resources of the system. Most of the links connect textual documents, but the system can be used to distribute audio, video, and custom data as well. Links make navigation to other documents easy. The user simply clicks a link in the document, and the browser interprets that as a request to load the referenced document or resource in its place.

A Web application builds on and extends a Web system to add business functionality. In its simplest terms, a Web application is a Web system that allows its users to execute business logic with a Web browser. This is not a very precise definition, but most people's conception of a Web application is not, either. There is a subtle distinction

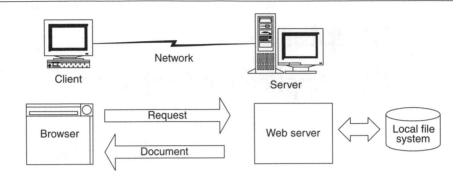

FIGURE 2-1 Basic Web system

between a Web application and a Web site. For the purpose of this book, a Web application is a Web site where user input—navigation through the site and data entry—affects the state of the business: beyond, of course, access logs and hit counters. In essence, a Web application uses a Web site as the front end to a business application.

HTTP

Browsers and Web servers use a special protocol, called the HyperText Transfer Protocol (HTTP), which specifies how a browser should format and send a request to a Web server. The client browser sends a document request consisting of a line of characters terminated by a CR/LF (carriage return/line-feed) pair. A well-behaved server will not require the carriage return character. This request consists of the word GET, a space, and the location of the document relative to the root of the Web server's file system. When a Web server/site is configured, it is usually set up to use a particular directory on the host machine's local file system as the Web site's root directory. Documents are found relative to this directory.

Document Identification

The full identifier for referencing and obtaining the document is called a uniform resource locator (URL). It identifies the protocol (HTTP), host machine name, optional port number, and document name/location. A URL is a single word with no white space. Any further words found on the request line are either ignored or treated according to the full HTTP spec.

A URL is a way to specify an object, or resource, on the network. A URL is like the network equivalent for specifying a file name on a file system. A URL can be used to request many types of objects with different protocols. In addition to HTTP, common Internet protocols include news, FTP, Gopher, and file. Each protocol is specific to the type of information or resource it represents.

When HTTP is specified, the object is a Web page. The following URL requests a Web page from a host identified by www.wae-uml.org:

```
http://www.wae-uml.org/specs/wd/cav43.html
```

The document name is `cav43.html` and is located in the directory `/specs/wd/`. This directory is relative to the Web site's root directory on the Web server.

A more explicit reference to this page could include the port number; however, the default port number, 80, is usually assumed for all HTTP requests:

```
http://www.wae-uml.org:80/specs/wd/cav43.html
```

It is possible to configure the Web server to listen to a port other than 80. This is often done to create a "private" Web site. Some Web servers monitor an additional port and use it for Web configuration. This allows Web masters—those responsible for managing a Web server and site—to remotely manage a Web server's configuration with just a browser. This type of configuration tool is an example of a small Web application.

Domain Names

A domain name is simply the textual name used to look up a numeric Internet address. The Internet addressing system in use today is the Internet Protocol (IP).[1] When a client requests a URL, the request must be made directly to the host computer. This means that the host name identified in the URL must be resolved into a numeric IP address. This process is done with a domain name server (DNS). A DNS is a network computer that the client has access to and that has a known IP address. Network infrastructure software on the client knows how to request the IP address from a DNS for a given domain name.

The host name www.wae-uml.org is made up of two distinct parts. The rightmost dot in the name is used to separate the host name from its top-level domain (TLD), in this case com. The wae-uml part is the subdomain. The term domain name often refers to the combination of the top-level domain and the subdomain. In this case, the domain name is wae-uml.org, and it is this name that I "own." As owner of this domain name, I am responsible for ensuring that an IP address is associated with the domain. Reserving a domain name and not using it to host a Web site or application is referred to as "parking" the domain name, with the expectation that a real host will soon respond meaningfully to this domain name.

When I registered that domain name, I used one of the official registrars delegated the authority to assign domain names. In order to reserve a domain, I had to supply the

---

1. The version in use today is version 4 (IPv4) and is a 32-bit number. The next version, 6 (IPv6) — version 5 was skipped—is a 128-bit number and is expected to replace IPv4 in the coming years.

IP addresses of two name servers (DNS) that would act as the authoritative source for translating the domain name into a valid IP address. It is on this server that I have the rights to adjust, as necessary, the IP address that I want associated with the domain name and all its mutilevel variations. So in my case, I created records in the DNS to equate `wae-uml.org`, `www.wae-uml.org`, and `test.wae-uml.org` to the specific IP address of my host computer.

The `www` and `test` parts are third-level domains, and their usage is up to the discretion of the host owner. The convention is to use `www` for HTML Web sites, `ftp` for FTP servers, `nntp` for Usenet news servers, and so on, although this shouldn't be confused with the protocol specification part of a URL (see discussion of protocols in this chapter). Third-level domain names serve only as a convenience to host machine administrators and are not part of the domain name ownership process; nor do they impact types of protocols that are used.

Any host can receive the requests for multiple domains. When it makes an HTTP request for a resource to a server, a client application typically includes the full URL that was used to resolve the IP address. The server, with a single IP address, can receive a request and look at the URL to determine which application or separate Web site should handle the request. This is how many Internet service providers (ISPs) can offer basic hosting capabilities to customers with custom domain names on shared machines. I've set up my server to point to a portal application when the request is for `wae-uml.org` and `www.wae-uml.org` and to a simple test HTML Web site for `test.wae-uml.org`.

The two types of top-level domains are generic and country specific. An additional one, `.arpa`, is dedicated to Internet infrastructure. Recently, the list of generic top-level domains was expanded; however, `.com`, `.edu`, `.net`, and `.org` continue to be the ones most of us recognize. Each domain is intended for a particular type of use. For example, `.com` domains are for commercial businesses; `.net`, for Internet service providers; `.org`, for nonprofit organizations; and .edu, for educational institutions.

Country-specific domains are managed by organizations in individual countries and can define the usage of the second-level domain in any way they want. For example, the `.uk` top-level domain of the United Kingdom defines a number of second-level domains, such as `.co.uk`, `.me.uk`, `.org.uk`, `plc.uk`, and `ltd.uk`, each with its own expected uses. It isn't until the third-level domain is specified that individual organizations can claim ownership.

TLDs are managed by a single authority: Internet Corporation for Assigned Names and Numbers (ICANN, www.icann.org), with the distribution of Internet numbers managed by Internet Assigned Numbers Authority (IANA, www.iana.org). In the vast majority of situations, you will work through an official registrar—a company responsible for selling domains—or an ISP rather than work directly with these organizations.

Resource Identifiers

Related to the URL is the uniform resource identifier (URI) and the uniform resource name (URN).[2] Simply put, a URI is a superclass to URLs and URNs, whereas the URI is simply an identifier of a resource on the Internet, nothing more. A URL, on the other hand, is a name that includes an access mechanism: name of host server. The URN is required to "remain globally unique and persistent even when the resource ceases to exist or becomes unavailable."[3] For all practical purposes, we as Web application developers are interested mostly in URLs since it is these identifiers that we use to connect our Web pages to form a system.

Fault Tolerance

One important design goal of Web systems is that they be robust and fault tolerant. In the first Web systems at CERN, Web documents, computers, and network configurations were often subject to change. This meant that it was possible for Web pages to contain links to documents or host computers that no longer existed. It is even possible for the HTML specification itself to change, by adding elements, or tags. The browsers and Web servers of the system have to deal gracefully with these conditions.

This desire for a high degree of fault tolerance led in part to the decision to use a connectionless protocol, such as HTTP, as the principal protocol for managing document requests. HTTP is considered a connectionless protocol because as soon as the request is made and fulfilled, the connection between the client and server is terminated. The connection is broken by the server when the whole document has been transferred. The client can abort the transfer by breaking the connection before the transfer completes, in which case the server doesn't record any error condition. The server doesn't need to store information about the request after disconnection. This enables hosts and clients to act more independently and is more resistant to temporary network outages.

HTTP runs over TCP (Transmission Control Protocol), but could run over any connection-oriented service. TCP, a lower-level network protocol used by the Internet and many company networks, enables computers to make connections and to exchange information with one another. TCP, usually combined with IP, is an implementation of layers in the OSI (Open Systems Interconnection) model for network communications.

---

2. An excellent, detailed discussion of URIs by Tim Berners-Lee can be found at http://www.w3.org/DesignIssues/Axioms.htm.

3. The World Wide Web Consortium (W3C) report "URIs, URLs, and URNs: Clarifications and Recommendations," at http://www.w3.org/TR/2001/NOTE-uri-clarification-20010921/, is an excellent resource for exploring this topic further.

HTTPS—HTTP with Secure Sockets Layer (SSL)—is related to HTTP but uses encryption to help "secure" the communication. HTTPS is used on the Internet for handling sensitive data such as personal and financial information. More detailed discussion of security and encryption is in Chapter 5, Security.

HTML

Browsers, in addition to establishing the network connections and protocols for document interchanges, need to render the document on a display. TCP/IP and HTTP don't address this at all. The rendering of content is managed by the browser. This is where the Hypertext Markup Language (HTML) fits in. HTML, used to express the content and the visual formatting of a Web page, is a tag language based on the Standard Generalized Markup Language (SGML), which is a much broader language used to define markup languages for particular purposes. HTML is simply one specific application of SGML, suited to the presentation of textual documents. HTML contains tags that define how text is to be formatted—font, size, color, and so on—on the display. Tags are used to point to images to include in the display, as well as to define links to other Web pages. Like HTTP, HTML is an evolving standard managed by the World Wide Web Consortium standards body. The current W3C recommendation is HTML 4.01, which is based on the earlier HTML 3.2 and HTML 2.0 specifications.

One important thing to note is that HTML is a language that specifies how documents should be displayed on a computer screen. This raises several problems when the Web system needs to enable users to print formatted documents. Many documents, especially forms, have strict printing requirements. If a Web application needs to allow users to print forms or documents in which the typesetting is important—page breaks, font sizes, margins, and so on—additional elements will have to be added to the system. HTML does not address printing in detail. Several attempts to make HTML more suitable for printing have been made, but so far with little more than page break support, so Web applications that need strict printing capabilities must include additional components in their architecture.

HTML defines a set of tags that can be used either to tell the browser how to render something or to define a link to another Web page. All tags are enclosed by angle brackets (< and >). Tags are usually used in pairs, with a beginning and an ending tag. For example, to make a word italicized, the emphasis tag—<em>—is used. A sample sentence and the HTML to render it follow:

```
This is really neat.
This is really <em>neat</em>.
```

Some tags accept parameters, which are placed inside the brackets and are usually a parameter name, followed by an equal sign and then the value enclosed by double quotation marks. The following HTML for a hyperlink to another Web document uses the anchor tag, `<a>`:

```
The HTML 4 spec can be found at the <a href="http://www.w3c.org">W3C Web site</a>.
```

Most browsers render the hyperlink with an underscore:[4]

```
The HTML 4 spec can be found at the W3C Web site.
```

The anchor tag uses the parameter `href` to define the location and the type of the link.

HTML pages are usually text files on the Web server's file system. The language was originally intended to be easy to learn, so that people interested in publishing content could easily specify how the content should be rendered. The key points here are "easy to learn" and "any display terminal." Because a Web system is, potentially, made up of many types of computers, a device-independent way was needed to specify basic formatting commands. For example, specifying a font by name would be a problem if the browser's computer didn't recognize the font name or didn't have the ability to render that font.

This was not a problem for early Web page writers, who were more interested in content than presentation. The language was simple enough to express only the basic formatting capabilities expected for the scientific community. The first generation of Web pages were all written manually, without the aid of WYSIWYG editors.

When the Internet and the Web became commercial, this simple language and its limitations did become a problem. Exact formatting of pages is very important to companies, especially e-commerce companies on the Internet. As in print advertisement, the look of a Web page is very important to potential customers and clients. HTML evolved to meet these needs, enabling more precise formatting of content by introducing new tags and parameters to the language.

What didn't change, though, was that the document content and the presentation information are coupled. The content of an HTML-formatted Web page is a mix of document content—the text or pictures that are displayed by the browser—and rendering instructions, such as bold, indent, font size, and so on. Figure 2-2 shows how HTML renders in a browser.

All the formatting commands are embedded with the content of the document. It is possible to separate some of the formatting specifics from the content with style sheets; even with their use, however, complete separation is not possible. A related term and technology—content management, discussed in Chapter 7, Defining the Architecture—provides more concrete examples of how the separation of content from formatting is an ongoing and important topic to Web application developers.

---

4. This is the default behavior. For any given Web page and browser instance, this behavior is determined by a combination of browser default settings and style sheets referenced or included in the HTML document.

(a)
```
<p>The <em>new</em> <strong>HTML
4.0</strong> specification includes
additional support for</p>
<ul>
    <li>Style sheets </li>
    <li>Internationalization </li>
    <li>Accessibility </li>
    <li>Tables and forms </li>
    <li>Scripting and multimedia </li>
</ul>
```

(b)

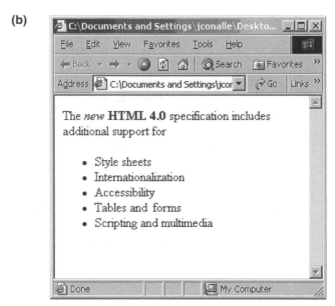

FIGURE 2-2   (a) HTML content (b) rendered in a browser

Style sheet specifications allow Web page authors to define a separate layout, such as color, font, and margins, template that could be used by many other content documents. This helps maintain a consistent look-and-feel across a Web site.

It should be noted that some browsers, especially older and nontraditional browsers, such as PDAs (personal digital assistants) and mobile phones, do not support the use of style sheets. Even so, the W3C recommends the use of style sheets, and is continuing to refine HTML so that in the future, there will be an even further separation of content and presentation. The emergence of XML (Extensible Markup Language), discussed in Chapter 4, Beyond HTTP and HTML, plays a key role in this separation.

One mechanism for separating the content of an HTML page from its presentation is server-side includes (SSI). The NCSA (National Center for Supercomputing Applications) has defined a simple tag that can be used to include HTML fragments that need to be shared across a number of response pages. Typically, these are standard prologs, epilogs, or legal disclaimers and copyright notices. By spreading the content on several shared pages, it is possible to manage a single point of update.[5] The tag simply specifies the name of a file in the Web site's file system:

```
<!--#include file="banner.html"-->
```

HTML has special tags that allow the Web page author to use multimedia information such as images, sound, and video, in addition to textual information. Instead of embedding the multimedia data in the page with the text, the tags specify separate URLs for each item. This means that the browser will make an additional request and connection to the server for each image or multimedia item mentioned in the original Web page. To the Web application architect and designer, this means that certain exceptions need to be taken into account when designing the application. These situations usually are invalid URLs or missing files. It also implies that Web applications with lots of images and multimedia types may cause significant network performance penalties when establishing so many discrete connections. Remember, the choice of a connectionless protocol benefits the robustness of the system, not its performance.

A full discussion of HTML and its tags will not be presented here; the topic is beyond the scope of this book and has been done very well in countless other books. What does need to be discussed here is the architecturally significant elements of the language, especially as they relate to Web applications. Like separating content from presentation, the architecturally significant elements of a Web page need to be brought out and modeled as such. For example, a design model of a Web application is not very interested in the font size or color of the text used in a display, but it is very interested in the sets of Web pages that can be navigated to. The following sections discuss these important elements of HTML.

Anchors

A hyperlink to a Web page is created with the HTML anchor tag: `<a>`. The tag uses several parameters, the most important of which is `href`. This tag can be used without an `href` value, but in this case, the tag is being used as an internal bookmark of the page and as such is not architecturally significant to the design model but could be significant in the user experience model (see Chapter 9). The `href` parameter, which specifies the linked document's URL, may contain a relative URL, which doesn't specify the full URL, including the host's name, but rather expects the browser to use as the host the host that supplied the page containing the hyperlink. For example, the following anchor tag is perfectly acceptable:

```
We have a full line of <a href="prod.html">products</a> to choose from.
```

---

5. See the discussion on content management in Chapter 9, The User Experience, for additional ways to manage content as separate from the rest of the system.

In this example, the link is to a page on the same machine and in the same directory as the current page.

In addition to the location and the name of the Web page, an anchor can pass along parameters with the page request. When parameters are specified in a page request, it usually means that the requested page is executable. The requested Web page is capable of accessing the parameter information and using it to build the returned page. Parameters are passed with the request as name/value pairs separated by the ampersand symbol (&). The parameters are separated from the Web page by a question mark (?). The following page request passes along two parameters: `ProductID` and `RateCode`. The `ProductID` is assigned the value 452, and the `RateCode` is given a value of B.

```
http://www.mystore.com/catalog/products.jsp?ProductID=452&RateCode=B
```

The requested page is `products.jsp`. The extension of the Web page gives a clue that the enabling technology used by the executable page is JavaServer Pages.

In addition to `href`, the other significant parameter is `target`. When a hyperlink is selected, it typically loads the new document in the same browser window as the original document. This is not always the case. When frames are used to divide up a browser's display area, each frame displays a separate Web page. Frames are discussed in detail later.

When frames or multiple browsers are used, it is possible for a hyperlink to specify a frame or browser instance to load in. Frames and browser instances can be assigned any name, although a few target names are reserved.

_blank	Makes the link load into a new blank browser window. The new window is not assigned a name.
_parent	Makes the link load in the immediate frameset parent of the document. It defaults to _self if the document has no parent.
_self	Makes the link load in the same window the anchor was clicked in. This is the default behavior of an anchor.
_top	Makes the link load in the full body of the window. It is a way to "break out" of a frameset.

In the following example, the anchor tag specifies a named `target`: `maindoc`.

```
<a href="chap1.html" target="maindoc" >
    Chapter 1, Web Application Basics.
</a>
```

Forms

HTML form elements distinguish a Web site from a Web application. The HTML form part of a Web page can accept user input. An HTML form is a collection of fields that allow users to enter text or to select from a list. In addition to text boxes, form fields can be rendered by buttons, check boxes, and radio buttons. If a Web page has a form in it, the browser will render that form with the appropriate user interface controls and allow the user to enter and to change its values. Most forms have a special button in them that, when clicked by the user, submits the form and its contents to the Web server as part of another Web page request. The Web server receives a request for a special Web page, or executable module, that is capable of reading the form's field values and processing them on the server. The ultimate result is a new HTML page that is sent back to the requesting browser; see Figure 2-3.

More detailed discussions of form-processing enabling technologies are given later in this book. The general concept, however, is that the executable page is used by the Web server to process the form's values and to produce a new HTML page to send back to the browser. Most often, the processing involves communicating with objects on the server or with databases. Forms are a key mechanism in the interaction of Web application users but by no means the only one. More sophisticated mechanisms for getting user input are discussed in Chapter 3, Dynamic Clients.

A form is defined by the `<form>` tag. The two principal parameters are `action` and `method`. The `action` parameter is the URL of the executable Web page that processes the form. The `method` parameter specifies how the data will be sent to the server. The two valid values are `GET` and `POST`. When `GET` is used, the values of all the fields in the form are appended to the URL as parameters. The Web server sees the form submission as a typical `GET` request, as if it were from a standard anchor tag. The W3C does not recommend using `GET`, as it has some internationalization problems and will not work for large forms. Instead, the value `POST` is preferred. The `POST` method tells the browser to package up the field values in a special section of the request called the data body.

Plain-vanilla HTML has only a few core form elements: `<input>`, `<select>`, and `<textarea>`. The `<select>` tag specifies either a list box or a drop-down list from which the user can select something. The `<textarea>` tag is a multiline text input

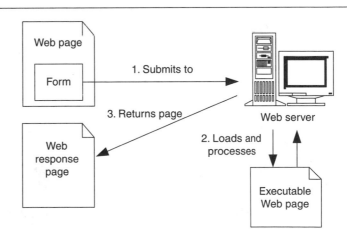

FIGURE 2-3   An executable Web page processing a form's data

control and allows users to enter in large blocks of text. The <input> tag is really an overloaded tag that could be configured to act like a push button, a check box, a radio button, or a single-line text entry field.

The <input> tag's name parameter identifies the field's name. This name is used by the executable Web page when processing the form's data. The <input> tag's type parameter determines what type of user interface control should be used and what type of data to accept. The most common values are:

Checkbox   Displays a check box. If the user checks the box, the field's value will be assigned the value specified by the <input> tag's value parameter.

Hidden   Does not display a user interface control. Values are usually set here by either the executable page that created it or client-side scripting and dynamic HTML.

Password   Displays a password-style entry field. Characters entered here are not displayed to the user.

Radio   Displays a radio button. The tag's name value defines the radio button group. When selected, the field associated with the radio button group is assigned the value specified by the value parameter.

Submit   Displays a push button. When the user clicks this button, the form and all its values are submitted to the server.

Text   Displays a single-line text entry box.

Other types exist, but these define the core set of input types that are used and available in most browser implementations. The key point here is that simple forms collect textual information from the user—either directly or by translating a check box, a button, or a list box selection into one—and define the mechanism by which it gets submitted to the server.

The following HTML fragment defines a simple form for collecting log-on information:

```
<form method="POST" action="cgi-bin/logon.pl">
<p>Username:
<input type="text" name="username" size="10"></p>
<p>Password:
<input type="password" name="password" size="10"></p>
<p>Logon as:</p>
<p>
<input type="radio" name="Role" value="Supervisor">Supervisor<br>
<input type="radio" name="Role" value="Clerk">Clerk<br>
<input type="radio" name="Role" value="Guest">Guest
</p>
<p><input type="submit" value="Logon" name="LogonBtn"></p>
</form>
```

The browser's rendering of the form is shown in Figure 2-4.

Username: [   ]

Password: [   ]

Log on as:

⦿ Supervisor
○ Clerk
○ Guest

[Logon]

FIGURE 2-4   Rendered HTML form

Frames

A controversial element in the HTML arsenal is a frameset. A frameset divides up the browser's display area into rectangular regions, each rendering its own HTML document. The `<frameset>` tag defines the number of frames the display should be broken up into and their sizes or proportions. Separate `<frame>` tags identify each of the frames with a `target` name. The `<frame>` tags also tell the browser which Web pages to request for each frame when initializing the page. Once a frameset page is loaded, with all its individual frames loaded as well, the user can work with the page. The user can select a hyperlink in any of the displayed pages. The link might specify a new document for the frame that it is in or a page to be loaded in another named frame.

The most common use of frames is to define a table of contents and main document frame. The Web page in the table of contents frame is typically a long list of table of content entries, each a hyperlink to an area of the Web site. Each of the links specifies that the "main document" frame, or target, is where the linked Web page should be rendered. The output produced from the JavaDoc application is another excellent example of the use of frames.

The parameters `cols` and `rows` of the `<frameset>` tag define the initial size and the number of frames in the set. For example, the value `"20%,50%,*"` specifies three frames to be defined. The first occupies 20 percent of the screen; the second, 50 percent; the third, the remaining space, 30 percent. Instead of percentages, explicit widths can also be defined, and that's where the `*` value becomes useful. Of course, it is entirely possible for a frame to contain another frameset. This allows designers a little more freedom from a simple matrix frame design and can be used to produce any combination of rectangular regions in the browser's display.

The following HTML fragment defines a simple table of contents–like page. The table of contents appears in the leftmost frame and occupies 20 percent of the display.

```
<frameset cols="20%,80%">
    <frame name="toc" src="toc.html">
    <frame name="maindoc" src="intro.html">
</frameset>
```

Names are specified for each frame. A link in the table of contents frame would specify `"maindoc"` as the target for the link. For example, clicking on the following HTML link would display the Chapter 1 page in the main document frame. The table of contents frame would remain the same.

```
<a target="maindoc" href="chapter1.html">Chapter 1. Web Application Basics</a>
```

The frameset Web page itself typically doesn't contain content like other Web pages do. Most do contain enough content to tell the user that a frames-capable browser is needed to view the page and to provide a link to a page that doesn't require one. This is sometimes necessary on the Internet, as not all browsers support frames.

The controversy over frames centers on user interface preferences and complexity. Some people don't like frames. Frames do, however, raise the level of complexity a bit, as now multiple Web pages are interacting with the user at the same time. This is what makes frames an architecturally significant element.

Web Applications

Web applications use enabling technologies to make their content dynamic and to allow users of the system to affect business logic on the server. The distinction between Web sites and Web applications is subtle and relies on the ability of a user to affect the state of the business logic on the server. Certainly, if no business logic exists on a server, the system should not be termed a Web application. For those systems on which the Web server—or an application server that uses a Web server for user input—allows business logic to be affected via Web browsers, the system is considered a Web application. For all but the simplest Web applications, the user needs to impart more than just navigational request information; typically, Web application users enter a varied range of input data: simple text, check box selections, or even binary and file information.

The distinction becomes even more subtle in the case of search engines, on which users do enter in relatively sophisticated search criteria. Search engines that are Web sites simply accept this information, use it in some form of database SELECT statement, and return the results. When the user finishes using the system, there is no noticeable change in the state of the search engine—except, of course, in the usage logs and hit counters. This is contrasted with Web applications that, for example, accept online registration information. A Web site that accepts course registration information from a user has a different state when the user finishes using the application.

The architecture for a Web site is straightforward. It contains the same principal components of a Web site: a Web server, a network connection, and client browsers. Web applications also include an application server. The addition of the application server enables the system to manage business logic and state. A more detailed discussion of Web application architectures is given in Chapter 7, Defining the Architecture.

Client State Management

One common challenge of Web applications is managing client state on the server. Owing to the connectionless nature of client and server communications, a server doesn't have an easy way to keep track of each client request and to associate it with the previous request, since each and every Web page request establishes and breaks a completely new set of connections.

Managing state is important for many applications; a single use case scenario often involves navigating through a number of Web pages. Without a state management mechanism, you would have to continually supply all previous information entered for each new Web page. Even for the most simple applications, this can get tedious. Imagine having to reenter the contents of your shopping cart every time you visit it or to enter in your user name and password for each and every screen you visit while checking your Web-based e-mail.

To address this common problem, the W3C has proposed an HTTP state management mechanism.[6] This mechanism, more commonly known as "cookies," has received quite a bit of attention from privacy advocates in the past few years and will most likely continue to as more and interesting uses of this mechanism are found. This book isn't about privacy concerns but rather is focused on the technology around Web applications, so I'll focus on describing the technology and leave the philosophy to you.

Cookies

A cookie is a piece of data that a Web server can ask a Web browser to hold on to, and to return every time the browser makes a subsequent request for an HTTP resource to that server. Typically, the size of the data is small, between 100 and 1K bytes; however, the official limit is around 4K. Initially, a cookie is sent from a server to a browser by adding a line to the HTTP headers:

```
Content-type: text/html
Set-Cookie: sessionid=12345; path=/; expires Mon, 09-Dec-2002 11:21:00 GMT; secure
```

If the browser is configured to accept cookies, the line is accepted and stored somewhere on the client's machine, depending on the browser vendor. After that, each and every HTTP request to the server is sent back the values of these cookies.

When it is sent to a client, a cookie can have up to six parameters passed with it:

- Name (required)
- Value (required)

---

6. All the gory details of this mechanism can be found in the RFC 2109 document at http://www.w3.org/Protocols/rfc2109/rfc2109.

- Expiration date
- Path
- Domain
- Requires a secure connection

The Set-Cookie header is a string that contains characters, including white space, commas, and the semicolon. The name and value parameters are required and must not contain white space, commas, or semicolons. The expiration date tells the browser how long to keep this information. The path and the domain are a way of determining which servers, or domains, to send the cookies back to. If the domain is not set explicitly, it defaults to the full domain of the document creating the cookie. The path helps organize cookies within a domain. Only when a resource is requested in the domain under the path will the cookie be sent back to the server.

The server sending the cookie must be a member of the domain that is specified. Thus, a server in the domain www.myserver.com cannot set a cookie for the domain www.otherserver.com. If it could, one company would be able to set cookies in another company's domain.

The server can send multiple Set-Cookie headers with an HTTP response. When the browser responds with the Set-Cookie header, all cookies for the domain and the path are returned. For example, the server could have included the following Set-Cookie headers:

```
Set-Cookie: sessionid=12345; path=/; expires Mon, 09-Dec-2002 11:21:00 GMT
Set-Cookie: colorPref=Blue; path=/; expires Mon, 09-Dec-2002 11:21:00 GMT
```

When it requests a URL in the path / on this same server, the client sends with its HTTP request the following:

```
Cookie: sessionid=12345; colorPref=Blue
```

When the response is returned, the server might set another cookie with:

```
Set-Cookie: rateCode=B; path=/order
```

When it requests a URL in path /order, a client sends:

```
Cookie: sessionid=12345; colorPref=Blue; rateCode=B
```

Note that all three cookies are sent with the request because the first two are in a higher path and are "inherited" in the mapping.

In addition to the server's being able to set a cookie value, so too can JavaScript. Chapter 3, Dynamic Clients, describes the capabilities of client-side scripting in more detail; here, however, it is sufficient to say that cookies can be set and obtained in multiple ways. The specific mechanisms for setting and accessing cookies are typically provided by the development environment and architecture, by a single function call to an accessible object.

This mechanism is not without faults. Privacy advocates point to cookies as the primary mechanism supporting the tracking of unknowing users across multiple Web sites. In fact, while writing this chapter, I wanted to look at some sample cookies on my machine. When I scanned the list, I was surprised to find a few cookies from domains that I know I had never visited. Of course, this piqued my curiosity, and as I looked at the data in the cookies, I noticed name/value pairs that included URLs from sites I do remember visiting. Investigating a little further, I found out that these cookies were placed on my machine through the use of banner ads that appeared in the sites that I did visit.

The reality here is that the images in most banner ads are not hosted by the sites that referenced them. Rather, companies specializing in banner ads sell a service to Web sites. When someone visits those sites, the companies provide most of the content of the Web page, as well as a reference to an image stored on the advertisement company's server. Because the image is obtained with a standard HTTP request, the exchange of cookies also happens with this "other" server. So when you visit a Web page that has banner ads in it, they most likely are coming from another company's server and are being collected and managed by that company. After a while, you will visit enough Web sites using the same advertiser's server that the banner ad company can start to build a profile of the sites you visit most and begin to target more appropriate advertisement for you.

Using cookies in this way is very controversial and has led to the heated debate on the use of cookies, privacy, and the Internet. But we won't focus on that type of usage here. Instead, we'll look at how cookies were intended to be used: to manage client state in the context of a single use case or set of use cases.

Sessions

A session represents a single cohesive use of the system. A session usually involves many executable Web pages and a lot of interaction with the business logic on the application server. Because achieving a use case goal often requires the successful execution of a number of executable Web pages, it is often useful to keep track of a client's progress throughout the use case session.

The most common example of keeping client state on the server can be found on the Internet at any e-commerce site. The use of virtual shopping carts is a nice feature of an online store. A shopping cart contains all the items an online customer has selected from the store's catalog. In most sites, the shopper can check the contents of the cart at any time during the session. This feature requires that the server be capable of maintaining some state about the client across a series of Web page requests.

Session state in a Web application can be maintained in four common ways, two of which require the use of cookies:

1. Place all state values in cookies.
2. Place a unique key in the cookie and use with a server-managed dictionary or map.

3. Include all state values as parameters in every URL of the system.

4. Include a unique key as a parameter in every URL of the system and use with a server-managed dictionary or map.

When you place all state values in cookies, you are first limited by size (4K) and at most 20 cookies per domain. All state data must be encoded into simple text: no white space, semicolons, and so on. You can't directly use higher-level objects in the session state. The real limitation, however, is that many clients' security settings don't allow the automatic storing of cookies. If the application is an Internet application targeting the consumer market, you don't want to automatically turn away a significant number of potential customers without a good reason.

When a unique key is used in a cookie and then used on the server as a key into a dictionary or a map, any type of server-side object can be part of the session state. This is the default mechanism used by most Web application–enabling environments, such as ASP and JSP. It is very effective and flexible; however, like any cookie-based method, it depends on the willingness of clients to accept cookies.

URL redirection is the other class of session management. In this mechanism, all URLs in the system are dynamically constructed to include parameters that contain either the entire session state or only one key into a server-side dictionary.

Each mechanism has tradeoffs. Keeping a dictionary in memory for every user of the system could be very expensive if it never expired. For practical reasons, most session dictionaries are removed when the Web application user either finishes the process or stops using the system for a set period of time. A session timeout value of 15 minutes is typical. No matter what technique is used, the management of client state on the server is almost always an issue in Web applications.

Enabling Technologies

The enabling technologies for Web applications are varied and differentiated principally by the vendor. Enabling technologies are, in part, the mechanism by which Web pages become dynamic and respond to user input. Of the several approaches to enabling a Web application, the earliest involved the execution of a separate module by a Web server. Instead of requesting an HTML-formatted page from the file system, the browsers would request the module, which the Web server interpreted as a request to load and to run the module. The module's output is usually a properly formatted HTML page but could be image, audio, video, or other data.

The original mechanism for processing user input in a Web system is the Common Gateway Interface (CGI), a standard way to allow Web users to execute applications on the server. Because letting users run applications on your Web server might not be the safest thing in the world, most CGI-enabled Web servers require CGI modules to reside in a special directory, typically named cgi-bin. CGI modules can be written in any language and can even be scripted. In fact, the most common language for small-scale CGI modules is Perl (practical extraction and reporting language), which is interpreted each time it is executed.

Even though HTML documents are the most common output of CGI modules, they can return any number of document types. They can send to the client an image, plaintext—an ASCII document with no special formatting—audio, or even a video clip. They can also return references to other documents. In order for it to interpret the information properly, the browser must know what kind of document it is receiving. In order for the browser to know this, the CGI module must tell the server what type of document it is returning.

In order to tell the server what kind of document is being sent back—a full document or a reference to one—CGI requires a short header on the output. This header is ASCII text, consisting of separate lines followed by a single blank line. For HTML documents, the line would be

```
Content-type: text/html
```

If it does not build the returning HTML Web page, the CGI module can redirect the Web server to another Web page on the server or even another CGI module. To accomplish this, the CGI module simply outputs a header similar to

```
Location: /responses/default.html
```

In this example, the Web server is told to return the page `default.html` from the `responses` directory.

The two biggest problems with CGI are that it doesn't automatically provide session management services and that every execution of the CGI module requires a new and separate process on the application/Web server. Creating a lot of processes can be expensive on the server.

All the available solutions overcome the multiprocess problems of CGI by adding plug-ins to the Web server. The plug-ins allow the Web server to concentrate on servicing standard HTTP requests and deferring executable pages to another, already running process. Some solutions, such as Microsoft's Active Server Pages, can even be configured to run in the same process and to address space as the Web server itself although this is not recommended.

Two major approaches to Web application–enabling technologies are used today: compiled modules and interpreted scripts. Compiled-module solutions are CGI-like modules that are compiled loadable binaries executed by the Web server. These modules have access to APIs that provide the information submitted by the request including the values and names of all the fields in the form and the parameters on the URL. These modules produce HTML output that is sent to the requesting browser. Some popular implementations of this approach are Microsoft's Internet Server API (ISAPI), Netscape Server API (NSAPI), and Java servlets.

ISAPI and NSAPI server extensions can also be used to manage user authentication, authorization, and error logging. These extensions to the Web server are essentially a filter placed in front of the normal Web server's processing.

Compiled modules are an efficient, suitable solution for high-volume applications. The biggest drawbacks are related to development and maintenance. These modules usually combine business logic with HTML page construction. The modules often contain many print lines of HTML tags and values, which can be confusing and difficult for a programmer to read.

The other problem is that each time the module needs to be updated, or fixed, the Web application has to be shut down and the module unloaded. For most mission-critical applications, this is not much of a problem; the rate of change in the application should be small. Also, it's likely that a significant effort would have been made by the QA/test team to ensure that the delivered application was free of bugs. For smaller, internal intranet applications, however, the rate of change might be significant. For example, the application might provide sets of financial or administrative reports. The logic in these reports might change over time, or additional reports might be requested.

The other category of solutions is scripted pages. Whereas the compiled-module solution looks like a business logic program that happens to output HTML, the scripted-page solution looks like an HTML page that happens to process business logic. A scripted page, a file in the Web server's file system, contains scripts to be interpreted by the server; the scripts interact with objects on the server and ultimately produce HTML output. The page is centered on a standard HTML Web page but includes special tags, or tokens, that are interpreted by an application server. Typically, the file name's extension tells the Web server which application server or filter should be used to preprocess the page. Some popular vendor offerings in this category are JavaServer Pages, Microsoft's Active Server Pages, and PHP.

Figure 2-5 shows the relationship between components of the enabling technology and the Web server. The database in the figure, of course, could be any server-side resource, including external systems and other applications. This figure shows how the compiled-module solution almost intercepts the Web page requests from the Web server and in a sense acts as its own Web server. In reality, the compiled module must be registered with the Web server before it can function. Nonetheless, the Web server plays only a small role in the fulfillment of these requests.

The scripted-page solution, however, is invoked by the Web server only after it has determined that the page does indeed have scripts to interpret. Typically, this is indicated by the file name extension: `.aspx`, `.jsp`, `.php`. When it receives a request for one of these pages, the Web server first locates the page in the specified directory and then hands that page over to the appropriate application server engine, or filter. The application server preprocesses the page, interpreting any server-side scripts in the page and interacting with server-side resources, if necessary. The results are a properly formatted HTML page that is sent to the requesting client browser.

Even though JavaServer Pages are scripted, they get compiled and loaded as a servlet the first time they are invoked. As long as the server page doesn't change, the Web server will continue to use the already compiled server page/servlet. This gives JavaServer Pages some performance benefits over the other scripted-page offerings.

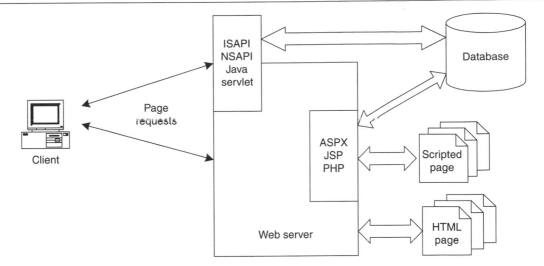

FIGURE 2-5   Web server–enabling technologies

The real appeal of scripted pages, however, is not their speed of execution but their ease of development and deployment. Typically, scripted pages don't contain most of the application's business logic, which instead is often found in compiled business objects that are accessed by the pages. Scripted pages are used mostly as the glue that connects the HTML user interface aspects of the system with the business logic components.

In any Web application, the choice of technologies depends on the nature of the application, the organization, and even the development team itself. On the server, a wealth of technologies and approaches may be used, many of them together. Regardless of the choices, they need to be expressed in the larger model of the system. The central theme in this book is that all the architecturally significant components of a Web application need to be present in the system's models. Servers, browsers, Web pages, and enabling technologies are architecturally significant elements and must be part of the model.

❑ ❑ ❑ ❑ ❑ ❑ ❑ ❑

Summary

❑ Web systems are hypertext document systems that are relatively new to the computing world.

❑ The fundamental elements of a Web system are the client browser, the network, and a Web server.

❑ A Web application is a Web system that delivers business logic.

❑ HTTP is the primary protocol for communication between clients and servers.

❑ HTTP is a connectionless protocol. Each time a client requests a document from a Web server, a new connection must be established with the server.

❑ As identifiers of network resources, URLs or URIs can reference Web pages, images, applets, and other resources on the network.

❑ Web pages are documents that are requested by the client and delivered by the Web server.

❑ The principal formatting language for Web pages is HTML. It tells the browser how to render the content on the screen.

❑ Forms allow users to enter input through a Web page.

❑ Frames allow multiple Web pages to be active for a user at the same time.

❑ Session management is the tracking of a particular user's progress through the application, even across Web pages. Cookies can be used to help manage client state on the server.

❑ Enabling technologies are development environments that provide the infrastructure for building Web applications.Some popular technologies are CGI, Active Server Pages, JavaServer Pages, servlets, and Web server APIs.

Discussion

1. What are the advantages of a connectionless protocol, such as HTTP? What are the disadvantages?

2. Discuss the differences in the main client tier—what happens exclusively in the browser—and the presentation tier—the handling of URL resource requests—paradigms of operation?

3. What types of side effects might you expect to see in a Web application when the client browser's Back and Forward buttons are used? How might bookmarked pages affect the application?

Activities

1. Examine the cookie file(s) on your machine. Look for and examine cookies left by advertising companies. Compare these cookies with other cookies from sites and applications that you know well.

2. Develop a long-term persistent session management strategy that will allow users to engage in a use case scenario over a period of days, with long breaks in continuity.

Chapter 3
Dynamic Clients

The great distinction between Web sites and Web applications lies in the use of business logic. In Chapter 2, the discussions of Web applications and their enabling technologies all centered on implementing business logic only on the server. The client browser was a simple, generalized user-interface device that played no role in the execution of business logic. In the history of Web applications, that model didn't last long. When system designers, especially client/server system designers, recognized the potential of the Web as a serious system architecture, they realized that it might be beneficial for client computers to share in the execution of the business logic. The idea was simple, but some problems needed to be solved, including those of deployment and platform independence

An important concept needs to be made clear when discussing dynamic clients and business logic. Business logic comprises the rules and processes that shape the business state of the system. It is field validations and data systems. For example, the computation of shipping charges is covered by business logic, since it involves the rules of the business, as well as those of the postal service. Presentation logic focuses on making the user interface easy for the user. It may accept any data that contributes to the business state of the system, but it is not responsible for it. For example, the use of a date-picker control—a user interface widget that pops up a minicalendar for the user to select a date from—does not constitute business logic. It is simply a device to capture user input; the device itself doesn't affect the business state of the system, just the data it collects. The use of the date, in computing an age or an expiration period, however, is business logic.

The simplest examples of business logic on the client are field and form validations. For example, a date entry field should never accept the invalid date February 30th, even though it is entirely possible to enter the words in an ordinary text box. Without client-side validation, this value would be submitted with the form to the server and only there be identified as an invalid value. When this happens, the entire form is usually sent back to the user for correction. This number of server trips is expensive because the time it takes for a form to submit itself to the server, receive processing, and get a response is on the order of seconds, not milliseconds.

In a traditional client/server system the date value would probably be checked as it was entered, when it lost focus, or when the form was completed. The validation of the field would be done by the client machine, possibly by the user interface, because the action does not require server resources. Another option for traditional client/ server designers is to use a specialized date input control, one that doesn't accept invalid dates.

It is not surprising that the movement to enable dynamic clients was not originally driven by the need to execute business logic on the client. It, like many other aspects of Web development, was driven by the need to enhance the user interface rendered by Web pages. Many Web users, already familiar with computers, sought some of the features found in their client applications: most significantly, a responsive and dynamic user interface. Plain-vanilla Web pages aren't very dynamic and were never intended to be. Therefore, to give Web surfers new reasons to visit sites and to lay the ground-work for serious use of the Web as an application platform, HTML became dynamic.

A number of technologies and mechanisms bring business logic to the client. These technologies can also be used to enhance the user interface. For the most part, they fall into one of two categories: scripted or compiled. All of them share some features.

- They are associated with the Web page and can access and modify its content.
- They are automatically deployed, or downloaded, to the client computer as needed.
- They address specific security concerns.

When minimal business logic needs to be used on the client, scripting is often an easy yet powerful mechanism to use. When truly sophisticated logic needs to run on the client, building Java applets, JavaBeans, or ActiveX controls is probably a better approach because these environments are more structured and powerful. ActiveX, however, is an option only when the client computers are Windows based. In an intra-net environment, this could very well be the case, and such an environment could take advantage of the increased performance of natively coded modules.

For most Web applications, the key to the use of business logic on the client, par-ticularly in the context of HTML pages, is that it has access only to the resources on the client. Implementing a business rule on the client that requires access to server resources doesn't make much sense because the rule can be implemented only by making additional page requests to the server.[1] The business logic that is implemented on the client needs to focus on the manipulation of the data in the Web page itself.

---

1. It is possible for client-side components to have persistent and asynchronous communications with server-side objects, however; this type of Web architecture is covered in detail in Chapter 7, De-fining the Architecture, and doesn't relate to HTML-page business logic.

Client-side enabling technologies can be sophisticated and highly object oriented if done properly. This depth of functionality is important to keep in mind when designing client-side activity. When giving the client a role in the business, it is essential to do so in a way consistent with the rest of the system.

The manipulation of content and function of the user interface in a Web page is the central focus of client-side scripting and dynamic activity. To truly enable business logic—or even user interface enhancements—to be useful, they need access to virtually every aspect of the page they work within. The key to enabling dynamic clients lies in the ability to make Web page content accessible to scripts and modules that can be executed on the client and delivered by the Web page. In keeping with the theme of this book, it is important to recognize that the technologies used to bring business logic to the client must be well understood and incorporated into the application model. Just because an element of the application uses JavaScript to perform some simple calculations on the client but the rest of the system relies on distributed C++ objects and CORBA (Common Object Request Broker Architecture) ORBs (object request brokers) doesn't mean that the script isn't important. If it implements a business rule or process, it needs to be included in the model.

Document Object Model

Regardless of the underlying philosophy for enabling the client, the technology relies on the Document Object Model (DOM), a platform-neutral interface to the browser and the HTML documents it's rendering. The specification has been defined by the W3C,[2] and most of the browser manufacturers have implemented it in their latest versions. The idea is to have a common API that Web page developers[3] can use to manipulate the content in the HTML and XML document, as well as the resources of the browser itself.

With the DOM, programs and scripts can dynamically access and update the content, structure, and style of documents. The document can be further processed by the browser and the results incorporated into the presented page. The browser is now responsible for both the rendering of the HTML in the document, which could change after being received from the server, and the execution of scripts in the document, as well as compiled programs specified by the document.

Figure 3-1 shows the relationships among the browser, HTML document, scripts, compiled modules, and the DOM. The browser contains an HTML document. Contained in the document are scripts—lines of interpretable code—that use the DOM interface. The HTML document also contains references to compiled modules, which also use the DOM interface. The browser is responsible for both rendering the

---

2. The World Wide Web Consortium (W3C) of technology vendors and institutions is responsible for HTTP, HTML, XML, XSL, DOM, and other important Web and Internet standards.

3. I use the term "developer" instead of "author" because we are discussing client-side execution of code, not just content.

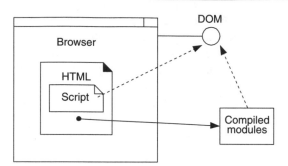

FIGURE 3-1   The Document Object Model interface

dynamic HTML document and implementing the DOM interface for scripts and programs to modify the HTML document.

The name Document Object Model was chosen because it provides an object interface to HTML and XML documents. The documents are manipulated as objects, possessing both data and behavior. The collaboration of these objects represents the structure of the document. Because a document is a collection of objects, it can be represented by an object model. Take as an example the following HTML fragment:

```
<body>
<p>The new HTML 4.0 specification
includes additional support for;</p>
<ul>
    <li>Style sheets </li>
    <li>Internationalization </li>
    <li>Accessibility </li>
    <li>Tables and forms </li>
    <li>Scripting and multimedia </li>
</ul>
</body>
```

In this example, the HTML expresses a simple itemized list. A simplified[4] class diagram, shown in Figure 3-2, represents the structure of this document. An object diagram, shown in Figure 3-3, shows the relationships among the instances of the "objects" in the document.

The key point here is that the DOM specification gives all these elements an object interface that is accessible by scripts or modules executing in the browser. The three principal goals of the DOM are to specify

- The interfaces and objects used to represent and manipulate a document

---

4. The class and instance diagrams are simplified; the actual diagrams contain a large number of other elements that might confuse the main point of the diagrams.

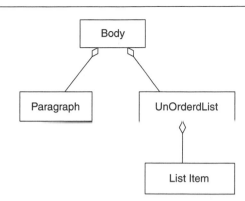

FIGURE 3-2   Class diagram of HTML document

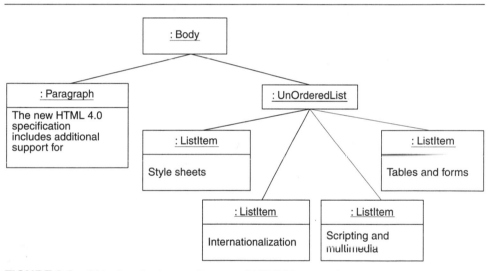

FIGURE 3-3   Object, or instance, diagram of HTML document

- The semantics of these interfaces and objects, including both behavior and attributes
- The relationships and collaborations among these interfaces and objects

Another key aspect of the DOM is that it is vendor and platform neutral. Even though it comes with bindings for the Java language, the specification is language independent. All the major browser manufacturers have implemented the DOM in the latest versions of their browsers. The two major browsers, Microsoft and Netscape, have provided an implementation of the DOM and have extended it with a few additional features.

Dynamic HTML (DHTML) is a term used to describe the combination of HTML, style sheets, and scripts that allows documents to be manipulated in a Web browser. DHTML is not a W3C specification or recommendation, so caution should be observed when designing systems that use incompatible elements of DHTML.

Scripting

The most common scripting technology in browsers today is JavaScript. JavaScript, one part of the Java technology revolution, is an implementation of a scripting language that has its roots in the Java programming language. JavaScript was intended to be easier to learn and to use than Java; the first users of JavaScript would be interested mainly in enhancing user interfaces and would have more of an authoring background than a programming one.

The JavaScript language resembles Java but does not have Java's static typing and strong type checking. JavaScript's runtime environment is also smaller and has fewer data types than Java does. JavaScript is object based, not objected oriented, meaning that it uses built-in extensible objects but does not support user-defined classes or inheritance. Because JavaScript is not compiled, it uses dynamic binding, and all object references are checked at runtime. JavaScript supports functions without special declarative requirements. This makes it easier for those new to programming to use.

JavaScript comes embedded in HTML pages, so it needs to coexist in the document, as does any other element of the document. The <script> tag, used to define regions of JavaScript, is an HTML extension that can enclose any number of JavaScript statements. The <script> tag marks the beginning of a JavaScript region; the end tag </script> is required to mark the end of the region. Because the <script> tag can be used to denote scripts in other languages, a language parameter is usually added; otherwise, the default scripting would be at the mercy of the browser. Anything between these tags is considered, from the DOM's point of view, written in the JavaScript language. The information between these tags is parsed by the JavaScript interpreter, not the DOM. In the following example, the HTML <script> tag identifies a simple JavaScript function call that displays a dialog box to the user.

```
<SCRIPT LANGUAGE="JavaScript">
    alert('Hello World.')
</SCRIPT>
```

Unfortunately, defining scripts is not as simple as that. Not all browsers are JavaScript capable, and even though a browser is built to be robust and fault tolerant, the earliest browsers do not gracefully handle JavaScript that they can't interpret. The problem stems from the fact that if it doesn't understand a tag, a browser ignores it. For the most part, this works well. For example, a browser that doesn't understand the <font> tag just ignores it and continues to use the default font. A problem occurs when an older browser ignores the <script> tag. The tag and its ending tag are

ignored, but the content between them, the JavaScript, is not. The browser attempt.
parse this information like any other part of the document. Because JavaScript doesn't
follow the same formatting or structuring rules as HTML, it is probable that an older
browser will react badly and report a large number of warnings or errors. To guard
against this situation, HTML and JavaScript comments are used to protect regions
where an error might be generated by a non-JavaScript browser. In the following
example, the <script> tag defines a function called isPositiveNum(). This function
is probably called by the form validation function prior to submitting it to the server.
The first line in the script block is an HTML comment token (<!--).

```
<SCRIPT LANGUAGE="JavaScript">
<!--- Hide script from old browsers.
function isPositiveNum(s) {
   return (parseInt(s) > 0)
}
// End the hiding here. -->
</SCRIPT>
```

The last line in the script block is a JavaScript comment and is there only so that
the HTML comment end token (-->) is ignored by the JavaScript interpreter. Like
polyglot programs that compile error free under multiple languages, this code needs
to behave well for both HTML and JavaScript.

JavaScript Objects

The Document Object Model, the main source of objects for JavaScript, puts an object
interface on both the HTML document and the browser. JavaScript can interact with
the browser to load a new page, examine the browser's history—previously loaded
Web pages—or interact with pages in neighboring frames.

The principal object to use when working with document content is the document
object. A reference to it can be obtained through the document property of the window
object, which is a globally available object in any JavaScript function. JavaScript uses
"dot notation" to navigate through the properties and references associated with the
document. For example, the following JavaScript function initializes a text field in a
form with the current day of the week:

```
today = new Date();
weekdays = new Array("Sun", "Mon", "Tue", "Wed", "Thu", "Fri", "Sat");
dow = weekdays[today.getDay()];
window.document.forms["demo"].elements["inday"].value = dow;
```

In this script fragment, the variable today is set to the current date. An array of all
possible weekdays is defined in the variable weekdays. The current day of the week is
obtained by calling the getDay() method of the Date object, which returns an integer
indicating the day of the week. This value is used to index into the weekdays array to

obtain the current day of the week as a string and to assign it to the dow variable. The last line sets the value of a field in a form. The form is named "demo", and the field is an input text control named "inday".

To access the field and to set its value property, the object hierarchy is navigated by beginning with the window object, a browser-supplied global object that more or less represents the browser itself. This object has a property, called the document, which represents the HTML Web page. The document object has a forms collection, since it is possible to define multiple forms in a page. This collection of forms is indexed by the name of the form: "demo". Forms contain form elements, or input fields, that can be accessed by indexing the elements collection of the form object. Once a reference to the field is obtained, its value property is set with the current day of the week.

Most JavaScript interactions behave in this way, first performing the business logic calculations and then accessing the appropriate DOM interfaces to update the document. The trick to using JavaScript is gaining an understanding of the objects and interfaces you have to work with. The Document Object Model standard is a good place to start. It defines the object hierarchy that page scripts use to access the information in the document and even the browser itself. Figure 3-4 shows the object hierarchy available to scripts in a page.

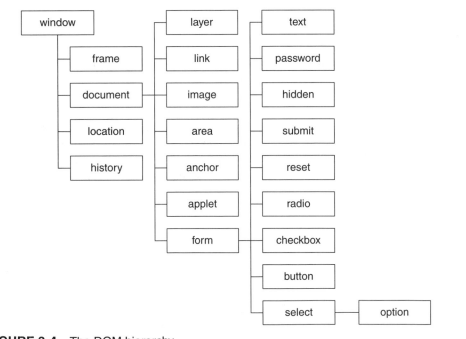

FIGURE 3-4   The DOM hierarchy

Custom JavaScript Objects

Even though it is not an object-oriented environment, JavaScript does provide a mechanism for encapsulation, or the ability to package and to hide data in an object. In JavaScript, you can create an instance of a generic object and assign it properties and even methods. For example, in the following JavaScript, a generic object instance called cartLineItem is created. Using the dot operator, four custom properties are defined and assigned values.

```
cartLineItem = new Object();
cartLineItem.productID = 'MG1234';
cartLineItem.productName = 'MGB Roadster (1935)';
cartLineItem.qty = 1;
cartLineItem.unitPrice = 36000;
```

The cartLineItem instance can be used later by any JavaScript with a reference to it. For example, the following statement displays a message to the user with the shopping cart line item's name and current quantity:

```
alert( 'You have ' + cartLineItem.qty + ' ' + cartLineItem.productName +
' in your shopping cart' );
```

Like properties, custom methods can be associated with objects as well. As long as it has been defined earlier in the document, the function can be assigned to an object. For example, the following function, total(), can be used as a member function of the cartLineItem instance. This function has access to its owning object through the operator this. In this function, the total() function computes the total amount for this line item: quantity times the price.

```
function total () {
  return (this.qty * this.unitPrice);
}
```

A function is assigned to an object, just like a property:

```
cartLineItem.total = total;
```

Once it has been assigned to the object, the function can be called directly from the object cartLineItem. For example,

```
cartLineItem = new Object();
cartLineItem.productID = 'MG1234';
cartLineItem.productName = 'MGB Mk I Roadster';
cartLineItem.qty = 2;
cartLineItem.unitPrice = 12500;
cartLineItem.total = total;
```

```
document.write( '<p>' + cartLineItem.qty + ' ' + cartLineItem.productName +
    ' will cost you $' + cartLineItem.total() + '</p>' );
```

The preceding JavaScript code produces the following output on the browser screen:

```
2 MGB Mk I Roadster will cost you $12500
```

To make things a little easier, a prototype can be defined. This is similar to a C++ constructor. The prototype is a function that creates a custom object and, optionally, initializes the object's properties. In the case of a JavaScript object, this must include the object's functions. The prototype for a LineItem[5] object would be

```
function LineItem( id, name, qty, price ) {
  this.productID = id;
  this.productName = name;
  this.qty = qty;
  this.unitPrice = price;
  this.total = total;
}
```

With a prototype defined, an array of LineItem instances could be created with the following JavaScript:

```
var cartLineItem = new Array();
cartLineItem[0] = new LineItem ('MG123', 'MGB Mk I Roadster', 1, 36000 );
cartLineItem[1] = new LineItem ('AH736', 'Austin-Healey Sprite', 1, 9560 );
cartLineItem[2] = new LineItem ('TS225', 'Triumph Spitfire Mk I', 1, 11000 );
```

Events

As mentioned, JavaScript is not an object-oriented language; neither, in a strict sense, is an HTML page. The DOM puts an object interface on an HTML page, but inherently it is still a document. JavaScripts embedded in an HTML page inherently suffer from some of the same problems. Like the document itself, JavaScript is read and interpreted in the order it appears in the document. Any script blocks that contain executable JavaScript statements outside of a function definition are interpreted in the order they are read. Writing in-line scripts that initialize the page before the user starts to interact with it might be OK to write this way, although I still wouldn't encourage it.

A more structured way to organize JavaScripts in an HTML page is to define functions that encapsulate very discrete behaviors and then have them executed as

---

5. Call it an old Smalltalk habit, but I like to capitalize the name of "class"-like objects and to use lowercase names for instances. In this example, the LineItem function is behaving like a constructor and so is "class"-like.

needed. A function would respond to an event; if the code needed to be executed when the document was first loaded, the event would be the onLoad event of the <body> element in the HTML page.

The concept and use of events in client-side activity is critical for most applications. An HTML or browser event is something that triggers a script or a module into action. Typically, some user interaction with the browser or document triggers an event, although in some situations, the browser itself might be the source for the event. The event handler parameter defines the name of the function that will handle the event when it is fired. Not all elements in an HTML document receive all events. A summary of common events and handler function names, taken from the "Netscape Java Script Guide,"[6] is given in Table 3-1.

TABLE 3-1   Summary of HTML Document Events

Event	Applies to	Occurs When	Event Handler
Abort	Images	User aborts the loading of an image, by, for example, clicking a link or the Stop button.	onAbort
Blur	Windows, frames, and all form elements	User removes input focus from window, frame, or form element.	onBlur
Click	Buttons, radio buttons, check boxes, Submit buttons, Reset buttons, links	User clicks form element or link.	onClick
Change	Text fields, text areas, select lists	User changes value of element.	onChange
Error	Images, windows	The loading of a document or image causes an error.	onError
Focus	Windows, frames, and all form elements	User gives input focus to window, frame, or form element.	onFocus
Load	Document body	User loads the page in the Navigator.	onLoad
Mouse out	Areas, links	User moves mouse pointer out of an area—client-side image map—or link.	onMouseout
Mouse over	Links	User moves mouse pointer over a link.	onMouseOver
Reset	Forms	User resets a form: clicks a Reset button.	onReset
Select	Text fields, text areas	User selects form element's input field.	onSelect
Submit	Submit button	User submits a form.	onSubmit
Unload	Document body	User exits the page.	onUnload

---

6. Available at http://home.netscape.com/eng/mozilla/3.0/handbook/javascript/index.html.

Client-side programming is event driven. Except in the case of in-line JavaScripts—discouraged—all JavaScript functions are executed in response to an event. The <body> tag of an HTML document defines the main textual content of the document and can generate the following events:

- Load
- Unload
- Blur
- Focus

Generally, these events are fired when the content is created and destroyed and when it receives and loses user focus. The main controller function would probably handle the Load event of the <body> tag. In the following HTML example, the onLoad event handler is assigned to the main() function. When the event is fired, the main() function is executed. This function overwrites the original content of the page. The result is a Web page that displays the text "I am in control now, ha ha ha!" instead of "This is the normal content."

```
<script>
function main() {
  document.write( 'I am in control now, ha ha ha!' );
}
</script>

<html>

<head>
<title>test page</title>
</head>

<body onLoad="main()">

<p>This is the normal content. </p>

</body>
</html>
```

One popular way of using JavaScript over the Internet today is to animate menu items or buttons in a Web page. JavaScript functions handle the click or mouse-over events of Web page elements, and alter the display to show nested menus, or new images. This type of JavaScript use, although important to the overall application, is not necessarily considered architecturally significant. When modeling JavaScript in an application's analysis or design model, it is important to separate business logic and presentation. JavaScripting is very useful for both. When JavaScript is used to execute business logic—enforce validation rules, perform calculations, and so on—they belong in the design and, possibly, analysis models. When the scripts are used to enhance the presentation, they belong in the user interface models and prototypes.

Java Applets

Java technology has invaded nearly every aspect of Web development. JavaScript and Java applets are used to make the client dynamic. JavaServer Pages and servlets are used on the server. JavaBeans, small reusable components that can be used to build larger Java programs and applets, have brought Java into the component world. The Java revolution has even extended into the application server arena, with Enterprise JavaBeans (EJB)—transactional objects—and Java Database Connectivity (JDBC). A full discussion of Java technologies is, of course, beyond the scope of this book, indeed any book; a complete discussion would take a library of books! What is provided in this section is an overview of Java applets and some of its interesting architectural elements as related to making clients dynamic.

Using JavaScript in an HTML page is a simple way to make the client dynamic, but it does have limitations. In addition to JavaScript compatibility problems, the use of scripts in Web pages can work only with the tools and information available in the page. Additionally, as the code becomes complex, the nice JavaScript features that make it easy to use and deploy become a problem. It is not difficult to have JavaScript code evolve into spaghetti code. This is where Java comes in.

Java is much better suited to solving the large problems that scripting is not suitable for. In addition to being able to access the DOM, Java has the ability to define its own user interface, something even JavaScript can't do. Being a true object-oriented language, Java defines classes and uses inheritance. Perhaps the most important feature of Java, though, is that it is platform neutral. This is particularly important to Web application developers, because Web applications often exist in heterogeneous environments. The Java enthusiast's mantra is "write once; run everywhere."

The use of Java on the client is usually in the form of an applet. An applet is more or less a user interface control that is placed in a Web page. An applet is made up of both system and custom classes. A custom applet extends, or inherits, from the Java applet class. Additional user interface capabilities are available with the Abstract Windowing Toolkit (AWT), a Java class library that contains most of the user interface primitives and tools. More advanced user interface functions can be obtained from the Java Foundation Classes (JFC) and Swing components.[7]

Because applets are referenced by a Web page, they need to be identified by a tag. The `<object>` tag is used to identify an applet and, most important, where it can be obtained.[8] In addition to being platform neutral, Java applets are a good fit for the Web because deployment of applets is almost automatic. An `<object>` tag's parameters define the type of object (Java), the name of the class file to load and run, and, optionally, the

---

7. In addition to basic user interface tools, 3-D user interface libraries and specifications are available for the Java platform.

8. Previous versions of HTML had a separate `<applet>` tag. This tag, however, has been deprecated, and the more general `<object>` tag is recommended instead.

location, or URL, where the file or files can be found on the network. In the following HTML example, an applet called Bubbles is displayed to the user. The text between the <object> begin and end tags is displayed in place of the applet for non-Java-enabled browsers.

```
<OBJECT codetype="application/java"
        classid="java:Bubbles.class"
        codebase="http://www.wae-uml.org/javaclasses/">
Java applet that draws animated bubbles.
</OBJECT>
```

In this example, the codetype parameter indicates that the object is a Java applet. The classid parameter identifies the class name of the applet—the object that inherited the applet interface. The codebase parameter indicates that the Java applet class file can be obtained from the server www.wae-uml.org in the javaclasses directory and with HTTP. This means that the browser can get the applet by making another GET request to the Web server www.wae-uml.org.

Parameters can be supplied to an applet within the context of the <object> tag. Separate <param> tags can be placed between the <object> begin and end tags. The browser allows the applet to access these parameters. In the following example, two parameters are defined for the applet:

```
<OBJECT codetype="application/java"
        classid="java:DatePicker.class"
        codebase="http://www.wae-uml.org/javaclasses/">
<PARAM name="format" value="mm-dd-yyyy" type="data">
<PARAM name="style" value="DropDown" type="data">
</OBJECT>
```

One nice thing about Java applets is that, once they are downloaded to the client, the next time they are invoked, they don't have to be downloaded again. Let's face it: The Internet is slow, and downloading large Java applets can be time consuming, especially over a slow modem. Caching applets on the client can save a lot of time. Each time the Web page is revisited, the browser checks to see whether the applet has already been downloaded and makes sure that it has the correct version. If the version has changed or the cached applet no longer exists on the client, it is downloaded.

When a Java applet is created, many class files usually make up the application. To help manage this, a Java Archive (JAR) file can be created to package all the class files into a single archive file. A JAR file is, essentially, a ZIP file that contains all the class and auxiliary files necessary to execute an applet. A JAR file compresses the files, making them quicker to transmit over slow network connections.

In addition to easier management of Java files, one advantage of JAR files is security. JAR files can be digitally signed. When a user accepts a digitally signed JAR file, the applet could be granted security privileges that it might not otherwise have on the client machine.

ActiveX/COM

ActiveX is Microsoft's answer to reusable components. ActiveX is built on Microsoft's Component Object Model (COM). COM is an infrastructure in which developers can build components, each in the language of its choice, and share these objects to build bigger, more complex systems. ActiveX is simply the brand name associated with a subset of these technologies. One key feature of COM is that ActiveX/COM components are reusable by any, not just Web-related, program in the system. COM is very much a part of the operating system. In fact, each release of the Windows operating system is increasingly coupled with the COM technology. When thinking about the Web, the brand name ActiveX, not COM, is often what's in people's minds.[9]

In order to use an ActiveX object, it must be installed on the computer that it is to run on. Installing an ActiveX object typically means copying the DLL (dynamic link library), EXE, or OCX[10] file to the local hard drive and adding a few entries to the registry. Because ActiveX objects often have dependencies on other ActiveX objects or DLLs, these too need to be installed on the computer.

ActiveX is used to extend client-side functionality in much the same way as Java applets do. ActiveX controls are placed in an HTML page with the <object> tag. ActiveX controls have some pretty significant advantages over Java applets. For one, their security model allows ActiveX controls full reign over client operating system resources. In an Internet environment, this might be a problem, but for secure intranets, they offer capabilities that Java applets do not.[11]

ActiveX components can be made aware of the DOM. Included in a Web page and invoked by a browser, they can access the object model of the HTML page, as well as the browser itself. This means that an ActiveX component can control the content of the Web page it originally came in with, just as the JavaScript examples did earlier.

In Web applications, ActiveX components can be used to do two things: enhance the user interface and implement business logic. One common use of ActiveX on the Internet is, not surprisingly, as a user interface control. ActiveX components, or controls, can capture user input that is difficult to do in standard text boxes and selection lists. One of the most useful ActiveX controls is the DatePicker control, which allows a user to select a date from a pop-up calendar.

One key feature that makes ActiveX suitable for the Web is that the components can be automatically downloaded when needed. When ActiveX is used on the client,

---

9. For the most part, ActiveX and COM can be used interchangeably. I tend to use the term ActiveX when talking about specific components in a Web application; COM, when speaking in general.

10. OCX, the original name for the first generation of COM components, is another file name extension valid for COM components.

11. Of course, Java applet access to client computer resources could be increased with the use of signed JAR files. Even so, ActiveX controls have more access to client computer resources.

the control is typically packaged in a cabinet (.cab) file, which is similar to Java JAR files and can be digitally signed. Digitally signing .cab files is pretty much the main security mechanism for ActiveX controls; once they are installed on the client, they are exactly like any other COM component on the system. ActiveX controls and COM objects in general are just program modules installed on the client computer. They can be invoked and used by the Web browser and other programs, unlike Java applets, which can be used only in the context of a browser.

❑ ❑ ❑ ❑ ❑ ❑ ❑ ❑ ❑

Summary

❑ Web applications implement business logic. Business logic is a rule or a process that affects the business state of the system.
❑ The Document Object Model is a platform-neutral interface to the browser and the HTML or XML documents it's rendering.
❑ The browser is responsible for executing client-side scripts.
❑ Dynamic HTML is a vendor term that describes a combination of HTML, style sheets, and scripts that allow documents to be manipulated in a Web browser. DHTML is not a W3C specification or recommendation.
❑ JavaScript is the most common scripting language supported in browsers today.
❑ JavaScript resembles Java but does not have its static typing and strong type checking.
❑ A custom JavaScript object is an attempt to create "objects" with JavaScript. It involves the bundling of discrete functions with generic JavaScript object instances.
❑ JavaBeans, small reusable components that can be used to build larger Java programs and applets, have brought Java into the component world.
❑ The use of Java on the client is usually in the form of an applet.
❑ ActiveX controls are the Microsoft solution to distributing custom components inside Web pages.
❑ An ActiveX control, or COM object, is a complete executable module that is executed by the browser.

Discussion

1. When is it appropriate to include client-side scripting in an application? When is it inappropriate?
2. Under what conditions would you decide to use applets, ActiveX, or JavaScript?

Activities

1. Visit several Web sites that use drop-down menus. Examine the scripting used by each and compare.
2. Create a simple JavaScript object—prototype and functions—that represents a line item in a shopping cart.
3. Create an HTML Web page that uses the JavaScript line item object and allows the user to dynamically change the quantities of the items. You should include initialization code in the page to provide a few line items to work with.

Chapter 4
Beyond HTTP and HTML

The basic architecture for Web systems includes a client browser, a Web server, and a connecting network. The principal protocol for communication is the HyperText Transfer Protocol (HTTP). The principal language for expressing the content between the client and the server is the Hypertext Markup Language (HTML). For many Web applications, these are enough on which to base a robust and sophisticated Web application. Internet applications especially benefit from this simplicity, since requiring sophisticated software and high-speed connections on clients is not always possible.

With the recent successes of Web applications, more and more architects are choosing this architecture for their next generations of systems. The significant advantages of easy deployment and minimal client configuration are well suited to organizations that maintain a varied array of computer types and models. This increased use of the Web as an architectural platform, however, has stretched the limits of the ability for HTTP and HTML to deliver the functionality required in relatively sophisticated software systems. This chapter discusses the limitations and extensions to these two principal elements of Web applications: HTTP and HTML.

Distributed Objects

From an object point of view, one of the biggest disadvantages of HTTP is its connectionless nature. Object-oriented architects and designers have been working for years with distributed object systems and are familiar with their architecture and design patterns. If we consider how most Web applications work, we know that a client browser navigates a system's Web pages, with each containing a certain content, either active or passive. At one level of abstraction, the pages in a Web application can be considered objects. Each possesses content—state—and may execute scripts, or behavior.

Pages have relationships—hyperlinks—with other pages and objects in the system: Document Object Model, database connectors, and so on). The fact that pages are distributed to clients, where they are executed, in a sense makes the simple Web system a type of distributed object system. In fact, the principal goal of this book is to show how to model the pages of Web applications and other Web-specific components in an object-oriented manner, consistent with the models of the rest of the system.

It should therefore be no surprise that architects and designers of Web applications have a natural affinity toward distributed object systems. Distributed object systems have certain advantages, including the ability to truly distribute the execution of the business logic to the system nodes that are the most appropriate to handle it. But because HTTP is connectionless, many existing distributed object design patterns are difficult to apply directly to Web applications. Most distributed object systems depend on a consistent network connection between client and server.

In addition to the connection issue, there is a limit to how much functionality can be delivered with plain HTML client-side scripting, even with applets or ActiveX controls. In many cases, the bandwidth to the server is too restricted by HTTP for sophisticated objects to perform business tasks on the server.

A classic example is the basic address collection interface. Many software systems that require the collection of personal and business addresses allow the user to enter a zip (postal) code and have the system automatically populate the state and city fields of the address. For a Web application to do this, either the entire postal code list needs to be accessible on or downloaded to the client, or the system must make an additional server request for the information. Neither solution is well suited for the Web, since the zip code list itself might be many megabytes and take several minutes just to download to the client, and an extra server trip is lengthy: on the order of several seconds. Additionally, the usability issues related to a several-second discontinuity in the data entry process of a common address block will prevent most designers from pursuing this route.

The solution for this common problem is beyond the ability of HTTP. The client needs a quick and efficient way to query the server for the city and the state of a given zip code. In a distributed object system, this is not a problem; a client object simply obtains a reference to a server-side object that can answer the query. The server-side object will have access to a database of postal codes and city/state mappings. The response time in such a system will probably be milliseconds—depending on network bandwidth—instead of the seconds that a full HTTP page request would require (see Figure 4-1).

Using distributed objects in a Web application can solve a lot of functionality and performance issues that are often encountered in Web application development. There are costs, however, the most obvious being an additional order of magnitude of complexity in the architecture of the system. The key to the use of distributed objects in a Web application is to incorporate the distributed object system without losing the main benefits of a Web architecture in the first place. The most notable benefit of the Web is its ease of deployment. For a Web application to make effective use of distributed

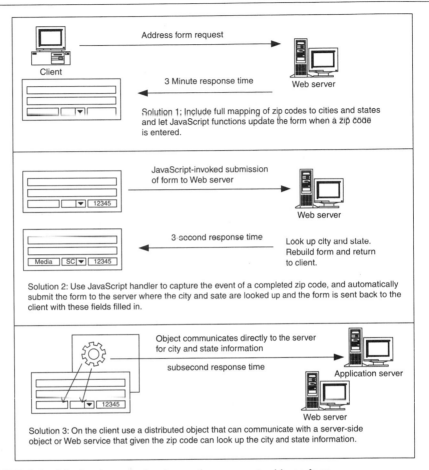

FIGURE 4-1 Mechanisms for implementing a smart address form

objects, there must be a way to automatically send to the client the objects and interfaces necessary for it to participate in the system without having the user stop the application and install special software.

Another benefit of Web architectures is the ability to leverage heterogeneous and minimally powered clients. Depending on the choice of distributed object infrastructures, there may be an impact on the types of clients that can participate in the system. In addition to the requirements on the client computer, using distributed objects in a Web application requires a reliable network; managing and designing for spotty network connections is often more trouble than it is worth.

At the time of this writing, two principal distributed object infrastructures are associated with Web application development: Java's RMI and Microsoft's DCOM. The goal of both is to hide the details of distributed communications and make them the responsibility of the infrastructure, not of the class designer or the implementer. They work on the principle of location transparency, which states that the object designer/implementer should never need to know the location of a given object instance. That decision is left to the architect or the deployment individual. Ideally, the designer of a class should not care whether a given instance of a class is located on the same machine, although the reality of distributed object design is that the actual location can be important, especially when designing to meet certain performance requirements.

The approaches taken by these infrastructures are for the most part the same. Each uses proxies, or stubs, as interfaces between the distributed object infrastructure and objects that use and implement the business functionality. Both provide naming and directory services to locate objects in the system, and both provide some security services. Bridges can even be built that allow objects from one infrastructure to communicate with objects in the other; however, these bridges are subject to severe functional limitations and performance consequences. The following sections offer an overview of these two infrastructures and how they are leveraged in Web applications.

RMI / IIOP

Remote Method Invocation (RMI), the Java standard for distributed objects, allows Java classes to communicate with other Java classes, which might be located on different machines. Java RMI is a set of APIs and a model for distributed objects that allows developers to build distributed systems easily. The initial release of the RMI API used Java serialization and the Java Remote Method Protocol (JRMP) to make method invocations across a network look like local invocations. Today, the use of Internet Inter-Orb Protocol (IIOP), a product of the CORBA[1] initiatives, as the transport protocol is preferred, making it easier to integrate with non-Java objects. Built-in support for this protocol is included in the latest releases of the Java Development Kit (JDK).

From the designer's point of view, the underlying transport protocol should have nothing to do with the design of the system's classes. This is not always the case, however. When IIOP is the underlying transport protocol, special care must be taken when designing operation signatures. Most CORBA implementations limit operation parameters to primitive types. Operations that accept Java object references as parameters might not be usable in IIOP-based systems. Also, the present release of the JDK does not support output and input/output parameters on operations. It is conceivable that existing CORBA objects might have operations that expect or require such parameters, and so it would be difficult for Java-based clients to use them.

RMI introduces two new types of object: stub and skeleton. The stub is a client-side object that represents the remote object and executes on the client machine. The

---

1. CORBA, like RMI and DCOM, is a distributed object protocol managed by the Object Management Group (OMG), the same group that manages the evolution of UML.

skeleton is responsible for managing all the details of being remote—responding to communications from objects on another machine—and exists on the server machine. The best part about these two objects is that you don't have to write the code for them yourself. They are automatically generated from a special compiler: `rmic`. This compiler creates the stub and skeleton classes from business objects that implement certain interfaces. For example, the `rmic` command would take the Java class `MyObject` as an argument and produce class files of the form `MyObject_Skel.class` and `MyObject_Stub.class`.

The goal is, again, to insulate the designer and developer as much as possible from the details of remote communication. Figure 4-2 shows an overview of the layered architecture for RMI.

To use a remote object, a client must first obtain a reference to it. This means that the client will need to know the name and the location of the remote object. This information can be expressed in terms of a URL. For example, a `CityStateServer` object existing on a machine called `myhost.com` would have the URL

```
rmi://myhost.com/CityStateServer
```

The `rmi:` part of the URL indicates its type or protocol. Clients wishing to communicate with an instance of this object use the Java Naming and Directory Interface to look up and obtain a reference. Obtaining a reference and using an instance of a `CityStateServer` object in an applet is as simple as

```
CityStateServer cs = null;
cs = (CityStateServer) Naming.lookup("rmi://myhost.com/CityStateServer");
aCity = cs.getCity(zip);
aState = city.getState();
```

The `Naming` instance is a well-known remote object that connects to the remote server and requests an instance of the object. It returns the object stub, which the client program uses to invoke methods.

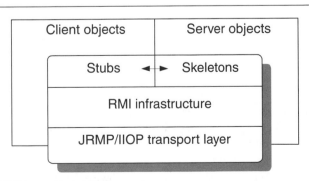

FIGURE 4-2   RMI layered architecture

One of the most significant features of RMI is that if it doesn't exist on the client, the stub for the remote object will automatically be downloaded to the client in accordance with the policies of the security manager. Every instance of an RMI-enabled program must install and run a security manager object. Applets, however, have the option of defaulting to the existing `appletSecurityManager` instance.

On the server, an interface is defined for the remote object as follows:

```
package myapp.CityStateServer;

import myapp.Address.*;
import java.rmi.Remote;
import java.rmi.RemoteException;
public interface CityStateServer extends Remote {
    City getCity( String zip ) throws RemoteException;
}
```

Each method call of the remote object must throw a `RemoteException`. All parameters passed to remote methods must be serializable (they will eventually get sent over the network).

Setting up a remote object server involves three steps:

1. Start a security manager class so that the server can accept stub classes from other machines and, in effect, become a client to another machine.
2. Create one or more instances of the server object.
3. Register at least one of the server objects with the RMI naming registry so that it can be found by client programs.

Presently, only Java applications, not applets, can be remote object hosts. This makes sense when the normal use of applets is in HTML Web pages that are quickly created and destroyed. The following code fragment for an application's `main` function shows the `CityStateServer` getting registered on a host:

```
public static void main( String [] args ) throws
    RemoteException, java.net.MalformedURLException,
    RMISecurityException
{
    System.setSecurityManager( new RMISecurityManager() );
    CityStateServer css = new CityStateServer();
    Naming.rebind("rmi://myhost.com/CityStateServer", css );
}
```

The designer and the implementer are not completely isolated from the RMI infrastructure; remoteable server objects must implement a certain interface and throw special exceptions. Clients must catch these exceptions and handle them gracefully. Additionally, all parameters passed as arguments to the interface's functions must be serializable, able to send their state out in a stream. The implementer also has other responsibilities; for the most part, however, it does isolate the designer and the developer from the complex issues of remote procedure calls, networking, and deployment.

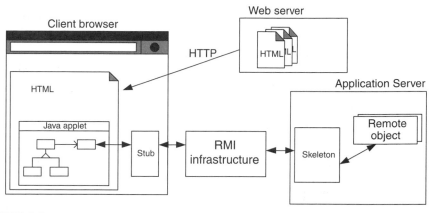

FIGURE 4-3   Applets using RMI

In a Web application, RMI is typically used as a communication mechanism between an applet and an application server. The applet is delivered as part of a Web page that the user navigates to. All that is required on the part of the client is a Java-enabled Web browser. All the classes necessary to invoke and to use remote objects will be downloaded to the client as necessary. Once the client applet is run, it can contact the remote server, request a remote object instance reference, and begin to invoke methods on it as if it were a local object instance. All marshalling of protocols is handled by the stub and skeleton classes and the RMI infrastructure. Figure 4-3 shows how applets and remote objects work together.

DCOM

Microsoft's solution to the distributed-object problem is provided by Distributed COM (DCOM), an extension to the popular Component Object Model (COM). Microsoft describes DCOM as COM with a longer wire. Most of the effort in making COM objects distributed is in their deployment and registration.

Just like RMI, DCOM isolates the object developer from the details of distributing an object. DCOM goes even farther by providing facilities to make COM-only objects live on remote servers. Unlike RMI, in which server objects must implement certain remote interfaces, DCOM gives the object developer independence from the distributed-object infrastructure.

COM object implementations are assigned special class identifiers (CLSID). Clients who want instances of a particular COM object request them with the CLSID from the operating system. When the client machine has the DCOM-supporting facilities installed, it is possible for these objects to be located on a remote server. When a client creates an object instance, the following happens:

1. The client calls `CoCreateInstance()` on a CLSID supported by a local server.

2. The DCOM runtime, working with the SCM (service control manager), determines whether the requested local server is running and can be connected to.

3. The client is provided with a reference to an interface proxy to the object. If an existing instance of the object is available, it will be used; otherwise, a new instance is created.

The principal responsibility for locating objects rests with the service control manager. The SCM will locate or create the object instance on the local machine or across the network, if necessary.

Once an object reference is obtained by the client, it can invoke operations on it. In normal COM, the communication between the client and the server objects that are in different process spaces is managed by the distributed computing environment's (DCE) remote procedure call (RPC) mechanism. When the objects are located on different machines, the DCOM infrastructure enters the picture and marshals the messages and replies over the network.

DCOM uses a scheme similar to RMI and CORBA, creating proxy and stub objects to act as interfaces between the client program, or server object implementation, and the COM infrastructure. The existence of these objects, invisible to the implementer, is provided by DCOM. Figure 4-4 shows an overview of the DCOM architecture.

The principal strategy for deploying these objects is to either manually install the object proxies on the client or use the code-downloading capabilities of Internet Explorer (IE) to do it for you. IE versions 3 and higher are capable of requesting and downloading COM components from servers. The download is, of course, subject to the security policies set up on the client. The objects that are downloaded are complete COM

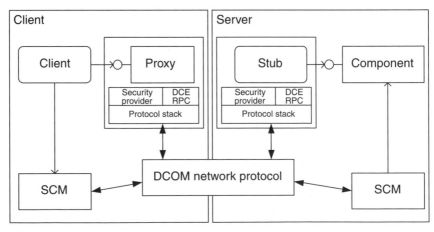

FIGURE 4-4　Overview of DCOM architecture

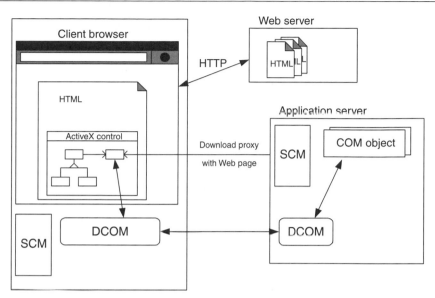

FIGURE 4-5   Use of distributed objects in a Web application

objects that can run entirely on the client. This means that if it is possible to download a COM object, it is possible to download proxies for remote objects as well.

When DCOM is used in a Web application, Web pages contain ActiveX controls that are downloaded to the client and executed. Along with these controls, proxy objects can be downloaded and registered to point to implementation objects on the appropriate application server (see Figure 4-5).

The biggest disadvantage of using DCOM instead of RMI or CORBA is the client requirement of running the Windows operating system. Even though COM and DCOM are public specifications, the reality is that only Windows-based operating systems support them. Additionally, Microsoft's Internet Explorer is the only major browser that has native support for COM. For intranet applications, however, this may not be a problem.

XML

The Extensible Markup Language (XML) does for HTML what distributed objects do for HTTP. XML is the creation of the W3C, which also controls the evolution of HTML. XML offers Web application developers another way to express Web page content. One of the principal problems with HTML is that content and presentation details are woven into the same document. XML documents don't contain presentation information; instead, a separate document, formatted with the Extensible Stylesheet Language (XSL) or a cascading style sheet (CSS) document, is referenced in order to render the document in a browser. In most situations, XML documents are not rendered only in browsers but are used as a cross-platform way to managing and communicate data between systems.

A lot of hype surrounds XML, as well as a lot of confusion as to what XML is and how it relates to Web applications. It is true that XML is powerful and will be a significant player in the next generations; however, it is not a technological silver bullet. XML is just a language, or rather a metalanguage. To be effective, therefore, it requires agreement by all parties using it. Additionally, XML is not dependent on Web architectures; nor are Web architectures dependent on XML. Although their evolution has been tightly related, they are separate technologies and concepts.

Basically, an XML-formatted document is a text document that defines a hierarchical collection of elements. An element is one part of a document and usually contains a textual value. An element can have child elements and thus form a hierarchy. Every XML document begins with one root element. Elements can be enhanced with attributes, which are just key/value pairs. Elements have bodies that can contain free-form text, with some restrictions.

The beauty of XML, and the reason that so many people are interested in it, is that you can define your own element types and associate your own semantics with it. In effect, XML offers the basic rules for formatting generic documents so that simple parsers can read and validate their contents. With the availability of free parsers, development teams are more likely to adopt XML document structures as a standard.

Most content of an XML document is textual; however, elements of the document can point to, but not directly contain, nontextual resources, such as images or applications.[2] By describing documents with XML, generic XML parsers can be used to extract the document's structure. Individual applications will still have to apply semantic meanings to the elements. A document that obeys XML formatting rules is considered well formed and can be parsed by any generic XML parser.

XML, like HTML, has its roots in the Standard Generalized Markup Language (SGML), the mother tongue for a whole group of document-formatting languages. XML formats its content with tags. An XML element is expressed with a pair of tags: a beginning tag and an ending tag. The following XML document could be used to express a postal address:

```
<?xml version="1.0" encoding="UTF-8"?>
<address>
    <street>123 Pine Rd.</street>
    <city>Lexington</city>
    <state>SC</state>
    <zip>19072</zip>
</address>
```

---

2. Of course, a binary file can be encoded into normal text, but this is beyond the scope of XML. In the majority of situations, XML documents contain references to binary data only through URLs or relative file system paths.

A proper XML document begins with a heading that indicates the version of XML and the encoding character set. As in HTML, tags are surrounded by angle brackets (< >). White space outside of tags is optional, so the indenting of the address's child elements is strictly for human reading. Space between an element's tags is not ignored, however. Ending tags are denoted by a slash as the first character, followed by the tag name. The text between these tags is the element's value. An element's value can be any combination of text or child elements. In the preceding example, the <address> element has four child elements, each of which contains textual information.

Unlike HTML, elements cannot have open-ended or overlapping tags. Every beginning tag must have an ending tag, or the tag can be constructed in a shorthand form:

```
<pobox/>
```

The tag for pobox is both a beginning and an ending tag. This tag on its own conveys no information, except its existence. Additional information can be tied to an element through the use of element attributes. For example, the tag pobox might have the attributes id and rural defined:

```
<pobox id="1234" rural="false"/>
```

When these attributes are included, the usefulness of the pobox tag becomes clearer.

The trick to successfully using XML in an application and across applications is in obtaining agreement on the structure and the semantics of the documents that will be used. The preceding address element is intuitive to a human being, at least to U.S. residents, but an automated application must be programmed to accept address information in this form. Take as an example a healthcare provider that has an application that exchanges patient information with an insurance company. The insurance company might expect address information in the preceding form, but the healthcare company might supply addresses in the following form:

```
<?xml version="1.0" encoding="UTF-8"?>
<patient-address>
    <street>
        <line1>123 Pine Rd.</line1>
        <line2></line2>
    </street>
    <city name="Lexington"/>
    <state abbrev="SC"/>
    <zip base="19072" plus4=""/>
</patient-address>
```

The insurance company application will not automatically associate the proper semantic meaning to the document and will not be able to use it. In order for XML to be used as a general data interchange medium, a mechanism is needed to help coordinate and to define the construction. The answer lies in a DTD.

A document type definition (DTD) is a document that defines the syntax for a particular type of XML document. DTDs are used to determine whether any given XML document is valid; that is, its structure is defined by a DTD. A DTD is a document that can be embedded in an XML document or exist as a file on the network and be referenced in the document. DTD syntax rules are a little different from those of XML.

A DTD is not required for a parser to read the document. Our first XML address document example is a well-formed document that can be read and parsed; however, it is unclear whether it is also a valid document. For this, it must be checked against a DTD. If the DTD was included with the first version of the address, the XML document would be as follows:

```
<?xml version="1.0" encoding="UTF-8"?>
<!DOCTYPE address [
    <!ELEMENT address (street, city, state, zip)>
    <!ELEMENT street (#PCDATA)>
    <!ELEMENT city (#PCDATA)>
    <!ELEMENT state (#PCDATA)>
    <!ELEMENT zip (#PCDATA)>
]>
<address>
    <street>123 Pine Rd.</street>
    <city>Lexington</city>
    <state>SC</state>
    <zip>19072</zip>
</address>
```

The DTD, beginning with the keyword !DOCTYPE, specifies five element types. The root element—and name of the document type—is specified to contain four child element types. All the child elements contain only parsed character data (#PCDATA). Parsed character data is text that does not contain special markup characters, such as <, >, and &. This XML document, with embedded DTD, can be validated with a validating XML parser.

Instead of embedding a DTD in every XML document, it is possible to reference it and give the parser the option of fetching it— use a cached copy—to perform the validation. The second address XML document could be constructed with a referenced DTD as follows:

```
<?xml version="1.0" encoding="UTF-8"?>
<!DOCTYPE patient-address SYSTEM "http://dtd.mycompany.com/paddress.dtd">
<patient-address>
    <street>
        <line number="1">123 Pine Rd.</line>
        <line number="2">Apt B116</line>
    </street>
    <city name="Lexington"/>
    <state abbrev="SC"/>
    <zip base="19072" plus4="4501"/>
</patient-address>
```

In this document, the DTD can be obtained with the URL specified after the SYSTEM keyword. This particular URL happens to specify also the machine name and protocol that can be used to obtain the document.

As XML becomes more popular and standards become defined, there is a greater chance that element names might collide. Because anyone can create elements, it is possible that a banking application, for example, might define the element <state> to mean the state of the account—open, closed, pending, and so on. Another application, dealing with psychological things, might define state to mean "normal," "depressed," "schizophrenic," and so on. While these elements remain in their own documents, there is not much of a problem. But a problem does arise for the designer of the Mental Health Home Banking application. The situation might be contrived, but it does illustrate the possibility of instances in which multiple XML documents get packaged together and name collisions occur. The element <state> could now have three meanings: part of an address, account status, or mental condition. This reuse of the element <state> would be very confusing for a validating parser.

To help parsers resolve this dilemma, the W3C has recently defined a namespace mechanism. In an XML document, a namespace can be defined that will allow us to continue to use the element name of <state>, but in each instance, we can define the namespace it belongs in. Each namespace is identified with the special attribute xmlns and requires a unique identifier, which is usually a common URL. For example, our address element might define a default namespace for the document:

```
<?xml version="1.0" encoding="UTF-8"?>
<address xmlns="http://mycom.com/postaladdress/" >
    <street>123 Pine Rd.</street>
    <city>Lexington</city>
    <state>SC</state>
    <zip>19072</zip>
</address>
```

In this example, a default namespace is defined for all elements of the address: the root element.

Namespaces can be qualified and multiple namespaces used in a single document. For example, our banking application might use a document like the following:

```
<?xml version="1.0" encoding="UTF-8"?>
<client xmlns="http://crazybanking.com/accounts/"
        xmlns:mental="http://mymind.com/mental/"
        xmlns:postal="http://mycom.com/postaladdress/" >
    <name>jim conallen</name>
    <accountno>123456789</accountno>
    <mental:mind>
        <mental:state>normal</mental:state>
    </mental:mind>
    <postal:home>
        <postal:street>123 Pine Rd.</postal:street>
        <postal:city>Lexington</postal:city>
```

```
            <postal:state>SC</postal:state>
            <postal:zip>19072</postal:zip>
        </postal:home>
</client>
```

In this example, three namespaces are defined, with one as the default. When referencing an element that is not part of the default namespace, the element name is pre-
fixed with the namespace. With the namespaces defined, a validating parser has a
much better chance of understanding and validating the document against a DTD.

Although DTDs are useful in Web applications, they have shortcomings.

- DTDs don't allow the specification of data types, such as numbers or dates.

- DTDs cannot be reused or combined to form new document definitions.

- The grammar of a DTD is different from that of XML and can be difficult to
  understand, especially by new users.

- It is not easy to expand the DTD with new features.

The next step for describing XML document structures is XML schemas. XML
schemas were introduced by Microsoft but are now under the management of the
W3C. An XML schema, like a DTD, describes the structure of an XML document and
also happens to be a valid XML document in its own right. In addition to describing a
valid XML document, an XML schema can go further to define element data types.

The XML schema that describes the second version of the postal address might
look like the following:

```
<?xml version="1.0" encoding="UTF-8"?>
<xsd:schema xmlns:xsd="http://www.w3.org/2000/10/XMLSchema"
elementFormDefault="qualified">
  <xsd:import namespace=" "/>
  <xsd:element name="patient-address">
    <xsd:annotation>
      <xsd:documentation>Comment describing the element </xsd:documentation>
    </xsd:annotation>
    <xsd:complexType>
      <xsd:sequence>
        <xsd:element name="street">
          <xsd:complexType>
            <xsd:all maxOccurs="unbounded">
              <xsd:element name="line">
                <xsd:complexType>
                  <xsd:attribute name="number" type="xsd:integer" use="required"/>
                </xsd:complexType>
              </xsd:element>
            </xsd:all>
          </xsd:complexType>
        </xsd:element>
        <xsd:element name="city" type="xsd:string"/>
        <xsd:element name="state" type="xsd:string"/>
        <xsd:element name="zip" type="xsd:string"/>
      </xsd:sequence>
```

```
    </xsd:complexType>
  </xsd:element>
</xsd:schema>
```

The details of the syntax are beyond the scope of this book; however, it is important to note that this entire schema is itself a valid XML document. The same parser that parses XML documents can be used to parse the schema document. In this document, data types are specified for some of the elements. There is also a place to include element descriptions, which can be captured by the parser. (Comments in DTDs are often skipped over by parsers and don't have obvious connections to the elements they describe.)

The use of XML in an application can get very complex. Just as this book advocates the modeling of Web applications with UML to help understand Web-centric architectures, it is possible to model XML with UML.[3]

Web Services

The term Web services is the latest hot phrase in development circles. Although the term has the word Web in it, it is not a Web application–specific technology. Instead, it uses Web technologies, such as Web servers and HTTP, to provide a set of services that can be invoked by other programs on the network.

The concept of Web services dates back to the early 1990s with Sun Microsystems's "the network is the computer" campaign. The idea was that with a strong and reliable network as the infrastructure, business problems could best be solved by distributing the solution of discrete problems to specialized components across the network. This decentralization of the processing mechanism has significant advantages as the system evolves, because relatively fewer places need to be updated when things change. Standards-based Web services first got some serious attention when Microsoft unveiled its .NET strategy. Web services play an important part in .NET applications.

Simply put, a Web service is a collection of functions packaged and published on a network for use by other client programs. From the highest levels of abstraction, a Web service is simply another type of remote procedure call (RPC). The difference, however, is what Web services bring to the concept of RPC. Much as component models—COM and JavaBeans—have made component reuse practical, Web services make RPC practical by providing a set of standards for discovering and invoking the services.

Component models define how components interoperate and how they can be found and examined programmatically. Both COM and JavaBeans have an introspection mechanism that allows other components to bind to them late and programmatically construct the appropriate function calls. Web services define a similar mechanism for the discovery of functional metadata.

---

3. See David Carlson, *Modeling XML Applications with UML: Practical e-Business Applications* (Boston, MA: Addison-Wesley, 2001).

Any Web service can interact with any other Web service. They can aggregate themselves to provide higher-level functions. After all, they are software components themselves, and all components have the potential to invoke Web services.

SOAP

One key to making all this practical is the Simple Object Access Protocol (SOAP).[4] SOAP is built on top of XML; that is, a SOAP message is simply an XML-formatted document that validates against a certain DTD or schema. When used with HTTP, SOAP messages—documents—can be sent to Web servers, which invoke the specified function defined by the Web service.

A SOAP message consists of a mandatory SOAP envelope, an optional SOAP header, and a mandatory SOAP body. The envelope is the top element of the XML document. The header is a way messages can be extended in the future with prior knowledge, similar to the use of the <META> tag in HTML. SOAP defines namespaces for the envelope and the encoding used by the communicating parties to ensure that the message is interpreted correctly.

In general, a SOAP message specifies three parts:

1. An envelope, which is the main container of the message

2. A set of encoding rules for application-defined data types

3. A convention for representing remote procedure calls and responses

In the following example, the address-lookup problem discussed earlier in this chapter might have been solved in part with a Web service. An example of the SOAP message that might have been used follows:

```
POST /CityStateLookup HTTP/1.1
Host: www.wae-uml.org
Content-Type: text/xml; charset="utf-8"
SOAPAction: "http://www.wae-uml.org/examples/CityStateLookup"

<SOAP-ENV:Envelope
  xmlns:SOAP-ENV="http://schemas.xmlsoap.org/soap/envelope/"
  SOAP-ENV:encodingStyle="http://schemas.xmlsoap.org/soap/encoding/">
  <SOAP-ENV:Body>
      <m:LookupCityState xmlns:m="http://www.wae-uml.org/examples/
          CityStateLookup">
          <zip>29072</zip>
      </m:LookupCityState >
  </SOAP-ENV:Body>
</SOAP-ENV:Envelope>
```

---

4. The full specification for SOAP 1.1 can be found at http://www.w3.org/TR/SOAP.

The SOAP response to this message is:

```
HTTP/1.1 200 OK
Content-Type: text/xml; charset="utf-8"

<SOAP-ENV:Envelope
  xmlns:SOAP-ENV="http://schemas.xmlsoap.org/soap/envelope/"
  SOAP-ENV:encodingStyle="http://schemas.xmlsoap.org/soap/encoding/"/>
    <SOAP-ENV:Body>
      <m:LookupCityStateResponse xmlns:m="http://www.wae-uml.org/examples/
          CityStateLookup">
        <City>Lexington</State>
        <State>SC</State>
      </m:LookupCityStateResponse >
    </SOAP-ENV:Body>
</SOAP-ENV:Envelope>
```

The rules and encodings for more complex data structures can get a little involved and are beyond the scope of this simple introduction. Fortunately, most tools today make the use of Web services very easy. In fact, in some tools like Visual Studio .NET make it is possible to couple an application to a Web service with simple drag-and-drop operations and a minimal amount of coding.

UDDI

In order to make Web services practical, you need more than SOAP. You also need a mechanism for publishing and describing Web services to potential clients. This mechanism is a standard. Universal Description, Discovery, and Integration (UDDI). A UDDI Business Registry is a set of replicated registries of information about Web services on the network. Registration of a service involves four core data structure types: business information, service information, binding information, and specification information.

- *Business information:* General information about the business, such as a unique identifier, the business name, a short description of the business, contact information, categories that describe the business, and a URL that points to a Web site with more information about the business.

- *Service information:* A list of related business services offered. Each service contains a description of the service, a list of categories that describe it, and a list of references to information related to the service.

- *Binding information:* With each service entry is a list of binding templates that define the access point and point to construction specifications for invoking the Web service.

- *Specification information:* A service type is defined by a tModel, which can be shared by multiple businesses. A tModel specifies additional categorization information and pointers to technical specifications for the service type, which might be a WSDL document (see the next section).

The general usage scenario is for a programmer to use a Web-based interface or specialized tool to query the UDDI registry via its inquiry API. The programmer can read about the business, search by categories, and follow URLs with a browser to obtain more detailed information. After finding the service that will do the job, the programmer selects an appropriate binding template and tModel. With this information and the information that it points to, the programmer can write the code that will use the Web service in an application.

This information described in a UDDI business service is packaged in an XML structure as defined by the UDDI specification and managed by UDDI registries. In general, this information categorizes and points to URLs that describe Web services but doesn't provide enough detail for a programmer to code a system that can accept and send SOAP-based Web service messages.

WSDL

What is needed next is a more detailed specification of the SOAP interface. The UDDI specification is focused only on finding the right service, not on explaining how to use it. The tModel structure in the service description points to the next specification and document in the mix, the Web Services Description Language (WSDL).[5] The WSDL specification describes in detail how to invoke a Web service and what to expect when it responds.

A WSDL description defines a Web service as a collection of network end points, or ports. Each port defines a collection of operations that can be invoked. Each operation includes a set of input and output messages: the parameters. A binding maps a port type to a specific protocol, HTTP, and data format, SOAP. A port instantiates a port type and binding at a specific network address.

A WSDL document contains five major elements:

1. *Types:* The `<types>` element defines the data types used in messages.

2. *Message:* Each `<message>` element defines input and output structures for operations. In the case of SOAP messages, these are the method parameters.

3. *Port type:* Each `<portType>` element defines a set of operations, whereby each `<operation>` element defines an operation and the input and output messages associated with it.

4. *Binding:* Each `<binding>` element maps the operations and messages to a protocol—HTTP—and data-encoding system: SOAP.

---

5. At first, I too felt overwhelmed by the number of specifications and document types that need to be managed to understand all the details of Web services; come to think about it, I still am.

5. *Service:* Each `<service>` element defines a collection of related ports. The `<port>` child element specifies the location of an instance of the Web service.

In general, the first three elements are an abstract description of the service. The binding connects these abstract descriptions and associates them with transport and encoding protocols. The service element provides the final piece of information and the instance of the Web service.

When all the pieces—UDDI, WSDL, and SOAP—are put together and with the right tool support, Web services can become a reality. Figure 4-6 shows how an application developer uses a UDDI registry to find and to locate a service that will make the development of the client application easier. With this service and by following the link to the WSDL document that provides the details, the developer can either use a tool or do the appropriate coding that will allow the client application to use the Web service. In the running client application, SOAP and HTTP are used to communicate with an instance of the Web service.

In Figure 4-7, a Web service developer codes—builds—a Web service and deploys it to an appropriate host. A WSDL document that describes in detail how to use this service is created. Also created is a UDDI document that describes the business and is used to publish the Web service on a UDDI registry.

Like distributed objects and XML, Web services are not required by Web applications; nor is the use of Web services only for Web applications. The two are independent. Web services might be an important part of your Web architectures. Those services

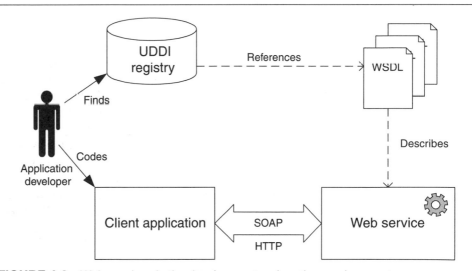

FIGURE 4-6 Web services in the development and runtime environment

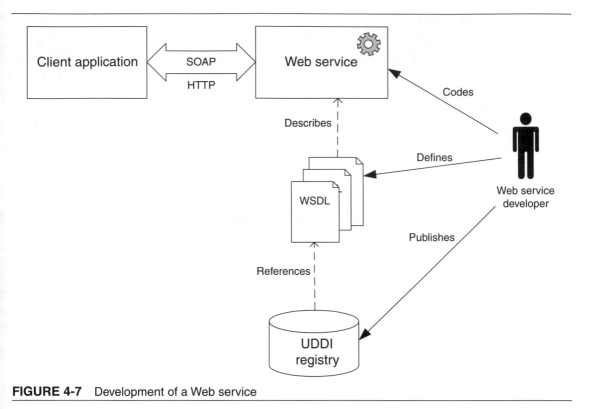

FIGURE 4-7   Development of a Web service

depend on HTTP, as do Web applications as a principal communications protocol. In many ways, Web services can be thought of and even modeled as a Web application. For the most part, Web applications produce HTML responses to HTTP requests, whereas Web services provide SOAP responses to HTTP/SOAP requests.

What makes these two technologies truly akin is that they use HTTP, a connectionless protocol designed for scalability and robustness. Many issues related to modeling and designing Web applications are a direct result of the use of HTTP. It should not be a surprise that the same issues can be found in modeling and designing Web services. Although this book is not directly devoted to an exploration of how to build Web services, it is hoped that an understanding of the issues involved in building Web applications can be applied to the building of scalable, robust Web services.

Summary

❑ HTTP and HTML are the principal protocol and language, respectively, in use on the Internet today. They form the backbone of a Web applications architecture.

❑ Web applications can be augmented with distributed objects that enable objects on the client to communicate directly with objects on the server, without using HTTP or going through the Web server.

❑ Remote Method Invocation (RMI) is a Java-based distributed object infrastructure that can be delivered to new clients in the form of applets.

❑ DCOM is COM on a longer wire. DCOM is Microsoft's infrastructure for distributing objects on different machines.

❑ XML, like HTML, is an SGML-based language and can be used for expressing content in Web pages.

❑ XML documents have many other uses, including metadata descriptors for Web services.

❑ The Extensible Style Language (XSL) defines formatting instructions for rendering XML documents on displays.

❑ You can define your own tags in XML. This gives designers the ability to tag document elements with special semantic meanings.

❑ A document type definition (DTD) defines the structure of an XML document. XML schemas provide a richer description of XML document structures.

❑ A Web service is a collection of functions published on a network for use by other client programs.

❑ Web services are invoked by sending SOAP-encoded documents to the Web service via HTTP.

❑ Web services can be searched for and examined in some detail through UDDI registries.

❑ Web services are described in detail with a WSDL document.

Discussion

1. What conditions should drive the decision to use distributed objects in a Web application? How do relative complexity, maintenance, functionality, and performance contribute to the decision to use distributed objects?

2. What limitations does the use of HTTP and SOAP place on Web services, specifically when used as an RPC?

Activities

1. Summarize the main advantages and disadvantages of using distributed objects in a Web application.
2. Explain how the use of XML and XSL makes it easier to separate content from presentation in a Web application.

Chapter 5
Security

If you are building an Internet application, security is a concern. Even if you are building an intranet application—one protected behind a company firewall—security should still be a concern. Security is the term we use to describe the protection of our data and systems. A secure system is a properly functioning software application that does only what it is supposed to do, without compromising the integrity of our data to those who are not authorized to have that information.

If our systems did only what they were supposed to do, security would not be an issue. So why is security a problem? Because our software and business processes often do things that we don't want or intend them to do. Unscrupulous individuals with even limited access to your system will take advantage of any side effect of the system to gain access to potentially valuable information—customer profiles and credit card numbers—or will simply bring your system down as a test of personal skill and pride. The threat is very real, and with Web applications taking on more mission-critical roles in corporations today, the need to understand the security risks and to manage them becomes even more critical.

The alt.security newsgroup FAQ[1] summarizes the issues of security by answering the following common question:

Q: What makes a system insecure?

A: Switching it on. The adage usually quoted runs along these lines: "The only system which is truly secure is one which is switched off and unplugged, locked in a titanium lined safe, buried in a concrete bunker, and surrounded

---

1. This FAQ is maintained by Alec Muffett (Alec.Muffett@uk.sun.com), with contributions from numerous others.

by nerve gas and very highly paid armed guards. Even then, I wouldn't stake my life on it."

This paints a bleak picture for system architects and designers, but as in all forms of engineering, compromises need to be made, and a delicate balance of functionality and security requirements must be maintained. This balance is unique to each software project and is not something that can be dictated by a book such as this.

Instead of presenting a complete security strategy suitable for all Web applications, this chapter introduces the issues and the nature of security risks specific to Web applications. Because security is a huge topic and the subject of many texts,[2] a full discussion is beyond the scope of this book. This chapter does, however, outline the security issues and topics that every Web application architect and designer needs to be familiar with when building Web applications.

One of the best sources of current information on security can be found on the Internet. The Usenet newsgroups are a valuable source of current information about security issues for both the new and the experienced. In particular, newsgroup FAQs are an excellent way to get introduced to issues facing a Web system architect. Much of the information in this chapter has come from reading these FAQs, and it is highly recommended that Web application architects and designers make a regular habit of monitoring the activity in these newsgroups.

Types of Security Risk

To understand the areas of risk in our application, we need to understand where our systems are vulnerable. The basic Web system architecture, being a variant of a client/server architecture, has three principal architectural elements: the client, the server, and the network. Each is vulnerable to attack (see Figure 5-1).

- Our *clients* are at risk from software that damages the client's system or compromises private client-side resources, such as personal information and files.

- Our *servers* are at risk from unauthorized access to the server, which may result in the capture of confidential information, the execution of damaging programs in the server, or even the temporary disabling of server functions.

- Our *networks* can be monitored and data communications between the client and the server can be intercepted.

It is the job of the chief architect and designers to understand and to manage these risks. Managing security risks in a software application happens at two levels: technical

---

2. Three excellent security reference books are Lincoln D. Stein, *Web Security: A Step-by-Step Reference Guide* (Boston, MA: Addison-Wesley, 1998); Simson Garfinkel and Gene Spafford, *Web Security & Commerce (Nutshell Handbook)* (Sebastopol, CA: O'Reilly, 1997); and Li Gong, *Inside Java™ 2 Platform Security: Architecture, API Design, and Implementation* (Boston, MA: Addison-Wesley, 1999).

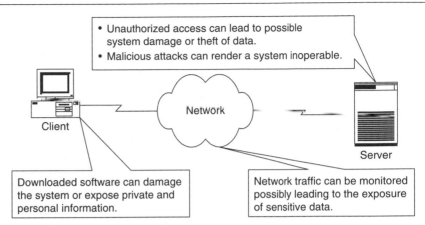

- Unauthorized access can lead to possible system damage or theft of data.
- Malicious attacks can render a system inoperable.

Client

Network

Server

Downloaded software can damage the system or expose private and personal information.

Network traffic can be monitored possibly leading to the exposure of sensitive data.

FIGURE 5-1   Areas of risk in a Web application

and procedural. Technical risk, the focus of this chapter, deals with risk presented by the technical components of the system—hardware and software—and is the domain of the architect. This type of risk is managed by a good understanding of the system and its deployment and by adding to the design certain technical measures that make it more secure.

Procedural risks, on the other hand, represent areas that are a result of poor operating practices. As any security expert will tell you, many of the security holes in your system are a result of human error and confusion. A classic story told in security circles is about a top-notch security expert called in to examine the latest security precautions at a banking institution. The institution was proud of its security precautions, which were a comprehensive set of the latest and most advanced technologies. The expert managed to gain access to the system by simply making a call to a new employee at the bank. The expert, claiming to be a member of the bank's IT department, asked the new employee for his name, office location, phone extension, and computer password, claiming to be updating the employee's status on the system. The new employee gave the expert the required information, and within minutes, the expert had gained access to the system.

This story emphasizes the point that security is more than a technical issue. In order to maximize the security of our systems, we need to be aware of both the technical and the human aspects of our system's vulnerabilities. Establishing proper security policies and training users of a system is as important to its security as any technical component.

Technical Risk

To understand the technical security risks of a system, architects and designers need to understand the nature of these risks in order to prevent problems. The nature of risks in our systems can be categorized into four major areas:

- Improperly configured systems
- Buggy software
- Poor authentication, or insufficient password requirements
- Lack of encryption in network traffic

The primary reason that any given part of a system is a security risk is improperly configured, or buggy, software. An improperly configured system, or a system with a bug, opens a security hole that can be exploited. One of the most famous security breaches has been chronicled by Clifford Stoll in his book *The Cuckoo's Egg*, in which he describes the eventual capture of a successful West German cracker.[3] The cracker managed to gain privileged access to a number of systems throughout the world by exploiting a bug—unknown feature—in a common text-editing program. The program allowed users of the system to save a file to a particularly important area of the file system. Files in this directory were automatically executed with root-level privileges and considered normal parts of the operating system. Once there, the hacker's file was run, giving the intruder a secret and unmonitored account on the system, which he used to anonymously examine the system for important information, and as a jumping-off point to the next unconquered system. This bug has long since been fixed, along with many other bugs that have been discovered as a result of a security breach.

Anonymous attackers are not the only worry of a security-conscious designer. A disgruntled employee can cause even more damage to a system than an intruder who has only the most basic knowledge of the system. It is therefore important to establish the identity of the users of the system as best as practically possible. At a minimum, separate user accounts and private passwords need to be established.

In a Web application, proper authentication of a system's users can happen at several levels. At one level, the client computer itself can be authenticated for use with the system. A Web application can be designed to allow only clients with certain IP addresses. My previous Internet service provider (ISP) uses this type of authentication to protect certain Web pages in the technical support section of its Web site. Because I travel a lot, I often need to look up the local access numbers for the city I am visiting. This information is important to the ISP's customers but represents a minor potential for abuse from noncustomers, by tying up these lines trying to gain unauthorized access. This particular page is set up such that anyone whose IP address is one of the ISP's own addresses is allowed full access to this page, whereas others are diverted to a page that contains only partial access numbers: just enough to determine whether an access line might be a toll call for a customer. This type of authentication is not perfect, but the complexity it adds to the system does balance out with the risks involved.

---

3. Not to be confused with the term *hacker*, a cracker is someone who maliciously breaches a system's security, whereas a hacker is someone who is considered an authority on computer-related things.

The most common form of authentication is a simple password. Users of a system are given a log-on ID—a publicly known identification of the user—and a secret ID (password). To gain access to the system, the user must use both. After the first access to the system, the user is usually prompted to change the password to something that only the user will remember. Passwords are usually the first line of defense in a system and help prevent interactive attacks on the system.

This type of authentication has many problems. From a purely technical point of view, a user ID and password tell the system only that a user who knows that combination is requesting access to the system, not necessarily that it is the person who is supposed to have that knowledge. What a system is really authenticating is a user with knowledge of a valid user ID and password combination, not the real identity of the person requesting access to the system.

This problem is exacerbated by the practice in some organizations of creating "group" accounts, in which a number of individuals use the same user ID and password combinations. In these situations, an individual user's identity is never really known, and any given password is likely to overlap with the introduction and expulsion of employees. So it is likely that at any given time, valid user ID and password combinations are known by unauthorized individuals.

In Web systems, especially Internet systems, anonymous users are the norm, and a special account is often created for this type of user. Popular systems may have many thousands of simultaneous users, all using the same account ID. In many Web applications, one user ID/password pair is used to gain access to the application and the business logic resources but to share another common user ID/password pair for access to the database.

In many situations, knowing a particular log-on account won't gain a cracker immediate access to all a system's resources. Typically, user accounts are restricted to allow access to only those system resources necessary to perform the user's responsibilities. Of more interest to a cracker are the administration passwords, root or administrator. With this level of access, the entire system's resources are open for exploitation.

Administrator-level access can be gained to a system by obtaining a copy of the system's password file. The default configurations of many UNIX and NT systems allow this. The cracker can then use special software programs to "crack" the password file's encryption and thus obtain access to the system's more interesting administrator and root accounts.

Simple passwords can be cracked with programs that repeatedly guess passwords from dictionary words and combinations of numbers or other common symbols. Short passwords are especially vulnerable because fewer combinations of letters and numbers exist. The best passwords are combinations of letters and numbers that are truly random. The problem, however, is that a human is less likely to remember a completely random sequence of digits than one that has some semantic meaning to the user. Once a semantic meaning is placed in a password, it stops being purely random and is more likely to be cracked.

When creating passwords, you should not base your password on

- Your name or any part of your name
- Any part of a dictionary word or proper name
- Acronyms

In general, any systematic way of producing a password is subject to be repeated by an unscrupulous cracker. The following passwords are all considered bad because they can be cracked easily with common password-cracking software:

pba	Too short
jimc1	Based on user name
merlin	Dictionary word
bilbobaggins	Dictionary word
qwerty	Dictionary word and easy to see when typing
aaaaaa	Dictionary word and easy to see when typing
4tune	Prepending character to dictionary word
tune4	Postpending character to dictionary word
hIho	Capitalization in a dictionary word(s)
c001	Substitution of numbers for characters in dictionary word

The best passwords are those that the individual creates on a purely personal and random basis. The practical trick in password usage, however, is using passwords that can be remembered. I worked in one environment in which the passwords were distributed by the company's network administrator, who used a special piece of software that he believed produced very random and difficult-to-guess passwords. To increase security—in his mind—he changed them every three months. He assigned passwords to users of the system, expecting us to quickly remember them and to destroy written copies. The passwords were cryptic and difficult to remember. The result was that half of the users ended up writing down their passwords on Post-it notes and sticking them on their monitors. In the end, this was not very secure, yet there was very little that the common user could do.

The trick to the use of passwords is not to consider them the ultimate security tool but simply a first line of defense. To be effective, passwords need to be as close to random as the user is capable of remembering. Additionally, users need to be the ones to create the password; any systematic and organization-wide method of producing passwords is more likely to be cracked than are isolated and uniquely derived ones.

The final general category of security risk is lack of encryption. In this type of risk, intruders monitor network traffic, collecting the dialogs of communication between clients and servers. The most common network protocol on the Internet today is TCP/IP. When designed, security was not foremost in mind; the Internet, being the world's largest public network, does not prevent anonymous users from monitoring the general traffic passing through their systems. Crackers can use "sniffers" to monitor and to analyze the network traffic to a specific server or client and, possibly, to reconstruct

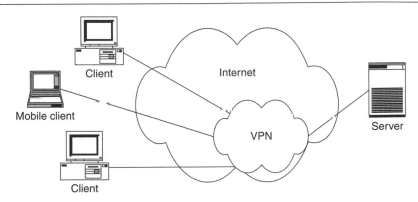

FIGURE 5-2   Virtual private networks

important information useful in gaining further access to the system or simply picking up a few valid credit card numbers.

To counter this risk, the traffic between the client and the server can be encrypted. Encryption is discussed in more detail later in this chapter, but the general idea is to encode the network traffic between a specific client and server so that the traffic cannot be understood by any listening third party.

One major use of network encryption is in virtual private networks (VPNs). In a VPN, a public network, such as the Internet, is used as a private network. All members of the private network use encryption to communicate with other members of the private network. From the user's point of view, the network looks like a private network, as might be seen in a small business with a local area network (LAN); see Figure 5-2.

VPNs have the distinctive advantage of allowing small companies to give private network access through the public Internet to individuals remotely located, rather than through more expensive private leased lines. Using VPNs places most of the security responsibilities, such as network traffic encryption, on the infrastructure rather than on the individual applications. Some Web applications may use VPNs as part of their security measures. VPNs can be implemented with a combination of software and hardware or with software alone.

Server-Side Risks

Once placed on a network, a server is vulnerable to attack. When placed on a public network, such as the Internet, a server is even more likely to be attacked. The major goal of an attack is to either gain control of the server or extract valuable information from it. Achieving the first will make achieving the second trivial.

The specific risks of Web application servers—those processing HTTP Web requests—are like those for most systems and relate to improper configuration, or bugs, in the software. A cracker will exploit a bug in a server's software or an improperly configured system. The most common configuration mistakes involve the enabling of optional features not required for the application. For example, one common feature of a Web server is directory browsing. This feature allows anonymous users to examine the contents of whole directories on the Web server instead of only the contents of the files it is supposed to serve.

A cracker uses as much information as can be obtained about a system to break into it. The more information a cracker has, the more likely that the system can be cracked. Allowing directory browsing gives the potential cracker more information about the system. This information can include backup files of sensitive scripts that contain source code to the applications modules.

EMACS, the popular UNIX-based editor, by default maintains a backup copy of files that it is working on, usually in the directory where the original file exists. A sloppy developer might have used EMACS to correct a bug in a CGI Perl script on the production machine and forgotten to remove the EMACS-generated backup file. Recognizing this file in a directory listing of the CGI directory, a cracker would examine it. The file contains source code to the application and valuable information about the Web application's server-side resources.

Allowing the use of symbolic links to directories elsewhere in the system is another dangerous feature. Symbolic links, such as /etc, to sensitive areas of a server are very dangerous. Unless the application requires the use of symbolic links, it is best to keep this feature turned off.

Another major security hole is the use of server-side includes (SSI). An SSI is a directive that is embedded in an HTML page. When a user requests this page, the Web server processes the embedded command(s) before sending back the HTML page. Some server-side includes allow the execution of general operating system commands or scripts. These "exec"-style directives are a major security hole and should be allowed only when absolutely necessary. They open up the possibility of an attacker's embedding a command that might e-mail out the system's password file or do other forms of malicious damage.

In addition to improperly configured servers, bugs in the Web server and associated software—even including the operating system itself—are a major security risk. Take, for example, one of the early versions of Microsoft's IIS and Active Server Pages running on a Windows NT 4.0 server. When the Web server used an NTFS-formatted file system, partition clients could request the source code to all the ASPs by simply appending :$DATA to a Web page request. In fact, clients could even request the raw contents of the special application configuration file (global.asa). This particular file often contains important configuration information normally hidden to users of the application.

One of my first ASP commerce applications was susceptible to this bug. My jaw virtually dropped to the floor when a friend, who had been notified of this bug when the word first went out, e-mailed me the contents of my global.asa file, which contained important information on the structure of my application. Of course, the first thing I did was to navigate to the Microsoft Web site: http://www.microsoft.com/default.asp:$DATA. For the next 36 hours, the entire ASP development community was abuzz in activity; by the time the fix came out from Microsoft, we had all come to the collective realization that none of us could write decent code. Fortunately, neither that file nor the contents of other dynamic files in the system alone were sufficient to allow the novice cracker unwanted access to the system. But the mere fact that the information was available was dangerous to the security of the system. Even before the official patch came out, several workarounds had been posted to the Net immediately after the bug was publicly known.

When a company makes its first plunge into the world of Internet commerce, the question that is often asked is: Are some operating systems and Web servers more secure than others? The simple answer is yes, qualified with "at any given time." It is impossible to say which operating systems are the most secure at this moment; things could be completely different in a few months. In general, the older and more stable the operating system is, the more secure it is because most of the obvious bugs have been discovered and patched. Of course, with each patch comes the potential for newer bugs and incompatibilities to be introduced. This cycle of operating system patch and upgrades eventually leads to a refinement of the system, ideally one with greater stability. Unfortunately, the cycle resets itself each time a new set of features, or a significant upgrade, is introduced.

Client-Side Risks

Just as servers are, clients too are at risk in Web applications, especially those on the Internet. It is possible for Web browsers to unknowingly download content and programs that could open the client system to crackers and automated agents all over the Net. Malicious programs could collect and send sensitive and private information from the client machine to Net programs and servers that collect such information.

As a general rule, pure HTML 3.2, without client-side scripting, is rather secure. There is little that a Web page designer can do to extract or to breach a client's security. Client-side risk usually involves the following technologies:

- Cookies
- JavaScript
- Java applets
- ActiveX controls
- Plug-ins
- MIME-type viewers

Cookies

Except for cookies, each of these technologies is used by Web site and application designers to make the client itself more dynamic: animation, fly-over help, sophisticated input controls. Cookies represent a direct risk only when Web application designers use them to hold sensitive information, such as private IDs and passwords.

As discussed in Chapter 3, cookies are little pieces of information that a server can request a client to hold on to, thereafter passed back to the server on all subsequent HTTP requests. Cookies can be either transient, ending with the browser session, or retained on a near permanent basis. Typically, cookies are used by Web application environments to help the server keep track of a single client browser's session as it navigates the Web application's pages. Permanent cookies can be used as virtual admission tickets. When visiting a site for the first time, a user enters certain information to allow access; all subsequent accesses to the system request the cookie and, if valid, immediately give the client access.

Cookies can become a serious risk when one application gets access to another's cookies. An unscrupulous Web site might trick a browser into thinking that it was a another site and request the cookie for that site. If the cookies contained personal identification information—admission tickets—this would allow the Web site owners to impersonate a validated user of that system.

In addition to data security, another type of security issue may be important: privacy. The proliferation of banner ads centrally controlled by a few companies means that these companies can begin to track a given browser's visited Web sites. Advertisers are interested in this because it enables them to target more suitable ads to Web site visitors. Privacy advocates are concerned because this type of tracking typically is unknown by the user and, when combined by some of the other threats, can lead to a serious security breach of personal information.

JavaScript

JavaScript, not to be confused with Java, which is a completely different technology, can be a serious threat to the integrity of personal information on the client. Since its introduction, JavaScript bugs and security holes have appeared at a consistent rate. Most of the security breaches have been the ability for scripts to gain access to files on the client machine, or to obtain sensitive information from the browserlike navigation histories or information in other frames.

One of the many early bugs and security holes detected in first-generation JavaScript-enabled browsers was the file upload hole. In this bug, it was possible for a script to trick the browser into uploading any file on the local system by a submitting a form to a server. Password files and other sensitive files could be unknowingly sent to servers.

Although not as obvious a threat to security, client scripts can collect information on the navigation histories of the user by monitoring a user's session. Some variants of this hole capture all the URLs that a user visits, including any information used to fill out forms. Even though data or software located on the user's machine cannot be modified, the detailed knowledge that can be gained is a violation of a user's privacy.

Java

The use of Java on the client is typically in the form of applets.[4] Security issues relating to applets usually center on

- Reading and writing files on the client
- Making network connections to any machine other than the originating host
- Starting other programs on the client or making native operating system calls

In the original JDK, the security model was fairly restrictive and described by the sandbox model. Remote Java code was allowed access to only a restricted set of functions on the client. Essentially, Java was allowed to play in the confines of a small sandbox.

In general, applets loaded over the Net are considered "untrusted" and prevented from reading and writing files on the client file system and from making network connections except to the originating host. In addition, applets loaded over the Net are prevented from starting other programs on the client. Applets loaded over the Net are not allowed to load libraries or to define native method calls. If an applet could define native method calls, it would have direct access to the underlying computer. Figure 5-3 shows the security model for the JDK 1.0 release.

For some applications, this model was too restrictive. Under pressure to provide more functionality, the JDK 1.1 security model was expanded to allow digitally signed applets to be treated as if they were local code (Figure 5-4). As discussed later

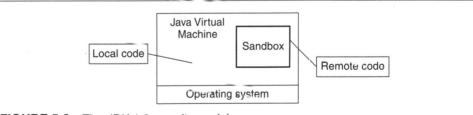

FIGURE 5-3   The JDK 1.0 security model

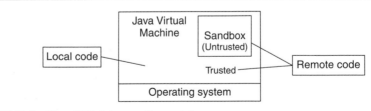

FIGURE 5-4   The JDK 1.1 security model

---

4. A good source of current security information related to applets and Java in general can be found on the JavaSoft Web site: http://www.javasoft.com/sfaq.

in the chapter, a digital signature encrypts a software module such that it is possible to determine, with reasonable certainty, that the code originated from the specified author without modification by a third party. A certificate authority (CA) is a third-party organization that can be trusted by both the server organization and the individual client.

Signed applets, together with their signatures, are delivered to the client in JAR (Java Archive) files. JAR files combine multiple Java files into a single file, which can then be signed and delivered to the client (Figure 5-5). In JDK 1.1, unsigned applets still run in the more restrictive sandbox.

The user has the option of accepting signed applets and examining the signature to determine whether the source can be trusted. If the applet is accepted, the Java code will run as if it were local code and will have all the privileges of any other application running on the client computer.

With the latest Java release, Java 2 (JDK 1.2), the security model has evolved to allow more control over which privileges any given component has access to. Even Java applications originating on the local machine are subject to implementation of custom security policies. The class loader is responsible for locating and fetching the class file, consulting the security policy, and defining the class object with the appropriate permissions (Figure 5-6).

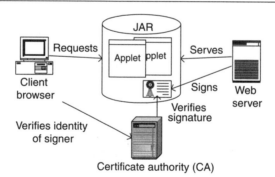

FIGURE 5-5   Delivery of digitally signed applets as JAR files

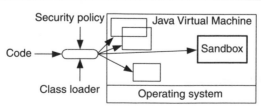

FIGURE 5-6   The Java 2 security model

Despite all this attention to security by the designers of Java, the problem remains of bugs and poor implementation of the Java Virtual Machine, which can make even the most restricted applets dangerous. Because the most serious security bugs are in the implementation of the virtual machine, the security issues resulting from bugs are usually related to a particular operating system and version. One of the most glaring of these is the bug in the Windows NT 4.0 SP3 version of the virtual machine, which results in the infamous Blue Screen of Death (BSOD). It seems that when even a trusted applet attempts to draw outside the bounds of a Java canvas, the entire operating system crashes.

ActiveX

The issues related to security for ActiveX content are similar to those for Java applets. The risks to the client are generally damage to the system or theft of private information. An ActiveX control embedded in an HTML page is essentially a compiled module, with free access to all the resources on the client. The potential for serious damage to the client operating system is slightly more than with applets because ActiveX controls execute only on Windows platforms,[5] and consequently, knowledge about the client operating system is more detailed.

ActiveX controls are COM objects; thus, they are binary modules that execute directly on the operating system (Figure 5-7). There is no virtual machine to insulate operations and to provide a security buffer. The principal security mechanism for downloaded ActiveX controls is code signing. There are no restrictions to what the ActiveX control can do once it is loaded and executed on the client. All implementation of security measures happens at the point the component is being requested to load on the client. Some security precautions are implemented by the browser. Internet Explorer can be configured to automatically reject all requests to load ActiveX or Java components. These settings can be configured to prompt the user each time a control is loaded or to trust everything.

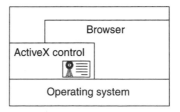

FIGURE 5-7   ActiveX security model

5. Emulators may be available to execute COM objects on non-Windows platforms, but the general rule remains: ActiveX content is for Windows-based clients.

Internet Explorer also has the concept of security zones. In a security zone, a subset of the network domain, the user can identify all the hosts in it as trusted or not. For example, hosts on a company intranet can often be considered secure and therefore ActiveX content on these hosts implicitly trusted. Hosts on the public Internet, however, are by default considered untrusted. The user has the ability to identify regions of the Internet, using the domain name server (DNS), as secure. For example, I might trust Microsoft and set up my browser to implicitly trust all sites in the microsoft.com domain.

ActiveX controls are packaged in Cabinet (.cab) files and digitally signed by the author. The signature, like those for JAR files, is verified by a trusted third party, such as VeriSign or Thawte Consulting, using public key encryption technology. It is very important to understand that code signing verifies only the identity of the author and that the module has not been tampered with. It does not impose restrictions on its execution or imply that the component is safe for use on the machine.

Plug-ins and MIME Types

A plug-in is an external program or module that is manually installed by the user to augment the functionality of the browser. Plug-ins were the original way to extend the browser's feature set with Netscape's Navigator. Plug-ins are operating system dependent; separate versions of a plug-in are required for each operating system.

The most common use of a plug-in is to act as a viewer of special MIME types (Figure 5-8). MIME (Multipurpose Internet Mail Extensions) is a freely available set of specifications that enable e-mail and Web sites to work with media types other than text: images, sound, video, and so on. Originally defined for e-mail, MIME has been used widely on the Web. The list of public MIME types is continually increasing. For each MIME type, the client must either natively be able to render the information, as with GIF and JPG files, or have an external viewer installed and configured to render the information.

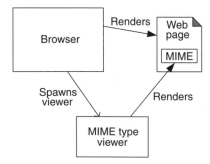

FIGURE 5-8   Plug-ins are often used as MIME type viewers

Plug-ins have the same security issues as ActiveX controls, because they too are implemented as native executables. The principal security mechanisms for plug-ins are built in to the plug-in itself. The browser can do little to restrict a plug-in once it has been loaded and executed.

Depending on the plug-in, additional security issues might arise about the content it renders. For example, a PostScript viewer may be tricked into changing the password of a printer that has not been assigned one yet. All further requests to print will then be denied until the password can be reset manually. Other MIME types and viewers may have similar security concerns.

Security Strategies

In general, we make our systems more secure by

- Limiting access to the system by means of firewalls, passwords, and so on
- Understanding the system and security requirements
- Keeping up to date on the latest patches and security alerts

Of course, the easiest way to limit access to a system is to disconnect it from any public network, such as the Internet, and physically secure all the points where the network meets the real world. This type of security measure might be fine and appropriate for military systems, but for Internet e-commerce systems, it wouldn't do much to help business.

Another option to limit access to intranet-based Web applications is to establish a firewall between the intranet and the Internet. Most companies maintain a firewall to insulate their internal systems from the external world; they are relatively easy to install and maintain. Firewalls, however, are no guarantee that an intruder or a disgruntled employee won't gain access.

Firewalls get their name from the steel wall between the driver's compartment of an automobile and the engine compartment. The idea is that a fire in the engine will have a difficult time spreading to the rest of the automobile. A network firewall is designed to prevent unwanted traffic from going into or out of an internal network (Figure 5-9). Typically, firewalls use a proxy server to monitor ingoing and outgoing traffic. Traffic can be limited a number of ways: by type—HTTP, FTP, or e-mail—or by address—www.waste-employee-time.com, and so on—as well as by others.

Perhaps the most important precaution you can take to protect your system is to have a realistic password policy. This policy should include training system users about the basic security risks and emphasizing the seriousness of keeping passwords private. All too often, passwords are shared and exchanged over the phone. The password policy must take into consideration the relative security risks and consequences with the personal considerations of the user. For example, 30-character passwords with nondictionary words and updated every two weeks are certainly more secure than 8-character passwords left completely up to the users' discretion and that never

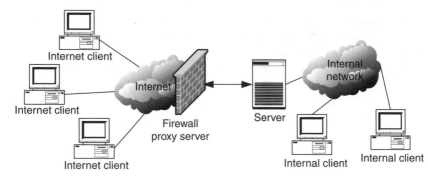

FIGURE 5-9   Firewall placement

expire, although 30-character passwords are often difficult to remember, especially for infrequent users. The password requirement can be configured to require at least one numeric character and periodic changes and to prevent the reuse of passwords.

In addition to complex password requirements, workers today are continually being requested to remember more and more unique passwords for various systems. I have to remember passwords for half a dozen Internet sites, my company network account, the HR intranet application of my employer, and several e-mail accounts that I continue to use. Even though it is insecure, I have little choice but to duplicate passwords or variants across systems just so that I can remember them. This is practical reality, and any password policy needs to consider this.

An additional option to authenticate a user can be done with personal certificates. Just as with code signing, individual users of a system can be required to authenticate themselves with a digitally signed certificate. Personal certificates, which can be obtained from the major CAs for a small fee, are of two levels. At one level, the certificate verifies only that the person claiming to be a specific user name has applied and paid for a certificate. The other, more expensive level verifies that the CA has checked into the identity of the applicant and has verified—usually via a government agency—that the person is who he or she claims to be.

Instead of relying on public certificate authorities, large organizations can distribute their own certificates to users of their system. These certificates, however, imply an existing trust relationship between the user and the company acting as its own CA. Distributing your own certificates is a cost-effective way to authenticate users of intranet systems.

Encryption

Certificates and code signing rely on digital cryptology. This same technology can be used to help secure the underlying network traffic in a Web application. Because many Web applications use the public Internet to connect clients and servers, crackers can monitor and decode network traffic and, with some effort, determine access patterns and confidential information, such as passwords and credit card numbers.

To make client and server network traffic more secure, it can be encrypted. The push to e-commerce has prompted the emergence of several schemes to protect confidential information over the network. The two most promising are Secure Sockets Layer (SSL) and Secure Electronic Transaction (SET).

SSL was introduced by Netscape Communications Corporation and is a low-level encryption scheme used to encrypt higher-level protocols, such as HTTP and FTP. SSL requires that the server present a certificate from a CA to verify its identity and can, optionally, verify a client certificate as well. SSL is implemented on most of today's browsers, and nearly all e-commerce applications use it to provide a measure of security for their users.

SET, a relatively new scheme to process credit card orders over the Internet, is being proposed by Microsoft, Netscape, Visa, and Mastercard. SET uses a complex system of CAs to verify the identities of everyone involved in the transaction: the customer, the merchant, the card issuer, and the merchant's bank. The key benefit of SET over other schemes is that it goes to great lengths to protect the identities and information in the transaction from those who don't need it. For example, the merchant doesn't have access to the type of payment the customer is presenting, only the item, cost, and approval of payment. Also, the card issuer has access only to the purchase price, not to the item purchased. This level of security protects the customer from being placed on specialized marketing lists, based on purchasing preferences.

Encryption technology today is based principally on the concept of public/private key pairs. A message is encoded by using a public key, which can be obtained by anyone from a CA or is usually distributed by the person who owns the key pair. Once the message is encoded, the only way to decode it is with the special private key. Not even the original public key can be used to decode the message, thereby keeping it safe. The only way the message can be decoded is with the matching private key, which the owner should guard jealously (Figure 5-10).

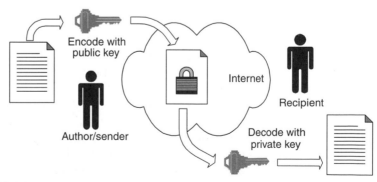

FIGURE 5-10   Public/private key encryption

The one disadvantage of public key technology is that the key is usually a long and cryptic code that can't be memorized by an individual. Therefore, keys are managed by copying and moving key files. So, just as with physical keys, a private key can be stolen or copied, and its protection is only as good as the protection of your physical machine. For example, anyone who can gain access to my personal computer will be able to decode encrypted messages sent to me at that machine.

Best Practices

Relying on technology alone is no way to ensure the security of your application. Making a secure application requires constant attention and awareness throughout the process of developing and maintaining the application. One of the first things that should be done when building a Web application is to create a written security policy. The mere fact that a policy is written down will help keep everyone involved aware of the issue.

A security policy should include at least the following:

- Who is allowed access to the system
- When they are allowed access
- What they are allowed to do with the system
- How users get added to the system and how they get removed
- System-monitoring procedures: types of logs and frequency of review

As with any policy manual, a security policy needs to be simple and easy to read. The policy manual should be read by every member of the development team and the users of the system. The purpose of the manual is to give everyone a better understanding of the issues related to the security of the system.

When configuring a Web application system, it is always a good idea to make the server as lean as possible. This will typically increase execution speed, but the fewer unused modules and features installed on the server, the fewer potential software bugs and security holes there will be. For example, if the application doesn't use CGI, turn it off. If directory browsing is not part of the designed application, turn it off.

Proper management of user accounts on a Web application server is also very important. As a general rule, I create a number of accounts or groups for particular roles in the development and maintenance process. The privileges for each account need to be carefully examined to ensure that they are sufficient to complete the user's tasks, and no more than that.

During the development process it is also useful to create a security view in the architecture model. A security view would contain such elements as users, policies, authentication, and so on. As with any other model in the system, a security model abstracts part of the system into something more easily understood. For a typical e-commerce application, the model will contain entities for customers, account managers, certificate authorities, policies, and so on.

Keeping a system secure goes beyond its design. System administrators need to be ever vigilant and actively monitor the popular security forums on the Web and Usenet newsgroups. The most up-to-date information about security holes and software bugs that might affect your system can be found on the Internet.

Modeling Secure Systems

Because this book is about how to build systems with UML, this might be a good place to briefly discuss appropriate ways to model the security interests of an application. In general, the security of a software system is defined by the countermeasures it implements. Five fundamental countermeasures and one organizing countermeasure are common to most secure systems:

1. *Access control:* Limiting system functionality to specific users.

2. *Authentication:* Identifying someone who has access rights to the system. Related to authentication is identification, which is the attempt to determine a specific identity.

3. *Audit:* Logging system activity, especially the activity of a system's users.

4. *Intrusion detection:* Detecting unauthorized use of the system.

5. *Encryption:* Converting data into a form that cannot be easily understood by those not authorized to view it. Decryption is the process of converting encrypted data into a form that can be understood.

6. *System assurance maintenance:* Managing system countermeasures and other functions that are related to security.

Countermeasures are best modeled as collaborations that involve system elements or roles. UML collaborations don't own classes or packages but rather express the behavior of a set of objects as they accomplish a common goal. To help distinguish security-related collaborations from others, the stereotype «countermeasure» can be applied (Figure 5-11).

Collaborations express the dynamic behavior of a system in terms of a particular arrangement of objects. Collaborations have both a static and a dynamic representation.

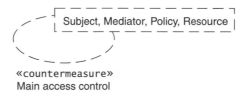

«countermeasure»
Main access control

FIGURE 5-11   Access control collaboration stereotyped «countermeasure» identifies a security-related behavior

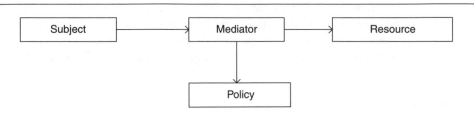

FIGURE 5-12   Static part of an access control collaboration

The static part is represented with a class diagram that shows the principal objects or roles participating in the collaboration (Figure 5-12). The dynamic part is represented as a sequence, or activity, diagram that uses the objects specified in the static part to express a scenario of behavior (Figure 5-13).

In the case of access control, Figures 5-12 and 5-13 show abstractly how a subject—user or client application—invokes a function on a resource. A mediator is used as a go-between and is responsible for checking the access control policy to determine whether this access of the resource is allowed. The access control policy is either hard-coded in the mediator or implemented as a property set or a file system document that is consulted each time a resource function is requested.

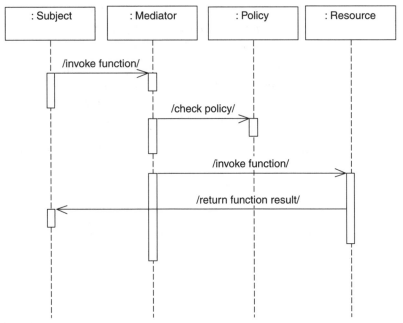

FIGURE 5-13   Dynamic part of an access control collaboration

Each countermeasure should be at least addressed in the software architecture document if not implemented. For each, there may be many different implementations, and if they are all stereotyped and organized properly, a security audit would be able to assess the ability of an application to counter any threat.

Modeling and even providing implementations of all the standard countermeasures is no guarantee that a system will be secure, but doing so will make it easier to determine relatively how secure one will be. Ultimately, the security of a system is at the mercy of the current state of software in general. Careful monitoring of all software versions—operating systems, infrastructure components, and so on—and of the most recent security bulletins is the only practical way of ensuring that any software application can maintain that balance of functionality and security.

❏ ❏ ❏ ❏ ❏ ❏ ❏ ❏ ❏

Summary

❏ Security is an issue that every Web system architect, designer, and manager needs to be concerned with.

❏ Usenet newsgroups are an excellent source for discussion of the current security issues of interest to system administrators and maintainers of Web applications.

❏ Security risks are present in all parts of a system: client, server, and network.

❏ The most common sources of security holes are a result of improperly configured software, or bugs.

❏ Passwords are the most common form of protection. Password policies should be managed so that they are practical for both the system and the user.

❏ Virtual private networks and firewalls are two ways to limit access to a network.

❏ Encryption technology can be used to authenticate users and to encode sensitive network traffic.

❏ Significant security issues must be understood when designing applications with dynamic client content.

❏ JavaScript, Java applets, ActiveX controls, and plug-ins all represent a certain degree of risk to the client.

❏ The use of cookies to store important and private information, such as passwords, poses a significant risk.

❏ To manage the risks of security, best practices need to be implemented, including the creation of a security policy document and a security model, or view, of the system.

Discussion

1. What factors help decide the balance between functionality and security when designing an application?
2. Discuss the advantages and disadvantages of excessive logging when a system is under a security attack.
3. Discuss which countermeasures are most important for specific types—business domain—of applications.

Activities

1. Develop a simple security policy document for an e-retail store.
2. Examine a cookie file on your machine, and look for identifiers and codes that may be used to track your movements on the Internet. Search your cookie files, that is `grep`, for multiple instances of these codes across different domains.
3. Change the security settings of your browser to warn you every time a cookie is placed on your browser, and then try to use some Internet-based Web applications.

Part Two
Building Web Applications

Chapter 6

The Process

If you are looking for a cookie-cutter recipe to success, forget it. Developing applications is hard work and relies heavily on the skill and the ability of everyone involved. Even so, a strong process is important. Heroic efforts on the part of a development team can often bring a project to maturity; however, heroic efforts and strong process can do so repeatedly and reliably.

A single chapter of a book is hardly sufficient to explain any software development process in detail, but it is enough for one to get an overview of the process and be able to identify and to explain its key points. This chapter introduces a software development process, explains its terms and concepts as applied to the development of a Web application, and goes on to establish the context and vocabulary for the remaining chapters.

First-generation Web applications have been created, for the most part, in the absence of a real process. They were the products of small teams—even teams of one—and had a limited scope of functionality. It was possible, and some would say even practical or optimal, to create these early projects without a strong process. However, current-generation Web applications are becoming more complex and are inserting themselves in more mission-critical roles. The demands for rapid development and high quality are stronger and more important than ever. All this means that the development teams are becoming larger and team members' skills are now more specialized. Developing these types of applications without a very robust, well-understood process would be foolish.

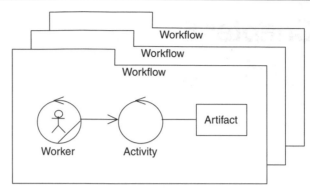

FIGURE 6-1   Roles in the software development process: workflows, workers, activities, and artifacts

Overview of Software Development

A software development process has four roles.

- Provide guidance about the order of a team's activities.
- Specify artifacts that should be developed.
- Direct the tasks of individual developers and the team as a whole.
- Offer criteria for monitoring and measuring the project's products and activities.[1]

A software development process is packaged as a set of documents, or it could be an online hypertext system. The process defines the workflows, activities, artifacts, and workers in the development process (Figure 6-1). A worker in this sense is a role performed by an individual in the process. In many projects, any given individual may perform the activities of several of these workers (roles).

A workflow is set of activities—requirements, analysis, design, implementation, testing, and deployment—that ultimately produce a tangible and observable result. Workflows are things. Each workflow typically requires several workers to complete and a number of activities and artifacts.

Workflows define a set of activities that the workers engage in. Activities are the things that the workers do to produce the output artifacts of the workflow. An artifact is any persistent piece of information that is produced by the workers during the process. Artifacts are models, model elements, source code, and documents. An important property of an artifact is that it can be version controlled. An artifact often undergoes significant change during the process, and an accurate history of its evolution is critical to the process as a whole. Another key aspect of version control, or configuration

---

1. See Grady Booch, *Object Solutions: Managing the Object-Oriented Project* (Boston, MA: Addison-Wesley, 1996).

and change management, is the association of change control and project tasks with discrete artifact versions.[2] This level of artifact traceability allows team members to track discrete tasks with artifact versions and enables project management to estimate realistic costs of activities throughout the process.

The process discussed here has its roots in the Rational Unified Process (RUP)[3] and the ICONIX Unified Process.[4] Both are essentially refinements of earlier object-oriented processes and methodologies based on the work of Grady Booch, Ivar Jacobson, and Jim Rumbaugh: the "three amigos."[5] The process has also evolved somewhat from the one described in the first edition of this book. Since that time, I've had the opportunity to work with various groups of architects and Web application developers. I've tried to collect these experiences, distill some of the good development practices I've seen, and incorporate them into this latest version of the software development process for Web applications. If you are serious about using a scalable and well thought-out software development process, my recommendation is to get the Rational Unified Process or one of its tailored variants.[6] These processes are not the only formal processes in use today but are the ones I am most familiar with, ones that I have used successfully, and unsuccessfully.

One additional process that deserves mention is significantly different from the ones already mentioned: eXtreme Programming (XP).[7] I have never worked in an XP-driven project, so my knowledge of it is limited; however, like most modern software processes, it includes a healthy respect for visual modeling and quality control. So if you are doing XP, much of the modeling content of this book is still applicable.

The key aspects of the process described here are that it is

- Use case driven
- Architecture-centric
- Iterative and incremental

Like most modern development processes, this one is iteratively based (Figure 6-2). This means that each workflow—requirements, analysis, design, implementation, test,

---

2. See Brian A. White, *Software Configuration Management Strategies and Rational ClearCase: A Practical Introduction* (Boston, MA: Addison-Wesley, 2000).

3. An introduction to the process is provided by Philippe Kruchten, *The Rational Unified Process: An Introduction, Second Edition* (Boston, MA: Addison-Wesley, 2000).

4. See Doug Rosenberg with Kendall Scott, *Use Case Driven Object Modeling with UML: A Practical Approach* (Boston, MA: Addison-Wesley, 1999).

5. A more recent view of their collaborative work, and a useful companion to *The Rational Unified Process*, is Ivar Jacobson, Grady Booch, and Jim Rumbaugh, *The Unified Software Development Process* (Boston, MA: Addison-Wesley, 1999).

6. See http://www.rational.com/rup.

7. Refer to Kent Beck, *Extreme Programming Explained: Embrace Change* (Boston, MA: Addison-Wesley, 1999).

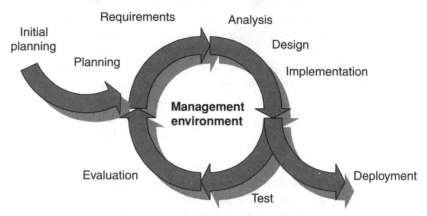

FIGURE 6-2 Iterative process (*Source:* Philippe Kruchten, *The Rational Unified Process: An Introduction, Second Edition* (Boston, MA: Addison-Wesley, 2000, p.7)).

evaluation—of the process is repeated and refined until it meets the system's requirements and is deployed. This is a significant departure from the traditional waterfall process, in which each project workflow was completed before the team moved on to the next one. Iterative processes came to be by simply acknowledging that software isn't created in a strict waterfall fashion. In all but the most exceptional cases, each phase of the project discovers issues and circumstances that question, and even change, decisions made in earlier phases. In the past, those changes were dealt with informally. Today, they are acknowledged and even planned for in the process.

The process outlined here is not intended to be used directly. In practice, any process needs to be tailored for each organization that uses it. Processes that are taught or found in a book are basically abstract. Implementing a development process is a process itself. It's very unlikely that you can walk into an organization, plop down a book, and say, "This is our software development process; read it, and we begin tomorrow." It won't work: not for the obvious reason that a day isn't long enough to read and digest a book but for the fact that the process needs to take into account a number of factors not available to the authors. A process must consider the following in order to be tailored to the task.

- *Makeup of the company and organization.* Large companies with pools of specialized talent may be more successful with an artifact-heavy process. In these types of organizations, team members perform one role and a small set of activities that are particularly suited to their talents and experience. Because of the large number of people involved, the need for formal communications among project team members is important. This means that the artifacts of the process must be complete and comprehensive. A greater emphasis on the review process might be appropriate because it is unlikely that team members will be participating in downstream activities and be able to provide explanations of earlier decisions.

At the other end of the spectrum, small project teams may prefer a more relaxed process. Teams that have worked successfully together in the past and whose group dynamics include good communications may not need the rigor of an artifact-laden process. These types of organizational structure rely on the proven abilities of the individual team members. This does not mean that a strong process is not required but rather that some aspects of the process, such as code reviews and formal meetings, play a less important role than others do.

- *The nature of the application.* What the application has to do can affect the structure of its development process tremendously. Human-critical applications, such as medical devices, spacecraft systems, and thermonuclear controls, obviously require a great deal of quality control. In these situations, strong emphasis is placed on quality assurance (QA), which includes reviews and testing. The rhythm of iterations in the process is established primarily by the successful completion of QA objectives.

  Given the present state of Web application technologies, it is unlikely that a human-critical Web application will be built soon. Still, other factors of the application can influence the process of building Web applications. For example, international applications may require significantly more up-front effort during analysis than others, placing a greater emphasis on the nonfunctional requirements and processes. Commerce applications have architectural and security implications that must be monitored during the process with additional reviews and exploratory prototypes. If the application's goal is to use a new technology rather than solve a specific business problem, defining strict requirements is not as important as allowing the team to take advantage of discoveries along the way.

- *The skill level of the development staff.* When implementing a process, the team's skill level should be taken into account. Relatively inexperienced teams require a more defined process, one in which peer reviews are more prominent. For these types of team, the development process is as much a learning process as anything else.

- *The relative priorities of feature set, time to delivery, acceptable defect count, and so on.* Whatever is important in the final system will obviously determine which elements of the development process are important. If getting the product to market first is the most important goal, reviews and inspections might be decreased, and the ability to remove requirements from the initial release might be given greater importance. The development process in this situation is tailored for quick delivery. When a rich feature set is important, it is important to ensure compatibility, and this means greater emphasis on analysis.

It cannot be stated strongly enough that the software development process has to work with the people and the goals of the effort if it is to be successful. A process is no good if it is not used. Huge monolithic processes that fill volumes of shelf space often go untouched because they didn't consider the people who had to use them. To be successful, a process must be accepted and used by the team.

While delivering seminars and working with Web application development teams over the years, I've had many opportunities to ask, "What are the most important issues facing you and your development effort?" Almost without exception, the issue of rapid development ranks number one. Other notable issues include quality, security, building the right application, and dealing with the rapid advancement of technology.

One additional issue facing these teams is related to the artistic aspects of the application. Internet applications today depend heavily on a good look-and-feel. In many situations, getting to the marketplace first is only the first step; maintaining a fresh look-and-feel, or user experience, is critical in keeping your customer base.

To handle the artistic and creative side of project, a new type of team—the user experience (UX) team—and new type of specialist—the information architect (IA)—have been introduced into the organization. Stan Ward of Context Integration and Per Kroll of Rational Software Corporation have done some excellent work in the area of integrating the "creative" input into the software development process.[8] A lot of the enhancements to the process here were influenced by their work, as well as by an examination of other cutting-edge Web development organizations.

The project goals of rapid development and high quality, along with the problems of the rapid pace of technology and reliance on artistic attributes, must influence the process. Additionally, the iteration schedule of Web applications is typically tighter than that of most other efforts, and the process must be suited to this fast pace of development. Fortunately, good sets of tools and frameworks exist today that maximize worker productivity.

Software Development for Web Applications

Since this book is based in large part on the expressive capabilities of UML, it would seem only natural to express the process itself in terms of a UML model. Using the business modeling extension[9] for UML, we can express the workers, workflows, artifacts, and activities of the software development process with UML elements.[10]

At the top of this model is the business use case view (Figure 6-3). The business actor Stakeholder represents all individuals outside of the project who have a vested interest in the project. They don't build the software; nor are they responsible for any

---

8. Stan Ward and Per Kroll, "Building Web Solutions with the Rational Unified Process: Unifying the Creative Design Process and the Software Engineering Process." A Context Integration and Rational white paper, available at http://www.rational.com/products/rup/prodinfo/whitepapers/dynamic.jtmpl?doc_key=101057.

9. The use of the business modeling extension is not completely accurate, because I pull out activities and represent them with analysis-level control classes. The official specification can be found on the Rational Software Web site as a PDF file under the title "UML Extension for Business Modeling."

10. The complete Rational Rose model is available from the Addison-Wesley Web site or from the author's Web site: www.wae-uml.org.

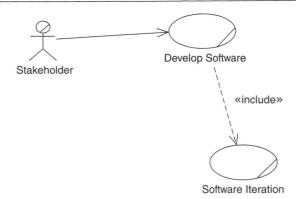

FIGURE 6-3   Top-level business use case diagram for the Web software development process model

artifacts of the process. Stakeholders do, however, contribute through interactions with the workers in the process. The Stakeholders are the customers, company executives, investors, and users: anyone with an active interest in the evolution and the delivery of the system.

A Stakeholder interacts with the "business" through the business use case Develop Software, which is the main use case of the process. A critical part of this use case is the included use case Software Iteration. Software Iteration describes the bulk of the work that we would normally consider as part of the development process. Develop Software provides the description of all the other stuff involved in the process, including the activities that start and complete the entire process.

Develop Software

The activities of the Develop Software use case are expressed in Figure 6-4. The development process begins with an analysis of the business and its perceived problems, at the same time developing a domain model. A brief description of each of these activities follows.

- *Manage artifact versions.* This activity is done concurrently with every other activity that involves the evolution and the creation of process artifacts. Essentially, it is the activity of the change management process and the use of a version control system.

- *Analyze business and perceived problems.* Take an objective look at the state of the business. Try not to be influenced by the perceived problems presented by the stakeholders. Too often the perceived problem, as presented by the stakeholders, only scratches the surface and hides the real problems, which are rooted far deeper. Only with an understanding of the business can you examine the real problems in a truly unbiased way.

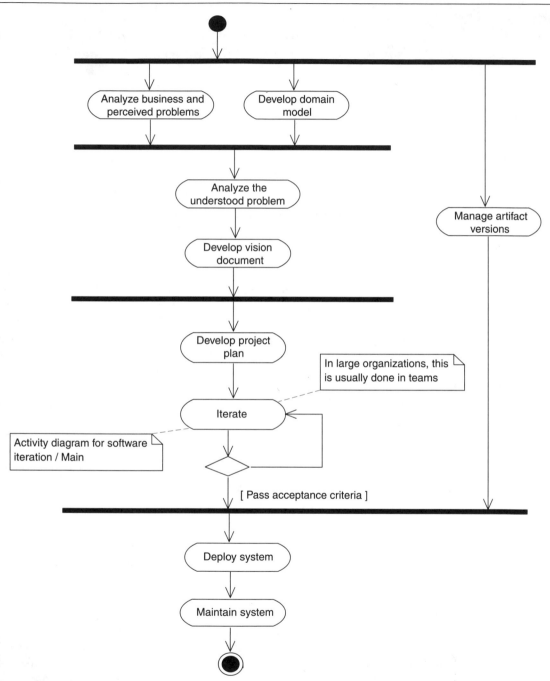

FIGURE 6-4   Activity diagram of develop software business use case

- *Develop domain model.* Use software development tools, such as UML, requirements gathering, and document management applications, to construct a model of the domain and the business. The UML extension for business modeling is the most appropriate way to express the major entities and processes of the business. The most important artifact of the domain model and the requirements model, however, is the glossary, which defines the key terms and concepts of the context that the system is working in.

- *Analyze the understood problem.* With a solid understanding of the state of the business and of the domain that it operates in, it is time to focus on the real problem, or at least the problem that the stakeholders are willing to let you work on.[11] Look at the problem without unnecessarily preconceived notions of the solution.

- *Develop vision document.* The vision document, the one that all else derives from, expresses the scope and the purpose of the entire software project. Typically, the vision document is focused on providing the principal features and acceptance criteria for the system under development.

- *Develop project plan.* The project plan outlines the activities of the entire software development effort, defining the major milestones and referencing appropriate standards documents, including the change and configuration management plan.

The project plan includes a first draft of the iteration plan. Planning iterations is key to the process. Iterations don't just happen; they are planned in advance. The project manager, with the architecture team, tries to identify the key high-risk areas for development. These areas are targeted for early iterations. The iteration plan describes in sufficient detail the activities that are expected to be carried out during the time period of the iteration.[12] The plan specifies the artifacts that should be delivered by the end of the iteration and, most important, the success criteria for each. The success criteria are important because in those situations, in which an encompassing artifact is evolved partially in one iteration, completeness may not be the goal, but rather a part or aspect of it is the real goal.

It is fully expected that the iteration plan will undergo significant revision by the time the project is completed. Ideally, the plans for the first and second iterations should be reasonably accurate, but the farther out you go, the more likely that the iteration goals become more vague, to be revised with more detail, as it is available, later on.

---

11. This may sound a little cynical, but on one project, it was pretty clear that the roots of the problem were that all the company's facilities were treated as cost centers, some of which were literally across the street from each other as a result of an acquisition binge. We, however, were tasked only with the creation of a centralized order fulfillment system that had to somehow be optimized for all peculiarities and differentiating features of each facility.

12. This assumes a time-bound iteration. For human-critical applications, the end of the iteration might be identified only as the completion of QA objectives and tests.

One of my favorite stories about the variability of project schedules is from a former colleague of mine. While toiling late hours and weekends to meet a "do-or-die" deliverable, Wayne confided that in his nearly 20 years of software development experience, he had never failed to meet a system delivery date. He went on to explain that when the date arrived, the current version of the system was shipped, and whatever was done next was called maintenance. This is not exactly how I would approach the concept of a variable project schedule, but it does express a common practice in many companies.

One very important goal of the process described in this chapter is to address risk early. Risk is the unknown; it is areas that rely on new, unproved technology or areas with which the development team is unfamiliar. Throughout the process, and especially early on, the project manager, the architect, and key members of the team review the current set of requirement and architecture artifacts, which include the use cases, and look for signs of risk. These areas are targeted for development in early iterations.

Instead of letting risk pop up uncontrolled, the process actively seeks out risky areas of the system and implements them first. The reason for this is to let use cases drive the process. Use cases are a resource for nearly every activity in the process. All workers typically review the use cases to validate decisions made during their activities. The use case–driven approach helps manage and attack risk by providing a focus for development and identifying deliverable targets for the iterations.

Use cases or sets of use cases that are determined to contain the most risk are targeted for early development. If they are included or are extensions, appropriate stubs and infrastructure are created so that they can be executed and evaluated. One by one, these use cases are elaborated and implemented, with their completion contributing to the incremental delivery of system functionality. Because most are delivered as executables—or at the very least as a set of semifunctional Web pages—they can be evaluated by the testing team. The testing team uses the iteration plan and the current state of the use cases and requirements to prepare test plans and scripts to evaluate each iteration delivery. The project manager assesses the results and uses them to make adjustments to the development schedule and the next iteration's plan. Under some circumstances, the project manager may use the results to reassess the minimal set of requirements to make the project a success and to adjust the requirement set to make a successful delivery of the system more realistic.[13]

Iterate

Perform one instance of an iteration. The exact nature and the makeup of the iteration are defined by the iteration plan. Throughout the phases of the process, the emphasis of activities shifts from one workflow to another, yet most are active throughout the entire effort. Figure 6-5 shows the activity levels throughout the phases and workflows

---

13. I know you're smiling; let's face it, this happens far more often than we would like.

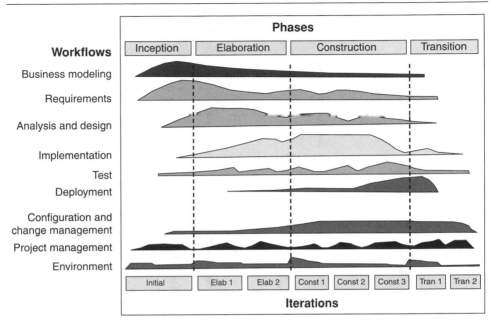

FIGURE 6-5   Phases and workflows of the Rational Unified Process. (*Source:* Philippe
Kruchten, *The Rational Unified Process: An Introduction, Second Edition* (Boston,
MA: Addison-Wesley, 2000, p. 46.))

of the Rational Unified Process. This activity is expressed in more detail in the Software Iteration activity diagram of Figure 6-6.

On large software projects, iterations can happen in parallel. Usually, this is practical only during the elaboration and later phases, after key subsystems and interfaces have been defined.

- *Deploy system.* Deliver and install the system. This may involve a phased rollout or simply mean turn it on. If involved in a phased rollout, additional activities and workflows should be completed during the construction phase, in preparation.

- *Maintain system.* System maintenance is essentially a miniversion of the process that developed it.

Software Iteration

The Software Iteration business use case describes those development process activities that involve the iteration of all artifacts that make up the stepping stones from the vision document to the collected artifacts that make up the final product. This use case is included, or invoked, by the Develop Software use case and appears in its activity diagram as the Iterate activity.

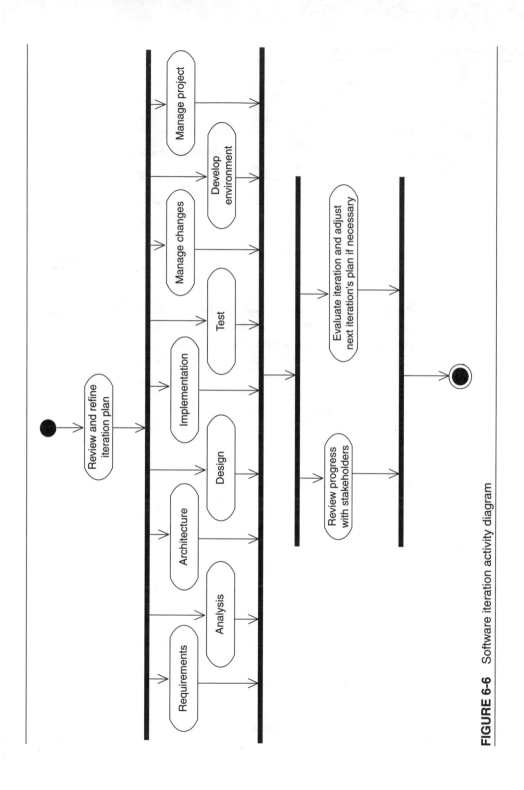

FIGURE 6-6 Software iteration activity diagram

The activities of the Software Iteration use case are described at a very high level by the activity diagram of Figure 6-6. The most significant feature of this diagram is that all the individual workflows happen in parallel. Before the iteration starts, the plan is checked. After the iteration is complete and has passed its success criteria, it is evaluated by the team. This is also a good time to update the stakeholders who are interested in the progress of the project.

A project manager experienced in this type of development process will realize that the use cases tackled in the first few iterations will typically take the longest to develop because they are often the learning mechanism for the team's junior members. Once the first few iterations are complete, the project's rhythm is established. Establishing a rhythm is crucial in the process. The project's rhythm is set by the periodic project activities that contribute to the creation of the system's artifacts. These activities include the weekly status meetings, the daily "stand-ups," the nightly builds, the morning's test reports, and any other periodic activity of the team. The rhythm is important because inevitably, something will go wrong. A date will slip or a technology will falter, and the natural reaction of an unseasoned team is to panic. With an established project rhythm, enough inertia will be built up to make it more difficult to toss away the process while concentrating on the fix of the "big" problem.

Nearly every organization starts with a process of some sort. The real test of a successful process-oriented organization is the continued use of the process even in the face of slipping schedules. I've seen it too many times: The organization starts well by defining, or at least accepting, a process and for the most part follows it. Technical problems pop up, requirements get changed, and the schedule starts slipping. The natural reaction of the team, still unsure about the process, is to temporarily drop it and concentrate on coding, hoping that a last-minute Herculean effort will bring the project back on schedule. What usually happens is that the team makes that one milestone on time but is left with a model and a set of project artifacts in such disarray that they are out of date, virtually unusable, and unable to help meet the next impending milestone. The cycle repeats, and the project continues to slip.

Ironically, in situations like this, when the schedule starts to slip, an even stronger commitment to the process is needed. In an incremental process, this slippage is considered an invaluable metric of the process. It guides future iteration plans. Slipping schedules and significant defects rates are key metrics to be monitored and are not meant to be hidden for fear of bad press. For iterations to be successful and to drive the project, each iteration result, whether good or bad, needs to be considered and used.

- *Review and refine the iteration plan.* Before the iteration, the team takes a look at the iteration plan. The project manager makes resource allocations, and the team makes its deliverable commitments.

- *Review progress with stakeholders.* Often the stakeholders are very interested in the progress of the project. Sometimes this review is required to retain funding. As a result, this activity can be either a dog-and-pony show with a lot of hand waving by an overextended and troubled team or an honest appraisal of the project's status. Needless to say, an honest review of progress is in everyone's long-term best interest.

- *Evaluate iteration and adjust next iteration's plan.* The team needs to do some serious soul searching and self-evaluation. Have the deliverables been made with the expected effort?[14] Is the level of quality what was expected by the team? Did it meet your personal expectations? These are all important measures that need to be reflected in the next iteration's plan.

The Artifacts

In many ways, software development can be thought of as the creation, evolution, and transformation of a series of artifacts that begin with the vision document and unambiguously lead to the final product. The process describes the required artifacts and often provides guidelines and additional help throughout their evolution. The business use case Software Iteration describes how and when the artifacts of the process are evolved.

Building software is all about decisions. The transformation of a software product from an idea into an executable system is nothing but the result of the many decisions made by the workers in the process. To help structure and communicate these decisions, artifacts documenting the work are created along the way. These artifacts end up being the stepping stones that lead away from the idea and toward the resulting system.

If getting to code in the fastest way possible is the most important goal of the application, I would recommend vi on UNIX systems, and Notepad on Windows systems. These tools can get you to the coding phase quickly, in approximately 10ms on Linux and in about 120ms on Windows.[15] Strangely enough, a lot of developers work this way. They look at the vision document or listen to a stakeholder's problems, make a mental picture of the problem, and instantly start realizing a solution and begin typing. It should be no surprise that this type of development philosophy results is a significantly high failure rate and doesn't scale very well.

To avoid a high failure rate and reach the desired goal, it is critical to develop the process and to define a set of artifacts to be produced that will ensure the delivery of the proper solution in the quickest way possible. The real trick is to select the right artifacts to create and work with; too many of the wrong ones will slow a team down, and too few artifacts may result in wasted time and backtracking.

At one end of the artifact trail is the vision document, which outlines in broad terms the goals of the project and places the effort in a context. The context may be further detailed with a domain and/or business model. At the other end is a set of components, scripts, deployment descriptors, installation, and maintenance documents

---

14. Count the number of nights the pizza was ordered for the team to support a late night of work that week the iteration deadlines were due. Having more than two nights of boxes is a not a good sign.

15. These informal timings are based on my home machines—Linux: 200MHz Pentium MMX, 128MB RAM; Windows 2000: Dell Latidude Cpx 500MHz, 256MB RAM.

that make up the delivered system. The artifacts in between are what really define the character of any given process. The rest of this chapter presents what I consider a minimal set of artifacts that a medium-sized Web application development effort should have.[16] A detailed discussion of each, especially those expressed with UML, appears in the following chapters.

Each artifact is created for a number of reasons:

• Traceability/transformation

• Communication

• Managing complexity

That aspect of the development process that strives for predictability and repeatability is most concerned with the traceability and transformation between artifacts. The rapid development of most Web applications also depends heavily on the clear and understood transformations from one artifact to another. Not having a clear path defined for transforming requirements into a usable system results in a lot of wasted time and the exploration of a lot of unnecessary development paths.

Communication is a fundamental part of the process. Large teams with specialists depend heavily on artifacts for efficient and clear communications. Each artifact is designed to be understood by those who will eventually consume or review it. Requirements artifacts will tend to be expressed in the language of the domain, whereas design and implementation artifacts involve a much greater deal of technology.

The system model is one of the most important artifacts of the process. Although it is an excellent communication mechanism, its principal responsibility is to help manage the complexity of the system under construction. A model is a complete representation of a system from a particular viewpoint. This book uses the term system model to mean the collection of models being developed for a particular system. Because they are all models of the same system, they must be consistent with one another, yet each can express a different viewpoint. This ability to be consistent with one another and to express different viewpoints is a very powerful mechanism for establishing traceabilities across the project's artifacts.

In the Web application development process described here, the recommended models are:

• Domain model

• Use case model

• Analysis/design model

• Implementation model

• Process model

---

16. A medium-size Web application can be visualized as a classic e-retail application with about 10 to 25 developers working for about six months.

- Security model
- User experience, or user interface, model

The system model is the abstract representation of the system that is to be built, the system being built, and the system that was built. This model is used by nearly every member of the team: from the stakeholders whose jobs will depend on the system to the implementers responsible for coding its components. Each worker in the development process uses or contributes to the model differently (Figure 6-7). Even though different workers have different views of the system, collectively it is one model and one system that is being developed.

The model is used to answer questions about the system. A good model tells which components are associated with which use cases and in what capacities. The model can also help predict the relative impact change requests might have on the system. Because the process is iterative, every artifact is subject to change at any time. Using the traceability links between the artifacts is critical to understanding and reacting to the change. During an iteration, when a discovery is made that questions something in an input artifact, the change management process kicks in. Before any official and lasting change can be made in the originating artifact, the consequences must first be determined and evaluated.[17]

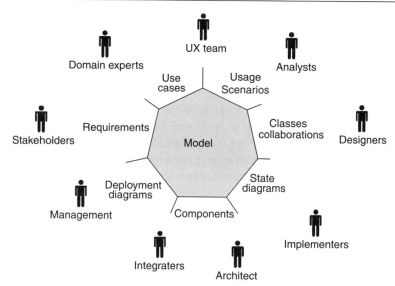

FIGURE 6-7   The model as a central artifact of the development process

---

17. The details and complexities of version control vary greatly. The management of merging and branching artifact versions is a topic well beyond the context of this book. It should be sufficient to state that if you are adopting a complex and flexible version control mechanism, don't skimp on the quality of talent that you have managing such systems.

Take as an example the situation when it becomes apparent during implementation that including detailed product descriptions in the search criteria would significantly reduce the performance of the system. This might be the case if detailed product descriptions are captured in a relational database text or BLOB (binary large object) type of column and are therefore not capable of being searched with the standard SELECT SQL (structured query language) statement. The possible solutions that the team comes up with vary from dropping the feature from the requirements to changing the design to use standard character column types to storing product descriptions, as well as others.

Before deciding what to do, the architect and interested members of the team need to examine the issues and make an informed decision. To identify the consequences, begin by examining the traceability links in the chain between the requirements and the implementation. A project with sufficient traceability should be able to easily identify all the analysis and design elements that resulted from the initial search requirements. Following that path, it might be discovered that the inventory, shipping, and ordering systems' designs all depend on the way the catalog system stores its products. The relative impact of any change in the design must be considered in the context of these other systems before a final decision is made.

Establishing traceabilities in project artifacts can be done in many ways: using a naming convention or leveraging special features of the tools the development team uses for creating the artifacts. UML in particular has several ways to establish traces from one element to another, most notably with dependency relationships. When the trace needs to go beyond the bounds of the UML model, the use of tagged values is useful for capturing the links to external artifacts.

Figure 6-8 shows the major artifact sets, which roughly correspond to the individual models of the system, and their principal dependencies on one another. It is important not to misunderstand the dependencies in this diagram; they represent only the principal traceabilities. For example, the reality is that nearly everyone on the project makes use of the use case model and specifications to help drive and focus work, even though hard traceability links may not be established to the use cases in the system model.

The remainder of this chapter introduces the activities and artifacts and identifies their transformations and traceabilities. A more detailed description of the workflows and activities of the process—in particular how the UML models are constructed and used—is given in the following chapters.

Project Management Set

The principal artifacts of the project management set are the project plan, the iteration plan, and the change management plan (Figure 6-9). Of course, any manager can tell you that plenty of other documents are in use when managing employees. These three, however, are specific to software development.

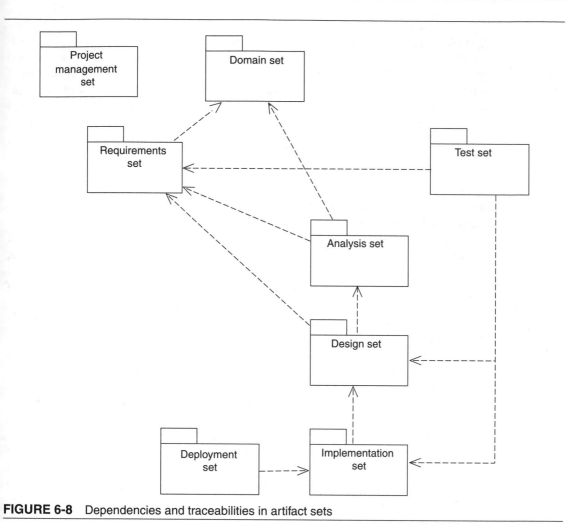

FIGURE 6-8   Dependencies and traceabilities in artifact sets

The project and the iteration plans outline the schedule for development and include such things as staffing, areas of responsibility, and major milestones. The project manager works with the architect on the technical details in the iteration plan. The goal of this collaboration is to define realistic expectations for the iteration, as well as to identify and to tackle the riskiest areas of the application in the earliest iterations rather than in later ones.

These plans, like every artifact in the process, are subject to change. Exactly *how* they change is the topic of the change management plan, which describes how artifacts are changed across iterations and workflows. This plan explains how to change an artifact that has already been used by another and where a dependency exists.

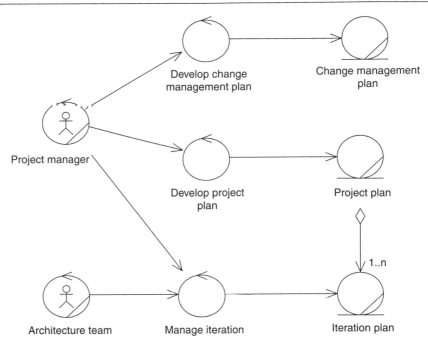

FIGURE 6-9 Project management set

The change management plan can be very simple. It might simply state that in order for a "nonowner" to change something in an artifact, that person must first go through the owner. If an owner of an artifact changes something in a version that has been released internally, some due diligence is required to ensure that the change doesn't adversely affect anyone already using the artifact. The last part of the plan should outline conflict resolution procedures, which might be as simple as letting the architect decide. Again, the key here is that the plan, like the process itself, doesn't have to be overbearing and complex; it simply has to work for the team that uses it.

Domain Set

The domain model and the glossary are the principal artifacts of the domain set (Figure 6-10). The domain model is a UML model that captures the essence of the context of the business and the domain that the system will be in and, possibly, doing work in. The UML business modeling extension is used to capture and to express the domain objects in terms of workers and entities.

The glossary captures definitions of key terms and concepts that are used in discussions of the business and, most likely, in those of the operations of the proposed system. The glossary should be easily accessible by all. Establishing an internal Web site for a project team is an excellent way to manage an evolving glossary.

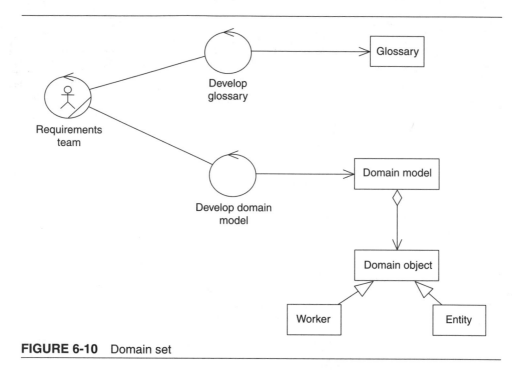

FIGURE 6-10   Domain set

Never underestimate the importance of a good, up-to-date glossary, and don't be surprised at how contentious this seemingly benign artifact might be. I have worked on several projects on which common terms were often misunderstood by team members. This has led not only to poorly designed systems but also to contention and frustration on the part of the team.

Requirements Set

A requirement is a statement of what the system must do. The collection of artifacts that make up the requirement set are shown in Figure 6-11. Gathering the system's requirements is an effort that extends beyond the requirements team; it includes the system analyst, the architect, and the user experience teams, as well as input from the stakeholders.

Although a number of roles are involved in requirements gathering, the principal role is the requirements team. This team, typically staffed with domain expertise, as well as analysis, design, and user interface skill sets, works to develop an accurate representation of the problem and the solution from the requirements viewpoint. The requirements viewpoint specifies a system solution independent of system architecture, looking at the solution and its context from the viewpoint of what we would like the system to look like from the outside.

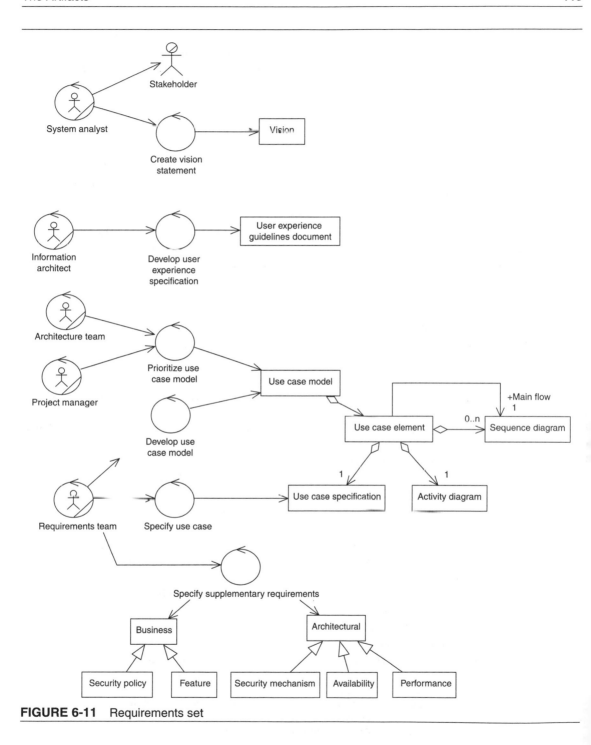

FIGURE 6-11   Requirements set

The most important document of the entire process is the vision document, or statement. This document, often started before the project starts in earnest, states the overall goal of the system and the context it is set in. It usually needs to be refined a bit early in the process but should remain stable through the project life cycle. Its development and refinement are shown in the activity diagram for the Develop Software business use case (Figure 6-4). The activity takes place formally after a minimal commitment has been made to at least investigate the project.

A system's requirements can be categorized into functional and nonfunctional. Functional requirements are captured with use cases and describe the visible functionality of the system as described by dialogs of activity. Nonfunctional requirements capture all other types of requirements that are not easily expressed in terms of usage scenarios.

The system's nonfunctional requirements can be further categorized into business and architectural requirements. Business requirements are derived solely from the business processes and include such items as how payroll calculations are performed or references to industry-standard documents. Architectural requirements tend to focus on specifying the limits of the technologies and include such things as acceptable response times and uptime percentages, as well as acceptable client configurations and Web browser versions.

Anyone who has ever written software for someone else knows that defining a system's requirements is not easy. People's mental pictures about the proposed system often differ. Even from a common vision statement, different users and stakeholders of the system can view it differently. It is therefore important to establish the system's requirements as clearly as possible.

It's OK to have requirements that are not 100 percent complete before the development team starts elaboration or construction; it's an iterative process. Rest assured, the requirements model will, over time, approach completeness. There's a fine line, one that experience is invaluable in determining, between when to start analysis and design activities and when to wait.

It's been my experience not to trust solely either the requirements analysts or the designers and implementers to make this decision. I've been on projects on which the analysts insisted on specifying the requirements to such a level of detail that months would go by before anyone was allowed to do anything with them. The justification was that complete requirements would in the long run lead to faster elaboration and construction phases, making up for any time lost earlier. On the other side, the vast majority of coders I've worked with are willing to start work with the barest semblance of a requirements specification.[18]

A key component of expressing requirements so that all concerned can understand them is use cases. Use cases are a somewhat formal mechanism for expressing

---

18. I am embarrassed to admit that I fall into this category. I can't help it; I like to code, and in times of weakness will begin analysis and design on a set of use cases far earlier than would be prudent. I suppose there's a 12-step program somewhere out there for us.

usage scenarios of the system. Use cases are represented by a textual document called the use case specification and with UML modeling elements. The text is written in the language of the domain so that it is easily understood by the stakeholders, who typically review the use cases to determine whether this is the system they really want built. The use case specification is associated with a use case UML modeling element (Figure 6-12). This association is a key connection between the world of the domain and the technical world of the system.

The use case specification also has formal traceability links to the project's glossary and with UML domain objects. Technically, these can be accomplished with hyperlinks between artifacts, which is becoming more common in today's development tools.[19]

Web application development has elevated the status of one artifact in the requirements set: the user experience document. This document, the modern version of the user interface standards document, defines the targeted look-and-feel for the application. This document defines the emotion that the application is trying to establish with the user. The user experience (UX) team is responsible for both developing and implementing this document.

The user experience document combines the technical and the creative. One document both explains navigational mechanisms implemented with JavaScript functions and describes style sheets and color schemes. Looking at this document is like looking at an artist's portfolio. Although this document might look like marketing literature, don't throw it away or dismiss it too quickly. In a Web application, this document has a tremendous effect on its design at the technical level. Because most Web applications are essentially systems that deliver and process Web page requests, the scope of the objects that live and die while processing page requests is defined by this look-and-feel.

Analysis Set

Analysis is often mentioned in the same breath as design, yet I prefer to separate the two workflows conceptually. The analysis set of artifacts (Figure 6-13) is elaborated by many workers. Often the same individuals contribute to these workflows, yet the activities and motivations are distinctly different. In the analysis workflow, the architecture team defines a core artifact: the software architecture document. It is also the time that the system is initially divided into subsystems. Only when subsystems are defined and clear areas of responsibility formed can there be true asynchronous team development.

---

19. In Rational's suite of tools, there is good integration between Requisite Pro—the requirements and document management tool—and Rose, the UML modeling tool. A low-tech way to establish this link can be created by simply including a URL hyperlink to the online glossary in the UML description fields.

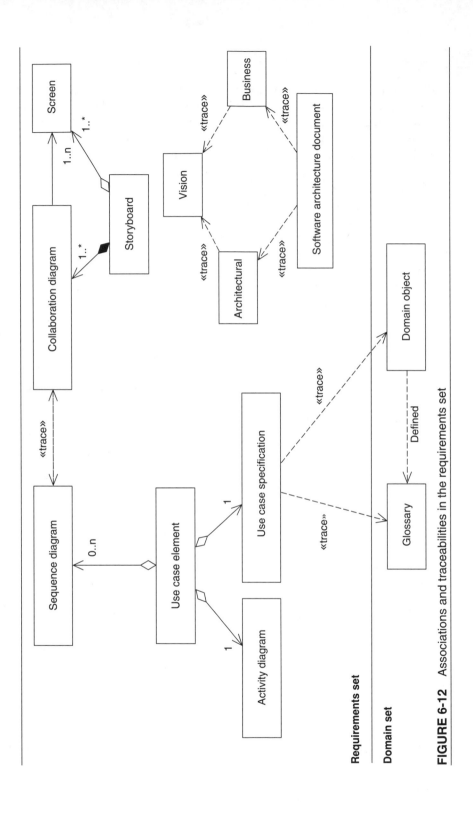

Requirements set

Domain set

FIGURE 6-12 Associations and traceabilities in the requirements set

118

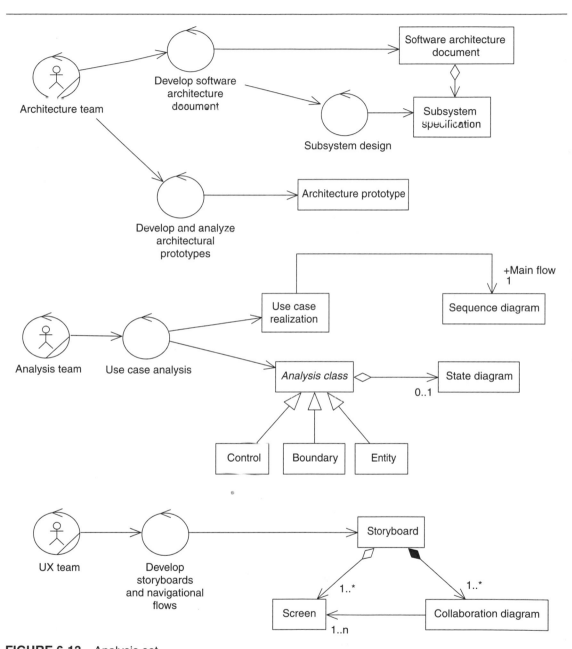

FIGURE 6-13   Analysis set

The software architecture document is refined with experiences from architecture prototypes. This is another key activity in the modern software development process: Prototype the architecture early. The rapid pace of technology has forced us all to adopt and to use the latest technologies long before a track record has been established, and all of its consequences are known. What gives many of us a technological advantage is also an area of high risk. Prototyping early can mitigate this risk.

The artifacts that the requirements team works on represent the logical shape of the system as it is abstracted from the architecture. Analysis artifacts can often be discussed with domain experts and educated users of the system, whereas once the architecture is applied in design, these artifacts often become too technical for the casual domain expert. These artifacts are the first in the process to truly describe the shape of the system to come.

Use case analysis is the process of examining the requirements—both use case and nonfunctional—and making a conceptual model of the system to be built as independently of the architecture as possible. The analysis of artifacts includes analysis classes, their structural relationships with one another, and their behavioral properties in the form of sequence and state diagrams.

The traceability links among the artifacts of the analysis and requirements set are shown in Figure 6-14. For the most part, the analysis model depends only on the requirements model, with the notable exception of connections to the domain model. During analysis, it is prudent to connect analysis-level classes with their domain model ancestors. Typically, the analysis class has the same name as the domain class; names, however, are subject to change. Establishing this traceability link will help if requests to change class names or responsibilities pop up.

Design Set

The design workflow takes the artifacts produced during analysis and applies the architecture to them (Figure 6-15). The principal goal of design is to make the analysis model of the system realizable in software. It is the first time that the hard realities of software architecture are introduced to the abstract business concepts.

In the design workflow, the architecture team builds on the subsystem model by defining a process view. This process model is a system view that expresses where and in what containers the objects of the system exist. For Web applications, this means which tiers in the application—client, Web, application, data, and so on—the object's life cycles reside in.

The design team, on the other hand, is busy defining the internals and details of these subsystems. The designers define design-level classes, operation signatures, and associations that participate in collaborations that fulfill the required business behavior. In Web applications, this extends to the business and logical behaviors of the Web pages and other client-visible resources of the system, such as XML document structures.

In Figure 6-15, the source of one of the new issues that face Internet application development teams can be seen. Both the designer and the information architect of

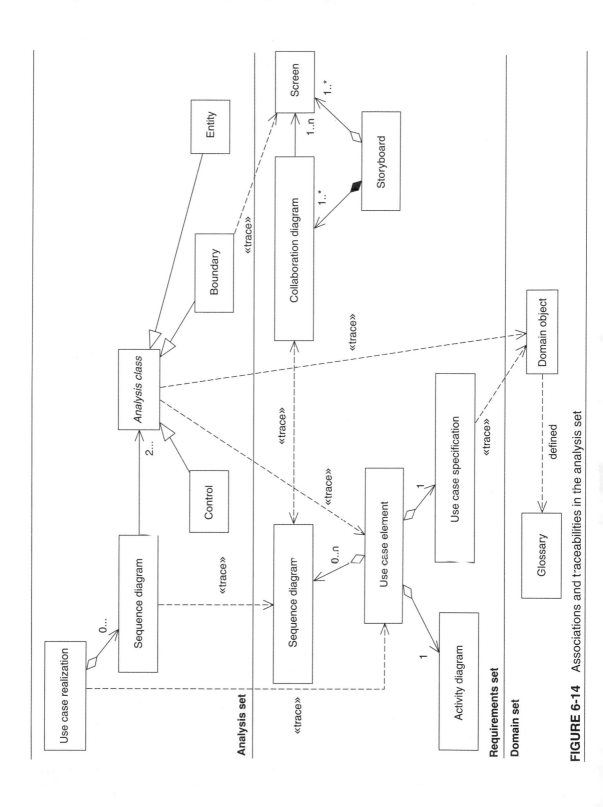

FIGURE 6-14 Associations and traceabilities in the analysis set

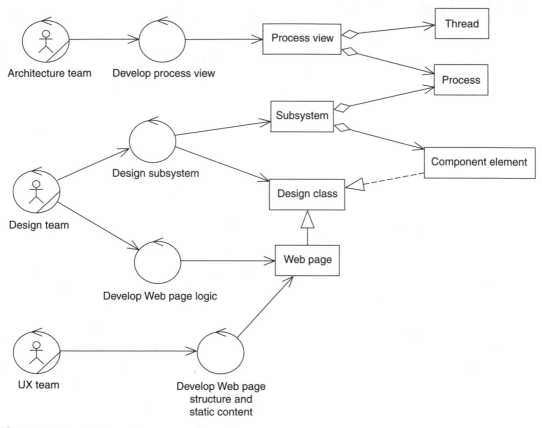

FIGURE 6-15   Design set

the UX team contribute to the design of the Web page. The designer is concerned with responsibilities of the page as a requestable resource on the server, as well as its transactional properties and interaction with the rest of the system's business state. The IA is more concerned with the page in the context of the navigational flows, both physical and workflow.

Normally, having two groups of teams work collaboratively on the same set of artifacts is not an issue. But in this case, the difference in cultures is so significant that it becomes an issue for the project management team and the architect. I like to joke about the typical UX team member being someone who wears black turtlenecks, is body pierced, and drinks only herbal teas. The UX has an iMac on the desk and a professional workspace covered with postcards of sixteenth-century Flemish art. On the other side, the typical designer is portrayed as an engineering geek with a pocket protector in a short-sleeved white buttoned shirt who carries around a full cup of strong coffee. Designers live in cubicles covered with taped-together UML models of "their" system and are surrounded by piles of trade rags littering the floor. The designer uses a Windows or UNIX machine that is rebuilt about every three to four months.

These stereotypes are obviously not completely accurate,[20] but the subtleties and backgrounds in culture do exist. The issues are rooted in the designer community's need for rigid logical rules and structures and the creative community's resistance to a stifling of its expressional capabilities. In one instance, I've seen this exhibited in the UX team's insistence on using Adobe Illustrator to create PDF files that document the user experience and storyboards. The design team then has to manually translate those artifacts from the printouts into UML models and HTML source code. In a tight iterative process, this leads to clashes and confusion over ownership of page content. As a general rule, I advocate allowing these two teams to work separately most of the time. When the time comes to collaborate, establish the playing rules early, and keep the meeting short. In Chapters 11 through 13 I discuss some tricks to ease—but, unfortunately, not remove—these issues.

Overall, the artifacts in the design set look very much like those in the analysis set. When examining the traceabilities of the design set (Figure 6-16), you can see the similarities in the two sets. This parity between the analysis and the design models is one reason that the Rational Unified Process recommends evolving the analysis model into a design model rather than creating and maintaining a separate design model. The arguments for either side of the debate are strong, and the correct decision on whether to maintain a separate analysis model is ultimately made on a per project basis.[21]

Implementation Set

The construction of a software system is more than writing and compiling code, although that is a large part of the workflow. The implementation workflow takes the artifacts of design and applies software development tools to them. The tools are typically editors and compilers, although the latest Web application environments come with a lot of other tools and frameworks that can be used. Figure 6-17 shows the major activities of the implementation workflow and the artifacts of the implementation set.

An important part of the construction phase and the implementation workflow is testing. Unit testing is critical to ensuring high-quality work. In fact, testing is a keystone of the XP development process.

Web applications often involve various technologies that need to be managed. The programming languages and skills for client-side development are principally HTML, JavaScript, Java, ActiveX, style sheets, and, possibly, some distributed object technologies. The languages and technologies on the server have a greater range and involve typical third-generation and object programming languages—C/C++, Java,

---

20. I happen to own several nonwhite shirts that I unashamedly wear into the office on wild Fridays.

21. I certainly weaseled out of that one, didn't I?

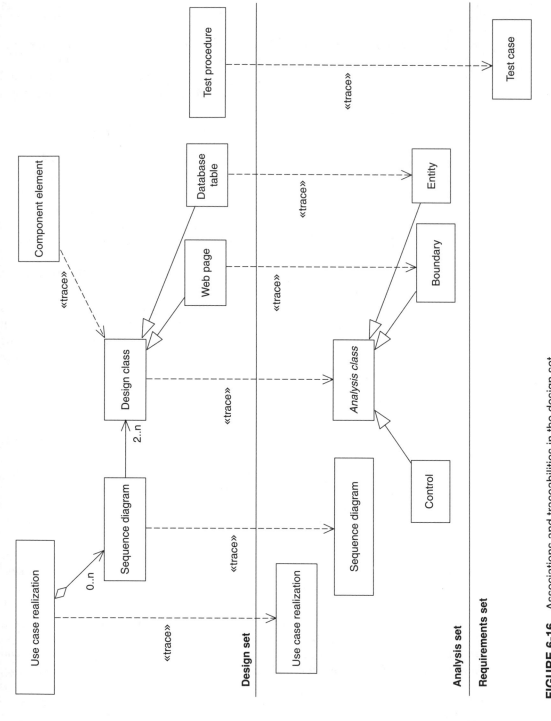

FIGURE 6-16 Associations and traceabilities in the design set

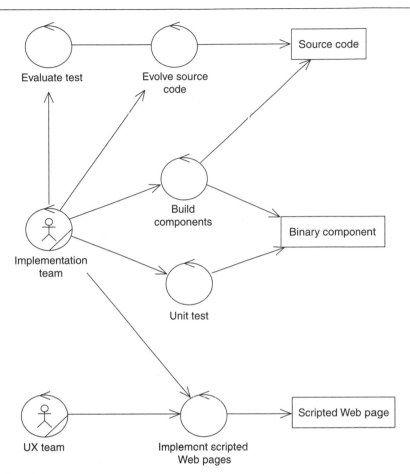

FIGURE 6-17   Implementation set

Smalltalk, Ada, Eiffel—as well as component technologies, such as Enterprise Java-Beans and COM+. The server side also deals with the traditional database, transaction-processing monitor (TPM), and messaging technologies. Beyond the Web server tier, the application is pretty much just like any other client/server system.

Nearly all implementation set artifacts trace themselves to design classes and component elements. The binary versions of the components and the other system deliverables ultimately map themselves to a design-level class in the model. The design class is the logical representation of the structure and the behavior of the target system.

The traceabilities between the system's runtime deliverables and the design model are significant; they represent the mapping from the abstract world of models and concepts to the physical world—if software could ever be considered physical. Because the trace links are most likely managed by the model, embedded as comments

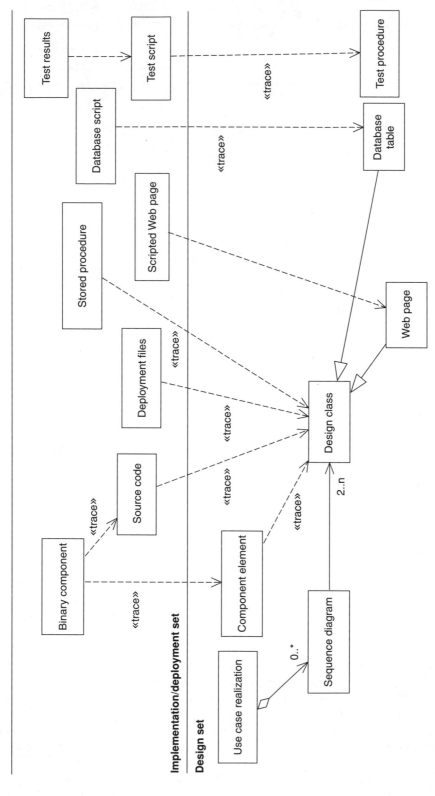

FIGURE 6-18 Associations and traceabilities in the implementation set

in the source code or in an external mapping document, an optimized binary would have no need of trace links to the model (Figure 6-18).

Test Set

The test workflow focuses on the evaluation of the executable artifacts of the system. Testing is separate from general quality assurance (QA). QA is more a frame of mind than a specific workflow, implemented through peer reviews, unit tests, standards documents, and so on. The test workflow and the test artifact set are pretty much limited to examining the executable system. This is not to say that testing is easy or a small part of the project effort. In fact, some organizations say that formal testing accounts for 30 percent to 50 percent of the project effort.

In many of these organizations, unfortunately, testing is usually done in an unorganized way. In fact, in one project I had the privilege of working on, the testing team, consisting of three full-time specialists, never even wrote a test plan! They simply got a release and started hacking. In fact, they didn't even use automated test tools. Clearly, only the most obvious errors in the application were likely to be caught in this situation. To make matters worse, we happened to be in a short development cycle, and changes to the application appeared rapidly. Whenever a nontrivial change or fix was put in place, it seemed as though half the time, it would get written up as a defect. Because there was no way to document the change and to update a test plan, the test team always seemed to find out about design changes during new bug report reviews.

Many different tests are made of the system. Each test tries to determine one quality of the system. Ideally, this quality of the system and its minimal acceptable value were captured in a requirement artifact. A performance test accesses the system's ability to function quickly and under heavy loads. Load testing specifically stresses the system and establishes the breaking point of the system, or just the performance curves under load. Functional tests determine whether specific functions, as defined in the requirements specification, have been implemented properly. Functional tests often are derived directly from use case specifications.

In an iterative development process, regression testing is very important. Regression testing is the retesting of a system that might have changed. Even though traceability in the model makes it easier to determine which use cases are affected with which code changes, there is always the possibility that a change to one part of the system will affect another, seemingly unrelated one. Regression testing mediates this risk by continually reapplying the same tests to the system. If a discrepancy is found, it might indicate an unknown connection in the model and needs to be explored.

Testing Web applications is pretty much carried out in the same manner as testing other systems (Figure 6-19 and 6-20). Often, the test team regards a system as a black box: What is inside is unimportant; how the box behaves, however, is. Depending on the nature of the Web application, testing may need to be carried out on a number of client platforms and browser configurations. Internet applications need to consider all the various browsers that might be used, even the platforms they run on. This fact alone is enough to limit the design of most Internet applications to the bare essentials.

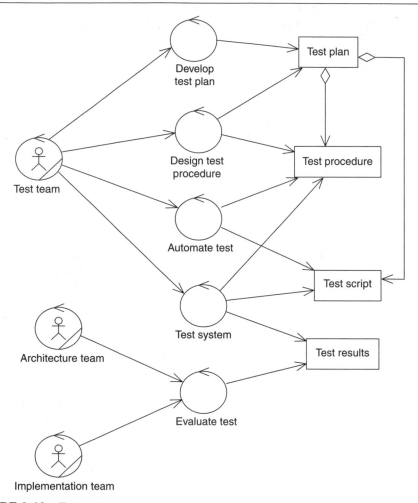

FIGURE 6-19   Test set

Deployment Set

Deploying a Web application can be real easy or very complicated. The deployment artifacts are essentially the deployment plan (Figure 6-21). The line is fuzzy between deployment scripts and installation instructions as part of the deployment set or part of the design set. To me, the point is academic. What is important is that a plan is thought out ahead of time and then constructed, long before the delivery of the system.

In that same project with the dysfunctional testing team, our earliest deliveries of system functionality were made in the absence of a proper deployment plan. When it came time to make the first delivery to an internal customer, the whole concept of delivering the system caught us by surprise and at the last minute. In the end, we had

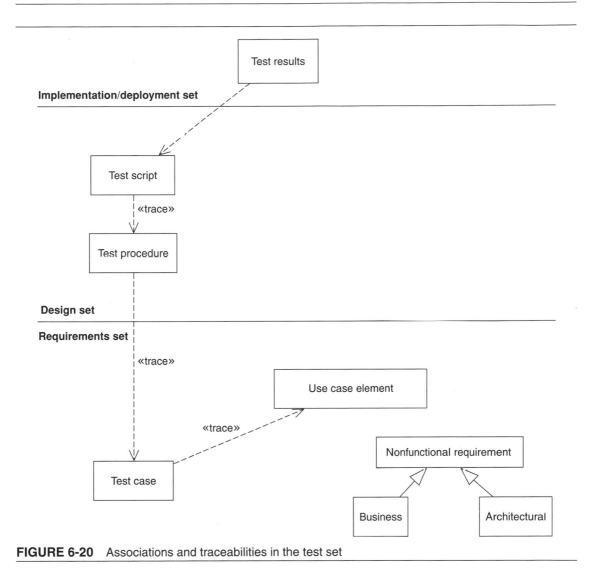

FIGURE 6-20   Associations and traceabilities in the test set

to build the server in our office and ship the server with one of the development engineers to the target location, which happened to be in another state and three hours away by air. Subsequent releases, however, had a full-time deployment plan and engineer.

The simple intranet application that runs on one server and leverages an existing network can be easy to deploy, and it might have a deployment plan that could fit in a memo. In this situation, only the server needs to be set up. Clients probably already have suitable browsers, and if the application is designed to use only the most basic client capabilities, there is nothing more to do.

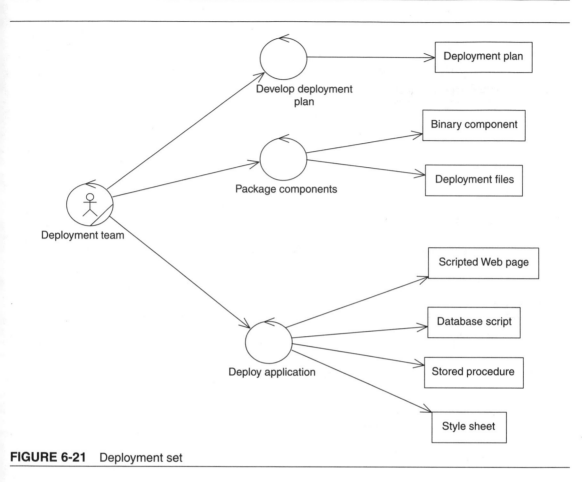

FIGURE 6-21   Deployment set

If the application, on the other hand, is to deal with security issues and heavy loads on the Internet, a significant amount of deployment planning is required. Additionally, many systems are phased in, and run concurrently with legacy systems. The handling of failover issues and load balancing as defined by the architecture often involves third-party and off-the-shelf components that need to be integrated. Internet applications also need careful planning of network resources and feeds. Most large Internet applications have redundant Internet connections and off-site backup systems. Deployment in these types of applications requires careful planning and management.

Summary

❑ Developing applications is hard work. A strong process helps bring a project to maturity repeatedly and reliability.

❑ The four roles of a software development process are to provide guidance to the order of the team's activities, define the artifacts of the process, direct the tasks of the teams, and offer criteria for monitoring and measuring the project's progress.

❑ The process described here is iterative and use case driven and relies on a strong architectural foundation.

❑ Iterations don't just happen; they are planned in advance.

❑ An important goal of the iterative process is to address risk early. Use cases representing risks are targeted for early elaboration.

❑ Establishing a rhythm helps build project inertia and thereby maintain the process.

❑ Every process needs to be tailored for the specific application and organization that uses it.

❑ To be successful, the software development process has to work with the people and the goals of the project.

❑ The model is an abstract representation of the system to be built, the system being built, and the system that was built.

❑ The model serves as a communication mechanism for the project team.

❑ Establishing traceability throughout the project's artifacts is an effective way to gauge and to evaluate the change that is inevitable in an iterative process.

Discussion

1. What are the principal benefits of a documented process? What are the potential drawbacks?

2. Which artifacts in the process described in this chapter can be removed for small development teams with fewer than six members? Which artifacts for large specialized teams?

Activities

1. Outline a vision document for a hypothetical Internet retailer.

2. List and name the artifacts that might be traced if a request is made to break a customer profile Web page into multiple pages. Identify the artifacts and describe what to look for in each.

3. Create an activity diagram describing details of the following activities:
    a. Implementing a requested change to a versioned artifact
    b. Use case analysis: deriving analysis objects from use case specifications
    c. Developing a storyboard scenario based on a use case

Chapter 7
Defining the Architecture

Architecture is about everything. This is just one of the reasons that it is especially difficult to define, not to mention describe. The term itself means different things to different people. For some, it is the set of middleware that the application uses. For others, it is much richer and describes all the significant decisions made in the process of developing the application.

The best way to approach the topic of architecture is to think about how it is going to be used and who its audience is. The architect or the architecture team has the sole responsibility of defining and communicating the system's architecture. The architecture's key role is to define the set of constraints placed on the design and implementation teams when they transform the requirements and analysis models into the executable system. These constraints contain all the significant design decisions and the rationale behind them.

An architecture description is either a single document or a set of documents and artifacts that describe the architecture. Because it contains key decisions for nearly every technological aspect of the system, an architecture needs to be communicated at various levels of abstraction and from many viewpoints.

My first introduction to visualizing architectures through views was in Philippe Kruchten's landmark paper "The 4 + 1 View Model of Architecture."[1] In this paper, architecture is described through a series of views: the logical view, the implementation view, the process view, and the deployment view. The one view that ties them all together is the use case view, which binds the other views of the architecture to the original reason for the system. In a way, the architecture represents the rationale for the decisions made in the other four views. If something in any of the views can't

---

1. Philippe Kruchten, "The 4 + 1 View Model of Architecture," *IEEE Computer* 12 (6), November 1995, pp. 42–50.

point to something in the use case view as justification, its existence in the architecture should be questioned.

The four views mentioned in the original article are not the only views allowed. Other views are included in the description as necessary. In Internet-based applications, the security view and the user experience view are commonly included.[2]

More recently, IBM has put forth an Architecture Description Standard (ADS),[3] which defines two major aspects: functional and operational. The IBM ADS leverages UML to help express these two aspects of the architecture. This standard is intended to support harvesting and reuse of reference architectures.

This book adopts the approach of defining multiple viewpoints. Viewpoints are a collection of views that share a set of concerns. Viewpoints provide the context and the meaning for each view. A view is a projection, or subset, of the system's models. A view addresses a stakeholder's or a worker's related concerns about the system. For example, the requirements viewpoint is concerned with representing the context that the system is being placed in and its principal risks. The design viewpoint, on the other hand, is concerned with the system's structure—subsystems—and interactions of its elements.

Each view is essentially a subset of the artifacts created in the development process. For example, the requirements viewpoint contains the domain view, the functional requirements view—use case model—and the nonfunctional requirements view. If this sounds familiar, don't be surprised. These views are essentially the categories of the principal artifacts for the requirements set and the requirements workflow.

In fact, if you look at all the viewpoints and their views, you will see a representative sample of nearly every artifact in the process. Architecture is about everything, after all! The one key differentiator is that all the content in this architecture description is "architecturally significant." Defining an architecture, then, becomes an activity of identifying what is architecturally significant and expressing it in the proper context and viewpoint. An architecturally significant requirement is a system requirement that has a profound impact on the development of the rest of the system. For example, the decision to limit the number of data collection fields on any page to no more than 15 is not an architecturally significant requirement. The decision to support international character sets on pages, however, is. This requirement affects not only the analysis process but also design, test, deployment, and so on.

Most documented software architectures I have seen have been focused on the selection of the vendor's middleware, the subsystem structure, and their principal interfaces, and that type of description was just fine. Some of the better architectures

2. The user experience view in this case is focused on the architectural aspects of the interface, specifically as they relate to browser-supported HTML, issues general to the Internet, and other related concerns rather than on the content, which is expressed in the use case view.

3. R. Youngs, D. Redmond-Pyle, P. Spaas, and E. Kahan, *IBM Systems Journal* 38, Nov. 1999. "A Standard for Architecture Description," available at http://www.research.ibm.com/journal/sj/381/youngs.html.

include design goals, success criteria, and the reasoning behind the architectural decisions. Another property of a good architectural description is prioritization. At some point during the process, direct application of the architecture might be ambiguous. With the architectural decisions prioritized, addressing the issue in an unbiased way would be easier. Even so, when a member of the development team catches an ambiguity in the architecture description, it needs to be brought to the attention of the architect.

Architectural Viewpoints

Looking at an architecture description is like looking at a condensed version of the entire set of development artifacts. Organized by viewpoint and view, the architecture description probably has accompanying models and possibly architectural prototypes as well. Many software descriptions have numerous references to vendors' specification sheets. Another important part of an architectural description is the mappings from one viewpoint to another. These mappings are the traceability links that associate an artifact in one view with one in another.

Requirements Viewpoint

The requirements viewpoint in an architecture description provides the support and the reasoning for the decisions made elsewhere. It is the viewpoint that in Kruchten's paper ties all the others together. The requirements viewpoint, concerned with the context of the system, is a representation of the significant architectural requirements (SARs), which influence the structure, arrangement, and constraints for all the other parts of the developing system. Although the views may seem like duplication of all the other documents under development, it should be pointed out that these artifacts represent the architecturally significant requirements, the ones that have driven the decisions made elsewhere in the software architecture.

The requirements viewpoint is organized into the following views:

- *Domain view,* or view of the business model. The domain view expresses the business context of the system. The domain view is expressed with business use cases, realizations, and objects, and it includes a glossary and may refer to other external documents, such as industry standards or regulations.

- *Functional requirements view,* which describes the "observable" of the system, typically from the perspective of an actor of the system. These requirements are usually expressed with use case models and specifications but can be expressed in any terms.

- *Nonfunctional requirements view,* or all those architecturally significant system requirements that are not expressed in the clear terms of functionality. Although they may be observable, these types of requirements, such as performance, robustness, and security, tend to be spread across the system. It is important to capture these requirements with discrete elements to enable traceability. When a decision is made in another part of the architecture because of a non-functional SAR, a traceability link can be made to it, thus providing important information to the team implementing that decision in the real system. The SAR explicitly states the justification for the decision. Should that decision ever be questioned late in the process, it can be traced to its rationale.

Design Viewpoint

The design viewpoint contains what most of us would recognize as an architecture document. The design viewpoint describes the system's major subsystems and processes, outlining significant third-party components and middleware to be used. Including this information about middleware vendors' specifications and documentation is important because the fact that components and frameworks are used implies that the application is subject to the design decisions and constraints that the vendor made to produce the components.

The reality of software development is that software teams don't write every line of code in the application. Today's software relies heavily on third-party components and frameworks, and this is generally a good thing. Because these third-party components are pieces of software themselves, their creation was subject to numerous design decisions. Unless the system that uses these components is willing to accept the design decisions of the component's maker, the component should not be used. Fortunately, most middleware and reusable components are made with a high standard of quality and are based on decisions geared toward the typical users of the components. Still, it is wise to understand exactly what you are using—its motivations, rationale, and purpose—before using it in your system.

Most content of the design viewpoint is expressed in a UML model. UML provides the rigid semantics to accurately express the type of content that concerns the design viewpoint. This viewpoint has two major views.

The *logical view* is the expression of the objects that make up the system. This view includes the structural relationships of logical objects that make up the system and their collaborations. This view is almost always in a UML model. The complexity of today's systems demands a visualization tool like UML for understanding them.

The *process view* focuses on the activities of the CPU (central processing unit). This view shows which processes and threads of control are active. Most important, the process view shows which activities are executing concurrently during the execution of the system.

Realization Viewpoint

The realization viewpoint expresses how the elements of the logical and process views are implemented in the system. This viewpoint, along with the design viewpoint, comprise the classic architecture specification. This viewpoint includes the UML deployment view, which encompasses the nodes of the system and their topology, and addresses the distribution aspects of the system, including not only the nodes of the system but also all communication mechanisms: CORBA, RMI, DCOM, SOAP, and XML. In discussions of these mechanisms, it is often a good idea to identify their performance limits and expectations.

It also helps to justify specific decisions in this viewpoint with rationale backed by elements in the requirements viewpoint. For example, because SOAP is more flexible and accommodating than the proprietary DCOM, the choice of less efficient SOAP over DCOM to communicate with the shipping department's system would be justified by the expectation that the shipping system will be replaced by an unknown system during the life expectancy of this system and by the low overall volume of traffic expected between the two systems.

Realizations of the logical and process elements of the system are associated with the system's nodes in this viewpoint. For example, it should be obvious which nodes in the system are responsible for managing personal account information. If any deployment unit—logical and component package—of the system is concurrently executed on multiple nodes, this section of the architecture must clearly express all the issues and strategies for managing concurrency. It might be as simple as letting the single database node manage concurrent entity instances, or there might be a complex strategy. As an architect, designer, or deployment engineer, if you are interested in concurrency and deployment issues, the realization viewpoint is one place in the architecture document where that information is expressed.

This viewpoint is also a key area for expressing some scalability strategies for the system. Scaling typically involves the addition of processing nodes. Just how the nodes of the system are arranged and how they would be altered to meet the system's scalability requirements is a core focus of this viewpoint.

This viewpoint might also refer to development environment issues, such as shared libraries, namespaces, and compiler and tool configurations. This might even extend to coding or naming conventions. For example, the EJB 1.1 specification requires certain naming conventions for property GET and SET methods. These conventions are required for Enterprise JavaBeans to work properly in standard containers. Similar conventions might be employed on projects developing in-house tools or postcompilers.

The final element of this viewpoint is the class and component implementations or source code. Because this is an architecture document, it obviously doesn't mean that the entirety of the system's source code is included. The system itself hasn't even been constructed yet. Instead, only key source code exemplars are necessary for the architecture document. These might include standardized ways to provide class GET and SET methods, handle variable association multiplicities—0..n associations—or acceptable sorting algorithms.

Test Viewpoint

The test viewpoint is considered a companion viewpoint because its artifacts play a special role in the development process. That role is to provide feedback to the development team and stakeholders. In its purest form, the results of the test workflow provide quality and performance measures of the evolving system against the system's requirements. The practical reality is that a well-integrated testing team will evaluate not only any distributable part of the system but also any artifact produced in the process.

In one of my earliest consulting experiences, I had the opportunity to work with a top-notch test engineer. The organization not only managed to find such an excellent individual but also had the foresight to ensure that this person reported directly to executive management, bypassing the project manager. This organization was serious about quality. Because testing was involved very early in the process, many of the requirements artifacts were reviewed with an eye toward their eventual use downstream by the testing team. This eliminated many ambiguities that might have had to be resolved when the testing occurred. The test engineer's influence also extended into other areas of the project's artifacts, such as coding, user interface, and design standards.

When an architect expresses an application's test viewpoint, the expected testing strategies and frameworks are included. This viewpoint essentially outlines the requirements for the creation of the test plan, which is the formal document that describes the purpose and the goals of the testing effort and outlines the team's strategies and scope. In the architecture document, the scope and the general strategies for testing are explained.

Of particular importance to Web and Internet applications is the scope of testing Internet-specific features. Delivering an application on the Internet is more than connecting a server to the Internet. Ensuring that the system meets the needs of the users might involve testing things outside of the scope of the organization's control. For example, some ISPs perform automatic page caching, and many organizations have firewalls that limit certain kinds of network traffic. The testing team needs to have a strategy for addressing and identifying these things outside the influence of the development team.

Viewpoint Mappings

Because only one system is being developed and all the views and viewpoints in the system's architecture describe this one system, the mappings among the views can provide significant architectural information. A mapping is the connection of one element in a view to another element(s) in another view. Some of these mappings are rather common and exist outside the architecture document. For example, use case realizations are a modeling element in the logical analysis model: design viewpoint. They express a use case's dynamic behavior in terms of analysis model objects.

Most of the valid mappings have been described with UML «trace» dependencies in the artifact set diagrams of Chapter 6. Their significance in the architecture document is that they enable conceptual connections among the views. Highlighting important mappings in the architecture document might fill some conceptual gap that would make understanding the system's architecture easier.

Architecture Activities

Architecture activities, like many other activities in the process, happen through all the phases of development. The key architecture activities are to

- Examine and prioritize use cases and look for significant architectural requirements
- Define and document a candidate architecture and prepare and evaluate prototypes
- Define a reuse strategy

Other activities of the architecture team include providing input to the project management team, participating in artifact reviews, and creating development standards documents. But identifying the SARs, developing the architecture, and being the number-one champion for reuse are principal activities.

Examining and Prioritizing Use Cases

One of the activities of the architecture team is to examine the use case model from a technical viewpoint. The use case model, as a view of the desired system's dynamic behavior, is prioritized according to perceived risk. The process is to address early the use cases that have greater risk and thus prevent unwanted "gotchas" later. A risky use case might involve a new technology or require a high degree of performance. For example, in an Internet-based commerce application, the use case writers might describe the collection of customer information as follows.[4]

> The system prompts the customer for name and address information. The customer enters his/her first and last names, then tabs to the address section of the screen. The customer enters a street address. The customer may enter a city and state or go directly to the zip code field and enter a five-digit zip code. When the customer enters a zip code, the system automatically fills in the city and state fields, if not already filled in.
>
> When the address is completed, the customer clicks the Next button to move to the next step in the order process.

Aside from the obvious implications that this Internet application is limited to U.S. addresses, this use case fragment describes some particularly risky dynamic behavior. Reviewing the use case means partitioning the behaviors into one of the system's tiers—client, server, or other. This is an Internet commerce application, so we can make the assumption that no special software is loaded on the client and that, for

---

4. This style of use case description is somewhat low level, describing the details of the user interface. Other use case styles might simply state that the user enters an address and that the system provides city and state or province information when a postal code is entered.

the most part, the activities described in this use case are happening in an HTML form on the client. The use case specifies that the customer can enter a zip code and have the system identify the correct city and state. If this is all happening on the client, it implies that the mapping of zip codes to cities and states must reside there as well. This is a problem because this mapping is continually changing and is huge: about 100,000 records! This amount of information would take minutes just to get to the client over normal Internet connections.

Because the use of client-side scripts is not a possible solution, the determined architect might consider the use of a Java applet or an ActiveX control that could asynchronously communicate with a server to get the city and state for a zip code and then update the HTML form fields. A small server process would manage the zip code information and provide the simple service of mapping zip codes to cities and states. But even this solution presents a certain amount of risk, because a new technology is being incorporated. Additionally, if the requirements state that this application should work on a large range of browsers, some of which might not have ActiveX or Java capabilities, it is not a possible solution. In this situation, the architect should reaffirm the priority of this feature—it's most likely that this is not a critical requirement—and a small rewrite to the use case is perhaps the least risky solution.

In other situations, the experienced architect might detect risk in the use case yet be constrained to keep and to overcome it in the application. For example, an account management application might allow users to open and to view several accounts simultaneously in different browser windows. Depending on the details of the architecture or proposed architecture, this may cause difficulties in the management of the client state by the server.

Web application development environments, such as Microsoft's Active Server Pages, use cookies to help manage client state. Cookies are key/value pairs that are placed in a browser when it first contacts the Web server. Cookies can persist beyond the single servicing of a browser's page request and offer a convenient mechanism to tackle the client state problem. The cookie usually contains a value that can be used as an index into a dictionary of objects and values: the client state. The architectural risk is that in some instances a new browser window inherits the originating window's cookie. This creates an instance in which two simultaneously open browser windows are sharing the client state on the server.

The disaster scenario might take the form of an account manager's opening a customer's profile, ready to make a slight change to it. The manager remembers that another customer has similar values and proceeds to open another browser window. This second window inherits the first's cookie and hence client state. As far as the server is concerned, the singular browser instance just switched to a new customer profile. The manager views the second customer's information and then switches to the first browser window, makes some changes, and submits them to the server. If the client state contained the primary key to the customer, the server might update the second customer's record with the first customer's data.

These specific scenarios don't represent limitations on the technologies, there are ways around the problems of both. At this stage of the process, it is simply important to recognize that the seemingly innocent use cases as applied to certain architectures may represent a risky aspect of the application. This being the case, they need to be addressed earlier rather than later.

Developing Candidate Architectures

In every successful project that I've worked on, the system's architecture was almost always a refinement of an earlier successful one that the chief architect had used or worked with. This is the unspoken secret of the industry: New projects don't always develop new architectures. Radical changes in software architecture are rare; in my experience, architects advocating new, untested ones are typically inexperienced or have a history of failure.

Even when the Internet popped up on corporate radar screens and Web-centric architectures started to become popular, they were almost always refinements of earlier, smaller-scale architectures. Web application architectures are specializations of the generic client/server architecture. The first-generation Web applications were also very simple. They either performed very little business logic or delegated that logic to an otherwise standard client/server middle tier. As architects became more familiar with the architectural issues specific to Web applications and as vendors started supplying more stable and sophisticated middleware, the scope and the criticality of Web applications expanded. Today nearly every major organization that depends on software technology depends in part on Web-centric systems.

Developing a candidate architecture begins with an understanding of the significant architectural requirements of the system. Ideally, the collection of these requirements alone should be enough to dictate a candidate architecture. But the reality of software development is that the makeup of the organization, its experiences, and skill sets are equally important. If, for example, the team has experience building only Visual Basic (VB) and COM-based two-tiered applications, adopting a Java applet–centric architecture would not be a good fit. Sending team members to a two-week intense Java course will not make them Java experts. In all likelihood, without proper mentoring, any resulting effort will end up with a system designed for Visual Basic and implemented with Java.

I had a very difficult time transitioning to Visual Basic from C++.[5] Without a mentor to guide me, I kept trying to design and to code my modules as I would with C++. I grew increasingly frustrated at VB's inability to provide true object-oriented inheritance. I relished Visual Basic's environment for building user interfaces and vowed never to build a UI (user interface) with Microsoft Foundation Classes (MFC)

---

5. Yes, I transitioned from Visual C++ and MFC to Visual Basic voluntarily. I believe that programming languages are not nearly as significant to the success of a project as the proper understanding of how to leverage the architectures and conventions to which they lend themselves.

again.[6] With proper mentorship, I'm sure I would have realized the relative merits of true inheritance and inheritance via implementing interfaces, as well as other important VB concepts, much sooner.

The architect needs to consider the development team when defining a candidate architecture. Introducing new architectures and technologies to a team can and does happen successfully. But this success depends on a combination of proper training, mentorship, and the target project. If it is desired to move a team's expertise from building Power Builder client/server systems to J2EE-based Web applications, the best approach is to pick a pilot project first. Create a success that the team can leverage and be proud of. Then, with the experiences learned from the pilot, tackle the larger and more important projects, using the pilot project team members in mentorship roles with the new project.

With the significant architectural requirements identified and prioritized and with an understanding of the skills and personalities of the development team, the team can explore candidate architectures. The architect usually starts with a well-known architecture that has worked well and determines whether it is good fit to meet the SARs. Key areas to examine are scalability and maintainability. The realities of Internet applications give these aspects a high priority. For many organizations, time to market is also critical, and this hinges heavily on the development team's skill set.

During this stage, the candidate architecture is expressed only in scattered sets of documents and in the minds of the architecture team's members. It is a time of discovery and exploration. Candidate architectures are poked and prodded conceptually; experience and research often are the only clues to its potential success. For all the academic importance of this stage, the truth is that it often happens quite quickly. Most of the time, the architect has a pretty clear idea of the candidate architecture, and this stage is mainly due diligence.

This is also the stage in which the beginnings of the software architecture document take shape. Sometimes, it begins with a slide presentation to upper management to obtain funding. All too often, the formal evolution of the architecture stops when funding is achieved. This happens so often that the term architecture by PowerPoint has been coined. I want to make it clear that I am not advocating that a candidate architecture shouldn't be proposed until its full documentation or prototype is completed. Given the fact that most architectures are refinements of earlier ones, proceeding with the development process is in no jeopardy with an incomplete architecture document. What I am saying, however, is that prototyping, investigating, and documenting the architecture need to continue even after funding has been obtained.

Prototyping: Knowing When to Stop

Every architectural prototype is created to answer a specific set of questions. A prototype should never be created until these questions are known. The two basic types of

---

6. That lasted about six months.

prototypes are experimental and evolutionary. Experimental prototypes are "throw-away" prototypes that are constructed solely to test a specific hypothesis. The questions are stated ahead of time. The prototype is built to answer these questions, and the results guide architectural and design decisions. The scope of the prototype is limited to testing the hypothesis and answering the questions that it was meant to answer.

Evolutionary prototypes, on the other hand, are intended to evolve during the life cycle of the development process. They too answer questions about the system and are intended to influence future design decisions. Because the evolutionary prototype is intended to be more permanent, there tends to be more formal design and rigor in its construction. Although initially not of production quality, the prototype is expected to evolve into something that is ready for production.

I do not favor this type of prototype. When schedules start to slip and management becomes nervous I've seen it happen all too often: the strong pressure to ship incomplete prototypes as the target system. Experimental prototypes, on the other hand, tend to be tightly focused and are not well suited to being transformed into an initial release of a system.

In addition to user interface prototypes, which are driven by the UX team, architectural prototypes are constructed to answer architectural questions. When constructing a prototype, first identify the set of questions it must answer, or propose a hypothesis. For example, architectural prototypes are constructed to

- Test persistence mechanisms
- Measure data throughput
- Prove or validate new middleware technology
- Prove or validate new tools
- Evaluate the level of effort necessary to create a specific artifact
- Test third-party interfaces, or connections to external systems

Only with the scope of the prototype defined is it safe to proceed with its development. If the prototype is experimental, little formal design needs to go into it. If the prototype is evolutionary, it is critical to ensure that proper change management procedures are in place and that good backups of the system are made in the event that the prototype fails and an earlier version of the system needs to be brought back to life.

Web Application Presentation Tier: Architectural Patterns

Real architectures are never created in a void. They always seem to evolve from something else or are assembled from well-known mechanisms and patterns. Nearly all architectural mechanisms and patterns that can be applied to the server tier of a standard client/server system can also be applied to Web application architectures. Some common structural patterns that are particularly suited to Web application architectures follow:

- *Façade.*[7] The dynamic information in any given Web page may have to be constructed from a collection of business objects and controllers. Façade classes pair up with dynamic Web pages. Each Web page has a specifically designed façade class that acts to consolidate all the business object orchestration and to provide a clear, easy-to-use interface for the Web page script writer to use.

- *Page composition.* Each conceptual Web page in the system is assembled at runtime from a set of independent smaller page fragments, which are often reused across pages in the system. For example, many Internet retail applications provide a quick way to enter product search criteria on every conceptual Web page. This pattern is one way to provide the functionality of HTML frames without using the framesets.

- *Templated page.*[8] This pattern defines a one-page template that all outgoing Web pages go through on their way to the client. Similar to the page composition pattern, the templated page pattern provides additional structure with formally defined templates and screens (conceptual pages). The Java Pet Store[9] provides an example of one use of this pattern.

Of course, many other patterns and mechanisms are commonly used and associated with Web application architectures. Unfortunately, detailed examination of these is beyond the scope of this book. Instead, the rest of this chapter focuses on three higher-level architectural patterns that help us classify and understand the basic forms of presentation tiers in Web applications.

An architectural pattern expresses a fundamental structural organization schema for software systems. It provides a set of predefined subsystems, specifies their responsibilities, and includes rules and guidelines for organizing the relationships among them.

The three most common patterns for the presentation tier are thin Web client, thick Web client, and Web delivery.

- The thin Web client is used mostly for Internet-based applications, in which there is little control of the client's configuration. The client requires only a standard forms-capable Web browser. All the business logic is executed on the server.

- The thick Web client pattern is used when an architecturally significant amount of business logic is executed on the client machine. Typically, the client uses

---

7. From E. Gamma, R. Helm, R. Johnson, and J. Vlissides, *Design Patterns: Elements of Reusable Object-Oriented Software* (Boston, MA: Addison-Wesley, 1995).

8. This pattern is described in detail as a sample asset of the Reusable Asset Specification, a specification being developed by Rational Software and others.

9. See Mark Johnson, Inderjeet Singh, and Beth Stearns, *Designing Enterprise Applications with the J2EE™ Platform, Second Edition,* (Boston, MA: Addison-Wesley, 2002).

dynamic HTML, Java applets, or ActiveX controls to execute business logic. Communication with the server is still done via HTTP.

- The Web delivery pattern is used when the Web browser acts principally as a delivery and container device for a distributed object system. In addition to HTTP for client and server communication, other protocols, such as IIOP and DCOM, may be used to support a distributed object system.

It is conceivable to apply several patterns to any specific system architecture. For example, an Internet-based e-commerce system may use the thin Web client pattern for its consumer sales use cases and use the thick Web client or the Web delivery pattern for the back-office maintenance use cases. This is likely because there is a degree of control of the client's configuration when you own the client but not so when you are soliciting business from Internet users all over the world.

Each of these patterns represents only the components of the presentation tier: the client browsers and the Web servers. Most real-world Web applications have additional middle—business—and data tiers. Architecturally, these back-end tiers are essentially unchanged from the way they appear in the more general client/server system. This is also where most of the system's business logic–processing components reside and most of the work of changing the state of the business happens.

The business logic tier of Web applications is where the bulk of the business objects do their work. This tier is typically a transactional tier, where objects can execute atomic changes in permanent state. The two most popular implementations/specifications are Microsoft's Transaction Server (MTS) and Enterprise JavaBeans (EJB). Both are essentially containers that manage transactional and nontransactional objects' life cycles and provide easy ways to execute database transactions. Both of these containers depend heavily on the data tier for providing the basic APIs to support transactions. The containers allow business objects to execute the logic of the business in a transaction-safe environment, even when multiple heterogeneous databases are used.

The focus of this book, however, is the Web and the architectural components specific to Web application development. The remainder of this chapter describes in more detail these three Web architectural patterns.

Thin Web Client

The thin Web client architectural pattern is useful for Internet-based applications, for which only minimal client configuration can be guaranteed. All business logic is executed on the server during the fulfillment of page requests for the client browser.

Requirements Viewpoint

The principal requirements governing this architecture revolve around the ability to deliver the system to as many types of user systems as possible. It is more important for an e-retail application to reach a large customer base with minimal client functionality than it is to deliver a technologically sophisticated one to a significantly limited number of customers. An e-retail business does not care about the type of systems its users have. Requiring complex functionality not critical to the execution of the system's business goals will limit the effectiveness of the application in meeting its business goals.

For this reason the thin Web client application requires only minimal capabilities on the client. In this type of architecture, the client's only responsibility is to be able to run a standard HTML Web browser that can request and render standard HTML-formatted pages. This includes the ability to accept and to submit simple data types—strings, Booleans, and selections—during some page requests.

Thin Web client architectures have additional restrictive requirements placed on them. Some have to operate with users who have disabled the ability for the browser to accept and to return cookies, which makes it impossible for some common client state management mechanisms to work. Many applications have to be able to operate in low-bandwidth environments, that is, modem Internet access.

In addition to the browser software, it is also recognized that many users of the system may be accessing it from behind a company or personal firewall. Firewalls often limit the type of access their users have with external systems. Many firewall configurations limit traffic to HTTP/HTTPS and only through the standard ports (80 and 443). Well-architected thin Web client systems recognize this and don't require nonstandard communications to the browser.

Design Viewpoint

When so much of the client is beyond the control of the development team and the principal requirements are to reach as wide a user base as possible, the only practical solution is to move all the system's business processing logic to one of the server tiers. The major components of the thin Web client architecture exist on the server. In many ways, this architecture represents the minimal Web application architecture. The major components are as follows:

- *Client browser:* Any standard forms-capable HTML browser. The browser acts as a generalized user interface device. Used in a thin Web client architecture, the only other service it provides is the ability to accept and to return cookies. The application user uses the browser to request Web pages, either HTML or server. The returned page contains a fully formatted user interface—text and input controls—which is rendered by the browser on the client's display. All user interactions with the system are through the browser.

- *Web server:* The principal access point for all client browsers. Client browsers in the thin Web client architecture access the system only through the Web server, which accepts requests for Web pages, either static HTML or server pages. Depending on the request, the Web server may initiate some server-side processing. If the page request is for a server-scripted page, CGI, ISAPI, or NSAPI module, the Web server will delegate the processing to the appropriate script interpreter or executable module. In any case, the result is an HTML-formatted page, suitable for rendering by an HTML browser.

- *HTTP connection:* The most common protocol in use between client browsers and Web servers. This architectural element represents a connectionless type of communication between client and server. Each time the client or the server sends information to the other, a new and separate connection is established between the two. A variation of the HTTP connection is a secure HTTP connection via Secure Sockets Layer (SSL). This type of connection encrypts the information being transmitted between client and server, using public/private encryption key technology.

- *Static page:* A Web page with UI and content information that does not go through any server-side processing. Typically, these pages contain explanatory text, such as directions or Help information, or HTML input forms. When a Web server receives a request for an HTML page, the server simply retrieves the file and sends it without filtering to the requesting client.

- *Dynamic page:* Web pages that go through some form of server-side processing. Typically, these pages are implemented on the server as scripted pages—Active Server Pages, JavaServer Pages, PHP, Cold Fusion pages—that get processed by a filter on the application server or by executable modules: ISAPI, NSAPI. These pages potentially have access to all server-side resources, including business logic components, databases, legacy systems, and merchant account systems.

- *Application server:* The primary engine for executing server-side business logic. The application server, responsible for executing the code in the server pages, can be located on the same machine as the Web server and can even execute in the same process space as the Web server. The application server is logically a separate architectural element since it is concerned only with the execution of business logic and can use a technology completely different from that of the Web server.

- *Database server:* The part of the system that maintains persistent state. To be a Web application, the system should ultimately change the state of the business. This state is maintained in the database. This server can be anything that logically manages state; in most situations, however, it is a relational database management system (RDBMS).

- *File system:* For many Web applications, the file system is a first-class citizen of the architecture, because its directory structure often mirrors the logical URL structure. In a Web application, the file system is responsible for managing HTML files—static pages—and scripted Web files—dynamic pages—for the Web and application server.

Figure 7-1 shows the structural relationships among these components. An additional abstract component, page resource, has been included to illustrate that both static and dynamic pages are essentially resources that can be requested by client browsers.

Two basic scenarios express the fundamental collaborations of this pattern. Figure 7-2 shows a sequence diagram that expresses the scenario of a simple static Web page

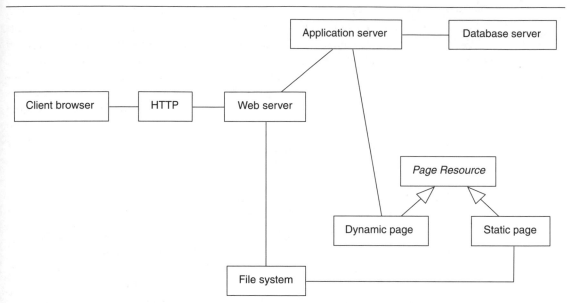

FIGURE 7-1   Principal participants in thin Web client collaboration

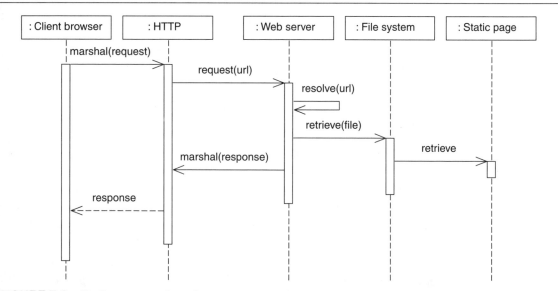

FIGURE 7-2   Static resource (page) request scenario

request. In this scenario, a client browser requests a page resource from a Web server. This request is marshaled by the network via either HTTP or HTTPS. The Web server must resolve the requested URL to a local file that is then retrieved and sent to the requesting client.

Figure 7-3 shows the sequence diagram that expresses the request and the fulfill-ment of a dynamic page—scripted or compiled—resource from the Web server. In this scenario, the client browser, as in the static page scenario, requests from the Web server a resource that is marshaled via the network. In this scenario, the application server processes the page, which in its own thread executes business logic, possibly changing the state of the business as captured in the database.

Realization Viewpoint

The realization viewpoint of a thin Web client architecture can vary greatly, depend-ing on the scalability strategy. In fact, the specifics of the entire system's architecture tightly hinge on this strategy. Discussing and describing all the ways a system can be architected to scale is definitely beyond the scope of this book. At the highest level, we can describe some points in the realization viewpoint that are common to all thin Web client systems.

Figure 7-4 shows the principal nodes in this architectural pattern: client, network, Web server, application server, and database server. Each of these server-tier nodes can be a separate physical machine or they can be colocated on the same machine. The client nodes, of course, are almost always many individual machines. Highly scalable systems often have multiple Web, application, and database nodes that are either clustered or cooperative (Figure 7-5).

Test Viewpoint

The major focus for testing any system is to verify that the system meets the needs of the stakeholders, as specified by requirements. For Web applications, many areas that need testing may not be mentioned in the requirements. Typically, these areas are a result of the system context, such as use on the Internet with unknown browser versions.

For thin Web client architectures, key areas that need to be addressed during test-ing are

- All supported browser versions
- Firewall settings: use of only standard ports and protocols
- Network latency
- ISP and browser page caching
- Cookie nature and use

Thick Web Client

The thick Web client architectural pattern extends the thin Web client pattern with client-side scripting and custom objects, such as ActiveX controls and Java applets. The thick

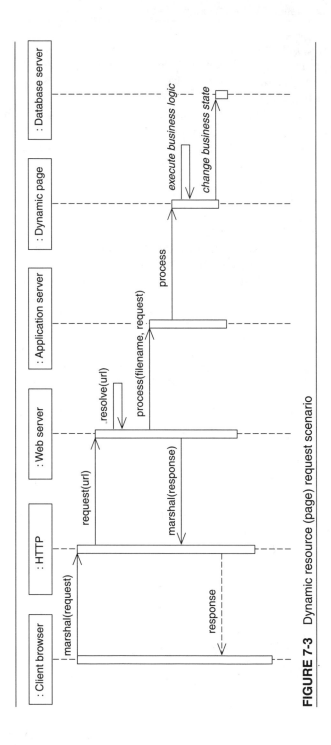

FIGURE 7-3 Dynamic resource (page) request scenario

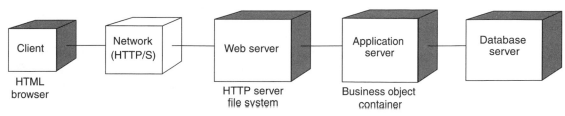

FIGURE 7-4 Deployment of simple thin Web client application

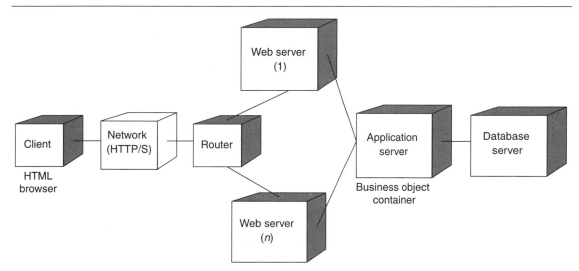

FIGURE 7-5 Deployment of scalable thin Web client application

Web client pattern is so named because the client can execute some of the business logic of the system and thus becomes more than a generalized user interface container.

The thick Web client architectural pattern is most appropriate for Web applications in which a certain client configuration and browser version can be assumed, a sophisticated user interface is desired, and/or a certain amount of the business logic can be executed on the client. Much of the distinction between the thin Web client and the thick Web client patterns lies in the browser's role in the execution of the system's business logic.

Requirements Viewpoint

The one additional new requirement that the thick Web client architecture addresses is the ability to execute some of the system's logic on the client. In many situations, this is desirable. The most basic example is that of a script or an applet that validates a form's fields prior to submission to the server. When possible, stopping invalid forms from being submitted to the server can improve the system's performance. Additional scripts and controls on the client can also provide intelligent assistance in filling out complicated forms or in navigating the system's pages.

In addition to executing business logic, the client's user interface experience can be enhanced with client-side activity. Sophisticated user interface controls, or scripting, can make the user interface easier to use or more attractive. Attractive interfaces are an important requirement in the tight e-commerce space, where the competition is only one click away.

Design Viewpoint

All communication between client and server, as in the thin Web client pattern, is done via HTTP or HTTPS. Because these protocols are "connectionless," most of the time, there is no open connection between client and server. Only during page requests does the client send information and requests to the server. This means that client-side scripting, ActiveX controls, and Java applets are limited to interacting with objects only on the client.

The thick Web client pattern uses certain browser capabilities, such as Java applets or ActiveX controls, to execute business logic on the client. Applets and controls are compiled executables that can be sent via HTTP and executed by the browser. Most versions of common HTML browsers also allow client-side scripting. HTML pages can be embedded with scripts written in JavaScript. This scripting capability enables the browser to execute—or rather interpret—code that may be part of the business logic of the system. The term "may be" is used because client scripts commonly contribute to only extraneous aspects of the user interface and are not part of the business logic.

The principal components in the thick Web client architecture are the same as those in the thin Web client, with the addition of scripts, applets, and Document Object Model (DOM) interface supported by the client browser. Figure 7-6 shows

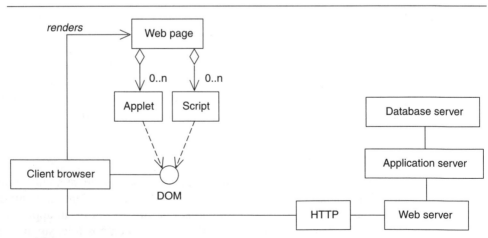

FIGURE 7-6 Principal participants in thick Web client architecture

these objects and their key relationships in a class diagram. Both scripts and applets interact with page content and the browser itself through the DOM interface.

Figure 7-7 shows an abstract scenario of the main collaboration in this pattern. Page resources are requested from the server exactly as they are in the thin Web client

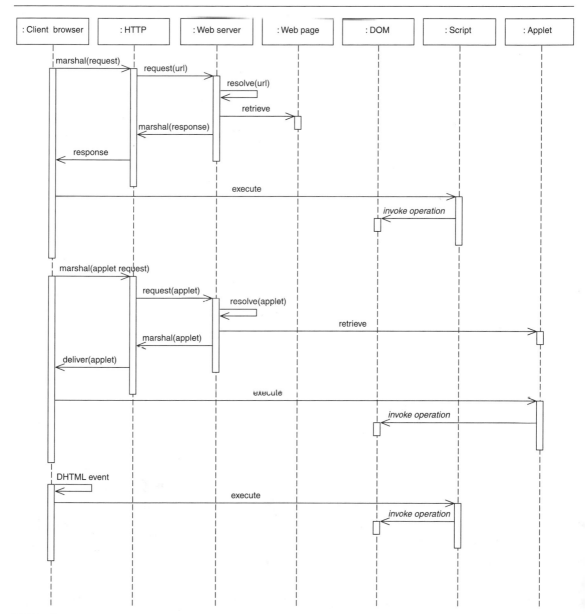

FIGURE 7-7 Basic applet and script execution scenario

architecture. They may or may not be dynamic page resources. As the page is received and rendered by the client browser, in-line scripts are executed, typically in separate threads of execution, not necessarily in the same thread of execution as the rendering operation. These scripts can interact with the page content via the DOM interface.

When applets are referenced, they are requested from the Web server separately and are executed. The browser is also generating events, as described by the various dynamic HTML (DHTML) implementations, which may be handled by embedded scripts. Both these scripts and the executing applets have access to the page content and the browser via the DOM interface.

Realization Viewpoint

The realization viewpoint of a thick Web client architecture is nearly identical to that of the thin Web client. Figure 7-8 shows these same nodes in this architectural pattern: client, network, Web server, application server, and database server. The only difference is that, in addition to rendering HTML, the client node is responsible for processing scripts and executing applets.

Test Viewpoint

The same testing issues described for the thin Web client are, of course, equally valid for thick Web client applications. However, testing and quality assurance need to address a few additional areas:

- Variations in vendors' scripting engines
- Access to support Java classes or libraries
- Network latency and its effects on multithreaded script processing
- Careful examination of fault situations, or missing applet components

Despite the efforts of the W3C to define browser interface standards, the reality is that browser vendors' implementations of this interface vary. Additional issues are related to each vendor's definition and implementation of the event mechanism.

One situation that developers often overlook is the system's behavior when certain resources, such as separate frames or applets, don't get loaded properly. This happens

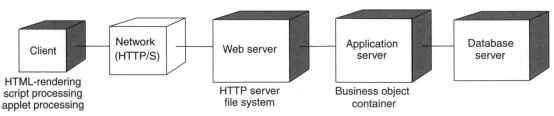

FIGURE 7-8   Deployment of simple thick Web client application

quite often in applications that operate over the Internet. The testing team needs to ensure that the system behaves gracefully when applets don't load in time.

Web Delivery

The Web Delivery architectural pattern is so named because the Web is used primarily as a delivery mechanism for an otherwise traditional distributed object client/server system. From one viewpoint, this type of application is a distributed object client/server application that happens to include a Web server and client browser as significant architectural elements. Whether such a system is a Web application with distributed objects or a distributed object system with Web elements, the ultimate system is the same. The fact that these two viewpoints are of the same system and that distributed object systems have always been seen as systems requiring careful modeling emphasizes the theme in this book that Web applications need to be modeled and designed like any other software system.

Requirements Viewpoint

HTTP can be a very limiting protocol for the most sophisticated applications. Its inherently connectionless behavior makes it ill-suited for situations in which quick and rich dialogs of communication must take place. For example, real-time device-monitoring equipment requires quick and voluminous data exchanges. The overhead required by standard HTTP traffic would make it impossible for many real-time equipment-monitoring applications to function on the Internet. Sometimes, good old-fashioned remote procedure calls or remote operation calls are the best solution.

The Web delivery architectural pattern is most appropriate when there is significant control of client and network configurations. This pattern is not particularly suited for Internet-based applications, where there is no or little control over client configurations, or when network communications are not reliable.

The greatest strength of this architecture is its ability to leverage existing business objects in the context of a Web application. With direct and persistent communications possible between client and server, the limitations of the previous two Web application patterns can be overcome. The client can be leveraged to perform significant business logic to an even greater degree.

This architectural pattern is unlikely to be used in isolation. More realistically, this pattern would be combined with one or both of the previous patterns. The typical system would use one or both of the first architectural patterns for parts of the system that do not require a sophisticated user interface or where client configurations are not strong enough to support a large client application.

Design Viewpoint

The most significant difference between the Web delivery and the other Web application architecture patterns is the method of communication between the client and the server. In the other patterns, the primary mechanism is HTTP, a connectionless protocol that

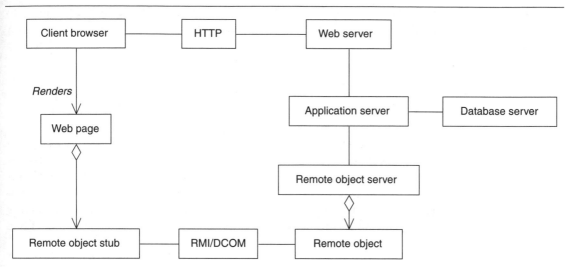

FIGURE 7-9   Principal participants in the Web delivery architecture

severely limits the designer when it comes to interactive activity between the user and the server. The architecturally significant elements in the Web delivery pattern include all those specified in the two previous patterns, as well as the following:

- *Remote object/remote object stub:* A conceptual object that can be interacted with, whose execution takes place on a remote machine. The stub is an object that executes on the client and has an identical interface to the actual object, which executes on the client. From the client's perspective, the object is local, but when methods are invoked on this object, they are marshaled over the network to the remote object server, where an instance of the business object is executing.

- *Remote object server:* A special server that hosts remote objects. It typically is responsible for managing the life cycle of the remote object instance and providing services to its objects by clients.

- *Remote object transfer protocol:* The protocol that allows efficient access to remote objects over standard networks. The two most common protocols for remote object use in Web applications are Microsoft's Distributed COM (DCOM) and Java's Remote Method Invocation (RMI) specification.[10]

Figure 7-9 is a class diagram showing the structural relationships among these components. The diagram shows that, at least conceptually, Web pages contain remote

---

10. Actually, the lower-level protocol for RMI use is either CORBA's Internet Inter-Orb Protocol (IIOP) or the earlier Java Remote Method Protocol (JRMP).

object stubs, which communicate with the server tier to a special remote object server through a separate protocol. Ultimately, however, the application server is the place where most of the real business logic gets executed. The objects executing in the remote object server mostly delegate their logic to the shared application server.

Figure 7-10 shows the main scenario of the pattern. In this sequence diagram, the Web page is obtained just as it would be in a thin Web client application. Any remote object stubs are requested via the Web server, similar to applets. Once on the client, any scripts or applets may invoke operations on the remote object stub. When an operation is invoked on a stub, the request is marshaled through RMI or DCOM to a remote object server. The server interprets the call and instantiates and invokes the methods on the actual object instance. Of course, this is a gross simplification of what goes on, but the essence is correct.

The key points to note for architects and designers is that remote objects use a protocol other than HTTP and can maintain open connections to a server so as to facilitate complex and long dialogs of activity.

Realization Viewpoint

The Web delivery pattern introduces a new node and device. The remote object server is responsible for making remote objects accessible to clients over the network. The protocol or method-invocation marshaling mechanism is the RMI or DCOM protocol, expressed as a device in the UML deployment diagram of Figure 7-11. It should be noted that in some situations, the application server and the remote object server might be one and the same in the realization viewpoint.

Test Viewpoint

The additional testing issues relevant to Web delivery architectures include all those for the previous patterns, as well as all those associated with normal distributed object systems. When associated with the Web, this includes careful monitoring of the infrastructure necessary to carry out the remote calls. Because the need for this pattern is often a result of the need for quick, long lasting, and reliable communications directly with the server, careful examination of network latency and fault tolerance are important when testing these applications.

The same testing issues described for the thin and thick Web clients are, of course, equally valid for Web delivery applications. However, testing and quality assurance must address a few additional areas:

- The use of additional ports for remote object communication through firewalls
- Performance over slow network connections
- Effect on underpowered client machines

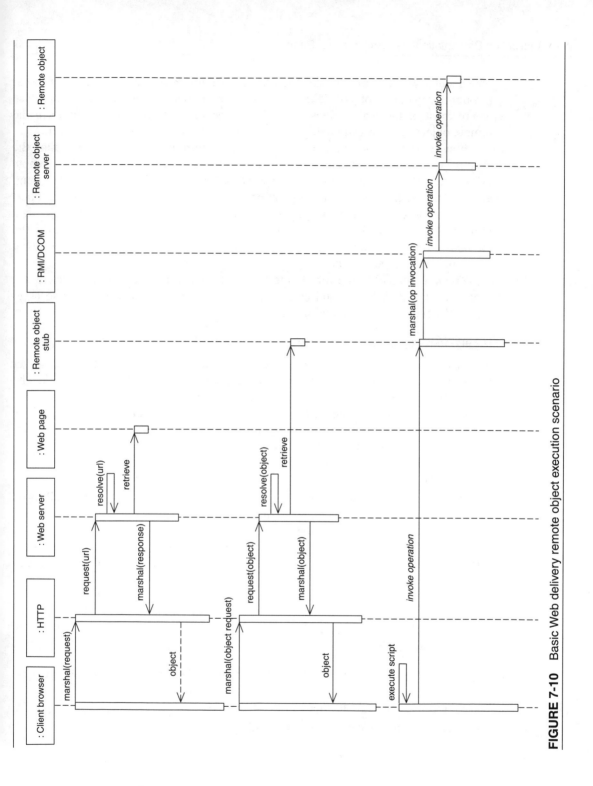

FIGURE 7-10 Basic Web delivery remote object execution scenario

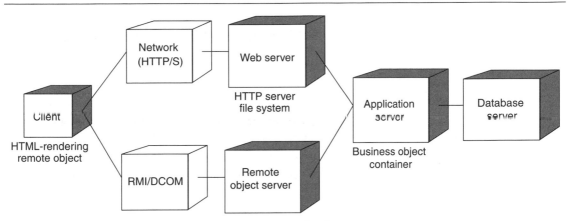

FIGURE 7-11 Deployment of simple Web delivery application

❑ ❑ ❑ ❑ ❑ ❑ ❑ ❑ ❑

Summary

❑ Architecture is about everything. An architecture description is essentially a selective and miniature version of the project artifacts.

❑ Software architecture is concerned with the significant architectural requirements (SARs). These are the requirements that influence the structure, arrangement, and constraints for all parts of the developing system.

❑ Architecture is expressed through viewpoints.

❑ The requirements viewpoint in an architecture description serves essentially as support and reasoning for the decisions made elsewhere.

❑ The design viewpoint expresses the logical components and their structural relationships. It also expresses their dynamics in terms of collaborations.

❑ The realization viewpoint expresses how the logical and process view elements are implemented in the system.

❑ The test viewpoint expresses the concerns relevant to the testing and quality assurance team.

❑ The architecture team examines the use case model from a technical viewpoint and prioritizes use cases according to perceived risk.

❑ The three most common architectural patterns for Web applications are thin Web client, thick Web client, and Web delivery.

Discussion

1. How do architectures evolve? What factors identify successful architectures?
2. What qualities are important in a chief architect?

Activities

1. Develop a rough architecture description suitable for solving the problem described in the prioritizing use cases section in this chapter.
2. Describe an appropriate testing strategy for a Web page that includes form validation code. Describe a strategy appropriate for testing a page that contains initialization scripts.

Chapter 8

Requirements and Use Cases

We build software applications to solve problems. In many situations, the problem and/or its scope may not be entirely clear. The primary goal of the first phase of software development—inception—is to provide good, reliable solutions to both of these issues.

The Vision

The solutions come as a set of artifacts, which include the vision document and the requirements. The vision document is the one document that all others should eventually trace back to. Created by the system analyst (Figure 8-1), the vision document is an overview of the entire project and is the source for the rationale that drives all the decisions made throughout the development process.

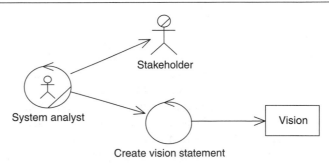

FIGURE 8-1   The vision, created by the system analyst with the help of stakeholders

The vision document contains several key elements:

- Description of the problem
- List of the stakeholders involved in the project and their views of the system
- Outline of the project scope
- Outline of the software solution: high-level features and key design constraints, driven directly by the problem domain

The system analyst responsible for drafting the vision document must accurately capture the nature of the problem and its context. For many projects, this is the development team's only view into the problem space. The language and the terms in this document come from the problem domain. This is important because the stakeholders typically are not technically oriented, yet it is vital that they grasp the development team's views of the problem and the business context.

The vision document captures the list of stakeholders and their views of the system so that the development team can understand whom the system is being built for and what their individual needs and expectations are. A stakeholder is anyone with an interest in the project. Most will be end users of the resulting system; however, there are other types of stakeholders, including senior management and even departments or organizations.

A good vision document recognizes the scope of the problem to be solved. Software systems, no matter how complex, are never sufficient to solve all business problems. In fact, the most successful systems are often those that have very limited scopes. The scope of the project begins by addressing the smallest set of stakeholder needs that absolutely must be met. This set grows as related needs and natural connections to other problems are identified. The idea is to define a project scope that is focused on the stakeholders' needs, not those of the project team.

I was on one project in which it was very clear what the stakeholders' needs were: to provide a software system for the management of home healthcare data. The project manager, however, made the development of a code generator the number-one feature and architectural requirement. The reasoning was that this code generator would be used by the development team to build the healthcare system. So for the vast majority of the time, the development team was focused on building this tool rather than on understanding the domain and building a solution for the real stakeholders' problem. In this case, the project's scope strayed from meeting the stakeholders' need and instead satisfied the project manager and architect's interests.

Determining the proper scope involves understanding not only the stakeholders' needs and the context of the problem but also resources and time. These two key factors influence a project's practical scope (Figure 8-2). A good vision document has some idea of the available resources and time frames involved to be able to scope the project appropriately. Often in a vision document, some features are separated and prioritized so that the scope of the project can be easily reduced, which is most often the case in the face of time, budget, and resource constraints.

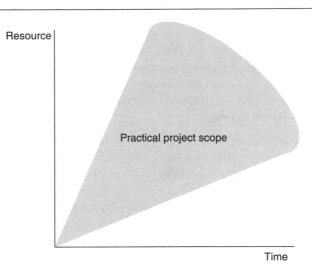

FIGURE 8-2   Project scope influenced by available resources and time

The shape of the software solution begins in the vision document with a list of high-level features. These requirements describe in broad terms bits of functionality that the solution is expected to have. Features are often a parent requirement to many detailed child requirements. The detailed requirements are collected and managed by the requirements team, which may or may not include the system analyst who created the vision document. The vision document acts as a basis for the detailed requirements, and all detailed requirements should be traceable to at least one system feature.

The vision document itself may include some detailed requirements, especially if they are significant and high enough in priority. Generally, however, the list of features is enough to describe the expected solution and to provide a basis for the detailed requirements collected later.

Because the vision document addresses the solution, albeit in very little detail, it is not unreasonable for it to contain some of the vocabulary associated with Web applications. Ideally, the vision document, like requirements as a whole, should be independent of the system's architecture. The reality is that in many cases, the architecture at a very high level is known. Most systems are built to leverage existing infrastructure. In fact, this is one reason that Web applications are so popular: The infrastructure needed to deliver them is usually already in place.

With this realization, it is not unreasonable to see some of the vocabulary of Web application architecture appear in the vision document. If the project is to build an online e-retail application, for example, the target architecture will most certainly be a Web application. When the target architecture is known in advance to be Web-centric, the vision document should include additional sections that address the following concerns:

- *Security.* Outline the level of security for the system as a whole, and detail areas where it is most relevant. Also attempt to establish the relative weight security has over functionality and performance concerns.

- *Supported client environments.* Describe the target client environment in some detail—browser version, operating system, screen capabilities, network bandwidth—and the relative importance for supporting other clients in the first and future versions.

These concerns will also appear in more detail later in the requirements; however, in the context of the vision document, they will influence the early architectural prototypes and set the expectations of the rest of the team during requirements gathering.

Vision documents are often used to obtain funding. For this reason, and in order to get it funded, they often exaggerate what the system will do. This is bad; these claims can threaten the success of the project as a whole. When writing vision statements, the stakeholders and the system analyst should make sure that the vision is realistic, not futuristic.

It is vital that a clear and understandable statement of the overall purpose and plan for the project be made. It must never be open ended. Visions that include such statements as "to utilize the latest technologies in establishing a competitive position" are a recipe for disaster. Perhaps the most important piece of the vision statement is the definition of success criteria. Concrete examples, such as "a gain of 15 percent of the marketplace" or "a 50 percent reduction in the processing of paper forms," are tangible success criteria and contribute to a clear vision statement.

Requirements

A requirements specification is a collection of artifacts—documents, database records, models—that attempt to unambiguously describe a software system to be built. Each document usually includes a description of the document's purpose, version number, contributors, and other administrative information, in addition to a list of specific system requirements. The specification can be a single document for small systems or can be distributed over multiple documents and databases. A system's requirements must always be available to nearly everyone connected to the project. An excellent way to do this is to make them available on an intranet via a Web server. If the application is going to be a Web application, the infrastructure for doing this is probably already in place.

A requirement is a constraint that the system must observe and is typically expressed as a statement that begins with a phrase like "The system shall . . . ." The purpose of a requirements statement is to express a behavior or a property that the system should have. More important than the phrasing, however, is the goal: to express the need for one very specific system behavior, in clear and easy-to-understand language. Requirements need to be understood by the development team and validated by the stakeholder and user community. A difficult-to-understand requirement doesn't help anyone.

One important quality of a good requirements statement is that it can be verified by the testing team when delivered. Only requirements that are objective and have clearly determined pass/fail criteria can be verified. Every requirement has the potential to be verified through a collection of test cases. Each test case formally defines a specific set of inputs, execution conditions, and expected results. A requirement that cannot be verified with a test case doesn't belong in the requirements specification.

In general, requirements can be categorized as either functional or nonfunctional. Functional requirements describe an action that the system should perform. They usually define both the stimulus and the response, or input and output. Functional requirements, the most common type of requirement, identify the things that the system can do, usually in response to external input. Examples of functional requirements are "The system should be able to compute international shipping charges for all products available for sale" or "The system shall automatically produce a summary report of all sales made for each week."

Nonfunctional requirements can be categorized to make them easier to understand and keep track of. Some common requirement categories are

- *Usability.* Usability requirements refer to those general aspects of the interface between the user and the system. These types of requirements are often related to look-and-feel user interface standards. For example, a common usability requirement defines the maximum number of clicks a user must make to complete a function of the application. Other requirements may constrain the Web page design: "The system interface shall not use HTML frames" or "The system shall be accessible by any browser that is forms capable and supports the use of the `<table>` tag."

- *Performance.* Performance requirements describe system execution performance and are usually related to time. A common requirement for Web application specifies a maximum load time for a page. For example, "Web pages should not take longer than 15 seconds to load in the browser during normal system usage."

- *Robustness/reliability.* All mission-critical applications need to clearly state the degree to which the application must be available. Most of these requirements affect only the architecture decisions. It would be nice if we could say that the system needs to be fully functional 24/7/52—24 hours a day, 7 days a week, 52 weeks a year—but building in that level of reliability is costly. What is more likely is a realistic expectation of maximum acceptable down time. It is not unreasonable for most applications to schedule 1 hour a week of down time for maintenance and upgrades. Robustness and reliability are also concerned with backup and storage issues. For example, a requirement of the system might be something like "The system should enable access to data on weekly backup tapes within a 2-hour window."

- *Security.* Security requirements tend to specify levels of access to the system and often map to human roles of the business. Security requirements should include access to the system by other "external" systems, if used. Security requirements are best described in the context of standard countermeasure mechanisms: access control, authentication, encryption, audit, and intrusion detection.

- *Hardware.* Hardware requirements often state the minimal hardware required to implement the system. These requirements should address hardware for each tier of the system: client, presentation, entity, and data.

- *Deployment.* Deployment requirements describe how the application is delivered to the end users. This element constrains how the system is to be installed, maintained, and accessed by maintenance staff. If scalability is important, the deployment requirements should address how hardware is added to running systems.

This list is by no means complete. Depending on the system's purpose, other categories might be appropriate as well. With so many categories, it is common for some requirements to naturally fit into more than one category. Because this is the reality for most applications, you should not place too much importance on how any individual requirement item gets categorized. Requirements should stand on their own, and categorizing them is a way to organize them, nothing more. Development team members should make a thorough review of all a system's requirements, even if they haven't been categorized in the area of their specialty.

An additional way to classify requirements is to define attributes that can hold extra information about a requirement, or metainformation. This metainformation can help categorize a requirement, provide an estimate of cost, establish a time frame for development, or even point to a reference source. Most tools for requirements management allow metainformation to be defined for requirements.

Another important property about requirements is their relationships with one another. A requirement, like a feature, is a parent requirement to a set of discrete and detailed requirements. This hierarchy of requirements makes it easier to manage them. For example, if a feature is scoped out of a particular release, all its child requirements can be easily taken out of scope. Of even more use are requirements that depend on other requirements. Before a feature is scoped out of a release, an automated check can ensure that the removal of the feature's requirements will not affect the remaining requirements of the system.

Take as an example one system feature to provide a native XML interface for browsers and use XSL (Extensible Stylesheet Language) for formatting. One of the child requirements is the creation of an XML subsystem and interface to the entity tier. For one reason or another, this feature is scoped out of the next release. The impact analysis, as required by the change management procedures for the project, identifies that another requirement of the system—the legacy system interface—

depends on the XML subsystem for access to the entity tier. The decision to scope out the XML interface now needs to be reevaluated in light of its other dependencies.

For small projects, most scoping decisions can be made and quickly evaluated. However, as the project team gets larger and the architecture more complex, having a well-structured requirements model is essential to ensuring the integrity of the development project.

It would be nice if it were possible to unambiguously specify a real system completely. In practice, however, some requirements are likely missing, overstated, or even wrong. This stems, in part, from an "impedance mismatch" between the problem space—the world of the domain—and the solution space—the world of the software system. Whenever you attempt to translate from one language or domain to another, there is always some information loss.

A system's requirements comprise a contract that binds the stakeholders to accept a system that meets the specified criteria and the development team that agrees to build that system. This sounds simple, and it can be. But the realities of software development always lead to changes downstream that affect nearly every aspect of the process and its artifacts. In an iterative and incremental development process, a system's requirements are living artifacts that evolve with the rest of the system artifacts.

Nonetheless, we write requirements expecting and hoping that they will not change. If the requirements team has done a good job, there should be very little change in the requirements of the system throughout the process. In fact, a very important metric of the process is the amount of change made to the requirements. If the requirements change significantly or waffle throughout the process, the requirements-gathering process is in need of some help.

Glossary

In my opinion, a project glossary is the most underrated project artifact in the entire development process. The glossary can be a document or a database. It is simply a collection of terms and definitions that the team can reference while creating and using the system's requirements. The glossary can start as an appendix to the vision, but as the project gains momentum, the glossary is most useful as a versioned document or database. This document is the authoritative source for all terms and definitions.

A good project glossary helps new team members come up to speed quickly. It can be used to help communicate subtle meanings across team boundaries. In general, this artifact is a resource for every member of the project. The cost of maintaining a project glossary is small compared to its benefits.

It may seem at first that everyone on the small team that begins the project has the same understanding of the major terms and definitions used in the project, albeit with slightly varying views of the details. When a vision document is created and distributed, it is also time to start the glossary. Appendix E is a functional glossary system that could be used; however, the ideal glossary repository is best when it is part of the larger requirements management system.

Gathering and Prioritizing Requirements

Requirements gathering is typically done in groups. It is not recommended that one person define the requirements of a particular part of the system, even if that person is the undisputed authority on the subject. Having varied skill sets in the team is also a plus. In Figure 8-3, the requirements team is responsible for developing most of the requirements artifacts, whereas project management and the architecture team are responsible for prioritizing them.

A requirements team is made up of at least one representative of the user or stakeholder community and a technical member of the development staff. The requirements are, after all, a contract between these two groups, and proper representation of both sides is important. Additional skill sets can complement the team. If the team has been appointed to examine the reporting and data-mining aspects of the system, a database expert should join the team.

The formatting of the documents is not of much concern, but the ability to tag, or identify, each requirement is important. Each specific requirement of the system should have a unique identifier that is used for traceability. The identifier might be something as simple as the chapter, section, and subsection numbers in an outline-formatted document. Requirements management tools provide a unique identifier for each and every requirement in a project and sometimes across projects.

The following example shows what a simplified fragment of a small system's requirements document might look like:

3. Performance Requirements

This section describes the system's performance requirements. These requirements usually relate to the execution speed and capacity of each component of the system.

3.1 Web server performance

The Web server performance section describes the expected performance of the Web server and network of the system.

3.1.1 Each Web server in the system shall be able to handle at least 150 simultaneous user sessions.

3.1.2 The system shall require no more than 3 seconds to retrieve and to respond to a client's request for a static Web page.

3.1.3 The system shall require no more than 8 seconds to respond to a dynamic page.

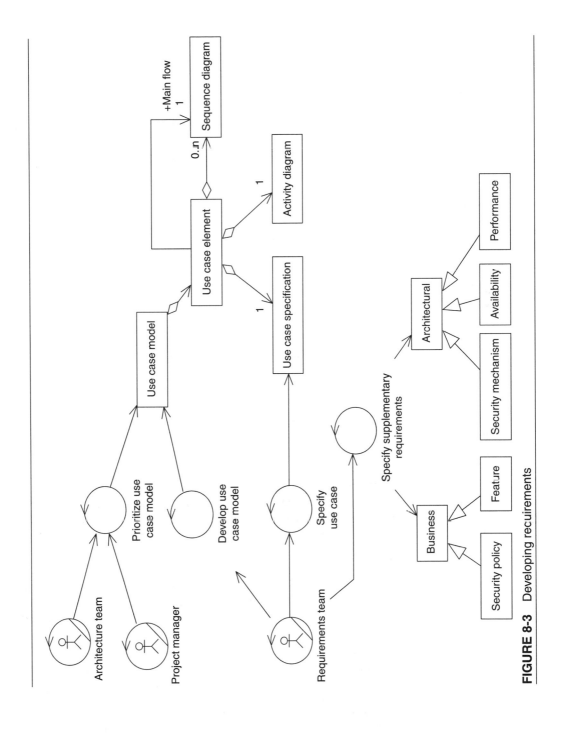

FIGURE 8-3 Developing requirements

Note that in this fragment, descriptive text introduces the sections and subsections. A requirements document should be self-explanatory, a document that can be given without additional explanation to any member outside the development team. Each requirement is by default assigned a unique ID. For instance, the "3-second page response" requirement would have an ID of 3.1.2. This ID is part of the traceability of the model. As the process goes on and the system gets designed, each element in the model traces back to at least one requirement. This is a key aspect of the entire process. Each and every element in the model must be able to point to a requirements item to support its existence.

I remember one project in which an engineer on a requirements team introduced a requirement that the system be constructed such that at runtime, additional attributes could be associated with certain entities, such as customers and purchase orders. The idea was that administrators of that system could easily add properties without redesigning or recoding the system.[1]

The feature is nice, and the design pretty slick, but the additional development costs were high, and unless it supports one of the system's key features, it should be questioned whether this is a real requirement. This is an example of how requirements get manufactured to support engineering interests, not necessarily business ones.

Later in the process, during design reviews, design model elements—classes and packages—are checked with the requirements to ensure that they point to at least one requirement and that they really capture the spirit of the requirements they point to. A reviewer might look at the requirement for dynamic entity attributes and compare it to other requirements in the system. Those features and requirements might simply state that the system needs to capture customer demographic information and even explicitly state the information to be captured. The reviewer then must ask, "Is this requirement necessary?"

Of course, it is entirely possible that the designer has realized something that the requirements team has missed. Perhaps the design team's experience in the domain has noted similar situations in the past and has a workable solution. In this situation, discussions between the analysis/design team and the requirements team need to take place. If this feature is desirable and the additional effort to implement it is minimal, the change control process kicks in. This process ensures that the appropriate people or departments are notified and consulted about the pending change. Depending on the scope of the change, this may affect a large number of people, and its impact needs to be examined and scheduled by the project manager.

The requirements fragment mentioned earlier contains some pretty specific knowledge about the architecture. For example, it references Web servers and the use of Web pages explicitly. Unless the use of a Web application was stated elsewhere in the requirements, these sets of Web-specific requirements probably evolved from others

---

1. Yes, this happened on a project I was on. The funny thing is that the architect at the time thought it was a good idea too, and we implemented the system this way. Of course, I can only speculate on the delay, if any, this type of architecture might have caused.

or were introduced during a later increment. For example, the usability section in the requirements for the first increment might have mentioned that the user interface response time should be less than 3 seconds. In a later increment, when it was realized that a Web architecture was going to be applied, the requirements might have been refined to include those items specific to Web applications.

Whenever it is determined that Web applications are involved, you will probably find new sets of requirements, especially in the hardware section. Once the architecture has been tentatively settled on a Web application, refinements and additions can be made to the requirements documents. Remember that artifacts in an incremental and iterative development process change, and we have to get used to the idea. The key, of course, is expecting, managing, and minimizing changes.

When writing a requirements statement, you should keep a few things in mind.

- Each requirement should be clear and concise. Avoid wordy descriptions that can be interpreted in a variety of ways.

- A requirements statement should focus on one point. The finer granularity enables better traceability through the model.

- Every requirement must be verifiable. "The UI must be intuitive" cannot be objectively tested and so is not verifiable.

Before the requirements can be used in any downstream phase of the process, they must be prioritized. It would be nice if all the requirements specified in the requirements documents were built into the system exactly as requested, but the realities of software development often force compromises between functionality and time to delivery. By prioritizing a system's requirements, both the stakeholders and the development staff know where it is important to spend valuable effort. Prioritizing also helps resolve conflicting requirements. For example, one requirement of the system might specify that the application must be functional on client computers with only a monochrome 640×480 pixel display. Another requirement might be for all invalid field validations to be identified with a red background. Clearly, if the system were used with a monochrome client, invalid fields would never be identified.

The requirements team would probably have made the screen resolution requirement relatively high, since another goal of the system is to leverage existing computing equipment in the organization. Using red to display invalid field values would probably have a lower priority because the use of specific colors in a user interface is often problematic. During the requirements review process, these inconsistencies would be noted. Having them prioritized makes it easier to decide how to handle the conflict.

Most systems can prioritize requirements with a few levels such as low, medium, and high. A high-priority requirement would be a "must-have" requirement. The system would not be functional unless it was met. A medium-priority requirement might mean that it is strongly desired but could be put off until the second release of the product. A low-priority requirement, of course, might mean that it is desired but optional. The system would be functional without it but would be a better system with it.

Of course, the definition and number of priority levels vary with each development organization.

Determining the priority structure is not as difficult as determining individual requirement priorities. This part of the process is probably one of the most stressful activities of the process, and some words on human nature need to be said. One can get a rather powerful feeling when defining requirements for a system. With seemingly little effort, our ideas can become pseudoreality. We can see it in our heads, and everything is perfect. These requirements or features of the system, in a subconscious way, become owned by their creators. When it comes time to prioritize the requirements, their creators tend to rate them high, whereas others think otherwise. The psychological battles ensue.

I can remember my first "real" object-oriented (OO) project. We were gathering the requirements for the customer demographics section of the application. The system was to replace an older DOS and file server–based system. I had suggested that instead of capturing a customer's street address in three separate attributes—line 1, line 2, and line 3—we could use a multiline edit box. Multiline addresses would be entered in the same control, by just pressing the Enter key to create a second line. From the system's point of view, it was just a single attribute of the `Address` object that, optionally, had line feeds in it. It caught on with my fellow requirements team members at the time, and we all agreed that the application might be simpler that way. That was my only unique contribution to the team's efforts, and I was prepared to defend it. Eventually, the team reversed the requirement, and we ended up using three separate street address attributes, owing in part to my junior status and in part to other, higher-prioritized requirements for deployment and legacy system compatibility. In retrospect, it was the best outcome for the system, and I learned a little about myself and the politics of requirements.

Even experience alone is not enough to ensure proper prioritization of requirements. In another personal experience, the project manager and the chief architect of a Web-based application had defined two requirements: that all users of the system would use browsers for system access and that there would be a common source code repository across all platforms. These two requirements were prioritized as the two most important ones of the entire system, even over every functional and usability requirement! It became a problem only when applied to the offline component of the system. Part of the system needed to be implemented with laptops and palm-top computers that would be temporarily disconnected from the main Web server. Because being a Web application and having a common source code repository were the top two requirements, a fully functional Web server had to be put on the portable devices. It was another case of envisioning the technology before the full scope of the problem was understood. Despite the arguments of nearly every other member of the development team, these two requirements remained a top priority. In the end, the application was never created. The constraints placed on the development team by these two seemingly laudable requirements meant, in the end, the death of the application.

It is important to objectively prioritize every requirement. If necessary, refer to the original vision statement of the project. Ask how important this requirement is in realizing the original vision of the system. Most requirements of a system are good and should be worked toward; however, tradeoffs often need to be considered: development time, complexity, compatibility, and so on. Requirements need to be weighed against the benefit that they add to the system. For example, one requirement might improve data entry speed significantly but increase the development time and complexity. Look at the vision statement for the project. If it emphasizes or discusses the importance of speeding up the process, it just might be a high-priority requirement. If the vision statement doesn't mention the need for fast data entry, prioritize it lower, and let it become part of the system without endangering other parts.

When dealing with requirements, especially the prioritization of requirements, we need to keep the human factor in mind. A good team is able bring these issues out early, when there is still time to accommodate everyone. Improper prioritization of requirements can lead to disastrous results. Proper prioritization of requirements can mean the difference between meeting or missing the delivery date.

Use Cases

Writing simple statements is an excellent way to capture and to prioritize performance, hardware, deployment, and usability requirements but is a little lacking for capturing functional ones. Functional requirements describe how the system behaves in response to user and external system input. They tend to be more dynamic and often require greater detail in order to clearly understand them. Use cases are a powerful technique for capturing and expressing detailed system behavior. Use cases were first put forward by Ivar Jacobson.[2] Other favorite resources of mine on use cases are Alistair Cockburn,[3] Larry Constantine and Lucy Lockwood.[4] Use cases are a formal way to capture and to express the interaction and the dialogue between system users, called actors, and the system itself. Because a full discussion of use cases is beyond the scope of this book, and I will concentrate on the highlights and most interesting points as they relate specifically to Web-based applications.

Jacobson uses the term *actor* to represent a generic role of user. The term *user* is reserved for instances of people using the system. Users may play the part of many actors of the system. An actor's name should represent the type of role it plays with the system. A typical actor of an e-commerce system might be *Online Customer*, or someone who uses the system to purchase items by using a browser and the Internet.

---

2. I. Jacobson, M. Christerson, P. Jonsson, and G. Overgaard, *Object-Oriented Software Engineering: A Use Case Driven Approach* (Boston, MA: Addison-Wesley, 1992).

3. A. Cockburn, *Writing Effective Use Cases* (Boston, MA: Addison-Wesley, 2000).

4. L. Constantine and L. Lockwood, *Software for Use: A Practical Guide to the Models and Methods of Usage-Centered Design* (Boston, MA: Addison-Wesley, 1999).

A use case is a textual description of the interaction between an actor and the system. A use case contains a narrative description of a specific usage scenario, one in which an actor supplies input and the system exhibits an observable output. A use case may contain more than one scenario; however, there is always one main scenario. The other scenarios are called alternative scenarios, or alternative paths.

A use case is written to express what a system should do, without constraining how it should do it. A use case describes the behavior of the system as viewed from the outside. All the behavior is in the form of observable results. Of course, the observable results don't have to be displayed on the user's screen; they could be in the form of a database change or the cutting of a bank check at the home office. The point is to maintain a focus on the input and output behavior of the system and to leave the details of applying the architecture and creating a workable design to the analysts and designers who will use the use case later on.

All use cases are named, and their names reflect their purposes, or goals. It is also helpful to number use cases for traceability because even use case names are subject to change. In addition to the required use case name and scenario description, most use cases capture other key information:

- *Unique ID:* Ideally, an automated number or a numbering system that will enable a use case name to evolve and yet maintain traceability throughout the process. The ID can be an intelligent key with the use case category—package—or other understandable information.

- *Goal statement:* A simple, one-line, if possible, statement that summarizes the goal of the entire use case. This goal, like a vision statement, is a useful reference as the use case evolves. If actions in the use case don't support the goal, their inclusion in the scenario should be questioned.

- *Authors:* The names of the requirements team members who have directly contributed to the text in the use case. Depending on how cynical you are, it could mean the people to contact when clarification needs to be made or the people to blame when things go wrong.

- *Assumptions:* A textual description of things that are assumed, that is, the state of the system. The assumptions do not constrain the system but rather are things that the use case writers have assumed to be true while writing the use case.

- *Preconditions:* A textual description of conditions that must be met before this use case can be performed. Unlike assumptions, preconditions must be satisfied before the use case can begin.

- *Postconditions:* A textual description of conditions that must be met before this use case can be completed. Postconditions typically refer to a state the system must be in for the use case to end, such as no outstanding error conditions.

- *Outstanding issues:* A collection of items that need to be resolved before the use case can be elaborated in analysis and design. This section of a use case should be used only during its construction and should be blank by the time it is used in any downstream process.

The formatting of the scenario is flexible, and there is no one right way to do it. Use cases can be highly structured, with tightly controlled phrasing and numerous section headings and enumerations to identify ordering. At the other extreme, use cases can be relaxed, and appear more like a story. I have worked with use cases at both extremes, and I can't say that I favor one over the other. The right style of use case is usually related to the type of application being developed and the dynamics of the organization building it.

A use case is written in the language of the domain. Remember, use cases are simply a technique to express requirements, and a requirement is a contract between the stakeholders/users and the development staff. Both parties need to be able to understand what is captured and meant by a use case. Use cases are also used by the technical writers as the basis for a user manual. In a well-managed project, user documentation should be complete about the same time as the software is, since both the software and the user manual are directly based on the use cases. Some processes even stress that use case descriptions be written in the form of a user manual. The testing group also makes use of use cases as the basis for the majority of the test scripts. Nearly every member of the development team uses the use cases for one reason or another. Use cases are a central artifact and drive all other aspects of the process.

I had one experience in which the initial requirements team consisted mainly of an analyst/developer, a database-oriented developer, and a domain expert (end user). We constructed a use case model and use case descriptions that were more or less as they were presented in the original text by Jacobson. The style was a compromise between the two extremes, and we all seemed to be happy with their format.

About a month after we had begun, the testing team had finally been assembled. The team members looked at our use cases—something that every new member of a development team should do—and determined that they needed a little more detail if automated test scripts were to be developed from them. We revised our use case descriptions, which became increasingly structured, to the extreme. The phrasing and terminology were so rigid and explicit that when one domain expert was asked if this use case was what she wanted the system to do, she had to say, "Well I think so; I'm not sure now since I really don't understand most of it anymore."

That raised a flag, and we immediately reassessed how structured we wanted our use cases to be. We made another compromise. We kept the general structure—numbered steps and simple sentences—but dropped a lot of the technical phrases and references to specific user interface elements. In the end, we had use cases the domain experts could read and, with some help from the design artifacts, something the testing team could read and build test scripts around.

A use case often contains multiple scenarios. One of them is always the basic flow scenario, or "happy path." The other scenarios represent alternative paths through the use case. These alternative paths may be exceptions or infrequently used options in the scenario. An exception would be something like the actor's deciding to cancel a transaction partway through it. An infrequently used option might be the capturing of additional information, required only for international customers. The common theme among the scenarios is the intent of the actor to accomplish the goal statement. Even an actor canceling a use case started it with the intent mentioned in the stated goal. In a use case document, the alternative scenarios are clearly indicated as such, and when appropriate, additional information is supplied to connect them to the main scenario. Similarly, the main scenario may refer to the alternative scenarios when appropriate in the narrative.

The Use Case Model

UML has special representations for use cases and actors. A simple ellipse represents use cases; simple stick figures, actors. A use case diagram expresses the system's use cases in relation to the actors that invoke them. I prefer to construct these diagrams with an adornment that draws a boundary around the system, placing the use cases within the boundary and the actors outside (Figure 8-4). This notation is convenient when multiple systems are being jointly developed, and it can be clearly seen which use cases are part of which system. The complete collection of use cases, actors, and diagrams forms a use case model, which, like individual use cases, is just one part of the system's requirements specification.

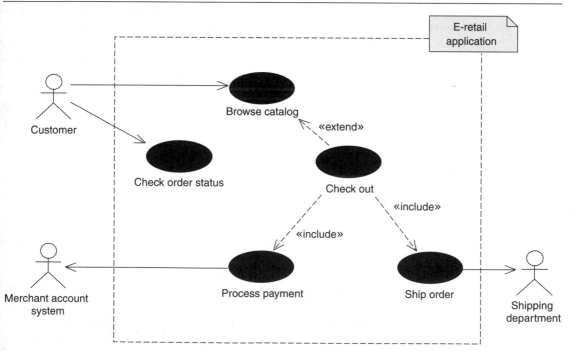

FIGURE 8-4   Top-level use case diagram for an e-retail system

Relationships between actors and use cases indicate that the actor can invoke a particular use case. Figure 8-4 shows that the actor can browse the catalog or check on the order status. This diagram also identifies two other actors: the Merchant Account System and the Shipping Department. These actors are in fact not individuals but rather external systems, or more accurately the APIs of those external systems. When the Process Payment use case is invoked, it initiates the dialogue between the Merchant Account System and this system; similarly, the Ship Order use case contacts the Shipping Department's system when invoked.

Relationships between use cases are also documented in the model and appear in a diagram as a stereotyped dependency relationship, or arrow-headed dashed line. The two major types of relationships between use cases are «includes» and «extends». Both indicate a dependency on one use case by the other; however, the subtle difference between the two has, in my experience, caused a significant degree of confusion.

In Figure 8-4, the use case Checkout extends the use case Browse Catalog. This means that the actor invoking the use case might decide to extend the dialogue with the system to include the activities described in the Checkout use case. The key word here is "might." Every invocation of the Browse Catalog use case does not necessarily include checking out. The relationships between the Checkout use case and the Process Payment and Ship Order use cases, however, are expected with every invocation of the Checkout use case. The «includes» relationship indicates that each invocation of the Checkout use case will invoke the included use cases at least once. This type of a relationship can be thought of as calling a subroutine.

The use case model shows the structural relationships between use cases but does not show dynamic relationships, or workflows. Dynamic behaviors are expressed with interaction diagrams: sequence, collaboration, and activity. It is important to keep that in mind when drawing use case diagrams. It's easy to start constructing use case diagrams as if they were workflow diagrams, since use case names often reflect major activities of the business workflow. Most associations between use cases in a diagram simply imply that one invokes the other, nothing more.

There's more to the use case model than this high-level diagram. I've recently begun to create a single activity diagram for each use case in the system. This activity diagram helps me sort out all the alternative flows in a use case and ensure that I haven't forgotten how any of them rejoins the basic flow. In the past, I helped draft a few use cases in which later iterations added alternative flows that seemed reasonable and addressed the issue at the time, but when it came to implementing them, it wasn't clear in what state those alternative flows would leave the system and at what point the normal flow of the use case scenario should resume. Properly created activity diagrams for a use case clearly identify all alternative paths as branches and even allow us to see the effects of repetition, or loops, in the flow that would otherwise be mentioned only in the text of the use case specification.

Figure 8-5, the activities for the Browse Catalog use case, shows a typical activity diagram for a use case that has some repetition. It is clear from this diagram that there is one main loop structure, labeled the Shop controller. Many of the branches are

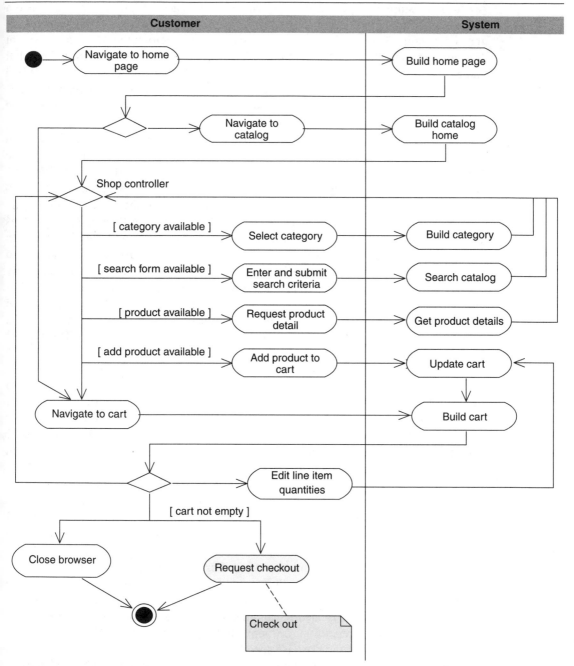

FIGURE 8-5   Activity diagram of the Browse Catalog use case

guarded with conditions—text between the brackets—and indicate the availability of an option that the actor can invoke.

As a notational convention, I add notes to the activity diagram at those points where the use case is extended or included. If the modeling tool you use supports the inclusion of hyperlinks to other diagrams, I highly recommend hyperlinking these notes to the relevant activity diagram to make it easier for the reader to follow the flow through all the related use cases.

The activity diagram of a use case clarifies the nature of the «includes» or «extends» relationships. In the case of an «extended» relationship, it should be possible for the actor to get from the start activity to an end activity without invoking the extended use case. Figure 8-5 demonstrates that it is possible for the actor to follow a path from start to finish without hitting the Request Checkout activity and thus invoking the Checkout use case.

When the actor does decide to check out, the flow of activities shifts to the Checkout use case. In Figure 8-6, the activities of the Checkout use case clearly show how the included use cases are part of the basic flow. Even though one possible path through the use case does not invoke the Ship Order use case, it is still considered an included use case because it is part of the "happy-path" scenario, or basic flow. It is the exceptional case, when the payment is not received, that causes the activities to bypass the commitment of the order.

Another recommendation is to create a sequence diagram for each named use case scenario: basic and alternative flows. Document each with text taken directly from the use case specification, if practical. This serves two purposes. First, it provides the template later models will use when constructing use case realizations; second, it helps you identify and pull out the most important statements in use case text. If you have particularly wordy use cases, the exercise will force you to simplify the text to fit in the sequence diagram. Figure 8-7 shows a sequence diagram for the Browse Catalog use case basic flow scenario. This diagram is simple and for use case readers probably doesn't provide much additional value; however, as the rest of the systems models evolve, this scenario will be referenced and elaborated on in each model's use case realizations. A use case realization is in part an explanation of how a use case is implemented with the elements of the specific model it is in. For example, in the design model, this sequence diagram would have a number of design-level objects instead of the System object and messages to and from the design objects that correspond to methods defined in their classes.

Avoiding Functional Decomposition

An extremely common mistake many new and experienced use case modelers make is to start thinking of use cases as primarily bundles of functionality, not dialogues of interactions between the actors and the system. *Functional decomposition* is the term for a use case model that describes bundles of system functionality independent of the user. Systems with many small use cases, such as Enter Payment Information, are examples of models that have degenerated into functional decomposition.

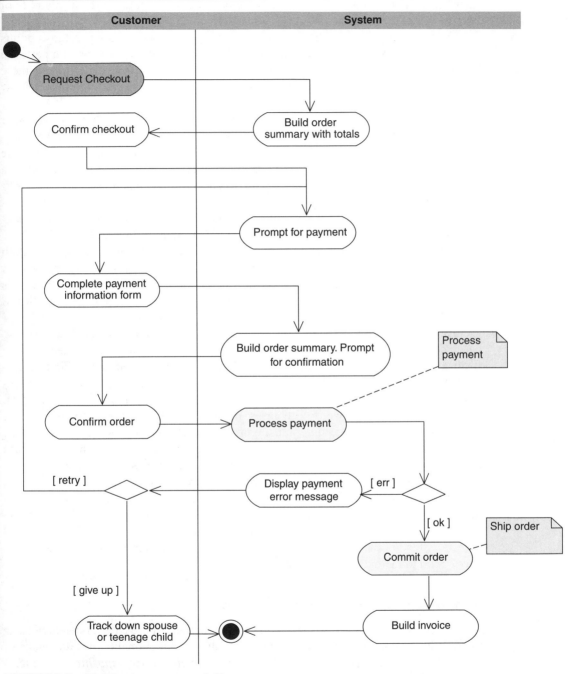

FIGURE 8-6 Checkout use case activities

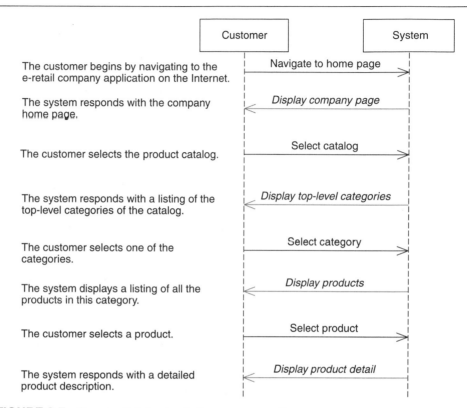

FIGURE 8-7   Browse Catalog basic flow sequence diagram

Even the most seasoned use case modeler can get confused at times. Ironically, while writing this chapter, I was also engaged in a discussion of how to model a certain set of use cases for a medium-size Web application. The two relevant use cases are Sign In and Create New Account. The Sign In use case is a classic log-on use case, which simply states that the actor enters a valid user name and password to change his or her state with the system:[5]

1. A user requests to sign in.
2. The system prompts for a valid user name and password.
3. The user supplies the valid user name and password.
4. The system validates the user name and password and sets the user's state to "signed in."

---

5. Yes, I know that many people consider a Sign In use case insufficiently large to warrant a use case by itself, but that argument has been going on in the industry for some time, and I am not about to get sucked into it myself.

The Create New Account use case scenario also is simple:

1. A user requests a new account with the system.
2. The system prompts for desired user name, password, demographic, payment, and e-mail information.
3. The system notifies the user that the account name and activation code have been e-mailed to the user.
4. The user reads the e-mail, with own e-mail client.
5. The user navigates back to the system and authorizes the system by entering the user name and activation code.
6. The system validates the code, activates the account, and signs in the user.

Figure 8-8 shows the use case model and an «includes» relationship between the Create New Account and Sign In use cases. This relationship was drawn because "logically," the Create New Account use case signs in the user when the account has been activated. The problem is, at no point during the invocation of the Create New Account use case has the user participated in the dialogue described by the Sign In use case. During account activation, the user does not need to enter a password, with the assumption that the activation code to validate the user is unique.

The point is, it may seem as though the Sign In use case is included when creating a new account; however, from the use case model point of view, the flow of events as described in the Sign In use case is never executed when creating a new account. Logically, the sign-in *functionality* is included when creating a new account but not the use case flow of events for Sign In. Figure 8-9 shows an early analysis model for these use cases. The analysis model, discussed further in Chapter 10, is a logical model, and it is here that we see how the Create New Account controller can invoke the functionality

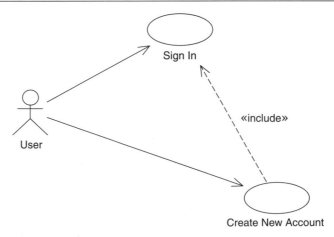

FIGURE 8-8   Use case model with functional decomposition

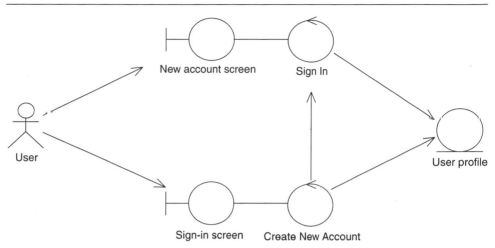

FIGURE 8-9   Analysis model showing logical connection between Create New Account and Sign In

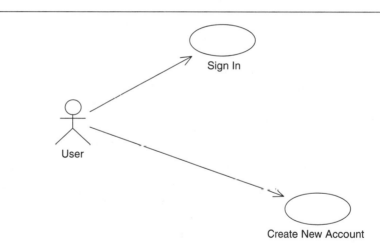

FIGURE 8-10   Use case model restructured to remove the functional decomposition

of the Sign-In controller through an association between the two. Figure 8-10 shows the correct use case model for these two use cases.

Use Case Model Structure

In the first iteration of the requirements-gathering phase, most of the attention is focused on the overall structure of the use case model. Even modest applications have a significant number of use cases: so many, in fact, that they need to be organized a little further.

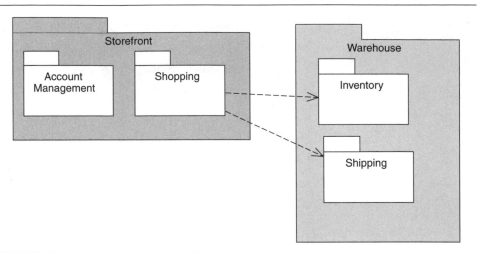

FIGURE 8-11   Use case package diagram

The idea of dividing a problem into smaller, more easily managed ones is not new. A use case model is often divided into packages. Each package owns a set of use cases or even other packages of use cases. A package is a UML mechanism for dividing a model into more manageable pieces. In a diagram, a package is rendered as a tabbed folder. Figure 8-11 shows a set of packages. The two top-level packages—Storefront and Warehouse—each contain additional packages that divide up the use cases inside of them across functional boundaries. In this diagram, some key dependencies are drawn between the packages, indicating that one or more use cases in the Shopping package have relationships with one or more use cases in the Inventory and Shipping packages.

As the use case definition activity progresses and a top-level use case diagram is completed, the project manager can assign separate packages and use cases to different requirements teams to complete. Careful coordination is necessary for those teams with packages and use cases that have relationships with those owned by other teams. In the initial iteration, this is usually accomplished by completing the goal statements of all the use cases involved and leaving the individual teams to fill in the use cases' details later. The goal statement becomes a temporary contract between the teams. Of course, during reviews, every use case owner will look carefully at all the available details of those use cases they depend on.

In the early iterations, requirements teams usually own packages, not individual use cases; at this point, many of the system's use cases have not even been defined yet. Each team treats the package as its own isolated system. The system, of course, has relationships with other systems via package and use case dependencies, but the focus is on the set of goals and use cases owned by the package.

The first pass of the use case model usually is a milestone indicator for the end of an iteration. It doesn't mean that all the use cases are complete; in fact, for moderate- or large-scale applications, they are rarely complete this early in the project life cycle. It does indicate that the next phase of development can continue on some of the architecturally significant use case packages. The determination of these architecturally significant use cases is made by the architecture team and project management.

The architecture team looks for use cases that possess a certain technical risk. Use cases that depend on new technologies or interfaces to external systems are targeted for early development. The architecture team also looks for use cases that exhibit "standard" functionality and that can be used as a future exemplar. Project management looks for use cases that will be easy to complete and for those that demonstrate some of the system's core behavior. It is important for the team to be successful in its first iteration of use case development, and it is also important for real progress to be demonstrated to the stakeholders. Together, the architect and the project manager pick use cases and packages of use cases to be developed first in the next phase of development.

The User Experience

At about the same time that use cases and supplementary requirements are being developed the UX guidelines document (UXG) begins its evolution (Figure 8-12). This document, which is owned by the information architect, outlines the intended look-and-feel for the application, and its purpose is to guide the team developing the user interface.

This document defines the general user interface metaphors. The look-and-feel might be menu driven, wizard driven, or, most likely, some combination of both. Other metaphors may be used, and it is the purpose of the UX guidelines document to explain these and to give guidance to those creating the user interfaces. This document will get technical and should include detailed specifications for fonts, sizes, colors, and artwork requirements. It also describes naming conventions for menus and titles.

If the look-and-feel divides the screen into defined regions, the document defines each of these regions, or compartments, and should define the rules for adding compartments, if needed. In general, this document describes everything that a Web page developer would need to know in order to specify and to create a new screen such that when added to the rest of the system, it appears to be a natural part of that system.

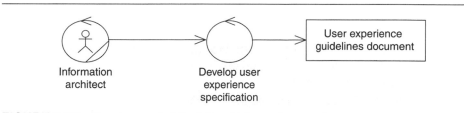

FIGURE 8-12   Development of the UX guidelines document

❏ ❏ ❏ ❏ ❏ ❏ ❏ ❏ ❏

Summary

❏ A requirements specification is a collection of documents and models that attempt to unambiguously describe the software system to be built.

❏ A requirements specification is a contract that binds the stakeholders to accept a system that meets the criteria specified in the requirements documents.

❏ A requirement is a constraint that the system must observe and is typically expressed as a statement that begins with a phrase like "The system shall . . . "

❏ It is important to prioritize every requirement objectively.

❏ Use cases are a powerful technique for capturing and expressing detailed system behavior. A use case is a textual description of the interaction between an actor and the system.

❏ A use case may contain more than one scenario; however, there is always one main scenario.

❏ A use case is written to express what a system should do, without constraining how it should do it.

❏ A use case is written in the language of the domain.

❏ Use cases are a primary input to documentation and testing activities.

❏ A use case realization is a UML collaboration that describes a use case in terms of the elements in a model. Realizations are created for analysis/design models and user experience models.

Discussion

1. Why is it necessary to separate functional and nonfunctional requirements? Are they used in the same ways during each phase or workflow in the process?

2. What are the relative merits of highly structured use case specifications versus free-form descriptions of the use case scenarios?

3. In what ways do Web architectures affect the process of gathering and expressing requirements?

Activities

1. Log on to the Internet and browse through the catalog of your favorite online retail store. Construct its use case specification. Be sure to identify any and all alternative scenarios.

2. Create a sequence diagram for each scenario in the use case.

3. Create an activity diagram that describes the entire use case.

Chapter 9

The User Experience

One of the first activities in the elaboration phase is to analyze the use case model and to identify the objects that will implement the behaviors described in the use cases. This activity is commonly called analysis, or more properly use case analysis. The activities of use case analysis begin with an examination of the use cases and the other requirements of the system. The analyst examines these documents and starts to identify objects that collaborate to deliver the functionality described by the requirements. For most client/server systems, this begins by identifying high-level objects that correspond to the system's entities, controllers, and boundary interfaces. These activities are described in more detail in Chapter 10. This chapter focuses on a new concept in modeling Web systems and introduces the user experience model to the Web application development process. The development of the UX model often happens in parallel with other analysis activities (see Chapter 6, Process).

The term *user experience (UX)* is receiving considerable attention in Web application development circles and is used to describe the team and the activities of those specialists responsible for keeping the user interface consistent with current paradigms and, most important, appropriate for the context in which the system is expected to run. The UX team is responsible for creating the look-and-feel of the application, determining principal navigational routes through the system's Web pages, and managing/organizing the structure of the content in the pages.

This group is responsible for developing the Web application's "emotion," which includes everything from the colors and fonts to the structure and positioning of the content, or information, on the screen to the navigational flows through the individual screens of information to any navigation to or use of external systems by the user. Some of this information is architecturally significant, whereas some is purely cosmetic. Because this book is about modeling Web-centric systems in UML and is not a book on art, we'll focus on the architecturally significant aspects of the user experience and how they connect with the rest of the software system. This isn't to say that the graphic arts, layout, and other artistic elements of the user interface aren't important; they remain a true art form and are less a science.

One specialist on the UX team is the information architect (IA),[1] whose focus extends the traditional user interface/human interaction (HI) skills and branches out to include the entirety of the "user experience." The IA is concerned with the information, content, of the screens, their organization, and their navigation. The IA brings some science to the user interface. In general, the IA is responsible for the overall layouts of the screens, the nature and limits of their content, and the flow of navigation through the application's screens.

The user experience is driven and shaped by two philosophies: the art and the architecture. The IA must balance the technical constraints of Web-centric architectures with the artistic requirements that make the application aesthetically pleasing. The principal artifact the IA is responsible for is the UX guidelines document. This document, developed at about the same time as the initial use cases, defines the overall look-and-feel and provides a foundation of rules and regulations for defining new screens and flows.

The tools of the UX team's trade are visual. Prototyping is perhaps the primary activity. Prototypes can take many forms. Some of the earliest prototypes are simple hand-drawn pictures. As they progress, they may take the form of wire frames, typically created with a drawing tool, such as Visio or Adobe Illustrator. Combined with use case specifications, these prototypes are good for storyboards describing specific scenarios of flow through the system's screens. The prototypes are also good for understanding the structure of compartmentalized screens and can give stakeholders an early and tangible view of the system.

In Web applications, the user interface is almost always a set of Web pages, with each page containing static and dynamic content. Use case scenarios are typically executed across a number of Web pages. The navigational routes through these pages become an architecturally significant element of the system.

Artifacts of the UX Model

Some of the artifacts the UX team is responsible for are

- Screens and content descriptions
- Storyboard scenarios
- Navigational paths through the screens

---

1. The Argus Center for Information Architecture is an excellent starting point for information on information architecture (http://argus-acia.com/index.html). Info.Design is another good resource for IA-related material (http://www.infodn.com/iares-print.shtml).

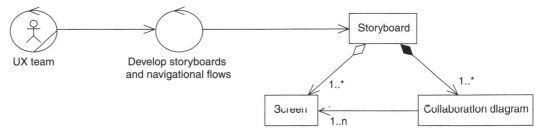

FIGURE 9-1   Artifacts developed by UX team: screens and storyboards

These artifacts are developed by the UX team (Figure 9-1) and are captured in the UX model of the system. The UX model is a separate model because it is a complete view of the system from a particular viewpoint; in this case, of the system through its screens. The architecturally significant properties of the screens and their navigational relationships are the principal elements in the UX model. Use case realizations, or UML collaborations, capture storyboard scenarios of the application in terms of the system's screens.

Capturing this information in a UML model is useful to the UX team; however, its real importance is for the other, "downstream" models of the system. The analysis/ design model, implementation, and test models will all provide mappings to the UX model. The UX model's storyboards are themselves mappings to the use case model.

Screens

A screen is something that is presented to the user. A screen contains the standard user interface infrastructure, such as menus and controls, as well as business-relevant content. Content, a generic term for business information that appears in a Web page, is a combination of static content—field names, titles, text, and images that are constant for each user of the system—and dynamic content—selected products, personal information, current status, and other computed information.

As defined in the UX model, the concept of a screen should not be confused with Web pages, which are the mechanisms that build and produce screens. The concept of a screen is strictly what is presented to the user. How it got there is not an inherent property of a screen. Usually, a screen is built and presented to the user by server-side mechanisms: Active Server Pages, JavaServer Pages, servlets, and so on. These mechanisms often interact with server-side components that produce the dynamic content in the screens. The static content is provided by templates and usually resides on the server's file system. This combination of template and dynamic content is what builds screens and is not the screen itself. It is also important to understand that whether a screen is produced as the result of a JSP's processing or dynamically assembled on the client from an XML document and style sheet, the resulting user interface experienced by the user is still a screen filled with content.

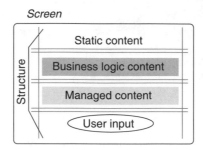

FIGURE 9-2   Screen properties

Overview of Screen Properties

A screen's properties (Figure 9-2) and its behavior with the user define the screen. These include

- Name and description
- Structure
- Static content
- Business logic content
- Managed content
- Input fields and controls that accept user input
- Description of user interactions with the screen

A screen's name and description should indicate its purpose and indicate to the rest of the team why it is important. The structure of a screen, best described by wire-frame prototypes, describes how the screen's information is laid out. Static, business logic, and managed content collectively represent the information that is presented to the user. Static content is all the embedded text and images that remain constant over time and with each user.

Dynamic content—business logic and managed—is described in the next section. The input fields and controls identify what information the users can provide to the system through the interface. Typically, these controls are a collection of the standard HTML-defined controls but in general can represent any customized control or user input element, such as Flash movie, applet, and so on.

Content Management

Dynamic content in a screen is a complex subject. In the last few years, the distinction between Web applications and Web sites has continued to blur. As a result, an entire new branch of software/information technology has emerged—content management— as well as a new class of off-the-shelf software systems: content management systems (CMSs). These systems have evolved to meet a primary business need: how to manage the change of the information presented to the users of Web sites and applications.

In the short history of Web sites and applications, the general mechanism for updating information on a company's public Web site or intranet has been to call the IT department's person responsible for managing the Web server. For small organizations, this worked. But the industry soon understood that the real owner of the information on the Web site was not the IT department but the various departments supplying the content. It wasn't right for the IT department to own and to be responsible for updating this content. Its responsibilities should remain in the technology, not in the business content.

It was also realized that as the sites grew and mingled with Web applications, coordinating changes to content was no longer a trivial matter. Even today, plenty of public Web sites have broken links to pages on the same site and have out-of-sync content. Without the proper infrastructure, the complexity of owning and managing content changes is beyond the ability of nontechnical business groups. Content management systems were developed to give control of Web site and Web application content back to the various business departments that own it and, most important, to provide a single mechanism and process for coordinating the content changes.

Content management systems bring two key ingredients to the solution: a workflow engine and the technological infrastructure to implement the process of coordinated change. Exactly how the numerous vendors in this market supply this varies widely. Some simply provide a toolset and minimal middleware to Web development teams, which then have to design and to implement a lot of customized software. This solution is appropriate for companies with existing Web development teams and that need to provide tight integration with existing proprietary systems. On the other end, near turnkey systems provide all that is needed to manage the content in relatively static Web sites. These types of solutions are appropriate to companies with little Web development expertise and that have relatively noncomplicated and static Web sites.

The picture gets more complicated when managed content mingles with content delivered by a Web application. In this situation, some of the content is managed by business processes and departments and has a typical duty cycle of days, weeks, or months. Example of this type of content are

- Public copyright statements
- Banner ads
- Help and informational messages
- Press releases
- Company and application FAQs
- White papers

The rest of the dynamic content is managed and delivered by the application. It's the application's main job to own the life cycle of this content. Business logic content in screens is often user session dependent. Examples of business logic content are

- Search results
- Shopping cart line items
- User preferences

In general, application content is any business state that is presented to the users of its Web interface. It is the responsibility of the Web application itself and any connected back-office applications to manage this type of content. Which type of dynamic content depends on which system—CMS or application—is responsible for managing its state.

Screens as Artifacts

Because it is so often referenced in use case specifications, the concept of a screen can be thought of as an artifact in the requirements set. However, many screens don't get fully described until analysis, and so it would seem natural for screen definitions to be in the analysis artifact set. In my opinion, exactly which artifact set it belongs to is academic. If the storyboards are used principally as a requirements artifact—the analysis and design teams are constrained to implement it—the screen belongs in the requirements set. As a requirements artifact, screens provide solid, concrete representations of the user interface that the analysis and design teams can support and that the stakeholders can immediately understand and comment on. If it evolves as a direct result of analyzing the use cases, a screen might best be thought of as an analysis artifact. In either case, the resulting UX model is the same. It's a complete view of the system from the viewpoint of the system's Web-based user interface.

Storyboards

When screens are combined and ordered, they can describe use case scenarios, or ministories of the behavior in an application, expressed in terms of sample screens. In any given "story," any screen may be visited many times, each time with a new set of dynamic data. Each scenario is an expression of a specific use of the system. There are no conditional expressions in scenarios, and real-life terms and names are typically used. The whole goal of a storyboard scenario is to express a typical use of the system through the eyes of the user.

Early in the elaboration phase, the screens might be simple hand-drawn diagrams or wire frames. As the process continues, these artifacts evolve into higher-fidelity mockups or HTML files. Eventually, these HTML files, or templates, make their way into the application's builds and are delivered by Web servers and contain static content and even dynamic content. Keeping and maintaining these scenarios throughout the development process is an excellent way for nontechnical stakeholders to keep in touch with the system's progress. On the flip side, it might also give these same stakeholders a false sense of completion, since these storyboards are almost always completed long before the rest of the system is ready.

Navigational Paths

One of the most architecturally important artifacts that the UX team produces is the navigational path map. These diagrams express the structure of an application's screens with their potential navigational pathways: a road map of the application's screens. An important characteristic of this diagram is that is expresses all the legal and expected paths through the system. The influence of the browser's Back button, or caching previously navigated pages, does not belong in this diagram. They are important issues to be considered when designing and architecting the system but do not belong in the navigational map.

When first thought of, the navigation path map seems like a good idea; even without UML, in fact, most Web developers produce some form of site map, which indicates all the application's screens and all the paths through them. In practice, only small or trivial applications produce nice and easy-to-read site maps that contain all possible navigational paths. This is why the navigational paths defined by the information architect are limited to the natural and expected paths, not every possible one. This is especially evident in menu-driven applications, in which the user is free to select any combination of menus and to roam in and out of any number of screens while trying to accomplish a task. On the other hand, wizard-driven applications often limit the ability of the user to roam through unnecessary pages when completing tasks and so are easier to develop path maps for.

UX Modeling with UML

A screen is represented in a UML model with a «screen» stereotyped class. UML's extension mechanism also makes it possible to give this new stereotyped class its own icon (Figure 9-3). Naturally, a screen's name is used as the class name and the screen's description captured as the class description. Like all UML classifiers, «screen» stereotyped classes are organized in packages, usually along functional or domain-relevant boundaries and as such are subject to normal namespace constraints.

Not all screen properties are appropriate to capture in the model, which is, after all, a simplification and an abstraction. Static content, such as label text and images, is not architecturally significant and so is not captured in the model. The structure, or content layout, also is not appropriate for the model and with the static content is completely within the domain of the UX team. Dynamic content, on the other hand, is an important element of the UX model. The UX team must incorporate dynamic content in the final presentation, and the engineering team must provide a mechanism to

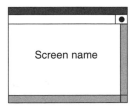

FIGURE 9-3   «Screen» class stereotype icon

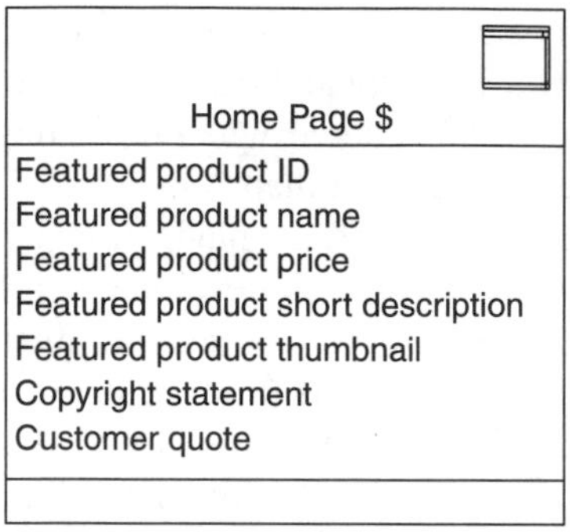

FIGURE 9-4   Simple dynamic screen content

access it. The simplest way to identify dynamic content is by enumerating it as attributes of the stereotyped class (Figure 9-4). Strict data types are not necessary; that is better expressed in the detailed design models. In this model, it is sufficient to identify the dynamic content by name and, perhaps, with a short description if it is not obvious by the name.

If it is expected that a content management system will be used in partnership with the application, it might be convenient to identify the type of dynamic content with the stereotypes «business logic» or «managed» or other stereotype (Figure 9-5). Depending on how managed content is handled in the architecture, the distinction of which type of dynamic content is part of a screen may or may not be important. For the remainder of this chapter, we'll focus on business logic content.

Mapping dynamic content to attributes is fine when only one instance of the content field appears in the screen. But for a shopping cart, for example, with its potential for multiple line items, using attributes is not that easy. This problem is solved, however, in the same way Java or C++ classes model such relationships: with array notation or

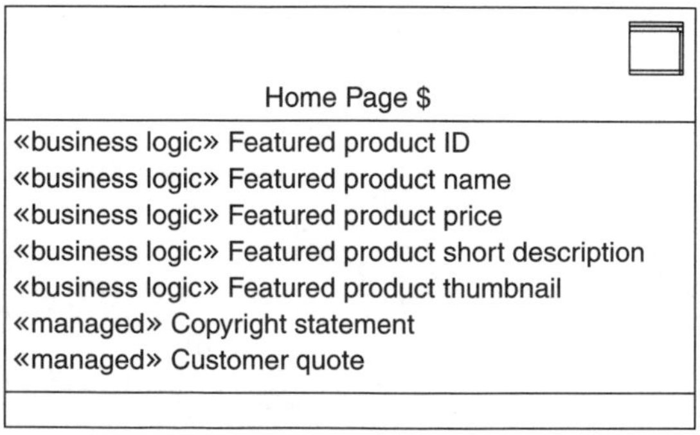

FIGURE 9-5   Screen with stereotyped attributes

a multiplicity on an association. Figure 9-6 shows a shopping cart screen that contains dynamic content modeled with array notation.

Not all screen content needs to be abstracted in a separate class; if there really is only one allowed instance of the content item in the screen, it's preferred to use the simplest mapping. In Figure 9-6, the content item for the total appears as a class attribute since there is only one occurrence of this value ever to be seen in the screen, whereas all the content in the line items is variable and changes with every user.

When the instances of content vary, it is often convenient to bundle them in discrete blocks, modeled as a class. Figure 9-7 shows how this same shopping cart page

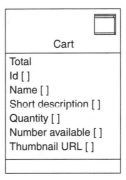

FIGURE 9-6   Variable-instance dynamic content model with array notation

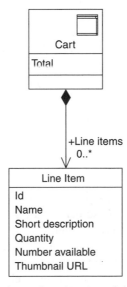

FIGURE 9-7   Variable-instance dynamic content model with contained class

can be modeled with a containment association. This allows the modeler to assign the multiplicity of the items consistently, since it is hardly likely that a shopping cart page would ever display four product names, three quantities, and five prices.

As with most objects, state is only half the picture. Screen behavior is the other important property of a screen captured in the model. The behavior of interest in the UX model is the behavior that the screen user can invoke. The behavior that went into creating the screen, like all behind-the-scene actions in the application, does not belong in the UX model but is best modeled in the analysis and design models. Of course, there are exceptions to every rule, and sometimes it may help the understandability of the model to include a few non-user-invoked behaviors of screens in the model.

Some behind-the-scenes operations in a screen are appropriate to capture and help make the expression of storyboards and, in particular, sequence diagrams of story-boards easier to understand. These operations can help quantify some of the creational things that go on. As a result, they are modeled as static operations—underlined in the diagram. For compartmentalized screens, behind-the-scene operations can be used to indicate which optional compartments are being created and hence available to the user or to indicate the preparation of special messages that are not typically in every instance of the screen.

One common "static" operation of a screen is `navigate to()`, which is called to create and to display a screen. Figure 9-8 shows a participants diagram for the story-board (Figure 9-9) describing the checkout scenario. Storyboards are discussed later in this chapter.

Screen behaviors are captured as operations on the screen. For the most part, these are operations that the user would invoke on the screen to alter its state or the state of the system. From the user's point of view, it doesn't matter which; from the architectural point of view, however, the difference between the two is significant. In Figure 9-10, the shopping cart screen has two operations defined that the user can invoke: update quantity and delete line item. Note that the operations are written in plaintext, and no attempt is made to use design model operations; the design model has yet to be constructed. The convention is to express the operation as a simple imperative sentence, where the implied subject of the sentence is the screen.

Operations whose only result is to navigate to a different page should not be included in the operation list of the screen; they are better modeled as an association to the navigated screen.

Screen Flow

Most Web applications get their work done by navigation from one screen to the next. The paths through the screens that participate in the scenarios are a key architectural element. Expected navigational paths are modeled with associations between screens. Figure 9-11 shows how a user might navigate to a Product details page. Two principal paths could be followed: directly to a featured product or through the Catalog and Category Item screens. Of course, each of these screens contains dynamic content, as

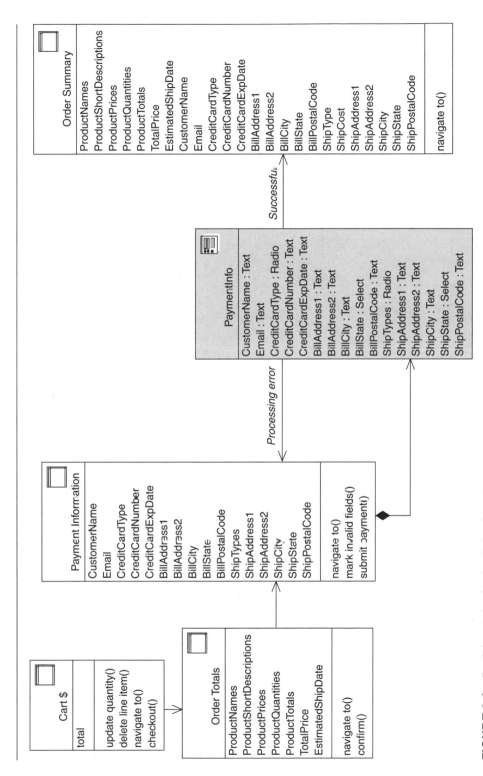

FIGURE 9-8 Participants in checkout storyboard

Cart $

total

update quantity()
delete line item()
navigate to()
checkout()

Order Totals

ProductNames
ProductShortDescriptions
ProductPrices
ProductQuantities
ProductTotals
TotalPrice
EstimatedShipDate

navigate to()
confirm()

Payment Information

CustomerName
Email
CreditCardType
CreditCardNumber
CreditCardExpDate
BillAddress1
BillAddress2
BillCity
BillState
BillPostalCode
ShipTypes
ShipAddress1
ShipAddress2
ShipCity
ShipState
ShipPostalCode

navigate to()
mark invalid fields()
submit payment()

PaymentInfo

CustomerName : Text
Email : Text
CreditCardType : Radio
CreditCardNumber : Text
CreditCardExpDate : Text
BillAddress1 : Text
BillAddress2 : Text
BillCity : Text
BillState : Select
BillPostalCode : Text
ShipTypes : Radio
ShipAddress1 : Text
ShipAddress2 : Text
ShipCity : Text
ShipState : Select
ShipPostalCode : Text

Processing error

Successful

Order Summary

ProductNames
ProductShortDescriptions
ProductPrices
ProductQuantities
ProductTotals
TotalPrice
EstimatedShipDate
CustomerName
Email
CreditCardType
CreditCardNumber
CreditCardExpDate
BillAddress1
BillAddress2
BillCity
BillState
BillPostalCode
ShipType
ShipCost
ShipAddress1
ShipAddress2
ShipCity
ShipState
ShipPostalCode

navigate to()

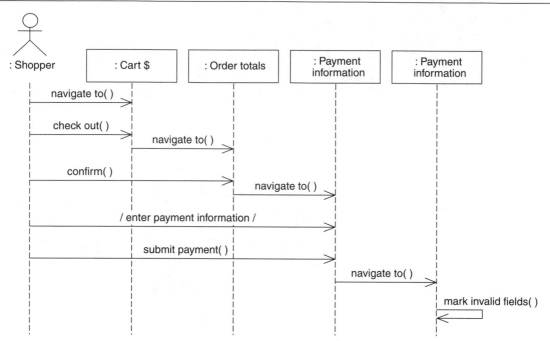

FIGURE 9-9   Checkout storyboard sequence diagram specifying static operations

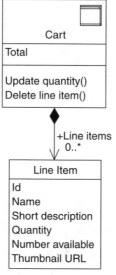

FIGURE 9-10   Shopping cart screen with defined operations

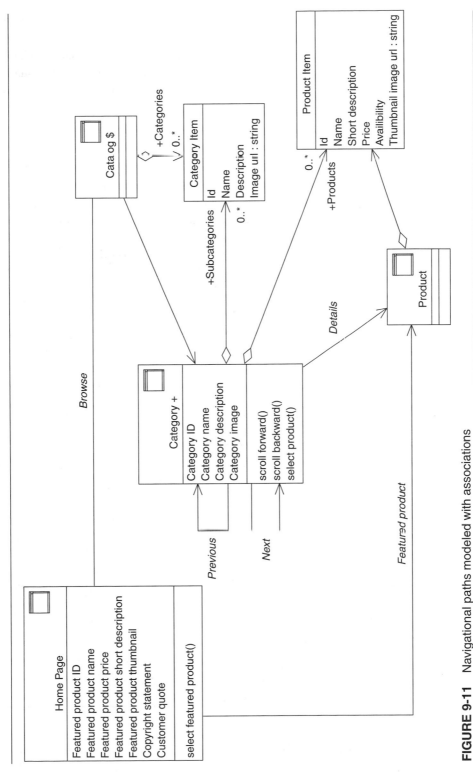

FIGURE 9-11 Navigational paths modeled with associations

shown by the containment relationships to the Category Item and Product Item classes, and the state of any given screen instance depends on the current state of the business. Association names can be used to help explain the user's intent or action that resulted in the navigation to the next screen.

User Input

User input in a Web application is typically managed with the standard HTML input controls. In the UX model, it is important to capture each named input field and, optionally, the type of control used to collect it. Input forms are modeled with a separate «input form» stereotyped class. Fields are captured as attributes and can be optionally typed with the type of input control they are.

An input form can appear as either an association class (Figure 9-12) or a contained class (Figure 9-13). Each has advantages and disadvantages. When modeled as an association class, the form is the relationship between one screen and another. Modeling input forms this way most closely matches what happens in the implementation, since values of the form itself make up part of the browser's request for the next screen. Modeling user input this way enables us to keep associations exclusively between screens. The big disadvantage is when the next screen is indeterminate. Often, the values supplied by the user will determine which screen is navigated to next. In Figure 9-14, the user supplies payment information and one of three screens is navigated to next.[2]

Modeling user input forms as contained classes and drawing associations from the form to the next screen allows us to model those situations in which the user input determines the next navigated screen. In Figure 9-13, a search form is part of the main Catalog screen. This screen contains dynamic content: multiple category items, where

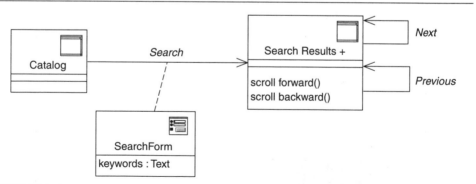

FIGURE 9-12   Input form modeled with an association class

---

2. Dynamic content and input fields attributes are suppressed to make Figure 9-14 easier to understand.

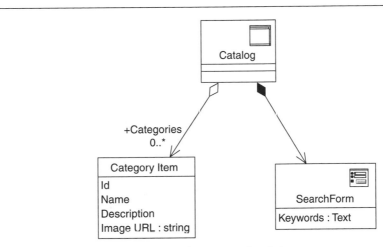

FIGURE 9-13   Input form modeled as a contained clas

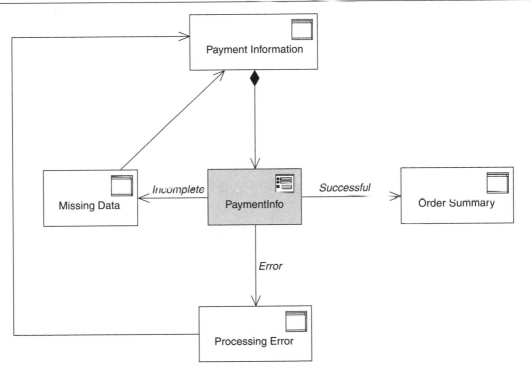

FIGURE 9-14   Navigational flow determined by user input

each category includes an ID, a name, a description, and a string that points to an image URL.

It is tempting to combine input fields and dynamic content, especially when the dynamic content is used to prefill the input form. The problem arises when only a subset of the form's fields are prefilled or when some dynamic content is not editable. Figure 9-15 shows a user profile screen that allows the user to update personal profile information. As a convenience to the user, most of the screen is prefilled with some, but not all, the current information, if available. For security reasons, it is decided not to display password information. The user may update the password, so input fields are available to enter a new password, but this is not prefilled. This screen also has an additional piece of content, a read-only status message. It is important not to confuse the dynamic content with user input. In many situations, these two appear to overlap and to some might seem like a duplication, but when examined in detail, these two concepts are very different and when mapped to the design model, they have a significant impact on the implementation of the screen.

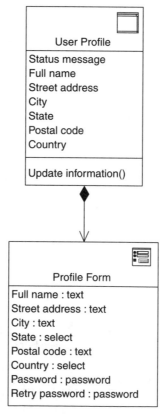

FIGURE 9-15   Input form with prefilled values

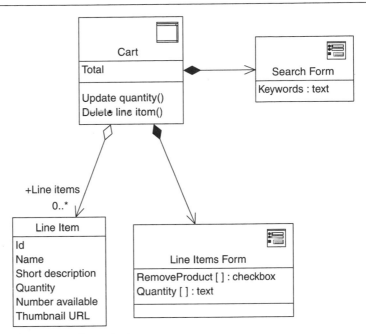

FIGURE 9-16   Multiple forms in the screen

Sometimes, a given screen contains multiple input forms. In these cases, each form is unique and designed with a completely different intent. In these situations, they are modeled with separate contained «input form» classes. Each input form defines the fields that are part of it and has a name that indicates its purpose. Figure 9-16 shows the shopping cart screen with an additional form embedded in it. This extra form allows users to enter search criteria and to execute a new product search without having to go back to the main home screen

Screen Compartments

The idea of divide-and-conquer has been successfully extended to UX design, as well as to modeling, warfare, and pizza. It is becoming common for information architects to define screens—and the look-and-feel as a whole—in terms of screen compartments, or subscreens: visual regions, each with a dedicated purpose that is expected to be combined with other compartments to make a whole screen.

Architecturally, there are several ways to implement this. Using HTML frames is the most obvious; however, `<table>`, `<div>`, `<span>`, or other HTML tags and positioning commands can also provide a sufficient mechanism to assemble screens from discrete components. These details are best left to the UX team. What is important to capture in the UX model is the definition of the compartment and its content.

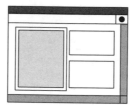

FIGURE 9-17   The «screen compartment» icon

Screen compartments are, for the most part, subscreens that are intended to be combined with other compartments to form a single screen. The main advantage of compartments is reuse. A compartment is most likely contained, or shared, by multiple screens. They are modeled with a «screen compartment» stereotyped class (Figure 9-17) and have attribute and operation definitions exactly like those of «screen» classes. Semantically, the only difference between a screen and a screen compartment is that a screen compartment is always contained by one parent screen that defines the complete user experience. The compartment, on the other hand, is a way to define reusable chunks of the user experience. Figure 9-18 shows an example of a home screen that is made up of three compartments: a menu, a header and a footer. The header contains an input form, and the footer contains a copyright statement as dynamic content. The screen still defines some of its own content.

Storyboard Realizations

A storyboard is a way to tell a story through the use of discrete static pictures. Each picture is one part of the entire story. Storyboards came to prominence as a mechanism for understanding and structuring scenarios following Walt Disney's success in the first animated feature film, *Snow White and the Seven Dwarfs*.[3] The concept, used for comic books since the beginning of the twentieth century, allowed the animation team to visualize and to understand what they were about to create. One nifty feature of storyboards is that the scenario can be quickly restructured by simply moving the boards around.

In a Web application, the screens are the individual boards that, when strung together, tell a story of the application. A UML storyboard is a collaboration and is best captured by collaboration diagrams. Collaboration diagrams are nearly identical to sequence diagrams semantically but represent time as a dimension in the diagram. Object instances can appear geographically anywhere in the diagram. Messages still connect one object to another. The advantage of using collaboration diagrams rather

---

3. David M. Boje, "Stories of the Storytelling Organization: A Postmodern Analysis of Disney as 'Tamara-land,'" *Academy of Management Journal* 38 (4), 1995, 997–1035.

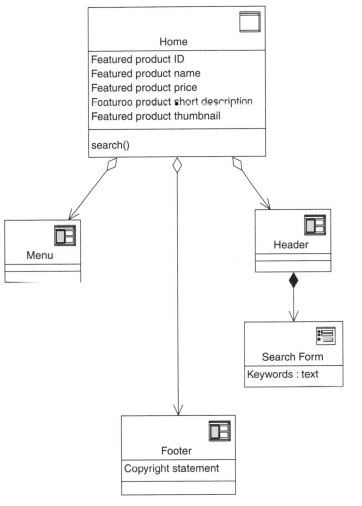

FIGURE 9-18   Defining screens with compartments

than sequence diagrams to express storyboards is that you can reposition the objects and organize them in a way that "looks" more like the traditional storyboards that Walt Disney might have used. Of course, the full expression of structured and static content is not evident in the UML storyboard. What *is* in the UML storyboard is a storyboard road map that is mapped to the use case model.

In Figure 9-19, the storyboard outlines the tale of browsing the online catalog for office supplies. It's preferred to use realistic names for object instances, especially when there are multiple instances of the same class. In this figure, the Category and Product pages are visited frequently, each time exhibiting new dynamic content. When

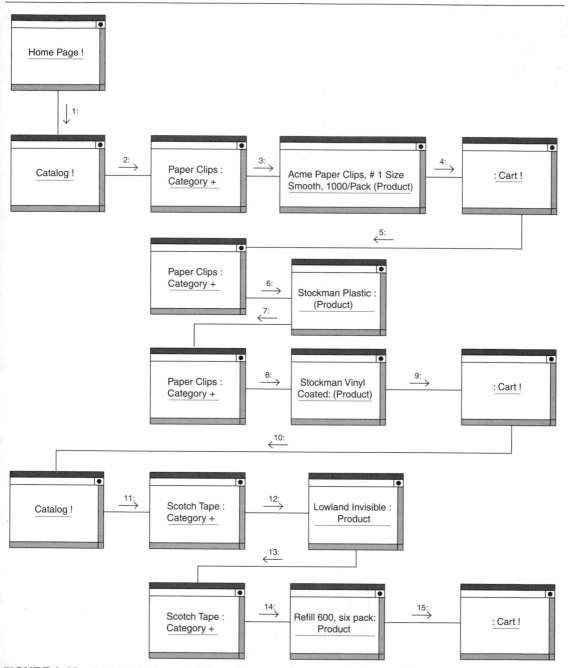

FIGURE 9-19   Storyboard scenario expressed as a UML collaboration diagram

convenient to do so, add notes to key screen instances to indicate special state information that might make the storyboard easier to understand.

The semantically equivalent storyboard expressed as a sequence diagram is shown in Figure 9-20. The main advantage of using sequence diagrams is that it is easier to supply narrative text on the side.

An additional way to express navigational flow, especially when the paths are dynamic and state-dependent is with an activity diagram. Figure 9-21 shows the activities of the shopper and the system for browsing the catalog. It is also a good idea to link screen instances to the activities when appropriate to trace activities to UX screens.

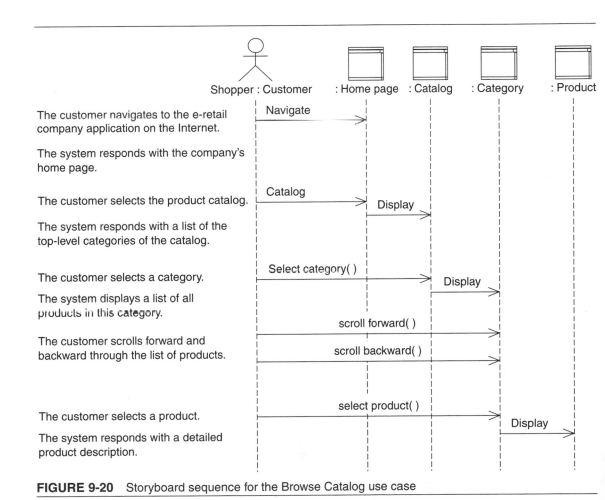

FIGURE 9-20   Storyboard sequence for the Browse Catalog use case

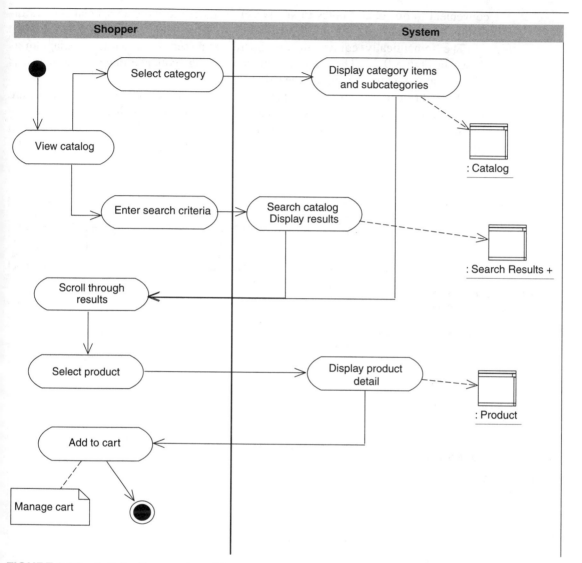

FIGURE 9-21   Activity diagram describing the Browse Catalog use case

It is also a good idea to define a participants diagram for all storyboards. This type of diagram is simply a subset of the main navigation map, usually with many of the screen's details—attributes and operations—shown. Figure 9-22 shows the participants diagram for the Browse Catalog use case.

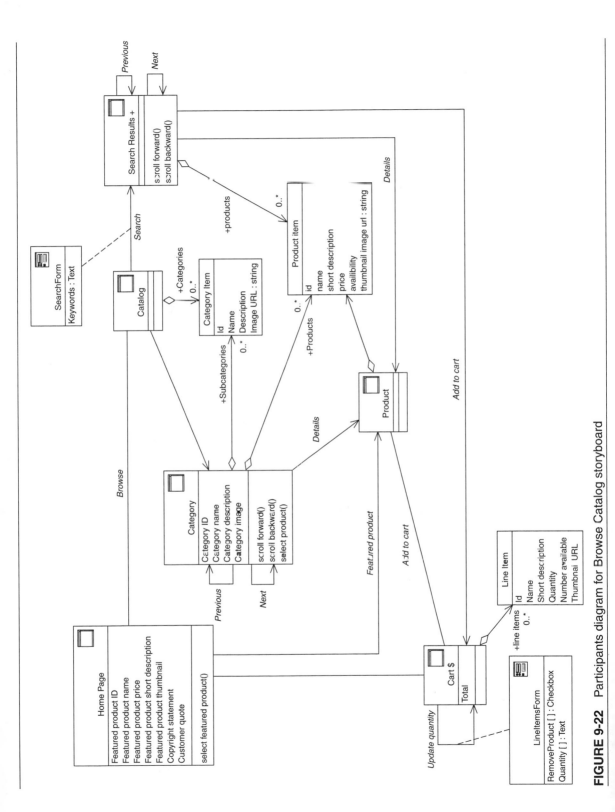

FIGURE 9-22 Participants diagram for Browse Catalog storyboard

Navigational Map

I find it useful to produce a top-level navigational map for a Web application. If the application contains fewer that 50 screens, this can be accomplished, with the right tools, in a single diagram. For larger applications, it's best to divide the map into several diagrams, each focusing on related use cases. In the navigational map, do not show screen details; if appropriate, render the classes with icons. This gives the cleanest top-level view of the "site." Figure 9-23 shows a simple navigational map for an e-retail application.

Adornments are visual notations that can be added to «screen» elements in the model to express special properties of a screen. For example, the screens in Figure 9-23 are color coded and use a special naming convention. A U.S. dollar sign ($) is appended to a screen name to indicate that the screen is navigable from any other page in the system, most likely from a common menu bar in the application user interface. Pages with a plus sign (+) appended to the name are "scrollable." These Web pages contain large lists of information that need to be paged through and have a limited number of items on any one page. Results from a search Web engine are an example of this type of mechanism.

Other notations can be used to express secure pages (SSL) or other types of project-specific information. A formal collection of these screen properties is not an official part of the UML profile; rather they are examples of local customizations that might be useful. The proper way to adorn screens with extra information like this would be to define tag values; however, it has been my experience that these are often hidden deep in the model and are easily overlooked if they are not shown by default in a diagram.

UX Model Stereotype Summary

The user experience model introduces two new class stereotypes: «screen» and «input form». The stereotyped classes can be rendered with the optional class icons in Table 9-1.

In addition to these class stereotypes, two optional attribute stereotypes—«business logic» and «managed»—can be used when a content management system is part of the architecture and it is important to distinguish between what the application manages and what the CMS manages.

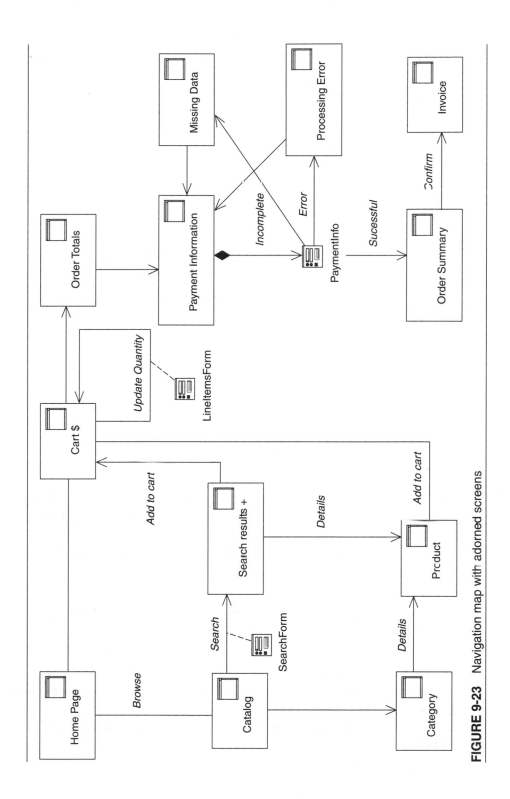

FIGURE 9-23 Navigation map with adorned screens

TABLE 9-1 Optional Class Icons

Stereotype	Icon	Decoration Icon
«screen»		Home Page ▢ Product special Product price Visitor count
«input form»		Payment Card holder : String Card number : String Expiration : String
«screen compartment»		Footer Copyright statement

❏ ❏ ❏ ❏ ❏ ❏ ❏ ❏ ❏

Summary

❏ The user experience (UX) is a superset of the normal user interface concept.

❏ An information architect (IA) is a specialist in the area of structuring and presenting information in Web-based systems.

❏ A screen is the complete display presented to the application's user.

❏ A screen contains structure and content.

❏ Content is the information displayed in a Web page.

❏ Static content refers to text labels and Web page artwork, or images, that do not change as the business state of the system is changed.

❏ Dynamic content changes over the life cycle of the application.

❏ Business logic content is dynamic content managed by the application.

❏ Managed content is dynamic content managed by a commodity content management system (CMS).

❏ The UX model is a complete view of the system from the point of view of the system's screens.

❏ The UX model contains only the architecturally significant aspects of the user experience. Layout, fonts, colors, and other details remain in the UX team's prototypes and documents.

❏ The UX model contains definitions for screens, storyboards, and navigational maps.

❏ The stereotypes «screen», «input form», and «screen compartment» are used to model the user experience.

❏ Storyboards are use case realizations in the UX model and are drawn as sequence diagrams or collaboration diagrams.

Activities

1. Create a UX model for a simple online auction application.

2. Define the storyboard for browsing the auction.

3. Define a storyboard for requesting an account that requires demographic information and payment information and uses a wizardlike approach. Compare the storyboard with the free-form browsing of the auction, and identify any high-level patterns.

4. Adorn the model with indicators for scrolled, secure, and globally accessible screens.

Chapter 10
Analysis

Analysis and design activities help transform the requirements of the system into a design that can be realized in software. Analysis and design can be done separately or combined as part of one set of activities. Use case analysis comprises those activities that take the use cases and functional requirements to produce an analysis model of the system (Figure 10-1). The analysis model is made up of classes and collaborations of classes that exhibit the dynamic behaviors detailed in the use cases and the requirements.

The model represents the structure of the proposed system at a level of abstraction beyond the physical implementation of the system. The classes typically represent

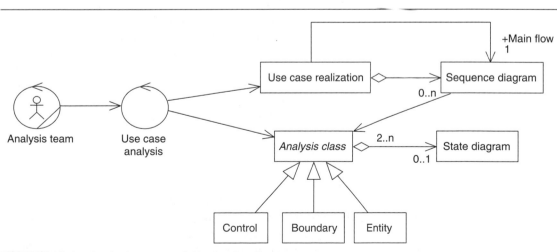

FIGURE 10-1   Analysis team activities and artifacts

objects in the business domain, or problem space: shopping cart, order, line item, product, and so on. Ideally, the level of abstraction is such that these same classes could be applied equally to architectures other than Web applications; however, in practice, some alterations are always necessary. Important processes and objects in the problem space are identified, named, and categorized during analysis.

Analysis focuses on the functional requirements of the system, ignoring for the moment the architectural constraints of the system. The emphasis is on ensuring that all functional requirements, as expressed by the use cases and other documents, are realized somewhere in the system. Ideally, each requirement item and use case is linked to the classes and packages that realize them. This link is important in establishing the traceability between requirements and use cases and the classes that will realize them.

Use case design, on the other hand, is primarily a refinement of the analysis model. Design activities use the nonfunctional requirements of the system and the constraints of the architecture to refine the analysis model into something that can be coded. The designer must take into consideration that nothing happens in zero time, that computers have limited memory, and that things can go awry. The designer is often the pragmatist of the team.

When done as separate activities, two models are produced: an analysis model and a design model. Because the analysis model is a direct-input design, either it can be kept as a separate model and maintained separately, or it can evolve into the design model.

A separately maintained analysis model is useful when the system is being designed for multiple target architectures. If the system is very complex, the additional abstraction layer provided by a discrete analysis model may be useful in understanding the system. It is especially useful for answering some of the "why did we ever do it that way?" questions that always seem to pop up late in a project.

The benefits of a separate analysis model must be weighed against the cost of maintenance. Often, the design activities and the realities of software development change things so they can be realized in software. Design activities almost always drive the evolution of the system's model away from the idealized analysis view. Maintaining the analysis model means evolving it with the design model. Eventually, the finer details of the analysis model will be lost, so even if it is maintained, it is best to keep only the most important domain classes and relationships. Once the analysis model becomes significantly out of sync with the design model, its usefulness is limited.

Iteration

Analysis and design activities usually get started with a nearly complete use case model and set of requirements. In an incremental development process, the entire use case model or set of requirements artifacts do not need to be completed before activities in subsequent phases of the development process can take place. This is not to imply that you can code while you're still gathering requirements and analyzing the problem.

It simply means that, given a fair understanding of the requirements, and completion of certain packages of the use case model, it is possible to begin analysis and design on them. It is important to understand that the more comprehensive the use cases and requirements are, the less likely that the analysis and design will have to be reworked.

Another important aspect of iterative development is the opportunity to address risk early. Risk is that unknown void where the team knows it has to tread but is unsure of the terrain. Risk is usually identified through the experience or lack of experience of the senior members of the team. Often, the unknowns are related to nonfunctional requirements, such as performance, security, and external system interfaces. For organizations venturing into new domains, however, the risk might be in the business processes themselves. Often, it is the architect and the project manager who identify the risky areas; however, any member of the team should be able to point out areas of uncertainty.

For example, the architect of an e-commerce system may recognize a new integration to the billing system and the use of an external merchant account system as an obvious area of risk. Perhaps the architect has never used this particular online merchant account system or has had troubles with it before. In an iterative development process, this area would be one for which the requirements and uses cases would be completed first and for which the analysis and design activities could begin before some other parts of the system had even completed their use case specifications.

When working in an iterative and incremental development process, it is important to have a solid change control process in place. When working in risky areas of the problem space, team members often make important discoveries that affect certain assumptions made in previous phases. When this happens during analysis, the use cases or requirements need to be questioned. For example, the requirements might state that new customers are automatically assigned new IDs that are a composite of their last names and phone numbers. The requirements might also state that every customer must have an ID. Yet elsewhere, the requirements might state that getting a new customer's phone number is optional. In practice, this simple scenario would most likely have been caught during requirements gathering, but if not, the analysis activities certainly would have caught it, and this would be reason to call for clarification of the requirements. "Does the ID have to use the phone number, or could any unique number do?" or "Is it unreasonable to require each customer to provide a phone number?" are questions that should be answered by the requirements team. No member of the development team should be shy about asking questions that could simplify the system.

Analysis Model Structure

One of the first activities of the analysis team is to create the package hierarchy of the analysis model. As for any complex system, one natural way to attack the task of representing the problem and solution space in a comprehensible way is to "divide and conquer." The UML mechanism for this is the package. A package is nothing more than a "chunk" of the model, a piece small enough that one can understand its purpose and significance in the model. Packages contain elements of the model: classes, diagrams, components, interfaces, and so on. Every element in the model is owned by exactly one package. This does not restrain model elements from appearing in the diagrams of other packages or from participating in relationships of elements in other packages. Classes in a package can be made public or private. A public class in a package is visible to and can be used by elements outside the package. In a way, these classes represent the public interface of the package and should be chosen carefully.

Packages themselves can be divided into more packages, and hence it is possible for a model to be structured into a hierarchy of packages. The most important property of a package is that it should be comprehensible. It should be possible for a person to understand and to comprehend a package's purpose, significance, major elements, relations, and relations to elements owned by other packages.

Packages are rendered graphically as a tabbed folder. Packages have names that are unique throughout the model. Each package forms a namespace, meaning that two elements can have the same name as long as they are owned by two different packages. Packages can have relationships. The two types of relations are dependency and generalization. A dependency relationship typically means that one package depends on, or has structural knowledge of, elements in the other. This relationship is drawn with a dashed line and an arrowhead pointing to the package that the other depends on.

A generalization relationship is like generalization in classes; the subpackages represent specializations of a package. For example, a user interface package might have two subpackages: ActiveX-Enabled UI and Java-Enabled UI. Both contain elements that support the goal of providing a user interface, but each subpackage does so with a different architecture.

Throughout the process, the package can also be used to denote ownership. Typically, a package is "owned" by one analyst or designer. The classes with public visibility in the system represent the package's interface to the rest of the system. The designer is free to add classes or to alter the methods of private classes in the package without impacting the rest of the team. Changes in public classes and operations, however, need to be agreed on. A properly maintained model should be able to quickly answer the question, Who uses this class's public interface? Because packages are "owned" by team members, they are convenient units of version control and are checked out of the configuration management system by the analyst or the designer when they are being worked on.

Defining the Top-Level Model

During the use case definition activities, the use case model was divided into packages. During analysis, the same package hierarchy could be used to model the structural view of the system. It has been my experience, however, that the hierarchy of the dynamic view of the system—use cases—may provide a start but usually falls short when defining the structural view of the system—classes. The reason is that it is likely

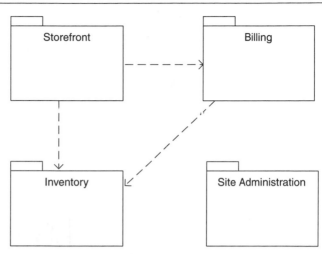

FIGURE 10-2   Top-level use case model diagram

that certain objects participate in many use cases and packages and logically can't be assigned to a single use case package.

At the highest level, the packages are often the same, but at the lower levels of the hierarchy, there are often better ways to divide the packages. For example, the top-level use case view of an e-commerce system might comprise the following packages: Storefront, Billing, Inventory, and Site Administration. The top-level use case diagram is shown in Figure 10-2.

This diagram could also be used for the top-level analysis model. At the lower levels—for example, in the Storefront package—additional packages may separate the principal functions of the system as available to the online user. The subpackages of Storefront (Figure 10-3) in the use case model might include packages for placing orders, tracking orders, and browsing the catalog.

On the other hand, the analysis model might have a very different Storefront package, with the following packages: Catalog, Shopping Cart, Customer Profile, and Product Customizations for engravings, color, and size. In the analysis model, the packages tend to represent things rather than actions. Dividing the analysis model to make it more manageable tends to place like things—objects—together instead of behaviors.

A good way to start the analysis model is to begin with the top-level use case diagram packages. From that point on, it is best to examine the use cases and functional requirements from a fresh viewpoint and to divide the model according to similar things, or classes, of objects.

One of the most important things to remember when creating the initial package hierarchy is this: We use packages to help us manage the size and the complexity of the model itself, not what we are modeling. The intent of any model's structure is not

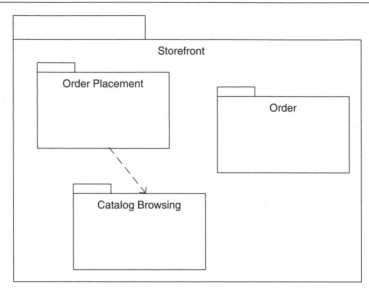

FIGURE 10-3   Storefront use case package

to mirror or abstract the structure of the business but rather to structure the modeling elements that do mirror and represent the business structures. This is a very fine point and is often confused because for most systems, the business's structure happens to provide a convenient and coincidental structure for the model. If this point is not properly understood, problems will arise later in the development life cycle, when elements and packages get refactored and competing teams fight for ownership of common entities.

Ultimately, the use of packages makes the model understandable. When defining packages, you should strive to ensure that they are

- *Comprehensible:* An individual is expected to comprehend the package's semantics, reason for existence, major elements, and responsibilities.
- *Cohesive:* Logically speaking, the classes belong together. At some abstraction, all the classes in the package form a natural group.
- *Loosely coupled:* Generally, each class has more relations with classes in the same package than with classes outside the package.
- *Shallow hierarchy:* Deep hierarchies tend to be difficult to understand because each level carries its own meanings. It is best to limit the number of levels to two or three.

Starting with a good model structure is important. Because the top level and possibly second levels in the hierarchy are important for all members of the analysis and design teams to understand, this activity should be done as a group and with an experienced member of the team leading. Throughout the analysis process, team members will be creating more packages, which will be refactored often, until a relatively stable structure is achieved and serious design activities begin.

Analysis Elements

Whether building Web applications or distributed object systems, the activities of analysis are pretty much the same. Analysis focuses on the functional requirements of the system, so the fact that some or all of the system will be implemented with Web technologies is beside the fact. Unless the functional requirements state the use of a specific technology, references to architectural elements should be avoided.

Analysis begins with the analysis team's examining the use case model, the use case specifications, their scenarios, and the functional requirements of the system that are not included in the use cases. The team identifies objects and classes of objects that can collaborate to perform the required behavior of the system. Because so many books discuss objects, classes, and the principles of object-oriented software, this one will not dwell on the details of these concepts but instead will give an overview of techniques and approaches to use case analysis.

CRC Cards

CRC (Class-Responsibility-Collaboration) card exercises are a simple, low-tech way to identify classes and their responsibilities.[1] A CRC card is an index card that contains the name of a class, its responsibilities, and its collaborations, or relationships with other classes. A CRC card exercise is a team brainstorming exercise; members of the team come up with possible classes and define their responsibilities, not their attributes and operations. Classes are matched up to produce collaborations that achieve the goals mentioned in the use cases and requirements. For some, it is an excellent way to begin the process of class discovery; for others, not. If you are having a difficult time discovering classes or are getting bogged down with too many classes and their details, CRC exercises might be helpful.

Role Playing

Role playing is another team-oriented mechanism useful in identifying and elaborating classes in a system. Team members play the roles of parts of the system. The roles can be users, the system itself, other systems, or even entities in the system. The group walks through scenarios in the use cases and discusses how the work of the system gets done. Each team member takes notes on the responsibilities of the role played. Role playing is often done alongside CRC card exercises.

---

1. R. Wirfs-Brock, B. Wilkerson, and L. Wiener, *Designing Object-Oriented Software* (Englewood Cliffs, NJ: Prentice-Hall, 1990).

Word Form Analysis

Word form analysis is another technique for identifying classes and objects. Use case and requirements texts are scanned for important nouns. These nouns indicate possible classes of objects. Verbs, on the other hand, indicate possible operations and processes. For example, consider the following use case fragment:

> The customer tells the system that he is ready to check out. The system examines the contents of the shopping cart and produces an itemized list of all the items that are ready to be purchased. The customer confirms the order and tells the system to process the order.

> Many important-sounding nouns would make good classes in the system: "customer," "shopping cart," "order," and so on. The verbs "check out" and "process" are also significant actions in the use case and are likely to be identified as operations on some of the objects.

Structural Elements

Ultimately, analysis identifies a preliminary mapping of required behavior onto structural elements, or classes, in the system. These activities begin with an examination of the use cases (Figure 10-4), especially the specification documents. At the analysis level, it is convenient to categorize all discovered objects into one of three stereotyped classes: «boundary», «control», and «entity», as suggested by Jacobson:[2]

Stereotype	Icon
«boundary»	
«control»	
«entity»	

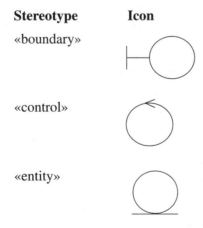

2. Ivar Jacobson, Magnus Christerson, Patrik Jonsson, and Gunnar Overgaard, *Object-Oriented Software Engineering: A Use Case Driven Approach* (Boston, MA: Addison-Wesley, 1992).

FIGURE 10-4 Browse Catalog use case

Boundary classes connect users of the system to the system. In a Web application, these boundary classes are the Web pages—screens—of the system. Most systems, however, also have connections to external systems—content management, merchant account, automated backup, and so on—that require boundary class interfaces. Control classes map to the processes that deliver the functionality of the system. Entity classes represent the persistent things of the system, such as the database. Entities are shared and have a life cycle outside any one use of the system, whereas control instances typically are created, executed, and destroyed with each invocation.

As a start, it is recommended to begin with one boundary and one controller per actor per use case.[3] With the introduction of a formal UX model, there is less emphasis on boundary classes in the analysis model, with the exception of boundaries to non-Web actors of the system. As a result, the emphasis during analysis is on entities and controllers. Figure 10-5 shows a first pass at the analysis model for browsing the catalog.

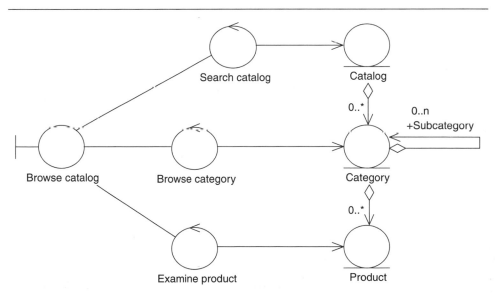

FIGURE 10-5 First-pass analysis model for the Browse Catalog use case

3. This is, of course, an oversimplification but nonetheless provides at least a start when looking at a blank diagram.

In this early diagram, the most important elements are the class names, the types, and the relationships. Each class's details will soon be fleshed out by detailed examination of the use case specifications and related supplementary requirements. The class diagram in Figure 10-6 shows the first-pass diagram elaborated with operations and attributes. As a general rule, controllers don't specify attributes. Initially, their operations are based on the verb phrases in the use case specification and tend to represent functionality that the user might invoke. .Entity properties tend to be mostly

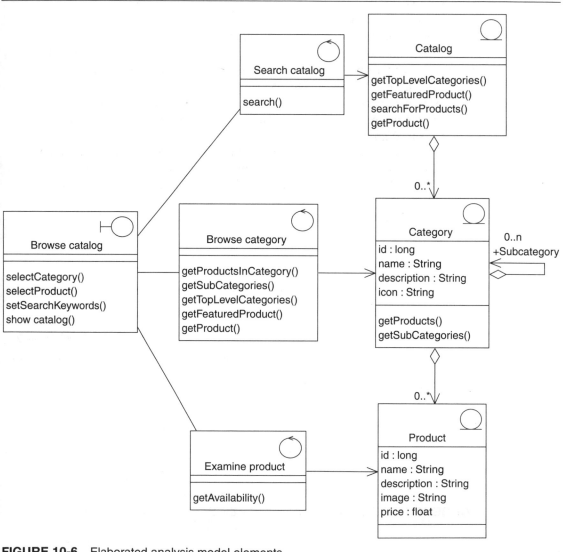

FIGURE 10-6   Elaborated analysis model elements

attributes, although operations that organize an entity's properties can often be found on them

Behavioral Elements

The discovery and elaboration of analysis classes is helped by the construction of behavioral diagrams that form the model's use case realizations. A use case realization is an expression of a use case's flow of events in terms of objects in the system. In UML, this event flow is expressed with collaborations, each with a set of sequence and collaboration diagrams. Figure 10-7 shows the collaboration Browse Catalog Realization with a realization relationship to the use case Browse Catalog.

A UML collaboration can realize a use case, describing the context in which the invocation of the use case executes. The collaboration describes the objects that are created, executed, and destroyed in order to execute the functionality described in the use case.

Development of the collaboration begins with the simple sequence diagram that was created when the use case was created (Figure 10-8). The System object in this diagram is replaced with the set of analysis objects in the analysis model. Messages corresponding to operations on the classes are drawn to correspond to the main narrative text alongside the scenario.

Figure 10-9 shows the same use case scenario as Figure 10-8 does but expressed in terms of the analysis classes in Figure 10-6. I have found the exercise of documenting use case scenarios with rich collaborations an excellent mechanism for discovering early the missing and sometimes forgotten bits of required functionality necessary for the smooth execution of use case scenarios.

Collaboration diagrams are semantically the same as sequence diagrams. Nonetheless, each diagram expresses the information with a different view. Sequence diagrams focus on the time dimension: Everything is rigidly placed along the time axis vertically, from top to bottom. In collaboration diagrams, the focus is on object instances, not time. Objects in a collaboration diagram can be placed anywhere in the

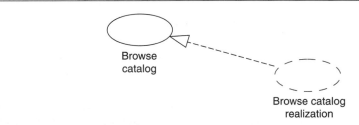

FIGURE 10-7   UML diagram showing a use case realization

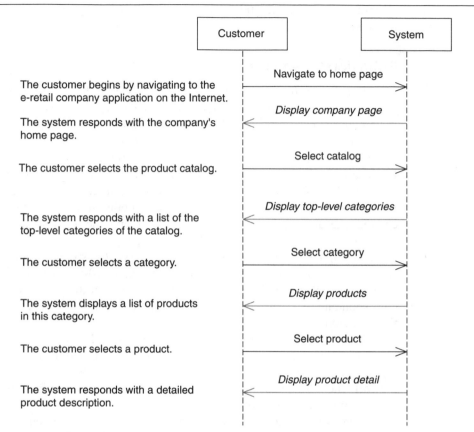

The customer begins by navigating to the e-retail company application on the Internet.

The system responds with the company's home page.

The customer selects the product catalog.

The system responds with a list of the top-level categories of the catalog.

The customer selects a category.

The system displays a list of products in this category.

The customer selects a product.

The system responds with a detailed product description.

FIGURE 10-8   Browse Catalog use case basic flow expressed as a sequence diagram

diagram, and a single line represents all messages from one object to another. Each message is numbered—to preserve the time dimension—and they are lumped together on the one association between each object. Figure 10-10 shows the sequence diagram of Figure 10-9, converted to a collaboration diagram.

Sequence and collaboration diagrams in particular provide a critical link of traceability between the scenarios of the use cases and the structure of the classes. These diagrams can express the flow in a use case scenario in terms of the classes that will eventually implement them.

An additional diagram that is useful for mapping analysis classes into the use case model is the activity diagram. As a general rule, I create one activity diagram per use

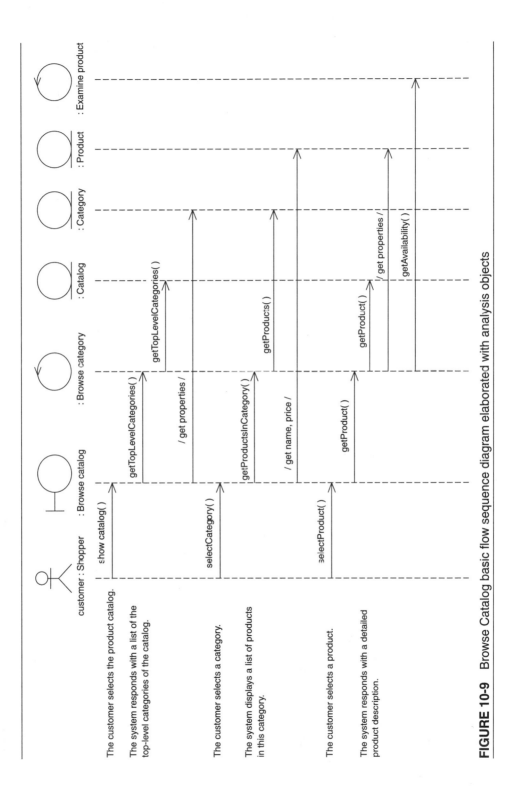

FIGURE 10-9 Browse Catalog basic flow sequence diagram elaborated with analysis objects

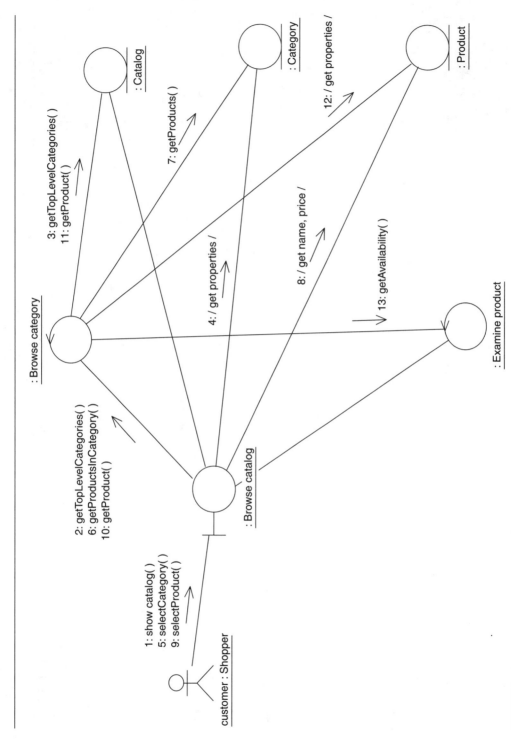

FIGURE 10-10 Semantically equivalent collaboration diagram of Figure 10-9

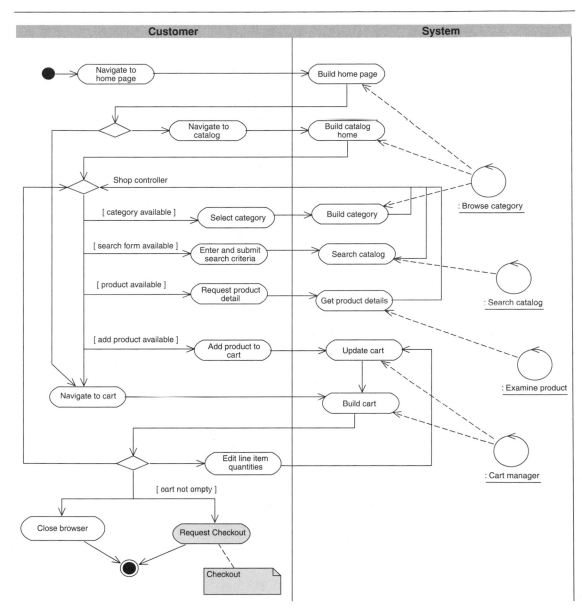

FIGURE 10-11   Use case activity diagram elaborated with analysis objects

case; as a result, I have diagrams ready to elaborate with analysis controller classes. By definition, activities are an execution of behavior. Activities map reasonably well to controller classes, where each controller executes one or more activities (Figure 10-11).

UX Model Mapping

A useful mapping to create is that between the UX and analysis models. The mapping is simple, expressed as dependencies from analysis boundary classes and UX screens. This mapping becomes more valuable as the analysis model evolves into a proper design model. However, creating this mapping early helps to ensure that both the UX and the analysis teams are working together on the solution to the same problem.

Figure 10-12 shows a simple mapping class diagram that can be found in the analysis model. The recommended procedure is to draw the mapping from the analysis/design class to the UX screen, which by default makes the owner of the mapping relationship the analysis model, not the UX model. The analysis model is the preferred owner because it's more likely for analysts and designers to be familiar with objected-oriented analysis and design than are UX team members, and therefore it is more likely for the mappings to be maintained properly.

In all but the most trivial system, analysis is carried out by a team. Each member of the team usually works on a package or set of packages independently and simultaneously. Early on, team members get together frequently to discuss and to negotiate their public interfaces. As the model is refined and the interfaces become more stable, these meetings are not needed as often. However, it is still important to have regular get-togethers and reviews to ensure that everyone is still marching in the same direction.

At some point, a package is considered completed and ready for design. This milestone is usually identified by having all the use cases and scenarios—both main and alternative flows—accounted for. The package should be reviewed before proceeding to design.

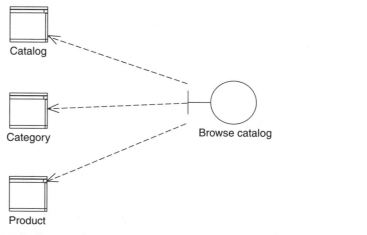

FIGURE 10-12 UX model mapping

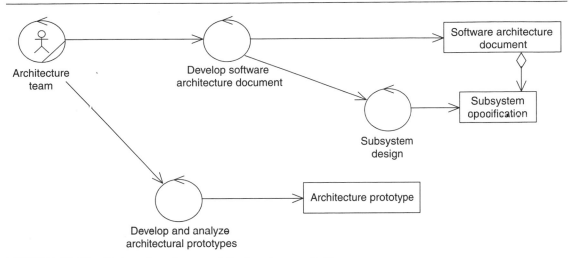

FIGURE 10-13   Elaboration phase architecture team activities

Architecture Elaboration

At the same time that the analysis model is beginning to take shape, the architecture team is busily examining the requirements as well, with an eye toward identifying and refining a target architecture (Figure 10-13). Certainly by this time, it is quite clear that the architecture is going to be Web-centric; what needs further investigation are some of the details. In particular, such issues as security, scalability, maintenance, and browser support need to be understood. The results of this analysis get documented in the software architecture document (SAD). The influences of the software architecture are described in greater detail in Chapter 11.

Summary

❏ The activities of analysis and design help transform the requirements of the system into a design that can be realized in software.

❏ Analysis begins with the analysis team's examining the use case model, the use cases and their scenarios, and the functional requirements of the system that are not included in the use cases.

❏ The analysis model is made up of classes and collaborations of classes that exhibit the dynamic behaviors detailed in the use cases and requirements.

❑ The analysis model and the design model are often the same artifact. As the model evolves, its elements change levels of abstraction from analysis to detailed design.

❑ Analysis-level classes represent objects in the business domain.

❑ Analysis focuses on the functional requirements of the system, ignoring the architectural constraints of the system.

❑ The analysis model defines mappings to the UX model.

Discussion

1. During analysis the software solution begins to take shape. Discuss how this is influenced by the use of the «boundary», «control», and «entity» stereotyped classes.

2. To what extent should the target architecture influence the development of the analysis model?

3. Describe some heuristics that can be applied to the analysis model to help determine when parts of the model are ready for the next stage of the process. Consider how much of the model needs to be complete before it is safe to start applying the rules of architecture to it.

Activities

1. Develop a set of analysis classes that could be used to implement a simple room-scheduling system. Include functionality to ensure that rooms are not double booked.

2. Construct a use case scenario for making a room reservation, and express the scenario in terms of the analysis objects.

Chapter 11

Design

Design is where the abstraction of the business takes its first step into the reality of software. Anything can be expressed in requirements and analysis models; I've even got a technical manual on the inner workings of the starship *Enterprise*'s Transporter System.[1] Yet even these well thought-out requirements and specifications are not likely to be implemented any time soon: what a shame! Design can be a humbling experience.

Design starts with the analysis model, the user experience model, and the software architecture document as the major inputs. The principal activity of design is to refine the analysis model such that it can be implemented with the components that obey the rules of the architecture. Even though this sounds straightforward, it can be the most complex phase of a development project, especially when significant advances in software technology are happening so quickly.

As with analysis, design activities revolve around the class and interaction diagrams. Classes become more defined, with fully qualified properties—name and type—and operations—complete signatures. As this happens, the level of abstraction of the class shifts from analysis to design. Additional classes, mostly helper and implementation classes, are often added during design. In the end, the resulting design model is something that can be mapped directly into code. This is the link between the abstractions of the business and the realities of software.

During analysis, we were content to work with only class diagrams and interaction diagrams. During design, a new view—the component view—and diagram are introduced. This view of the model expresses the physical—if anything in software can be considered physical—modules and executables that will be distributed as the system.

---

1. Rick Sternbach and Michael Okuda, *Star Trek: The Next Generation Technical Manual, Reissue Edition* (New York: Pocket Books, 1991).

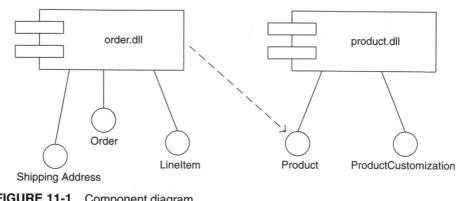

FIGURE 11-1   Component diagram

A component typically maps to executable files or files that are distributed as part of the runtime system, such as Java class files,[2] JAR files, static libraries, and dynamic link libraries (DLLs). A component is something that realizes a set of interfaces. An interface is a bridge between the logical view of the system and the physical view. Simply put, interfaces are public functions that can be called by outside components. An interface defines the name of the function, its parameters, and their data types, whether they are optional, whether they are input or output, and the function's return value type. A component can realize multiple interfaces.

The realization of a component is done with the classes and collaborations expressed in the logical view. Every class in the logical view is implemented by at least one component; abstract classes defining interfaces may be implemented by many components.

Component diagrams visualize components, interfaces, and their relationships. Components are rendered in a diagram with a set of rectangles (see Figure 11-1). Interfaces are rendered with a "lollipop," or a circle on a stick. Dependencies are expressed with dashed lines and arrowheads.

Class icons can be represented in component diagrams to express dependencies and realizations. Components realize classes, and this relationship is shown with a dashed line and an arrowhead. Figure 11-2 shows that the Shopping Cart component realizes the `ShoppingCart` and `ShoppingCartItem` classes.

During analysis, we were content to leave the interface between the actor and the system—as expressed in the interaction diagrams—as user interface. During design, the interface needs to be elaborated into a set of specific interfaces capable of handling the communication between the actors and the system, as well as supporting the flow

---

2. We treat Java class files as components only if they are individually distributed as separate files. If the class files are part of a Java Archive (JAR), it is the JAR file that maps to a component, and it is not necessary to treat the class files like a component.

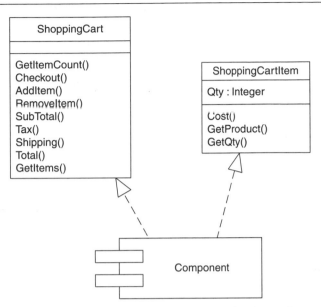

FIGURE 11-2   Shopping Cart component realizes `ShoppingCart` classes

of activity of business processes. In addition to elaborating the classes and collaborations, design activities include

- Partitioning objects into client, server, and other tiers
- Separating and defining user interfaces, or Web pages

When we partition objects into their tiers, we need to know what tiers are available for objects. This depends on the specifics of the architecture. For example, a Web application that uses only the thin Web client architectural pattern is not capable of supporting user-defined objects on the client. Therefore, all objects must exist somewhere in the server's tier; of course, depending on the complexity of the system, they may exist in many different "tiers" behind the Web server.

The basic architectural patterns of Web applications all involve Web pages. Web pages act as generalized user interface containers; Web pages are the glue that connects the browser with the rest of the system. Because one of the greatest uses of modeling is capturing all the elements of a software system and their collaborations so that they answer questions about the system, it is vital to capture Web pages as first-class elements in the model and to represent them alongside the classes and components that make up the rest of the model.

Representing Web pages in the model, however, is not as straightforward as we would like. It should be clear that Web pages are objects, just like any other user interface in a system. The modeling problem occurs when you consider a Web page that has scripts to be executed on the server. This type of Web page interacts with server-side resources before being sent to the client as a completed user interface. To complicate matters, this page can contain a separate set of scripts that execute on the client as well. When processed by the server, the page does one thing; when processed by the client, it does a completely different thing.

As they come out of the box, the building blocks of UML are not sufficient to express the necessary subtleties of scripted Web pages as objects in a class diagram. Yet because they perform important business operations and act as real objects of the system, they need to coexist with the classes and the objects of the system. The only solution is to modify UML.

Doing so may seem like a drastic solution, but the UML creators have built in a way to extend the language in a controllable way. They knew that in order for UML to last, it would have to adapt to the rapid pace of technology change in an orderly manner. They also understood that there will always be unique situations, especially in vertical markets, where tools right out the box might not be appropriate. To accommodate this need for flexibility, the UML creators defined an extension mechanism for UML.

Web Application Extension for UML

The Web Application Extension (WAE) to UML enables us to represent Web pages and other architecturally significant elements in the model alongside the "normal" classes of the model. Only by doing this can we accurately express the entirety of the system in a model and maintain its traceability and integrity.

An extension to UML is expressed in terms of stereotypes, tagged values, and constraints. Combined, these mechanisms enable us to extend the notation of UML, enabling us to create new types of building blocks that we can use in the model.

- *Stereotype,* an extension to the vocabulary of the language, allows us to attach a new semantic meaning to a model element. Stereotypes can be applied to nearly every model element and are usually represented as a string between a pair of guillemets: « ». However, they can also be rendered by a new icon.

- *Tagged value,* an extension to a property of a model element, is the definition of a new property that can be associated with a model element. Most model elements have properties associated with them. Classes, for instance, have names, visibility, persistence, and other attributes associated with them. A tagged value is rendered on a diagram as a string enclosed by brackets.

- *Constraint,* an extension to the semantics of the language, specifies the conditions under which the model can be considered well formed. A constraint is a rule that defines how the model can be put together. Constraints are rendered as strings between a pair of braces: { }.

A UML extension begins with a brief description, then lists and describes all the stereotypes, tagged values, and constraints of the extension. In addition to these elements, an extension contains a set of well-formedness rules. These rules are used to determine whether a mode is semantically consistent with itself. Appendix A contains the full specification for the extension. It also defines association types (Table 11-1).

Logical View

The logical view of a UML model consists mostly of classes, their relationships, and their collaborations. Some stereotyped classes define multiple icons. For practical reasons, the decoration icon is more manageable for modeling tools like Rose. The hand-drawn version simply shows that it is practical for hand drawings on whiteboards, cocktail napkins, and so on. The WAE defines three core class stereotypes and various association stereotypes.

Server Page

Metamodel class	Class.
Description	A server page represents a dynamic Web page that contains content assembled on the server each time it is requested. Typically, a server page contains scripts that are executed by the server that interacts with server-side resources: databases, business logic components, external systems, and so on. The object's operations represent the functions in the script, and its attributes represent the variables that are visible in the page's scope, accessible by all functions in the page.
Icon(s)	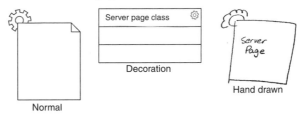

Normal　　　　Decoration　　　　Hand drawn

Constraints	Server pages can have only normal relationships with objects on the server.
Tagged values	None.

Client Page

Metamodel class	Class.
Description	A client page instance is an HTML-formatted Web page with a mix of data, presentation, and even logic. Client pages are rendered by client browsers and may contain scripts that are interpreted by the browser. Client page functions map to functions in tags in the page. Client page attributes map to variables declared in the page's script tags that are accessible by any function in the page, or page scoped. Client pages can have associations with other client or server pages.

Icon(s)

Normal   Hand drawn

Constraints   None.

Tagged values   • `TitleTag`, the title of the page as displayed by the browser.
                    • `BaseTag`, the base URL for dereferencing relative URLs.
                    • `BodyTag`, the set of attributes for the <body> tag, which sets
                      background and default text attributes.

HTML Form

Metamodel class   Class.

Description   A class stereotyped as a «form» is a collection of input fields that
                    are part of a client page. This class maps directly to the HTML
                    <form> tag. Its attributes represent the HTML form's input fields:
                    input boxes, text areas, radio buttons, check boxes, and hidden fields.

                    A «form» has no operations, as they can't be encapsulated in a
                    form. Any operations that interact with the form would be the
                    property of the page that contains the form.

Icon(s)

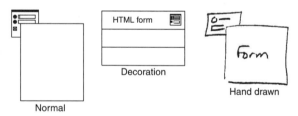

Normal

Constraints   None.

Tagged values   Either GET or POST: the method used to submit data to the action URL.

With these stereotypes in the logical view, we can model the basic architecture of
page-based Web applications. In Figure 11-3, we see the fundamental relationships
among the stereotyped classes. All the classes in this figure are implemented with a
single component: an ASP or a JSP file. The «server page» class models the page's
structure on the server. When the page component is requested, the Web server loads
the file for the page and executes its server-side functions. This process produces an
output stream, usually encoded in HTML,[3] which is then accepted by the client Web

---

3. Server pages can stream output in any format: XML, WML (Wireless Markup Language), image,
   audio, and so on.

TABLE 11-1   Association Stereotypes

Stereotype	Description
«link»	A relationship between a client page and a server-side resource, or Web page. The target may be a client page class or a server page class. A «link» association is an abstraction of the HTML anchor element, when the `href` attribute is defined in it. One important tagged value is defined for this stereotyped association: `parameters`. This value contains parameters passed along with the HTTP request. This tag value is formatted as a string and may contain implementation-specific encodings.
«build»	A directional relationship between a server page and a client page. This relationship identifies the HTML output of a server page's execution.
«submit»	A directional relationship between an «HTML form» and a server page. Similar to a «link» relationship, it references a server-side resource. However, when the resource is requested from the server, all the form's field attributes are submitted, along with the request where they are processed.
«redirect»	A directional relationship between a client page or a server page and another page. This association indicates a command to the client to request another resource.
«forward»	A directional relationship between one server page and another server page or a client page. This association represents the delegation of processing a client's request for a resource to another server-side page.
«object»	A containment relationship drawn from a client page to another logical class, typically one that represents an applet, ActiveX control, or other embeddable component. This association abstracts the HTML `<object>` and `<applet>` elements.
«include»	A directional association from a «server page» to another «server page» or «client page» class. During page assembly at runtime, this association indicates that the included page gets processed, if dynamic, and that its contents or by-products are used by the parent.

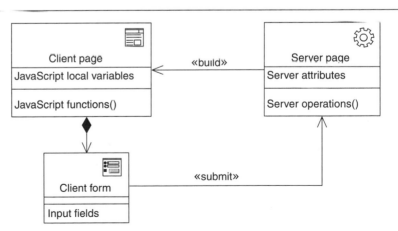

FIGURE 11-3   Basic relationships among WAE stereotyped elements

browser, which renders it. If the HTML includes client-side scripting—JavaScript—and the browser is configured to run scripts, the functions defined in the client page are invoked. Usually, the functions in an HTML page are event handlers and are fired in response to user gestures. However, some events, such as page loading, supply the necessary events to execute them.

One point to note, however, is that it is entirely legal to include scripting statements in line with the HTML, outside a function definition. Although many consider this bad form, it is legal and sometimes useful. These statements are not captured in the model. In fact, discrete statements are normally not captured in a structural class diagram, anyway. If they are architecturally important, the best way to model in-line scripts is with a behavioral diagram associated with class.

When modeling server pages, the goal of the abstraction is to reify the server-side scripts in the page. In most scripted Web page environments, when a page is processed, any code contained in it is immediately executed, and the page is more of a single function call than an object. So when designing server page classes, it needs to be understood that the attributes are simply variables that are accessible anywhere in the scope of the page, just like class member variables. Operations of the page should be thought of as strictly private helper functions; since they are almost all architectural, they are never called directly by objects outside of the page.

The «HTML form» stereotyped class is modeled as a contained class of the client page. The reason is that an HTML form cannot exist outside the context of an HTML page. It is an abstraction for just the HTML <form> tag, not for an entire page. Because it is legal for an HTML-formatted page to contain multiple forms, it is also allowed in the model (see Figure 11-4). Each form could submit its data to a different server page class.

In Figure 11-5, two client page classes are associated with a «link» stereotyped association. This association maps directly to the HTML anchor tag (<a href=...>) when the href attribute is supplied.[4] An important tag value on «link» associations is the parameters tag, which contains the extra information supplied with the hyperlink request, HTTP parameters. This value is formatted in a way that is often implementation specific. For example in Figure 11-6, the link to the server page FeaturedProduct specifies a single parameter: productId. The value of this parameter is <%=id%>, which in ASP and JSP notation, indicates a replaceable data value. When the page is executed, its real value will be substituted; if you were to look at the anchor tag href parameter, you would see a real value in its place.

Link stereotyped associations must originate from a client page and may point to either a server page or a client page class. The convention is that if a client page is dynamic—built by a server page—the «link» association should point toward the

---

4. Anchor tags do not require href attributes and when not specified are used primarily as an internal bookmark, or identifier.

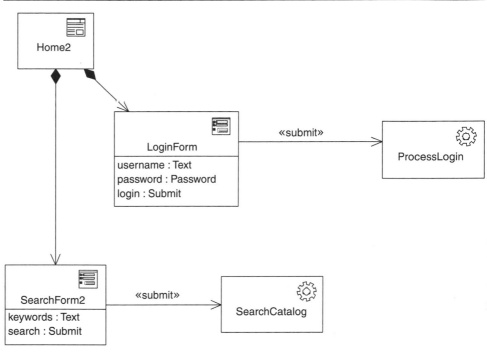

FIGURE 11-4   Multiple forms in client pages

FIGURE 11-5   Simple client page «link» associations

server page, not the client page. If the client page does not have dynamic content—is a static file, not processed by the server—the link should and can only point to the client page class.

When multiple server page components implement a single screen, as would be the case for UX models that define compartments, the «link» association may, optionally, go to a «screen» stereotyped class. This «screen» class can be the UX screen element defined in the UX model, or a fresh proxy for the screen can be created in the design model. Figure 11-7 shows a class diagram with «link» associations pointing to «screen» elements in the model.

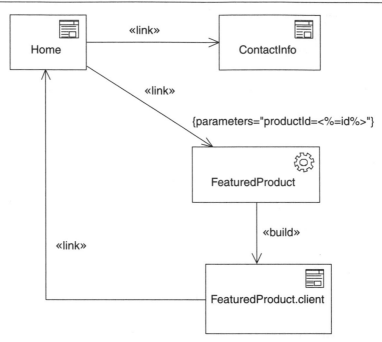

FIGURE 11-6   Stereotyped «link» associations originating from client pages

Component View

The component view of a UML model is concerned with distributable files that make up the runtime system. The WAE defines two component stereotypes. These stereotypes are essentially abstract, since it is expected that they would be replaced with language-dependent stereotyped components (e.g., «JSP», «ASPX», «ASCX», «XML», etc.). These language-specific components would have additional constraints particular to their language and environment. Since they are closely related to round-trip engineering, these stereotypes are best defined by the tool vendors. The two stereotypes «static page» and «dynamic page» are sufficient to capture the level of abstraction necessary to understand the major architecturally significant properties of page components.

Static Page

Metamodel class   Component.

Description   A resource that can be directly requested by a client browser. A static page performs no server-side execute and is delivered directly from the file system to the client intact.

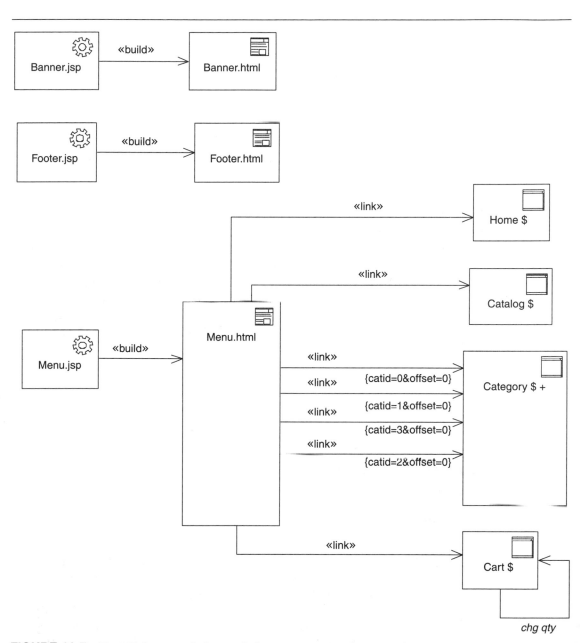

FIGURE 11-7   The «link» associations pointing to «screen» elements when screens
                  are compartmentalized

Icon

Normal

Constraints   Cannot realize logical components that execute on the server, that is, server pages. Static pages can realize only client pages.

Tagged values   None

Dynamic Page

Metamodel class   Component.

Description   A resource that can be requested by a client browser. When requested or delegated to via a «forward» relationship, server-side processing takes place. The results of this processing can change the state of the server and be used to construct some of the HTML that is streamed out to the requesting client. Dynamic pages can accept user input submitted by forms.

Icon

Decoration

Constraints   Must realize a single server page.

Tagged values   None.

Physical Root

Metamodel class   Component package.

Description   An abstraction of a file hierarchy that contains requestable resources. Clients request static or dynamic files directly from this hierarchy. A «physical root» package maps directly to a Web server file system directory. Tag values in this element identify the host name and the application context, which are necessary for resolving a component under this directory into a valid URL.

Icon

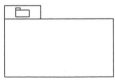

Decoration

Constraints   None.

Tagged values   • Host name, the name of the host of the Web server, such as
                       www.mycompany.com.
                     • Context, the application context. The context appears as a top-
                       level directory, such as www.myco.com/appcontext.

In the component view, the main responsibility of the model is to provide mappings between the physical files of the runtime system and the logical representations
in the logical view. Figure 11-8 shows the Page.jsp component realizing logical-
view classes. A single JSP is responsible for the server-side processing associated
with the «server page» class and its expected HTML output: client page and form.
Although technically, all three classes in this diagram are realized by the Page.jsp
component, it is usually sufficient for the component to realize the server page class,
since the «build» and containment relationships in the logical model are sufficient to
indicate that all three realizations can be found in the component.

In Figure 11-9, the «static page» component realizes a client page. Static components cannot realize server pages or any logical components that are processed on the
server. Static components are delivered to the client without server-side processing.

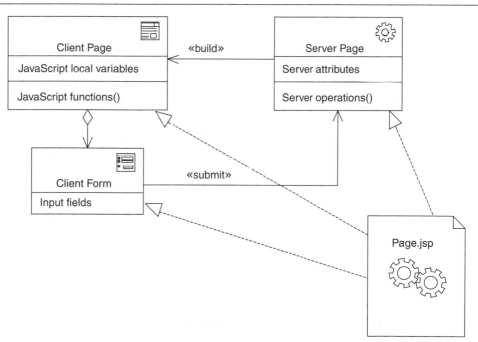

FIGURE 11-8   Logical-view classes realized by dynamic page component

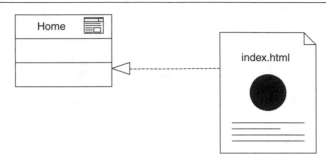

FIGURE 11-9   Client pages realized by static page components

Designing Web Applications

In Web application design, most of the activities are the same as for any client/server system: partitioning the objects into the system's tiers and developing the necessary infrastructure and helper classes to add to the analysis model. In Web-centric systems, Web pages are first-class objects, and the WAE gives us a notation for including them in our design models.

Proper partitioning of the business objects in a Web application is critical and depends on the architecture. Objects may reside exclusively on the server, the client, or both. In a sophisticated Web application, input field validation objects and specialized user interface widgets will likely run on the client, whereas container objects, such as a customer list or a product catalog, will exist only on the server. Some objects, such as an invoice, may have lives in both. For example, a customer invoice object could exist on the server, where its life cycle and persistence are managed. This object could be sent to the client in the form of an XML document. The XML document could be used as the invoice's state and bring to life a client-side invoice object. That object would have some of the interfaces that the one on the server has. Sophisticated behaviors like this are what make modeling so invaluable.

When the job is at hand, partitioning objects is straightforward. Thin Web client applications place all objects behind the server, running either on the Web server or on another tier associated with the server. Thick Web client applications allow some objects to execute on the client. There are, however, strict rules governing the use of objects on the client. Web delivery applications have the most freedom in the placement of objects, being essentially distributed object systems that happen to use a browser.

Thick Web Client Applications

When designing thick Web client Web applications, a large number of the objects discovered during analysis can be easily partitioned in the first pass. For the most part, persistent objects, container objects, shared objects, and complex objects all belong on the server. Objects with associations to server resources, such as databases and legacy systems, also belong in the server tier. Objects that maintain static associations or dependencies with any of these objects must also exist on the server.

It is easier to identify which objects *can* exist on the client than to identify those that can't. An object can exist on the client if it has no associations or dependencies with objects on the server and has associations and dependencies only with other client resources, such as browsers and Java applets. Candidate objects for the partitioning on the client are field validation objects, user interface controls, and navigation assisting controls.

When we first think of objects on the client, there is no stipulation on how they are to be implemented. They are simply objects that are invoked during the browser's processing of the Web page. Client objects can be implemented with JavaScript, JavaBeans, applets, ActiveX (COM), or even plug-ins. During analysis, these objects simply represent a mechanism to implement a requirement or a use case scenario. During design, however, they need to be given an architectural underpinning. They need to be realizable.

Web Delivery Web Applications

The Web delivery architectural pattern is essentially a distributed object system that is based on a Web site. This type of application uses client and server communication protocols other than HTTP. Real objects can execute in the context of the client or the browser and therefore have access to its resources. These objects can also communicate directly with objects on the server or even other browsers.

Partitioning objects for this type of architecture depends mostly on the nature of the individual objects. One of the primary reasons for distributing objects to the client is to take some of the load off the server. It is also natural to place objects in the part of the system where they will be most effective. Putting a date validation object on the server, for example, doesn't seem like the brightest idea a designer might have. A date validation object is most useful on the client, where it can notify the user of an invalid date immediately, avoiding all the communication overhead of a server trip.

As a general rule, I like to place objects where they have the easiest access to the data and the collaborations they require to perform their responsibilities. If an object can exist on the client and if most, if not all, its associations are on client objects, that object is a likely candidate for placement on the client.

Identifying Web Pages

While the objects are being partitioned, Web pages are also being defined. This activity involves the discovery of Web pages and their relationships with one another and with the objects of the system. This step too depends heavily on the architectural pattern of the application. For instance, it is entirely possible for a Web delivery type of application to use only one Web page! This particular page would most certainly be loaded with complex objects and applets, yet for some situations, it could be the best solution.

A perfect example of these types of applications are those that make extensive use of Macromedia's Flash plug-ins. For example, my young son is a fan of Nick Jr.'s online Web site (www.nickjr.com). This site offers plenty of activities for young children, including multimedia storytelling and games. On this site, the vast majority of the functionality is managed by the Flash movie plug-ins, not Web page client- or server-side mechanisms. Most Web applications, however, use many single-purpose Web page components.

Web page design elements—client and server pages—are discovered by first looking at the UX model and understanding the software architecture document, which outlines the rules for when to create new Web page design elements and what responsibilities each has. In the early generations of Web applications, Web pages mapped one to one to what we now refer to as UX model screens. Each page was responsible for preparing its output by interacting with server-side objects. Today, architectures are more complex. Today's development environments and frameworks enable us to build more robust, sophisticated Web applications with the same effort we used to create simple ones just four years ago.

The two predominant Web architecture frameworks available today are J2EE and .NET. Their approaches to managing Web page requests differ slightly. Both still maintain the concept of a Web page and are moving to treat Web pages even more like true objects. The major difference between these approaches is subtle. In the .NET framework, the Web page is cohesive. Although made up of a variety of actual components—.aspx files, Web page, code behind superclass, Web server–inserted client scripts, .resx resource files—the general idea is to have a defined Web page be responsible for handling all client-side events. This means that a Web page should be responsible for handling its own form submissions.

The .NET framework provides a lot of support code that the normal developer never sees to facilitate the creation of event handlers for client-side controls. When an ASPX page is created and ASPX controls are placed in it, the Microsoft Development Environment (MDE) makes it very easy to define validation functions and to specify event handlers that are executed on the server. Achieving this can be a little tricky. The general strategy is to include references to JavaScript files that include a number of functions that are assigned as event handlers to the HTML elements. When an event is fired, the JavaScript functions are called, and these make the determination, based on properties set in the page, whether to submit the page's form back to the server for it to execute the real event handlers on the server. [5]

In Figure 11-10, the ASPX file `myPage.aspx` is modeled with a «server page» stereotyped class. The C# code behind class `myPage.cs` is a superclass to the ASPX class and contains the majority of the event-handling code. The general strategy is for the code behind to contain the majority of the business logic interaction code and event-handling

---

5. The `do auto post back` property determines whether server-side event handlers are invoked immediately when the event is fired in the client.

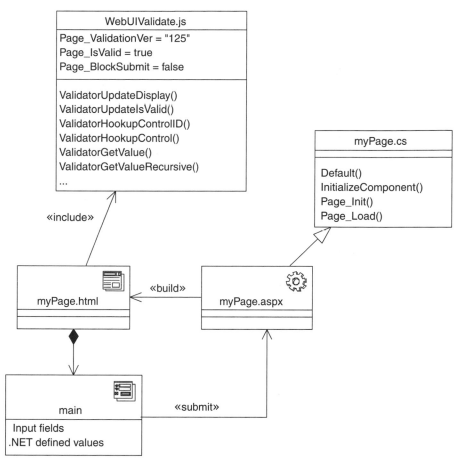

FIGURE 11-10   .NET paradigm for handling user input

code and to leave the ASPX file to focus on building the output page. The ASPX file is written mostly in HTML.

In Figure 11-10, the built client page includes a JavaScript file, WebUIValidate.js, which contains a number of JavaScript functions, some of which are assigned as event handlers to the client page's input fields and other HTML elements. The framework also inserts state information as HTML hidden input fields, used by the framework to synchronize the event handling.

Of course, not all user interaction is made with .NET-assisted event handling; many links point to other Web pages in the system. The general strategy is to have the code for accepting user input in the same page that delivered the page to the user.

In the J2EE world, the term *JavaServer Pages Model 2 Architecture* describes the general philosophy of separating the two mechanisms for accepting and processing input and building output. The general strategy is to use servlets for accepting all user-supplied input. A servlet is a completely Java-written component. There is no mix of HTML with the Java code, as in a JavaServer Page. With the submitted data accepted and processed, the servlet delegates the building of the response page to a JSP. Java-Server pages are more appropriate for building HTML output since the majority of the code in the component is often HTML. Figure 11-11 shows how a form submits its data to a servlet, which accepts the posted data, interacts with the necessary server-side objects—most likely EJB Session beans—to adjust the state of the server, and then forwards the remainder of the processing to a JavaServer Page.

Figure 11-12 shows a portion of a design model for a classic search engine. In this diagram, the Web page with the search form is not built by a server page, so there is the option of using a «static page» component for its implementation. The search form submits its data to the Search «server page», which is responsible for accepting the search request and processing it but not for building the response page. That is the job of the Listing «server page». When the Search page has completed the search, control is forwarded to the Listing page, which uses the built-in session management mechanism for J2EE applications (HttpSession). The SearchResults client page implements a page-scrolling mechanism—Paged Dynamic List, Page-by-Page Iterator—and has two «link» relationships to itself. The parameter tag value for each of these links has a value to indicate which direction to scroll: { parameters="scroll=next" } and { parameters="scroll=prev" }.

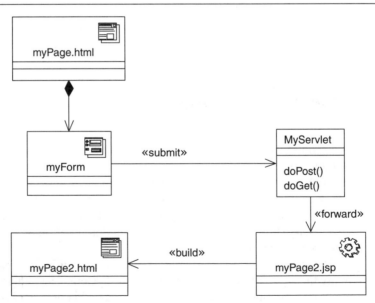

FIGURE 11-11   JavaServer Page Model 2 Architecture

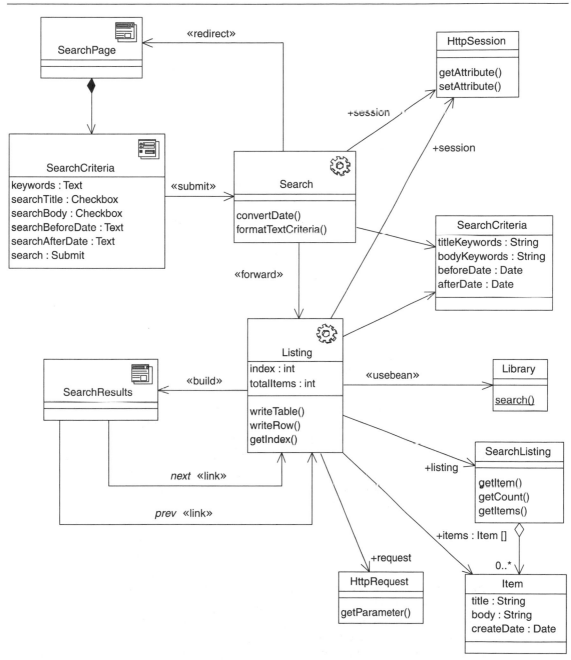

FIGURE 11-12 Design model fragment of catalog search functionality

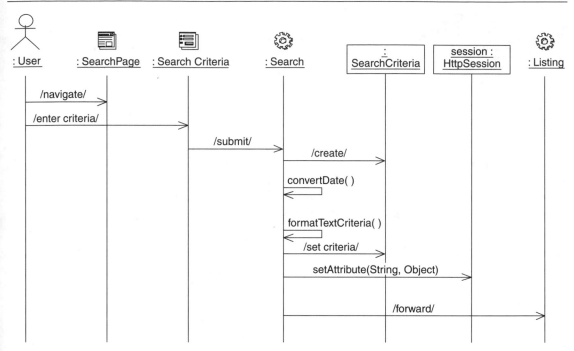

FIGURE 11-13 Search catalog sequence diagram using stereotyped elements

The expression of Web page designs is only half complete in class diagrams. Because they involve stereotyped classes, they can be referenced in interaction diagrams as well. Figure 11-13 shows the sequence diagram of a search collaboration. Even though this is a design model sequence diagram, nonoperation messages are sometimes drawn to simplify it. For example, the Search server page sends the /set criteria/ message to the SearchCriteria object. In reality, this is just an abbreviation of a number of setXXX() calls to the class, which are not necessary to enumerate in this diagram.

The scenario continues in another diagram since sequence diagrams at the design model level tend to get very wide because of all the object instances. It's a good idea to keep the breadth of your sequence diagrams manageable. If you have to scroll back and forth horizontally all the time, it makes it difficult to get any value out of the diagram.

Figure 11-14 shows how the Listing page builds the response HTML. This diagram shows how the list page is responsible for getting the current index: by examining the request parameters for the direction of the scroll and the current index cached in the session. The actual SearchCriteria object is stored in the session and passed to the Library, which returns a collection of items that the Listing page uses to build the table and rows in the response.

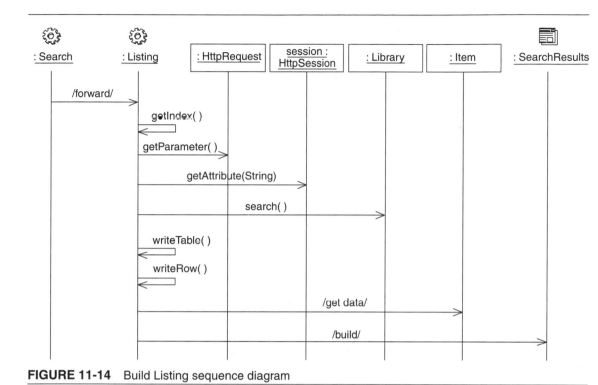

FIGURE 11-14   Build Listing sequence diagram

Figure 11-15 shows how the Web components match up with the classes. In this diagram, the components are all under the physical root at the same level. The physical root is named /store, which also happens to be the context. So a client browser would request the search page by using the URL http://localhost/store/searchform.html. (Of course, a real host name would need to be supplied to get this to work.)

Client-Side Scripting

Designing Web applications that have dynamic client pages requires careful attention to the partitioning of the objects. In thin Web client applications, there was no temptation to draw associations between client objects and server objects because there were essentially no user-definable client objects to begin with! Thick Web client applications, however, can have all sorts of objects and activity on the client.

Figure 11-16 shows a simple class diagram with a «client page» that has two defined JavaScript functions. This diagram also shows an «object» stereotyped association to the PolynomialView applet class. The client page also has an HTML form included with it. In this example, the applet is a second-order polynomial graph viewer. The applet draws a simple graph on the screen (Figure 11-17, based on the values supplied in the HTML form.

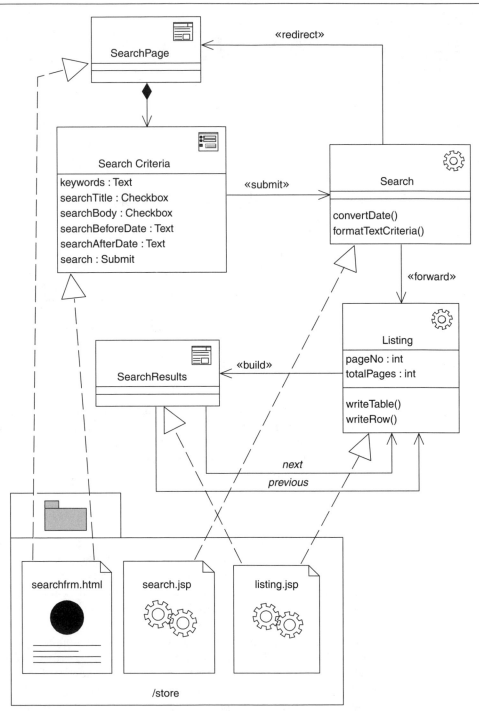

FIGURE 11-15   Component view realizations of logical-view classes

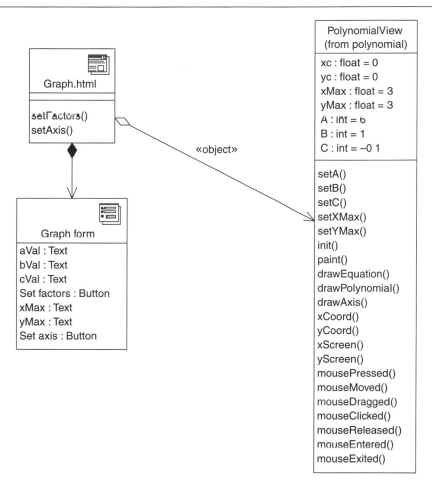

FIGURE 11-16   Modeling applets and other embedded controls

Figure 11-18 shows a sequence diagram that explains how JavaScript functions in the client page call operations on the applet. The message /enter factor/ is short-hand notation indicating that the user enters values in the form. The user clicks a button in the page, and the event handler for the click message, setFactors(), calls several setX() operations on the applet. Each of these set operations forces a repaint() of the display.[6]

---

6. After viewing this sequence diagram, it was clear that I had designed this applet poorly, but I'll leave it up to you to redesign. All the code for this example is available as a download at www.wae-uml.org.

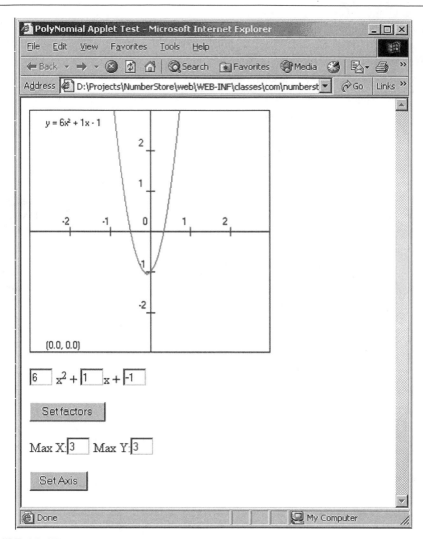

FIGURE 11-17   Applet as part of an HTML page

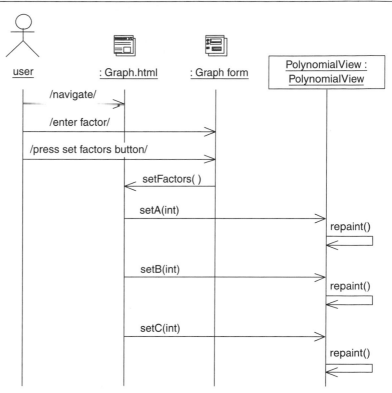

FIGURE 11-18   Sequence diagram showing applet and DOM communication

Mapping to the UX Model

Formalizing the user experience in a UML model is one way to establish this contract in a way that is understandable by the creative teams, which tend to be less formally trained in computer science. UML is visual enough for many nontechnical members to understand yet formal enough to have significant semantic value. The other advantage of a UML-based expression of the user experience is that it is possible for the engineering teams to establish and to maintain mappings directly between use case and design models to the UX model.

The mappings are captured in class diagrams that contain UX screens and design model classes with dependency relationships connecting them. These diagrams show which Web page classes realize which UX model screens. The complexity of the architecture can sometimes be determined by this mapping. Simple architectures have a one-to-one mapping between a Web page class—client or server page—and the screen. In more complex architectures, the mappings are not so obvious. This can happen when Web page classes are responsible for delivering multiple screens, as might be the case for applications that make heavy use of Flash and applet technologies.

Figure 11-19 shows a simple mapping between UX screens and server pages. In these diagrams, it is not necessary to expose all the properties of the elements; the dependency relationships are sufficient.

UX model screen compartments can also be realized by specific Web page elements in the design model. The implementation of the screen is responsible for including the separate and distinct JSPs that map to the compartments that make up the screen. Figure 11-20 shows a screen definition for an application home page, which is, by the way, navigable from any other page in the system, most likely from the link in the shared banner compartment.

As mentioned in Chapter 9, The User Experience, the UX model forms a contract between the information architect and the rest of the UX team and the engineering team. The UX team is responsible for assembling a functional, good-looking application. The engineering team, on the other hand, is more interested in providing access to business state and behavior and in processing new user input.

It has been my experience that traditionally, these two teams don't always play well together. In fact, in several organizations that I've visited, these two teams were located in separate buildings! Very often, one team will make a change that affects the other team, but that realization won't be noticed until far too late in the process. I've noticed a natural tendency for each of these groups of people to claim ownership of the entire Web page or screen, expecting the other team to miraculously keep up and to respond to hastily made changes via ESP or other supernatural means. A formal contract can help set expectations and enable these two teams to work together more effectively.

The way the contract works is that for each defined screen with dynamic content, the engineering team agrees to provide a mechanism for the UX team to easily and simply get the values of the content as defined in the UX model. If possible, the mechanism should use the names used in the screen definition. Whenever the UX team needs to add or to remove content items, the UX model is updated, and engineering is notified to confirm the change. Likewise, if engineering needs to change content items, the model is updated, and the change must be coordinated with the UX team.

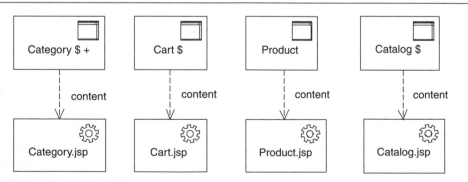

FIGURE 11-19 Design model mapping with UX model

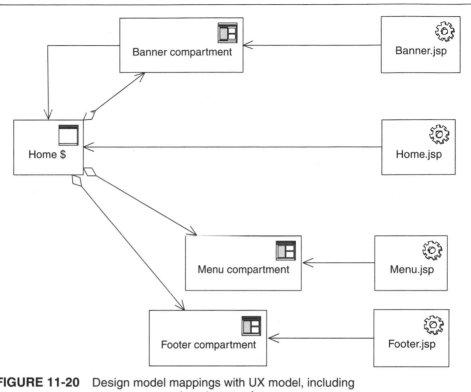

FIGURE 11-20   Design model mappings with UX model, including
«screen compartment» mappings

Periodically, the two teams' work needs to be integrated and tested. Ideally, the mechanism and architecture for providing access to dynamic content in the scripted pages should allow easy integrations. One of the simplest ways to provide access to named content is to define a server-side scripting variable for each dynamic content item. In Figure 11-21, a simple mapping is shown between a screen class and a JavaServer Page, with each dynamic content item having a scripting variable counterpart with a similar page. Some mandatory initialization code at the top of the page could set the values for the specific instance. In good designs, the code is minimal; ideally, making a single call to an external object would make the least impact to any construction code in the page itself. The UX team would then be able to use and to place the content anywhere in the HTML. The goal is to have the UX team own the HTML in the Web page and to let the engineering team own the API to get to the content.

This allows the two teams to work relatively independently. The UX team can develop the HTML and work with server-side scripts, under the assumption that access to certain named content is available. The engineering teams work with very simple and most likely ugly Web page skeletons during coding/debugging cycles. In fact, these simple Web pages are usually easier to test for accurate content because there is

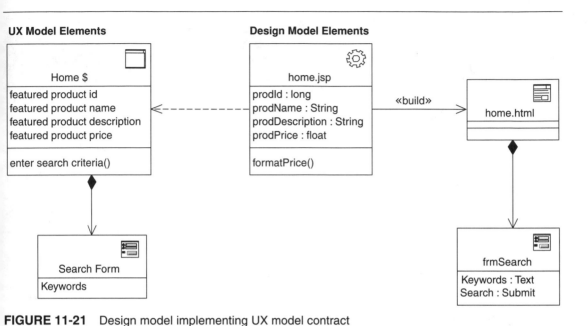

FIGURE 11-21   Design model implementing UX model contract

no attempt to make it look good. Whenever I build a Web application, I always start this way. Even late in the development process, when the completed HTML is available, I still append to each page the original engineering page stubs as a debug mechanism.[7]

In the .NET framework, the development environment makes it easy to bind user interface fields with database fields. If this is the target architecture, mappings to the UX model should include dependencies drawn between UX model screens and logical data model classes.

Another option I like to use in JSP-based applications is custom tags. It is possible to create custom HTML-like tags that can be used in JSP. I like this option because it keeps my JSPs looking like HTML, not a complicated mix of HTML and Java code. The Glossary reference application (Appendix E) uses custom tags and is discussed in the next chapter in more detail.

Integrating with Content Management Systems

A content management system (CMS) is just another software application. Fortunately, you don't have to write it; just install and use it, which for some of the early CMSs was just as difficult as writing one from scratch! Content comes in two basic

---

7. I used a similar technique to provide debug information in the Number Store Reference application (see Appendix B).

flavors: files and discrete items/values. File content includes images, documents, media files, and so on. There isn't much integrated in the design. The deployment of this type of content needs to be managed well, and this can be a difficult problem when the content needs to be distributed to multiple servers at the same time, but that's one of the reasons you buy a good content management solution instead of building your own.

When the content is in the form of discrete items, such as text fragments, there are two ways to incorporate it in Web application pages. CMS APIs can be called to get the content values each time the dynamic Web page is being processed. For content that changes hourly or daily, this is the most appropriate option. When the content changes annually, the overhead of calling potentially expensive CMS API functions for each user page request is not appropriate, and an alternative form of integrating content should be used. Most CMS systems provide a mechanism for Web page generation. If the CMS can generate ASPX or JSP pages with embedded content, these pages can be deployed just like file content whenever their values change.

Guidelines for Web Application Design

Regardless of how we strive to automate it, the art of design will always contain situations in which the designer has to make decisions based on his or her gut feelings. These situations may have compelling arguments for every possible choice. In the end, these decisions separate good designs from bad ones. Here are a few guidelines that may help the designer when making these types of decisions.

- Be wary of using the latest capabilities of browsers. The browser wars continue, and it is difficult to predict which features will eventually become standard. The W3C has finalized a Document Object Model (DOM) standard, which will, ideally, standardize the object interface of the browser. The standard is limited and missing some key elements, most notably an event model, and it is likely that each browser vendor will continue to have slightly different implementations. Just because it can be done doesn't mean that it should be.

- Think about how the page is going to be tested. Don't use visual cues to let the actor know when the page is safe to interact with unless these same cues are accessible by an automated testing tool. I have seen sophisticated client pages use all sorts of dynamic HTML functions to prepare a page for use in response to the load event. It took several seconds to complete, and only a few visual cues let the actor know it was safe to begin using the page. Unfortunately, there was no event that an automated testing tool could easily use to know when it was safe to begin the test script. Until this page was redesigned, all testing had to be done manually.

- Avoid the temptation to use multiple browser windows simultaneously. Although a useful feature for some applications, designing and maintaining two client interfaces requires more than double the effort. Try to keep client-side complexity low because the client is typically the component over which the development team has the least control.

- Keep the focus of server pages on the construction of the user interface. Avoid placing business logic code in the server page. Use external objects to encapsulate this type of logic.

❏ ❏ ❏ ❏ ❏ ❏ ❏ ❏ ❏

Summary

❏ Design is where the abstraction of the business takes its first step into the reality of software.

❏ Design starts with the analysis model, UX model, and software architecture document as its major inputs.

❏ Design activities revolve around the class and interaction diagrams.

❏ The design model can be mapped directly into code.

❏ The component view expresses the physical modules and executables that will be distributed as the system.

❏ Component diagrams visualize components, interfaces, and their relationships.

❏ The Web Application Extension (WAE) for UML is a set of stereotypes, tagged values, and constraints that allows Web applications to be fully modeled with UML.

❏ The core class elements of the WAE are «server page», «client page», and «HTML form».

❏ The core association elements are «link», «build», «forward», «redirect», and «object».

❏ The core component view elements are the «static page» and «dynamic page» components and the «physical root» package.

❏ Properly partitioning the business objects in a Web application is critical and depends on the architecture.

❏ Mappings between the UX and design models are useful and help establish the contract between the UX and engineering teams.

Discussion

1. Why is it necessary to model a single Web page with multiple classes?

2. How else can HTTP parameter information be captured in the model? Is it necessary to capture this in the model?

Activities

1. Redesign the `PolynomialView` applet (Figure 11-18) and its host page to make it more efficient when updating its values.
2. Design a simple auction application. Focus on the ability to place bids on items.

Chapter 12
Advanced Design

You can skip this chapter and nonetheless be an effective Web application designer/ modeler. All the discussions in the previous chapter are sufficient to express the designs of the vast majority of Web applications. This chapter focuses on those additional architecturally significant elements of the design that are a little more difficult to model, as well as on vendor/technology-specific concepts. This chapter discusses how to consistently model the use of HTML framesets in the client tier and how to model inconsistent URL and Web component hierarchies, Web services, and JavaServer Pages custom tags.

HTML Frames

One of the most difficult Web elements to model is the frame. Frames enable the Web designer to divide a browser window into subrectangular areas, each with a different Web page. On the Internet, frames are commonly used to divide the window into a navigational pane and a content pane. The navigational pane, or index window, displays an index of all the site's pages. Each item in the index is a hyperlink to a page. When the user clicks on one of these links, another pane is filled with the page. This type of link, a targeted link, requests Web pages for another pane or even another browser window instead of its own.

A frameset is a special type of Web page that divides its viewing area into multiple panes, each containing its own Web page. A frameset defines a rectangular grid of frames. Each frameset defines the number of rows and columns that divide its display area. Each of these frames is a potential target. A target is a named frame in a frameset that other client pages can request Web pages for. A frame can also be defined without a name, in which case the only way pages are rendered in it is via JavaScript calls to the DOM or by initializing the frame with a specific Web page and then calling normal hyperlinks in the page.

WAE Stereotypes for Modeling Framesets

Name	Frameset.
Metamodel class	Class.
Description	Abstracts an HTML page that contains a frameset element. This page divides the user interface into rectangular frames, or regions, in which each frame is rendered with a separate client page. Frames are optionally identified by a target.
Icon(s)	

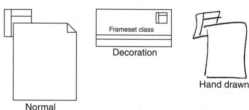

Constraints	Must contain at least one «client page» or «target» stereotyped class.
Tagged values	• Rows—the number of rows of frames to be defined. • Cols—the number of columns of frames to be defined.

WAE Stereotypes for Modeling Targets

Name	Target.
Metamodel class	Class.
Description	A specific named frame in a frameset. It is the "target" of hyperlinks, a targeted link class.
Icon(s)	

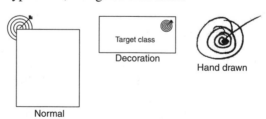

Constraints	None.
Tagged Values	• Row—the row number that this frame is rendered in. • Col—the column number that this frame is rendered in.

WAE Stereotypes for Modeling Targeted Links

Name	Targeted link.
Metamodel class	*n*-ary association.
Description	The target of a standard «link» association; however, instead of rendering the requested Web page in the same container that the request came from, the page is rendered in the referenced target.
Icon	
Constraints	• Must reference exactly one «target» class. • Must have a directional relationship pointing to exactly one Web page class: client, server, or frameset.
Tagged Values	None.

Figure 12-1 shows a conceptual metamodel of the WAE elements for framesets. This diagram shows that a frameset is a client page class, which is itself an abstract Web page, that adds containment associations to other client pages, which are potentially other framesets, and targets. A target is contained by a frameset and, optionally, references a Web page—client or server page—with a directional relationship. When a target references a Web page class, this page is used to initialize the frame when it is first loaded. It is also possible for an HTML form to submit an HTTP request that is targeted for a specific frame.

When a frameset contains a Web page, the Web page is rendered in one of the defined frames of the page but is not named. This means that the Web page cannot be used as a target. When a frameset contains a target, however, other client pages can draw normal «link» stereotyped associations to the target, with the result that the hyperlink request does not replace the current client page, as is the norm, but the response of that link is rendered in the frame that the target represents. This frame is resolved by examining the row and column tag values of the target and the number of rows and columns defined by the frameset that contains the frame.

The most common use of frames on the Internet is to implement a book outline metaphor. An index frame, or table of contents, occupies the left, or top, frame, with the main content displayed in the remaining space. This is similar to the Windows Explorer interface. The user clicks links in the index pane, and the requested pages are loaded in the content pane. Using the Web application extensions for UML, this arrangement of pages is shown in Figure 12-2.

The Book page is a frameset, and its tagged values define the size and the shape of the frames. A frameset aggregates client pages and targets. When the content of a frame remains a single page, as an index page might, there is no need to define a target for this frame, because it will never be used in a targeted link relationship. The content frame, however, is loaded with any number of pages and therefore requires a target to

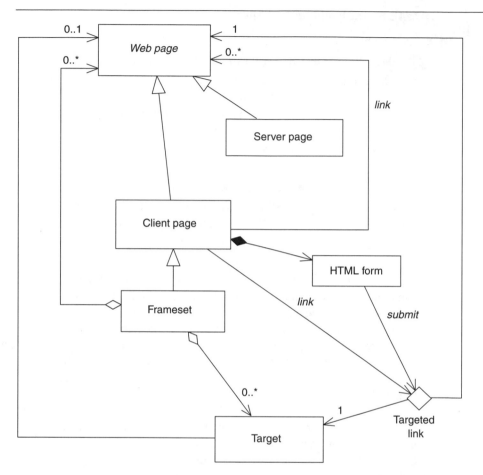

FIGURE 12-1   Conceptual metamodel for UML frameset elements

identify it. The index page defines a number of link relationships, each of which points to a targeted link. The «targeted link» *n*-ary association points to the requested page and the target for rendering.

The fact that a frameset class is a specialization of a client page is important when non-frames-capable browsers are used. In these cases, the browser renders a single normal client page. This alternative "normal" client page is modeled by the frameset class itself. So if a frameset class defines client-side scripts or has «link» associations to other Web pages, these are in effect only when the client browser renders the page as a single "normal" page. This page is often used to allow the user to navigate to a nonframes version of the application. In Figure 12-3, the frameset defines its own «link» to another page, and the main target defines an initial page to load.

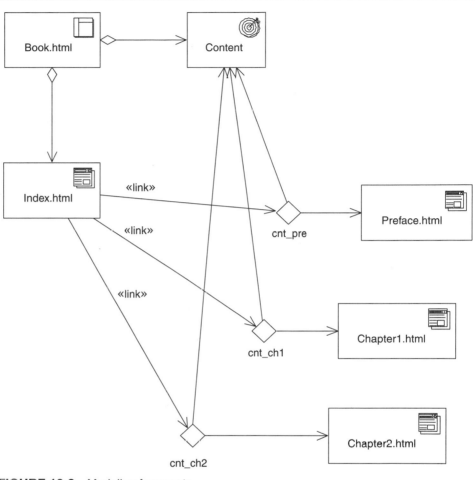

FIGURE 12-2 Modeling framesets

If a target class is not contained by a frameset, that frame is not part of a frameset but rather a separate browser window instance. Targeted links can reference this target as they do other targets.

Another type of frame that some browsers support is the <IFRAME>, an inset frame in a page. Instead of defining a rectangular grid for individual frames, it is possible to specify a single rectangular area that floats with the rest of the page's HTML content.

The idea behind an i-frame is simple. It defines a rectangular region of the current page and renders a separate client page. The size of the i-frame is controlled by the <IFRAME> tag in the containing page. In UML, this is modeled with a simple «iframe»

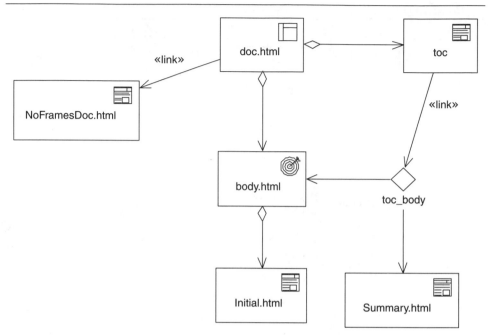

FIGURE 12-3 Frameset «link» associations and targets that define an initial page to load

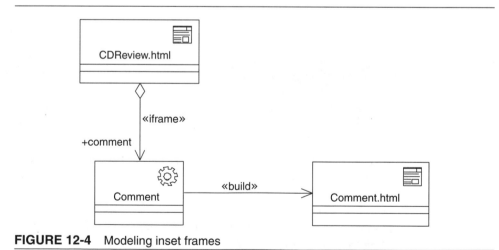

FIGURE 12-4 Modeling inset frames

stereotyped containment relationship. The name of the i-frame can, optionally, be specified with the association role identifier. Figure 12-4 shows a simple example of an «iframe» association. In this diagram, the CDReview client page contains a single i-frame that renders the dynamic page Comment.

Advanced Client-Side Scripting

Today's client-side scripts can get large and complex. Client-side scripting may use both script library classes and script library objects to handle such situations.

Script Libraries

Many scripts are reused over many pages in the system. When this happens, it is best to create and to maintain separate script library files (.js). These files contain a number of JavaScript functions that can be included in one shot by the client, making it easier to maintain common scripts. The following class and component stereotypes are used to model these client-side script files.

Name	Script library.
Metamodel class	Class.
Description	Defines a number of JavaScript functions and variables.
Icon	

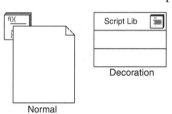

Normal　　　　　　Decoration

Constraints	None.
Tagged values	None.

Name	Script library.
Metamodel class	Component.
Description	Realizes one or more «script library» classes in the logical view.
Icon	

Constraints	None.
Tagged values	None.

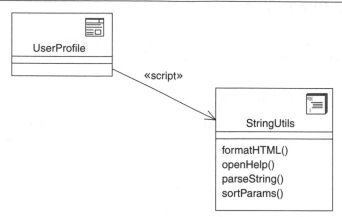

FIGURE 12-5   A script library with a «script» association in a client page

Script libraries are modeled very simply (Figure 12-5). A client page draws a directional «script» stereotyped association to a script library class in the logical view. In the component view, a script library component (.js file) is modeled with a «script library» component and exists in a «physical root» hierarchy.

A script library component realizes a script library class (Figure 12-6).

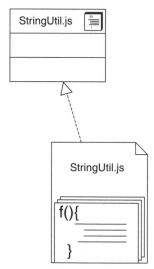

FIGURE 12-6   Script library classes, realized by script library components

Script Objects

JavaScript is not a pure object-oriented language, but it can be used in an object-oriented fashion, even to the point of simulating object classes (see Chapter 3, Dynamic Clients). An excellent example of a well-designed, well-implemented JavaScript object is the Menu object, created by Gary Smith of Netscape Communications.[1] JavaScript objects are modeled with a «client script object» stereotyped class, and their attributes and operations are, of course, modeled by the class's attributes and operations. JavaScript does not define types, so no typing is required in the model. If the types are specified, they should be used only as a reference to the implementer.

Name	Client script object.
Metamodel class	Class.
Description	A JavaScript object that has a prototype defined and usually defines a number of member variables and functions.
Icon	
Constraints	None.
Tagged values	None.

Figure 12-7 shows a class diagram with a «client script object» defined. The object is instantiated twice by the client page: browseMenu and actionMenu. This diagram also shows that the client script object uses several array instances for member variables. The Array class in this diagram comes from the class model of the JavaScript class library.

Virtual and Physical HTTP Resources

One of the many responsibilities of the Web server is to map URL requests to physical resources on the Web server: static files, scripted dynamic files, or compiled components and APIs. The simplest systems have a one-to-one mapping between a URL and a physical file, with the URL context mapping directly to a file system directory and all the directory paths in the location—text between the slashes, /—mirrored in the subdirectories of the file system.

Figure 12-8 shows a URL hierarchy; the root identifies the protocol (http:), the name of the host (localhost), and the application context (appcontext). Each of the requestable resources—HTML, JSP, GIF encoded files—is shown with the fully qualified

---

1. The full source code and copyright statement can be found in Appendix E.

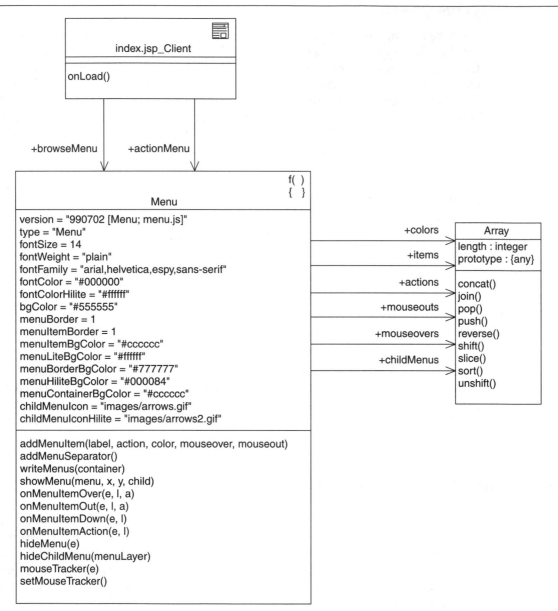

FIGURE 12-7   Class diagram of Menu client script object used by a client page and referencing a Java-Script Array object

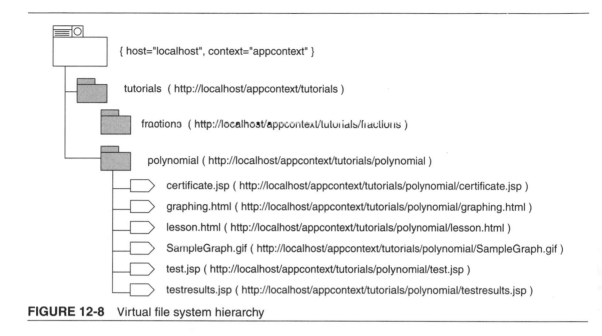

{ host="localhost", context="appcontext" }

tutorials (http://localhost/appcontext/tutorials)

fractions (http://localhost/appcontext/tutorials/fractions)

polynomial (http://localhost/appcontext/tutorials/polynomial)

certificate.jsp (http://localhost/appcontext/tutorials/polynomial/certificate.jsp)

graphing.html (http://localhost/appcontext/tutorials/polynomial/graphing.html)

lesson.html (http://localhost/appcontext/tutorials/polynomial/lesson.html)

SampleGraph.gif (http://localhost/appcontext/tutorials/polynomial/SampleGraph.gif)

test.jsp (http://localhost/appcontext/tutorials/polynomial/test.jsp)

testresults.jsp (http://localhost/appcontext/tutorials/polynomial/testresults.jsp)

FIGURE 12-8   Virtual file system hierarchy

URL. Note that regardless of the type of resource that is identified in the «virtual root» hierarchy, the «HTTPResource» symbol is the same because from the client's point of view, the nature of the file is irrelevant to making the actual request for the resource. For example, it is possible to specify a JSP resource as an image file. Of course, it is expected that the output of the correct MIME type will be set and that the JSP output is encoded as a binary image, not as HTML, which is the norm.[2]

In a simple mapping, each resource maps to a file, and the «physical root» maps to a directory in the Web server's file system. Figure 12-9 shows a Web server's file system in which the directory web maps to the «physical root» http://localhost/appcontext/.

Simple mappings are not always the case. For example, whenever servlets are used, their class files—or the JAR file they are contained in—are not located in this physical file system hierarchy with the rest of the system's JavaServer Pages. In J2EE applications, the mapping is located in the web.xml file, and each servlet can be mapped to an arbitrary URL.

These two hierarchies—the virtual URL hierarchy and the physical component file hierarchy—are not required to overlap, and can each be completely arbitrary. The mapping between the virtual resources (URL) and the physical file is architecturally significant and as such should be modeled. The only way to do this is to define two types of hierarchies: the «physical root» hierarchy, defined in the previous chapter,

---

2. This is a common mechanism for managing and delivering image files from a database instead of from the file system.

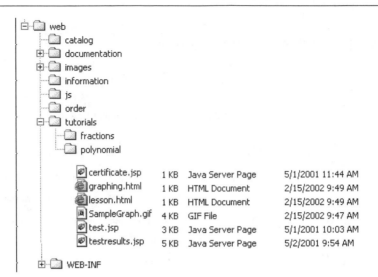

FIGURE 12-9   File system containing static and dynamic pages, as well as static resource files

and a new component hierarchy, the «virtual root», a hierarchy of component proxies. Each of these proxies is modeled in with an «HTTP Resource» stereotyped component. The two new WAE stereotypes are summarized as follows.

Name	Virtual root.
Metamodel class	Package.
Description	Contains Web components in a file system hierarchy that is visible to clients. The directory structure for requesting resources matches the physical directory structure.
Icon(s)	
Constraints	None.
Tagged values	• Host (optional), a host name that can be used to resolve contained elements into fully qualified URLs.
	• Port (optional), a port number used in URL resolution.

Name	HTTP resource.
Metamodel class	Component.
Description	A proxy to a real component(s) that maps to a requestable URL in the system. Each HTTP resource element represents a valid URL that can be requested and fulfilled by the system.
Icon	
Constraints	None.
Tagged values	Filter (optional), a regular expression that is used to match a set of URLs, such as *.scr.

When modeling systems that override the default URL resolution mechanisms, J2EE systems use servlets, or systems that use compiled binary components to filter or respond to specific URLs.

Figure 12-10 is Figure 11-12, redrawn to define the element Search as a servlet.[3] The component view for the Web elements—client pages, server pages, and servlets—is shown in Figure 12-11, in which the HTTP resource component Search is drawn with a dependency to a normal component, the Search servlet component. Both the virtual and the physical root packages have tag values that set their host and Web context values to be the same. This is often the case when there is a mix of servlets and JavaServer Pages.

Figure 12-12 shows the realizations of the logical classes in Figure 12-10 by the components in Figure 12-11. In Figure 12-12, the HTTP resource component does not realize a logical-view class directly but rather is a proxy to another component, the Search servlet component.

An HTTP resource component should identify what it is a proxy for, via a dependency relationship to another component or by realizing a logical-view element that eventually does get realized by a "hard" component of the system. In systems that rely heavily on reusable screen components, often no single JSP realizes any given screen and so any given URL. In these situations, it is convenient to model HTTP resource components as realizing UX model screens—or an equivalent logical-model construct—that in turn identifies the logical-view Web elements that make up the screens compartments. Each of these constructs is realized by a normal Web component in the system.

---

3. This icon and the stereotype «Http_Servlet» is the Rational Rose default for reverse-engineering servlets.

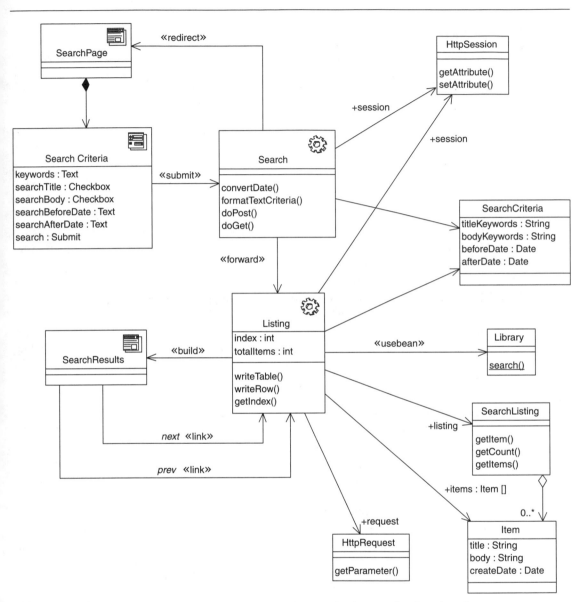

FIGURE 12-10   Class diagram with Web elements for standard searching functionality

Figure 12-13 shows how an HTTP resource can realize a UX model screen, which in turn is mapped to several design model logical elements: server pages and client pages. These page elements are eventually realized by Web page components, or servlets. In this diagram, the package owning the Web components is not stereotyped «physical root». The reason is that these individual Web components are not

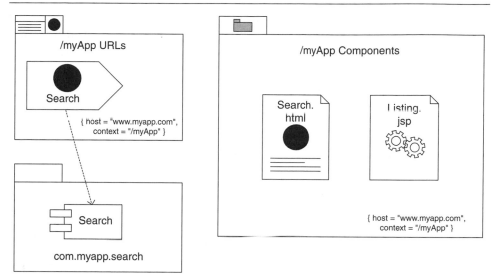

FIGURE 12-11   Component diagram showing components and URLs that realize
the classes in Figure 12-10

intended to be individually requested by the client but rather exist solely to contribute
to the realization of the screen.

In some situations, it might be useful to model resources other than Web pages.
The following components can be included in Web component packages.

Script library component: «script library», a file that
contains a number of JavaScript functions that are
requested directly by the client browser.

Image component: «image», an image file that can
be requested by the client.

Style sheet component: «stylesheet», a file that contains a number of style sheet definitions and that is
independently requested by the browser.

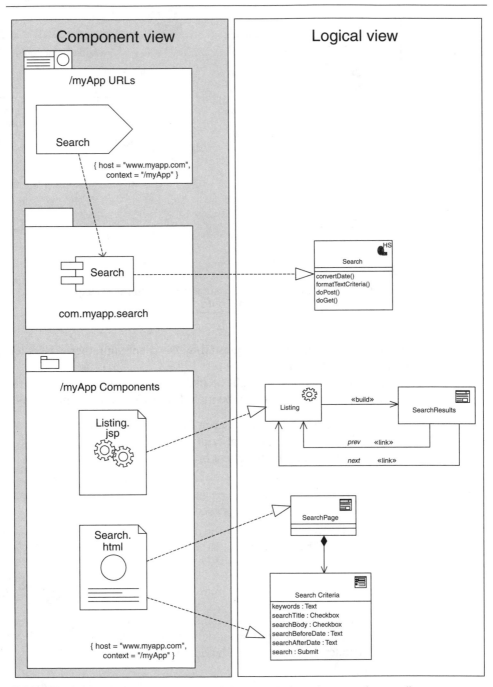

FIGURE 12-12 Web components and the logical-view elements they realize

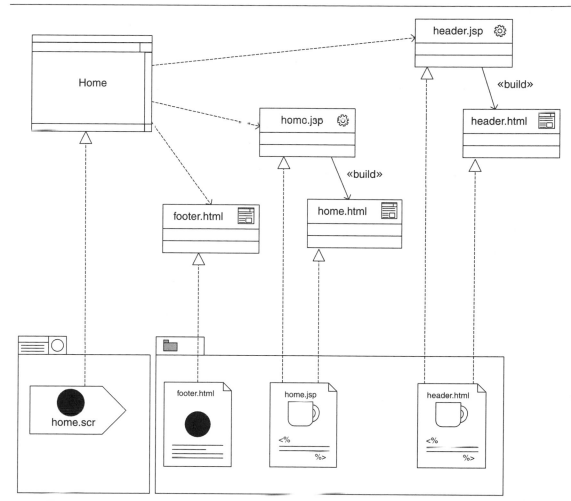

FIGURE 12-13   UX model screens can be realized by HTTP resource components

JavaServer Page Custom Tags

It took me a little time before I finally grasped the concepts and usefulness of JSP custom tags. My first real introduction to them was in the original Java Pet Store exemplar application.[4] I have to admit that the first version of this application had

---

4. The Java™ Pet Store Demo is a sample application from the Java™ 2 Platform, Enterprise Edition (J2EE™) BluePrints Program at Java Software, Sun Microsystems.

wonderful high-level documentation,[5] but when it came to matching up the code that I saw with the documentation in the book, I found myself scratching my head. Subsequent versions of this application are not only easier to read and understand but also make a lot more sense now that I understand the concepts of virtual roots and custom tags.

My problem in those early weeks of trying to understand the Pet Store was that the JSPs had what looked like relatively simple code. But behind the scenes, custom tags were doing a lot of work. The result was a relatively clean-looking JSP backed by some compiled and smartly written Java code inserted into the page via these custom tags. If you are not familiar with JSP custom tags and are doing J2EE Web development, I highly recommend getting a good book,[6] pulling down the official JSP specification,[7] or finding an online tutorial on the topic. Doing so may well change the way you design your J2EE Web applications.

The WAE defines the following stereotypes for modeling JSP tags.

Name	Tag library.
Metamodel class	Package.
Description	An abstraction of a JSP tag library as defined by the JSP tag library descriptor file. A library contains a number of «tag» definitions, each of which is made available to JSP server-side code.
Icon(s)	
Constraints	None.
Tagged values	None.
Name	JSP tag.
Metamodel class	Class.
Description	An abstraction of a custom HTML-like tag that can be used in JSP code. Each tag defines a number of attributes that can be assigned in the opening tag and a number of scripting variables that can be used in the body of the tag. These values are

5. Nick Kassem and Enterprise Team, *Designing Enterprise Applications with the Java™ 2 Platform, Enterprise Edition* (Reading, MA: Addison-Wesley, 2000).

6. Gal Shachor, Adam Chace, and Magnus Rydin, *JSP Tag Libraries* (Greenwich, CT: Manning Publications, 2001).

7. JSR-000053 Java™ Servlet 2.3 and JavaServer Pages™ 1.2 Specifications, available at http://jcp.org/aboutJava/communityprocess/first/jsr053/index.html.

defined as stereotyped attributes of the class: «attribute» and «scripting variable», respectively.

Icon	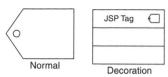 Normal Decoration
Constraints	• A «JSP tag» class must have exactly one «tag» dependency on a Java class that implements the javax.servlet.jsp.tagext. BodyTagSupport interface.
	• A «JSP tag» class may have an additional «tei» stereotyped dependency on a Java class that implements the javax.servlet.jsp.tagext.TagExtraInfo interface.
Tagged values	None.

Name	Tag.
Metamodel Class	Dependency.
Description	A «tag» dependency is drawn from a «JSP tag» class to its implementing Java class. The Java class must implement the javax.servlet.jsp.tagext.BodyTagSupport interface.
Constraints	None
Tagged values	None

Name	Tei.
Metamodel class	Dependency.
Description	A «tei» dependency is drawn from a «JSP tag» class to a class that defines the scripting variables it uses. The Java class must implement the javax.servlet.jsp.tagext.TagExtraInfo interface.
Constraints	None.
Tagged values	None.

Modeling JSP tag libraries begins with an abstraction for the library itself. From the view of the JSP page—or server page in the logical view—tags are referenced as a library of tags. Figure 12-14 shows the Entry Tags library referenced by two server

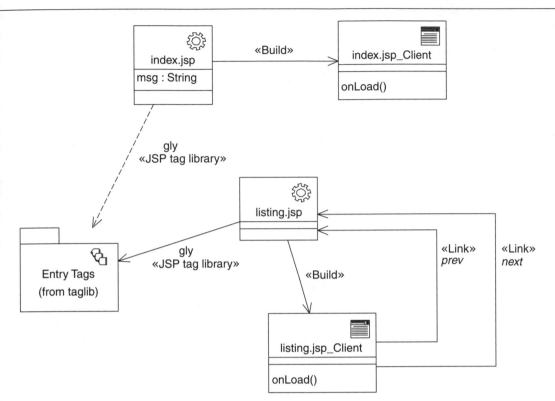

FIGURE 12-14   A tag library package referenced by server pages

pages by dependency relationships.[8] The name on these relationships, gly, is how the tag library is referenced in the context of the JSP code.

An individual JSP custom tag is modeled with a «JSP tag» stereotyped class. The class attributes are a combination of tag attributes and defined scripting variables. In Figure 12-15, Entry defines two tag attributes and seven scripting variables. The attributes are part of the opening tag, and tag values on them indicate whether they are required. The scripting variables are Java variables that can be safely referred to by JSP scripting code in the body of the tag.

This diagram also shows dependencies on the classes that implement JSP tags. The implementation classes are located in a different package because there is no restriction on the location of the implementing classes in the Java package hierarchy, and it is entirely possible for multiple tag libraries to reuse the same implementing classes.

---

8. The use of dependency relationships here is a result of a limitation on my modeling tool. It would be more accurate to draw a stereotyped association whose role name is the referenced name of the library used by the JSP code.

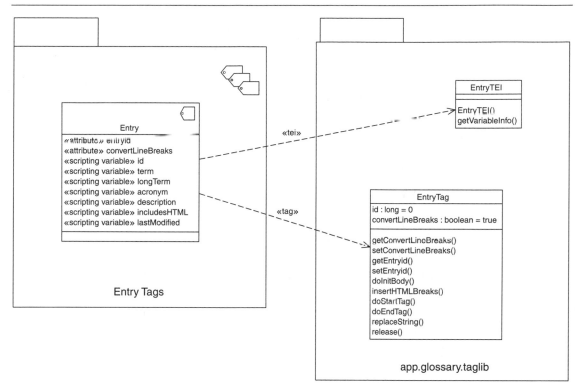

FIGURE 12-15   A JSP tag specifying its implementing class and the class that defines its scripting variables

❏ ❏ ❏ ❏ ❏ ❏ ❏ ❏ ❏

Summary

❏ A frameset is a special type of Web page that divides its viewing area into multiple panes, each containing its own Web page. A frameset is modeled with the «frameset» stereotyped class.

❏ A target is a named frame in a frameset that other client pages can request Web pages for and is modeled with the «target» stereotyped class.

❏ A «targeted link» stereotyped *n*-ary association is the link among a normal «link» association, a target, and the page to render in the target.

❏ A frameset is a specialization of a client page, and its attributes, operations, and «link» associations are used when the client browser does not support frames.

❏ The HTML <iframe> tag is modeled with a simple «iframe» containment association.

❏ A «virtual root» component package defines a URL hierarchy that is visible to requesting clients.

❏ Virtual roots define HTTP resource elements, which are proxies to the components that service the resource.

❏ «HTTPResource» components can realize UX model screens when screens are implemented with multiple Web page classes.

❏ JSP tag libraries are modeled with stereotyped packages.

❏ JSP tags are modeled with stereotyped classes and have UML attributes that define their JSP tag attribute and scripting variables.

Discussion

1. What are the implications of modeling JSP tag implementation classes in the «JSP Tag Library» package?
2. Why are HTTP resources modeled as components?
3. Under what conditions is it possible to model all the valid URLs of an application in the same package?
4. What are some alternative ways to model the use of framesets?[9]

Activities

1. Examine sample JavaDoc output. Construct a logical model of the frameset and a few of the class pages.
2. Construct a UML model of the sample SQL tags defined in the official JSP specification from Sun Microsystems.

---

9. If you come up with any really good ones, let me know!

Chapter 13
Implementation

The use cases have been completed, the problem has been analyzed, a candidate architecture has been drafted, and a suitable design has been defined. It is time to roll up the virtual sleeves and start implementing (Figure 13-1).

The activities of implementation include

- Mapping the design into code and components
- Building the code into binaries
- Unit testing
- Updating the model

At the same time, the UX team will be implementing the look-and-feel of the application in HTML.

The principal responsibility and activity of the implementer is to map the artifacts of design into executable code. The implementer, of course, uses more than the artifacts modified by design. A thorough knowledge of the use cases is required to ensure that their meanings and goals are not lost.

Every implementer is responsible for unit testing his or her own work. Some organizations may use pairs of implementers, and unit testing might be done by a partner. Either way, the goal is to have every delivered artifact, or component, unit tested before it is used by any other member of the team.

The final step in this cycle is to update the model when changes are made to the structure of the design as a result of the implementation. This is an iterative process, after all, and change is to be expected and planned for. An accurate model is important because the model is a view of not only the system to be built but also the system being built and the system that was built. Once the system and the model get out of sync, the model's ability to answer questions about the system is limited. Model updating can be as simple as a code review by the developer or designer and a manual updating

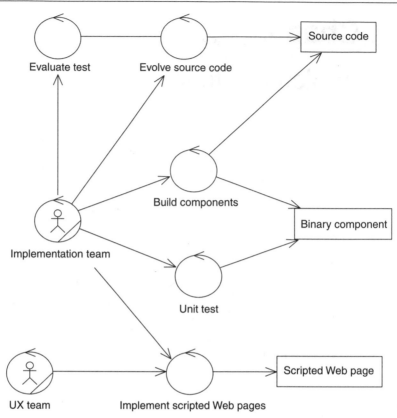

FIGURE 13-1 Activities during implementation

of the model. More sophisticated CASE tools have reverse-engineering capabilities built in and make this task much easier.

Most nontrivial Web applications have a development staff of more than one, so an important part of the development environment is to publish package interfaces as early as possible. This allows implementers to work asynchronously even when their own code is dependent on others. Each developer will stub out a public interface. In the case of Web page development, a suitable interface prototype can be created by implementing the pages, in their correct directory, with hyperlinks to the other Web pages that comprise the system's scenarios. These scenarios are, of course, owned by the UX team and are often a valuable reference and resource to the rest of the team.

For the most part, the implementation of all the server-side components—business objects, persistence layer, transaction components—is done in the same way as in any client/server system. Here, we'll concentrate on the construction of Web-specific components, most notably the Web pages of the system. Reiterating one of the main themes of this book: Web pages are architecturally significant components that exist in the model and in the executable system. Web page model elements map directly to Web page code. This chapter describes that mapping.

Web pages in a Web application can be implemented with scripted Web page files—ASPX, JSP, PHP—or with compiled components—CGI, Java servlets. In either case, the logical separation of client-side and server-side activity is the same. Implementing the client pages in the model is essentially the same, regardless of which server-enabling technology is used.

This chapter does not cover all the specifics of mapping the models to code. These details can be found in Appendix A, a detailed description of the WAE profile and its mapping to HTML and JSP code. Another excellent way to understand the mapping between models and code is to examine the two reference applications: Number Store and Glossary. This chapter covers a few examples from the reference applications and provides some explanatory text.

Microsoft's .NET framework with the next-generation Active Server Page server has been released. The details and their mappings to UML are not yet fully understood and therefore are not covered in much detail here.

Number Store Main Control Mechanism

Figure 13-2 shows the classes involved in the main Web page request and control mechanism. This diagram shows three «server page» classes, each of which is implemented as «JSP» components. The user session class is the J2EE HttpSession object and documents the key session state values used in this mechanism. The ScreenDefinition class, a simple wrapper of screen definitions, makes getting at all the discrete values of a single screen easy.

The RequestProcessor class is implemented as a Java servlet. This class, which uses the user's session and a UseCaseCoordinator class, is the main entry point for all user HTTP requests, and is defined by the web.xml configuration file and the fragment from this file (Listing 13-1).

The overall flow of user request handling is described by the sequence diagram of Figure 13-3.

Listing 13-1 Fragment from the web.xml file

```
<servlet>
  <servlet-name>screenRequestProcessor</servlet-name>
  <display-name>centralServlet</display-name>
  <description>no description</description>
  <servlet-class>com.numberstore.util.RequestProcessor</servlet-class>
</servlet>
<servlet-mapping>
  <servlet-name>screenRequestProcessor</servlet-name>
  <url-pattern>*.scr</url-pattern>
</servlet-mapping>
```

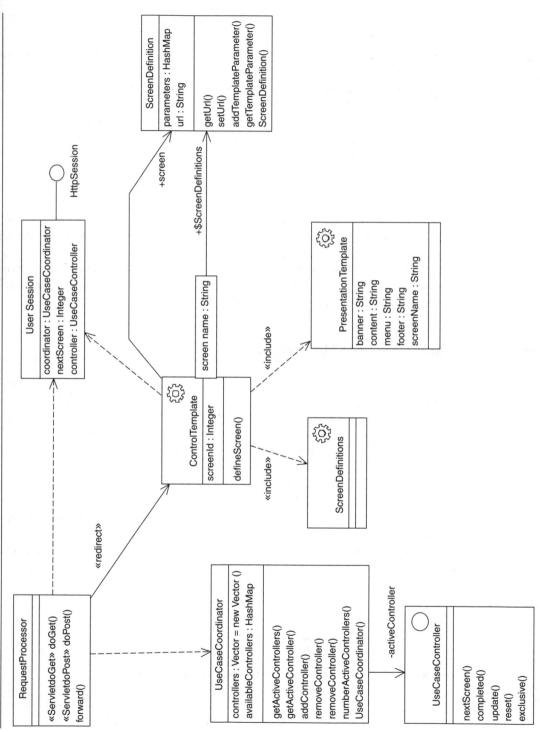

FIGURE 13-2 Class diagram of Number main control mechanism

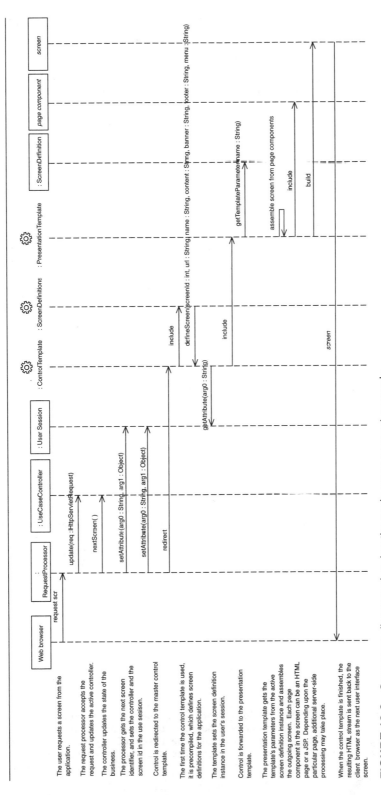

FIGURE 13-3 Sequence diagram showing the main page request scenario

The implementation for the `RequestProcessor` servlet follows. In this code, the main entry points and the operations that start the instance are the `doGet()` and the `doPost()` operations. These operations are called whenever a client browser requests a Web page with the extension `.scr` from the server. The `doPost()` operation delegates the processing to the `doGet()` operation, which is the main operation of the class.

In the `doGet()` operation, the `UseCaseCoordinator` is obtained from the user's session. If it is not there, a fresh one is created. The coordinator is asked for the current `UseCaseController` class. This controller is then asked to process the incoming `HttpServletRequest`. The controller manages the updating of business state in the entity tier. When finished, it is asked whether the scenario is completed. If it is, it is removed from the active controller stack, and the next controller on the stack is made current.

The current controller is checked to make sure that it doesn't require exclusive control, that is, won't allow another controller to be placed on top of it. If it is not exclusive, the incoming request is checked to see whether a new controller has been requested. If a new controller has been specified, it is made the current controller and given the chance to examine and to process the incoming request.

Finally, the controller is asked for the next screen ID that is set in the user session. The servlet then forwards the processing of the request, via the request dispatcher, to the `ControlTemplate.jsp` (Listing 13-2).

Listing 13-2   RequestProcessor source

```
package com.numberstore.util;

import java.io.*;
import java.text.*;
import java.util.*;
import javax.servlet.*;
import javax.servlet.http.*;

/**
 * The RequestProcessor is responsible for handling all incoming Http Requests for the
 * application.  It delegates the actual processing of the request to UseCaseController
 * instances which themselves are managed by a UseCaseCoordinator instance.  The Coordinator
 * is responsible for managing the collection of active use case controller instances. Once
 * the processing of the requests is completed the RequestProcessor forwards the request to a
 * controller JSP page, which uses information captured in the session to build the
 * appropriate response page.
 * @author jim conallen
 * @version 1.0
 * @see UseCaseCoordinator
 * @see UseCaseController
 */
public class RequestProcessor extends HttpServlet {

    /**
     * The doGet method is the main point of logic for the request processor.
     * The doGet method handles all incoming page requests for the application.
     * <p>The basic flow of this method is to first get the UseCaseCoordinator instance
     * from the session, creating one and placing it in the session if necessary. </p>
     *
```

```
 *  <p>Next the coordinator is asked for the active UseCaseController instance.  With
 *  this instance the system is updated with the incoming HttpServletRequest.  The active
 *  controller is responsible for updating the business state of the system.  Next the
 *  controller is asked if its task is completed.  If so the controller is removed from
 *  the coordinator's active stack.</p>
 *
 *  <p>Next the request is examined to see if a new controller has been specified as a
 *  parameter.  If it has, then the coordinator is told to add the new controller to
 *  the active controller stack.  Then it is asked for the active controller.  </p>
 *
 *  @param request incoming request for a page resource.
 *  @param response outgoing response.
 *  @see UseCaseCoordinator
 *  @see UseCaseController
 */
 public void doGet(HttpServletRequest request,
                   HttpServletResponse response)
     throws IOException, ServletException
 {
   // general algorithm: accept request, update business state through
   // the current controller, then delegate to the template indicating
   // the next page.

   HttpSession session = request.getSession();

   UseCaseCoordinator coordinator = (UseCaseCoordinator) session.getAttribute("coordinator");
   if( coordinator == null ) {
      coordinator = new UseCaseCoordinator();
      session.setAttribute("coordinator", coordinator );
   }

   UseCaseController controller = coordinator.getActiveController();
   controller.update( request );
   if( controller.completed() ) {
     coordinator.removeController( controller );
   }

   if( !controller.exclusive() ) {
     // if the active controller will allow a slight diversion to make
     // another controller the active one, and one has been requested,
     // then place it on top of the stack.
     String controllerName = request.getParameter("controller");
     if( controllerName != null ) {
       // inform the coordinator that a new controller has been requested
       coordinator.addController( controllerName );
       controller = coordinator.getActiveController();

       // check to see if we've been asked to reset the controller first
       String reset = request.getParameter("reset");
       if( reset != null ) {
         if( reset.equals("true") ) controller.reset();
       }

       // prime the new controller with any necessary parameters
       controller.update(request);
     }
   }
```

```
    int nextScreenId = controller.nextScreen();
    session.setAttribute("nextScreen", new Integer(nextScreenId) );

    // make this controller available to the JSPs as the default controller
    session.setAttribute("controller", controller );

    // if this is the last act of this controller then remove it from the
    // coordinator's stack.  But leave it in the session to process this last
    // request.

    forward( "/ControlTemplate.jsp", request, response );
}


/**
 * Overidden handler for post requests.  All post requests are handled by doGet().
 * Overidden handler for post requests. .All post requests are handled by doGet().
 * @param request incoming request for a page resource.
 * @param response outgoing response.
 */
public void doPost(HttpServletRequest request, HttpServletResponse response)
    throws IOException, ServletException
{
    doGet(request, response);
}


/**
 * Private method for redirecting the request to a JSP resource.
 * Private method for redirecting the request to a JSP resource. Uses the
 * RequestDispatcher for the redirection instead sendRedirect which would result in a new
 * client request, and most likely a stack overflow in the virtual machine.
 * @param url the relative url to pass control to.
 * @param req the incoming http request.
 * @param resp the outgoing response.
 */
private void forward(String url, HttpServletRequest req, HttpServletResponse resp )
    throws IOException, ServletException {
    // The pathname specified may be relative, although it cannot extend outside the
    // current servlet context. If the path begins with a "/" it is interpreted as
    // relative to the current context root. This method returns null if the servlet
    // container cannot return a RequestDispatcher.
    RequestDispatcher rd = req.getRequestDispatcher(url);
    rd.forward(req, resp);
}
}
```

The ControlTemplate's only responsibility is to define some static operations—bound in <%! ... %> blocks—that make it easy to define new screens. Included are the screen definitions files that use the defined operations in this file before obtaining the ScreenDefinition instance that will be used by the PresentationTemplate (Listing 13-3).

The template includes, via the @include directive, a ScreenDefintions.jsp file, which contains definitions for all the screens in the application. Each screen definition calls the operation defined in ControlTemplate. This operation packages the screen definition in a ScreenDefinition wrapper class and adds them to a static HashMap (Listing 13-4).

The HashMap stores all the screen definitions and uses their IDs as the key (Listing 13-5)

Listing 13-3 ControlTemplate.jsp source

```
<%@ page language="java" contentType="text/html" %>
<%@ page import="com.numberstore.util.*" %>
<%@ page import="java.util.HashMap" %>
<%!
private HashMap ScreenDefinitions = new HashMap();

private void defineScreen( int screenId, String url, String name, String content, String
banner, String footer, String menu) {
  ScreenDefinition screen = new ScreenDefinition();
  screen.setUrl( url );
  screen.addTemplateParameter( "name", name );
  screen.addTemplateParameter( "content", content );
  screen.addTemplateParameter( "banner", banner );
  screen.addTemplateParameter( "footer", footer );
  screen.addTemplateParameter( "menu", menu );
  ScreenDefinitions.put( new Integer(screenId), screen );}

%>

<%-- include screen definitions --%>
<%@ include file="ScreenDefinitions.jsp" %>
<%

Integer screenId = (Integer) session.getAttribute("nextScreen");
ScreenDefinition screen = (ScreenDefinition) ScreenDefinitions.get( screenId );

%>

<%@ include file="PresentationTemplate.jsp" %>
```

Listing 13-4 ScreenDefinitions.jsp source

```
<%
// definitions
defineScreen( (int) 0, "/home.scr", "Home", "home.jsp", "banner.jsp", "footer.jsp", "" );
defineScreen( (int) 1, "/catalog.scr", "Catalog", "catalog/catalog.jsp", "banner.jsp",
"footer.jsp", "menu.jsp" );
defineScreen( (int) 2, "/category.scr", "Category", "catalog/category.jsp", "banner.jsp",
"footer.jsp", "menu.jsp" );
defineScreen( (int) 3, "/product.scr", "Product Information", "catalog/product.jsp",
"banner.jsp", "footer.jsp", "menu.jsp" );
defineScreen( (int) 4, "/cart.scr", "Shopping Cart", "catalog/cart.jsp", "banner.jsp",
"footer.jsp", "menu.jsp" );
```

```
// order screens
defineScreen( (int) 5, "/checkout.scr", "Shopping Cart Summary", "order/checkout.jsp",
"banner.jsp", "order/order_footer.jsp", "" );
defineScreen( (int) 6, "/paymentInformation.scr", "Payment Information", "order/payment.jsp",
"banner.jsp", "order/order_footer.jsp", "" );
defineScreen( (int) 7, "/paymentConfirmation.scr", "Payment Confirmation", "order/
payment_summary.jsp", "banner.jsp", "order/order_footer.jsp", "" );
defineScreen( (int) 8, "/invoice.scr", "Invoice", "order/invoice.jsp", "order/
invoice_banner.jsp", "", "" );

// tutorial screens
defineScreen( (int) 9, "/addFractionLesson.scr", "Adding Fractions", "tutorials/fractions/
lesson.html", "banner.jsp", "footer.jsp", "menu.jsp" );
defineScreen( (int) 10, "/addFractionTryIt.scr", "Adding Fractions Try It!", "tutorials/
fractions/tryit.jsp", "banner.jsp", "footer.jsp", "menu.jsp" );
defineScreen( (int) 11, "/addFractionCheckWork.scr", "Adding Fractions Check Work",
"tutorials/fractions/checkwork.jsp", "banner.jsp", "footer.jsp", "menu.jsp" );
defineScreen( (int) 12, "/addFractionTest.scr", "Adding Fractions Test", "tutorials/
fractions/test.jsp", "banner.jsp", "footer.jsp", "menu.jsp" );
defineScreen( (int) 13, "/addFractionTestResults.scr", "Adding Fractions Test Results",
"tutorials/fractions/testresults.jsp", "banner.jsp", "footer.jsp", "menu.jsp" );
defineScreen( (int) 14, "/addFractionCertificate.scr", "Adding Fractions Certificate",
"tutorials/fractions/certificate.jsp", "banner.jsp", "footer.jsp", "menu.jsp" );
defineScreen( (int) 15, "/polynomialLesson.scr", "Graphing Polynomials Lesson", "tutorials/
polynomial/lesson.html", "banner.jsp", "footer.jsp", "menu.jsp" );
defineScreen( (int) 16, "/polynomialGraphing.scr", "Polynomial Graphing", "tutorials/
polynomial/graphing.html", "banner.jsp", "footer.jsp", "menu.jsp" );
defineScreen( (int) 17, "/polynomialTest.scr", "Polynomial Graphing Test", "tutorials/
polynominal/test.jsp", "banner.jsp", "footer.jsp", "menu.jsp" );
defineScreen( (int) 18, "/polynomialTestResults.scr", "Polynomial Graphing Test Results",
"tutorials/polynominal/testresults.jsp", "banner.jsp", "footer.jsp", "menu.jsp" );
defineScreen( (int) 19, "/polynomialCertificate.scr", "Polynomial Graphing Certificate",
"tutorials/polynominal/certificate.jsp", "banner.jsp", "footer.jsp", "menu.jsp" );

%>
```

Listing 13-5   PresentationTemplate.jsp source

```
<%
String banner = screen.getTemplateParameter( "banner" );
String content = screen.getTemplateParameter( "content" );
String footer = screen.getTemplateParameter( "footer" );
String menu = screen.getTemplateParameter( "menu" );
String screenName = screen.getTemplateParameter("name" );
%>
<html>
<head>
    <style type="text/css">
    a.:link { color: blue; text-decoration: none }
    a.:active { color: red; text-decoration: none }
    a.:visited { color: blue; text-decoration: none }
    a.:hover { color: green; text-decoration: underline }

    a.menu:link { color: white; text-decoration: none }
    a.menu:active { color: yellow; text-decoration: none }
    a.menu:visited { color: white; text-decoration: none }
```

```
        a.menu:hover { color: yellow; text-decoration: underline }
        </style>
        <title>The Number Store - <%=screenName%></title>
</head>

<body bgcolor="white">
<%  if( !banner.equals("") ) { %>
  <jsp:include page="<%= banner %>" flush="true"/>
<% } %>

        <table width="100%">
          <tr>
<%        if( !menu.equals("") ) { %>
            <td width=50 height=300 bgcolor="#3399cc" valign="top"> <jsp:include page="<%= menu
%>" flush="true" /></td>
<%        } %>
            <td height=300 width="*"><jsp:include page="<%= content %>" flush="true" /></td>
          </tr>
        </table>

<%  if( !footer.equals("") ) { %>
    <jsp:include page="<%= footer %>" flush="true" />
<%  } %>

<!-- ***********************************************************************************-->
<!-- **************** Development and Debugging information only ***********************-->

<table width="100%" bgcolor="Lime">
<tr><td>
    <small>
    <p><b>Debug/Development Information</b></p>

    <p>Screen Information</p>
    <blockquote>
        <p>Query String: <%= request.getQueryString() %> </p>
        <p> Screen: <%=screenName%><br>
            Screen Id: <%=screenId%> <br>
            Screen URL: <%= screen.getUrl() %> <br>
    <table border="1" cellspacing="0" cellpadding="2" >
      <tr><td align="center" colspan="2"<td><a target="jspsource"
href="sourcecode.jsp?source=<%=banner%>"><%=banner%></a> </td></tr>
      <% if( menu.equals("") ) { %>
        <tr><td align="center" height="80" width="200"><a target="jspsource"
href="sourcecode.jsp?source=<%=content%>"><%=content%></a> </td></tr>
      <% } else { %>
        <tr><td align="center" height="80" width="50"><a target="jspsource"
href="sourcecode.jsp?source=<%=menu%>"><%=menu%></a> </td><td align="center"
width="120"><a target="jspsource" href="sourcecode.jsp?source=<%=content%>"><%=content%>
</a> </td></tr>
      <% } %>
      <% if( ! footer.equals("") ) { %>
      <tr><td align="center" colspan="2"><a target="jspsource"
href="sourcecode.jsp?source=<%=footer%>"><%=footer%></a> </td></tr>
      <% } %>
    </table>
    </blockquote>
    </small>
```

```jsp
<%@ page import="java.util.Enumeration" %>
  <p>Session Attributes</p>
    <blockquote>
    <table border="1" cellspacing="0" cellpadding="2" >
<%
    for (Enumeration names = session.getAttributeNames(); names.hasMoreElements(); ) {
String name = (String) names.nextElement();
      Object value = session.getAttribute(name);
%>
      <tr><td><%=name%></td><td><%=value.toString()%> </td>
<%    } %>

    </table>
    </blockquote>
    </small>

<%@ page import="com.numberstore.util.*" %>
<p>Controller stack</p>
  <blockquote>
    <table border="1" cellspacing="0" cellpadding="2" >
    <tr>
      <td>Instance</td>
      <td>nextScreen</td>
      <td>completed</td>
    </tr>
<% UseCaseCoordinator coordinator = (UseCaseCoordinator)
session.getAttribute("coordinator");
    UseCaseController controllers[] = (UseCaseController[])
coordinator.getActiveControllers();
    for(int i=controllers.length-1; i>=0; i--) {
      UseCaseController controller = controllers[i];
      int nextScreen = controller.nextScreen();
      String instance = controller.toString();
      boolean completed = controller.completed();
%>
    <tr>
      <td><%=instance%></td>
      <td><%=nextScreen%></td>
      <td><%=completed%></td>
    </tr>
<%    } %>
  </table>
  </blockquote>
</td></tr></table>
</body>
</html>
```

The presentation template is the main template for all outgoing pages. This JSP maintains the overall application look-and-feel. The presentation template gets the current screen object from the user session and uses it to determine which JSP components will be used to fill the known compartments.

The presentation template itself doesn't do much more than define major screen components. Any one of these compartments is filled by individual JSPs.

The home.jsp is used to fill the main compartment of the Home screen. Because the compartments in this application are organized with HTML table tags, the individual JSPs that fill compartments do not specify <HTML>, <HEAD> and <BODY> tags (Listing 13-6).

Listing 13-6 The home.jsp source

```
<%@ page import="com.numberstore.catalog.*" %>
<%
  ShopController controller = (ShopController) session.getAttribute("controller");
  Product special = controller.getProductSpecial();
  int specialCategoryId = special.getCategoryId();
  int specialProductId = special.getId();
  String specialName = special.getName();
  String specialDescription = special.getDescription();
  String specialPrice = special.priceString();
  String specialUrl = response.encodeURL("product.scr?catid=" + specialCategoryId +
"&prodid=" + specialProductId );

%>
<table width="100%">
  <tr>
    <td colspan="2" align="center">
      <h2>Welcome to the Number Store!</h2>
    </td>
  </tr>
  <tr>
    <td colspan="2">
      <p>This fictional eRetail store offers for virtual sale some of the best
      and most interesting numbers on the market today.  The idea for the store
      is driven by two major factors.  Firstly I needed a sample J2EE application
      with sufficient complexity to illustrate how to properly model it with UML
      and the Web Application Extension (WAE).  Secondly, I needed something easy to
      build and something that didn't require a whole lot of additional software
      (EJB containers, databases, etc.).</p>
      <p>A more detailed description of the architecture of this application can be
      found <a target="NumberStoreArch" href="documentation/index.html">here</a>.
    </td>
</tr>
  <tr>
    <td colspan="2" height="20"> </td>
  </tr>
  <tr>
    <td width="10"> </td>
    <td>
      <b><a href="<%=specialUrl%>">Today's Special: <%=specialName%></a></b><br>
      <i><%=specialDescription%></i> <b><%= specialPrice %></b>
    </td>
  </tr>
</table>

<div align="center">
  <h3><a href="<%= response.encodeURL( "catalog.scr" ) %>">View our Catalog</a></h3>
</div>
```

The general strategy for all JSP components is to first get the current controller from the session and query it for all the dynamic content that fills the page. This keeps all access to the business state from Web pages located at a single source.

Glossary Application Tag Libraries

In the Glossary application, JSP tag libraries are used extensively. Figure 13-4 shows the main home page classes: index.jsp / index.jsp_Client. These classes are realized by the index.jsp component, which also uses the Entry Tags tag library and

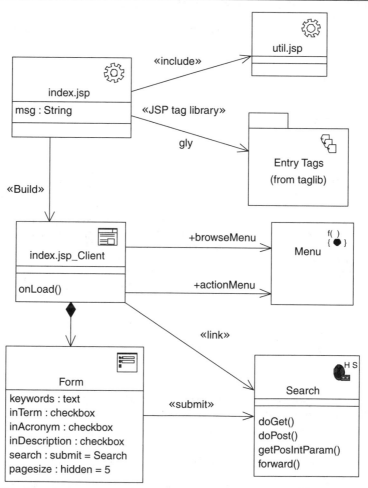

FIGURE 13-4   Class diagram including Glossary application's main home
                 page index.jsp

includes a utility page, which in this implementation contains a simple static operation definition to clip long strings when placing them in table cells. The source for the
index page follows (Listing 13-7).

Listing 13-7   The `index.jsp` source

```
<%@ page errorPage="error.jsp" %>
<%@ taglib uri="/glytlb" prefix="gly" %>
<%@ include file="util.jsp" %>
<%
String msg = (String) session.getAttribute("message");
if( msg == null ) msg = "";
%>
<html>
  <head>
    <title>Glossary Home</title>
    <script language="JavaScript1.2" src="menu.js"></script>

    <script language="JavaScript1.2">
    <!--
      function onLoad() {
        browseMenu = new Menu("Browse By Letter");
        browseMenu.addMenuItem("non alphabetic", "location='search?browse=0'");
        browseMenu.addMenuItem("A", "location='search?browse=a'");
        browseMenu.addMenuItem("B", "location='search?browse=b'");
        browseMenu.addMenuItem("C", "location='search?browse=c'");
        browseMenu.addMenuItem("D", "location='search?browse=d'");
        browseMenu.addMenuItem("E", "location='search?browse=e'");
        browseMenu.addMenuItem("F", "location='search?browse=f'");
        browseMenu.addMenuItem("G", "location='search?browse=g'");
        browseMenu.addMenuItem("H", "location='search?browse=h'");
        browseMenu.addMenuItem("I", "location='search?browse=i'");
        browseMenu.addMenuItem("J", "location='search?browse=j'");
        browseMenu.addMenuItem("K", "location='search?browse=k'");
        browseMenu.addMenuItem("L", "location='search?browse=l'");
        browseMenu.addMenuItem("M", "location='search?browse=m'");
        browseMenu.addMenuItem("N", "location='search?browse=n'");
        browseMenu.addMenuItem("O", "location='search?browse=o'");
        browseMenu.addMenuItem("P", "location='search?browse=p'");
        browseMenu.addMenuItem("Q", "location='search?browse=q'");
        browseMenu.addMenuItem("R", "location='search?browse=r'");
        browseMenu.addMenuItem("S", "location='search?browse=s'");
        browseMenu.addMenuItem("T", "location='search?browse=t'");
        browseMenu.addMenuItem("U", "location='search?browse=u'");
        browseMenu.addMenuItem("V", "location='search?browse=v'");
        browseMenu.addMenuItem("W", "location='search?browse=w'");
        browseMenu.addMenuItem("X", "location='search?browse=x'");
        browseMenu.addMenuItem("Y", "location='search?browse=y'");
        browseMenu.addMenuItem("Z", "location='search?browse=z'");

        window.actionMenu = new Menu("action");
        actionMenu.addMenuItem("Home", "location='index.jsp'");
        actionMenu.addMenuSeparator();
        actionMenu.addMenuItem("Create Entry", "location='edit.jsp?id=0'");
        actionMenu.addMenuItem(browseMenu);
```

```
        actionMenu.addMenuSeparator();
        actionMenu.addMenuItem("Help", "window.open('help.html','help',
'width=300,height=200,toolbar=no,menubar=no')");
        actionMenu.addMenuItem("JSP Source",
"window.open('sourcecode.jsp?source=index.jsp','src')");
        actionMenu.writeMenus();
    }
  //-->
  </script>

</head>
<body>
  <p><table width="100%" border=0 cellspacing=0 cellpadding=0>
    <tr bgcolor="#3B6EA5">
      <td><a href="javascript:window.showMenu(window.actionMenu);"
onMouseOver="window.showMenu(window.actionMenu);"><img border=0 src="images/
ActionMenu.jpg"></a></td>
      <td align=right><font face="arial,helvetica,espy,sans-serif" size=5
color="white">Home</font></td>
      <td width=20> </td>
    </tr>
  </table></p>

  <p><i><%=msg%></i></p>

  <b>Lastest Changes</b>
  <table border=2 cellspacing=3 cellpadding=3>
    <tr>
      <th>Term</th>
      <th>Description</th>
      <th>Last Modified</th>
    </tr>

    <gly:EntryList query="changes" length="3">
      <gly:EntryLoop>
        <tr>
          <td>
            <a href="entry.jsp?id=<%=id%>"><%=longTerm%></a>
          </td>
          <td><%=clip(description,100)%></td>
          <td><%=lastmodified%></td>
        </tr>
      </gly:EntryLoop>
    </gly:EntryList>
  </table>

  <h3>Search</h3>
  <form action="search" method="post">
    Keywords: <input name="keywords" size=30 maxlength="50"><br>
    <input name="inTerm" type="checkbox"> Term <br>
    <input name="inAcronym" type="checkbox"> Acronym <br>
    <input name="inDescription" type="checkbox"> Description <br>
    <input name="search" type="submit" value="Search">
    <input name="pagesize" type="hidden" value="5">
  </form>
```

```
<script language="JavaScript1.2">
<!--
  //For IE
  if (document.all) {
    onLoad();
  }
  //-->
</script>

</body>
</html>
```

In the source for this page, we see that the majority of the code appears to be defining the pop-up menu, which is a modeled with the «ClientScript Object» Menu class. This class is realized by the `Menu.js` script library component and included in the `<head>` element. This excellent example of a JavaScript class was created by Gary Smith of Netscape Communications, and the full copyright can be found in the source code file for the menu included in the application's files.

All the interaction with the entity tier is done via JSP tags (Figure 13-5). Three tags are defined. The `<EntryList>` tag, required to be the parent tag to the two other tags, provides the context—SQL result set—for the child tags. The `<EntryLoop>` child tag is an iterator tag and executes a loop, processing its body a certain number of times, specified as a tag attribute. The `<Entry>` tag provides access to a single entry.

The source code for the `<EntryList>` tag follows. This class extends the required `BodyTagSupport` class and provides `get` and `set` operations for all attributes defined in the tag library. Most of the functionality is in the `do start` and the `do end` tag operations. This class defines a helper operation to make the query to the entity tier. This tag expects to have a child tag access it and query it for the entry information (Listing 13-8).

One of the child tags, `EntryLoopTag`, follows—see Listing 13-9 starting on page 310.

Listing 13-8   `EntryListTag.java` source

```
Package app.glossary.taglib;

import javax.servlet.jsp.*;
import javax.servlet.jsp.tagext.*;
import javax.servlet.ServletRequest;
import javax.servlet.http.HttpSession;
import java.util.*;
import java.io.*;
import java.lang.Integer;
import app.glossary.*;

/**
 * <p>A logical representation of a query with multiple results.</p>
 *
 * <p>An entry list tag represents a particular type of query made to the
 * glossary. The query type is a tag attribute and must be one of { search,
 * changes, history }. This tag also examines the request object for the index
 * into the list and the page size to provide scripting variables for the next
```

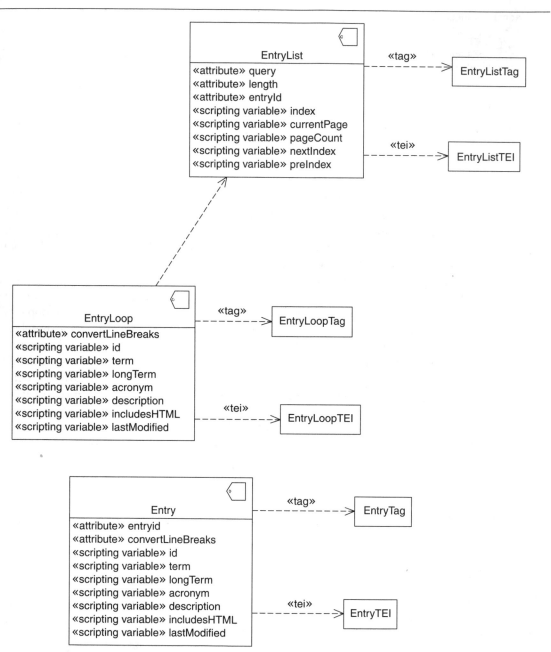

FIGURE 13-5   Modeled JSP tags

(Listing 13.8 continued)
```
 * and previous indicies.  In addition to the indices the total size of the
 * result set, number of pages and current page number is provided as a scripting variable.
 * </p>
 * @author jim conallen
 * @version 2.0
 */

public class EntryListTag extends BodyTagSupport {

  /** The type of query for the list { changes | search | history } */
  private String queryType = "";
  /** The starting index for the list loop. */
  private int index = 0;
  /** The current page number beginning this list */
  private int page;
  /** The index value beginning the next page. */
  private int next;
  /** The index value beginning the previous page. */
  private int prev;
  /** The total number of pages that this list spans. */
  private int pageCount;
  /** The size of each page in the list. */
  private int pageSize = 0;
  /** The total number of results in the list. */
  private int resultSize;
  /** The category id. */
  private long entryId;
  /** The category id. */
  private Enumeration entries;

  /**
   * Tag attribute that sets the type of query to be made in this list.
   *
   * @param queryType the type of query to be made for this list.
   */
  public void setQuery( String _queryType ){
    queryType = _queryType;
  }

  /**
   * Returns the type of query for this list.
   * Although not used directly by this application or the glossary code,
   * this getter seems to be required by the container.
   *
   * @returns The type of query this tag makes.
   */
  public String getQuery() {
    return queryType;
  }

  /**
   * Tag attribute that sets the entry id for a version history list.
   *
   * @param the id of the entry to list the versions for.  Should be parseable into a Long.
   */
```

```java
public void setEntryId( String _entryId ){
   try{
     entryId = Long.parseLong(_entryId);
   } catch( NumberFormatException ex ) {
     entryId = 0;
   }
}

/**
 * Returns the entry id set for a version history type of list.
 * Not required by the application, but it seems to be required by the servlet container.
 *
 * @returns The type of query this tag makes.
 */
public String getEntryId() {
   return Long.toString(entryId);
}


/**
 * Tag attribute that sets the page size for the loop of this page.
 *
 * @param the length in rows for this page.
 */
public void setLength( String _length ){
   try{
     pageSize = Integer.parseInt(_length);
   } catch( NumberFormatException ex ) {
     pageSize = 10;
   }
}

/**
 * Returns the page size for the loop of entries in this page.
 * Not required by the application, but it seems to be required by the servlet container.
 *
 * @returns The page size for this page.
 */
public String getLength() {
   return Integer.toString(pageSize);
}

/**
 * Called as the tag is first seen in a JSP page.
 * The query type should be set first, if it is a known type, then the appropriate query
 * is made to the database.  The requested index and page size is taken from the request
 * and if it is consistent with the results of the query, is set appropriately.
 * Ultimately the results of the query determine indices and sizes.
 *
 * @return EVAL_BODY_TAG if the query type is a known value, otherwise this tag is skipped.
 */
public int doStartTag() throws JspException {

   if( queryType.equals("changes") || queryType.equals("search") ||
queryType.equals("history")  ) {
      HttpSession session = pageContext.getSession();
      index = getIntFromRequest("index", 0);
```

```
          if( index == 0 ) index = getIntFromSession("index",1);
          if( pageSize == 0 ) pageSize = getIntFromSession("pagesize",10);
          if( index<=0 ) index = 1;
          if( pageSize<=0 ) pageSize = 10;

          executeQuery();

          if( !entries.hasMoreElements() ) {
            String message = "The query you requested resulted in no matches.";
            pageContext.getSession().setAttribute("message", message);
            next = 1;
            prev = 1;
            pageCount = 0;
            page = 0;
          } else {
            next = getNext();
            prev = getPrev();
            pageCount = getPageCount();
            page = getPage();
          }
          return EVAL_BODY_TAG;
      }

      return SKIP_BODY;
  }

  /**
   * Called just before the contents of the body are evaluated, all script variables are set
   * in this call.
   */
  public void doInitBody() throws JspException {
    pageContext.setAttribute("index", Integer.toString(index) );
    pageContext.setAttribute("currentpage", Integer.toString(page));
    pageContext.setAttribute("pageCount", Integer.toString(pageCount));
    pageContext.setAttribute("nextIndex", Integer.toString(next));
    pageContext.setAttribute("prevIndex", Integer.toString(prev));
  }

  /**
   * Called child tags that process the entries.
   * Child tags get the entries and typically iterate through them to provide lists of
   * results. This tag represents a query, while child tags implement the iterative loops
   * where each value is used.
   *
   * @return An enumeration of entries that meets the criteria of the list.
   */
  public Enumeration getEntries(){
    return entries;
  }

  /**
   * Called child tags that process the entries.
   * Child tags get the entries and typically iterate through them to provide lists of
   * results. This tag represents a query, while child tags implement the iterative loops
   * where each value is used.
   *
```

```
 * @return An enumeration of entries that meets the criteria of the list.
 */
private void executeQuery(){
  Glossary glossary = new Glossary();
  if( queryType.equals("changes") ) {
    index = 1;
    if( pageSize <= 0 ) pageSize = 5;
    entries = glossary.mostRecentChanges(pageSize);
  }
  else if( queryType.equals("history") ) {
    entries = glossary.history(entryId, index, pageSize);
  } else {
    HttpSession session = pageContext.getSession();
    EntryQueryCriteria criteria = (EntryQueryCriteria) session.getAttribute("query");
    if( criteria == null ){
      entries = new Vector().elements();
    }
    else{
      if( criteria.isSearch() ){
        entries = glossary.search( criteria.getTerm(), criteria.getAcronym(),
criteria.getDescription(), index, pageSize);
      } else {
        entries = glossary.browse( criteria.browseWith, index, pageSize );
      }
    }
  }
  resultSize = glossary.getResultSize();
}

/**
 * Utility method that gets an int from a request parameter.
 *
 * @return An int from the request
 */
private int getIntFromRequest(String param, int defaultVal) {
  String intStr;
  int intVal;
  ServletRequest request = pageContext.getRequest();
  intStr = request.getParameter(param);
  if( intStr == null ) {
    intVal = defaultVal;
  }else{
    try{
      intVal = Integer.parseInt(intStr);
    } catch( NumberFormatException ex ){
      intVal = defaultVal;
    }
  }
  return intVal;
}

/**
 * Utility method that gets an int from the session.
 *
 * @return An int from the session
 */
```

```java
private int getIntFromSession(String key, int defaultVal) {
  Integer intObj;
  int intVal;
  HttpSession session = pageContext.getSession();
  intObj = (Integer) session.getAttribute(key);
  if( intObj == null ) {
    intVal = defaultVal;
  }else{
    intVal = intObj.intValue();
  }
  return intVal;
}

/**
 * Determines the current page number given the index and page size.
 *
 * @return The current page (one based)
 */
private int getPage(){
  int page = (index / pageSize) + 1;
  return page;
}

/**
 * Determines the total number of pages in the result.
 *
 * @return The number of pages in the result set, given the page size.
 */
private int getPageCount(){
  int pageCount = (resultSize / pageSize) + 1;
  if( resultSize == 0 ) pageCount = 0;
  return pageCount;
}

/**
 * Determines the next starting index, given the current page, page size and total number of
 * results.
 *
 * @return The next index
 */
private int getNext(){
  int next = index + pageSize;
  if( next > resultSize ) next = index;
  return next;
}

/**
 * Determines the previous page's starting index, given the current page, page size and
 * total number of results.
 *
 * @return The prev index
 */
private int getPrev(){
  int prev = index - pageSize;
  if( prev <=0   ) prev = 1;
  return prev;
}
```

```
/**
 * Called when the end tag is identified.
 * The method simply writes out the processed body.
 *
 * @return The prev index
 */
public int doEndTag() throws JspTagException {
  BodyContent body = getBodyContent();
  try {
    body.writeOut(getPreviousOut());
  } catch (IOException e) {
    throw new JspTagException("EntryList: " + e.getMessage());
  }
  return SKIP_BODY;
}

/**
 * Clean up time, all internal variables are reset.
 */
public void release() {
  queryType = "";
  index = 1;
  page = 1;
  next = 1;
  prev = 1;
  pageCount = 0;
  pageSize = 10;
  resultSize = 0;
  entries = null;
}

}
```

Listing 13-9 EntryTag.java source

```
package app.glossary.taglib;

import javax.servlet.jsp.*;
import javax.servlet.jsp.tagext.*;
import javax.servlet.ServletRequest;
import javax.servlet.http.HttpSession;
import java.util.*;
import java.io.*;
import java.lang.Integer;
import app.glossary.*;
import java.text.DateFormat;

/**
 * <p>A loop of entries.</p>
 *
 * <p>This tag looks to a parent tag (EntryList) for a definition of a set of entries.  The
 * list is iterated through and for each entry a set of scripting variables is set.
 * </p>
 * @author jim conallen
 * @version 2.0
 */
```

```
public class EntryLoopTag extends BodyTagSupport {
private Enumeration entries;
private IEntry entry;
private boolean convertLineBreaks = true;

public String getConvertLineBreaks(){
  return new Boolean(convertLineBreaks).toString();
}

public void setConvertLineBreaks(String _convertLineBreaks ){
  if( _convertLineBreaks != null ) {
      _convertLineBreaks = _convertLineBreaks.toLowerCase().trim();
  if( _convertLineBreaks.equals("false") || _convertLineBreaks.equals("no") ){
      convertLineBreaks = false;
}
}
}

public int doStartTag() throws JspException {
//get the criteria and execute the query
  try{
    EntryListTag list = (EntryListTag) findAncestorWithClass(this,
      Class.forName("app.glossary.taglib.EntryListTag"));
    entries = list.getEntries();
    }catch( ClassNotFoundException ex ){
    throw new JspTagException("EntryLoop: " + ex.getMessage());
  }
  if(entries.hasMoreElements()) {
    entry = (IEntry) entries.nextElement();
    setEntryAttributes();
    return EVAL_BODY_TAG;
  }
  else {
   return SKIP_BODY;
  }
}

public void setEntryAttributes() {
  pageContext.setAttribute("id", Long.toString(entry.getId()) );
  String term = EntryTag.prepareHTML( entry.getTerm() );
  pageContext.setAttribute("term", term);
  String formattedAcronym = EntryTag.prepareHTML( entry.getAcronym() );
  pageContext.setAttribute("acronym", formattedAcronym);

  if( formattedAcronym.equals("") )
    pageContext.setAttribute("longTerm", term );
  else
    pageContext.setAttribute("longTerm", term + " (" + formattedAcronym + ")" );

  String description = entry.getDescription();
    if( convertLineBreaks && !entry.getIncludesHTML() ) {
      description = insertHTMLBreaks(description);
    }
  pageContext.setAttribute("description", description);
    if( entry.getIncludesHTML() )
      pageContext.setAttribute("includesHTML", "CHECKED");
```

```java
    else
       pageContext.setAttribute("includesHTML", "");

   pageContext.setAttribute("lastmodified",
      DateFormat.getDateInstance().format(entry.lastModified())));
}

public String insertHTMLBreaks( String str ) {
   return replaceString(str, "\n", "<br>");
}

public int doAfterBody() throws JspException {
   BodyContent body = getBodyContent();
   try {
      body.writeOut(getPreviousOut());
   } catch (IOException e) {
      throw new JspTagException("EntryLoop: " + e.getMessage());
   }
// clear up so the next time the body content is empty
   body.clearBody();
   if(entries.hasMoreElements()) {
      entry = (IEntry) entries.nextElement();
      setEntryAttributes();
      return EVAL_BODY_TAG;
   } else {
   return SKIP_BODY;
   }
}

private static String replaceString(String str, String sep, String rep) {
   StringBuffer retVal = new StringBuffer();
   int idx = 0;
   int jdx = str.indexOf(sep);
   while (jdx >= 0) {
   retVal.append(str.substring(idx, jdx));
   retVal.append(rep);
   idx = jdx + sep.length();
   jdx = str.indexOf(sep, idx);
}
   retVal.append(str.substring(idx));
   return retVal.toString();
}

/**
 * Clean up time, all internal variables are reset.
 */
public void release() {
   entries = null;
   entry = null;
}

public static String formatHtml( String str ) {
   str = replaceString(str, "<", "&lt;");
   str = replaceString(str, ">", "&gt;");
   return str;
   }
}
```

As with all tags, <EntryLoopTag> extends the BodyTagSupport class and provides operations for the start and end tag operations. What is notable in this class is how it gets a reference to its parent tag. This is done in the start tag operation by calling the findAncestorWithClass() base class operation. This tag iterates by returning the value EVAL_BODY_TAG each time the operation doAfterBody() is called and there is another row to display.

This class sets a number of scripting variables that are used in the JSP source as dynamic content items. The UX team is free to position and to format these values according to the UX guidelines document. The engineering team, on the other hand, is able to control all access to the entity tier through the custom tags.

❑ ❑ ❑ ❑ ❑ ❑ ❑ ❑ ❑

Summary

❑ The activities of implementation include mapping the design into code and components, unit testing, and, if necessary, updating the model.

❑ Client-side and server-side programmers deal with the implementation of business logic. Graphic artists provide the implementation for the look-and-feel of the user interface.

❑ When the enabling technology is scripted pages—JSP, ASPX, PHP—each server page maps to one scripted page file, or page component.

❑ Vendor/framework-specific component stereotypes make it easier to understand the component models.

❑ A significant amount of structural code can be mapped directly from the model; the vast majority of behavioral code must be created by the implementer.

❑ The implementer uses interaction diagrams—sequence, collaboration—and activity diagrams to understand and to implement the classes' operations.

❑ During implementation, the number of attributes and operations defined in a class almost always increases with the introduction of helper members.

Discussion

1. What are the advantages and disadvantages of using JSP tag libraries for separating UX and engineering team activities?

2. What types of debugging aids can be created to assist the code/build/test/model cycle?

Activities

1. Design and implement a simple applet that reacts to JavaScript events in a Web page.
2. Create a new tutorial section in the Number Store application.
3. Add paged list functionality to the Glossary application's entry history page.

Appendix A

Web Application Extension Profile Version 2

Overview

This document describes the mapping of UML and HTML from two viewpoints. The mapping is consistent between them. The first viewpoint expresses the mapping from HTML to UML and is targeted at explaining the reverse engineering of HTML into UML elements. The second mapping expresses the forward-engineering viewpoint.

Figure A-1 shows a conceptual overview of the class stereotypes defined in this profile. This metamodel diagram of the profile expresses the relationships among WAE profile elements. Figure A-2 shows which component stereotypes realize which class stereotypes in the profile.

HTML to UML

This section describes the modeling of HTML code with UML. All HTML elements in our context have two common attributes: ID and class. ID is a unique identifier that distinguishes the element from all the others in the document. The nonunique identifier CLASS assigns one or more class names to an element; the element may be said to belong to these classes. A class name may be shared by several element instances. The class element attribute has two roles in HTML:

- As a style sheet selector, when an author wishes to assign style information to a set of elements
- For general-purpose processing by user agents

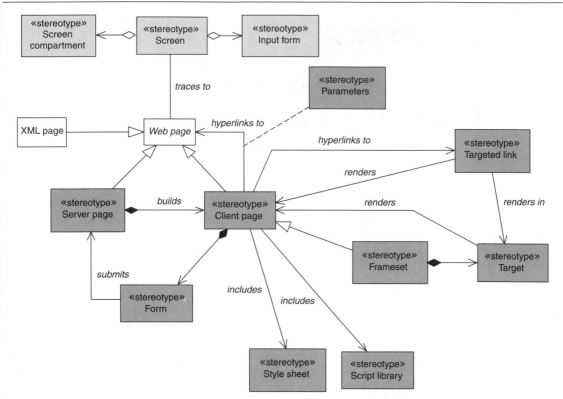

FIGURE A-1   Conceptual overview of WAE class stereotypes. Light shading indicates elements in the UX model; dark shading indicates design model elements.

The placement of logical-view classes in the package hierarchy is not important. Those classes can be placed in whatever package makes logical sense and supports the team development strategies. It is expected that during the model's evolution, classes may get moved into other packages. Placement of components, however, is semantically important and they should not be arbitrarily moved. The location of a WAE stereotyped component in the «physical root» is used to resolve URLs.

URL Resolution

When working with hyperlinks to URLs it is necessary to define a model package that will map to a Web context: www.myserver.com/context. The term *universal resource identifier* (URI) is a broad term for an address of content on the Web. A URI is a way of unambiguously identifying a resource on the Internet. A *universal resource locator* (URL), a type of URI, is a pointer to a particular resource on the Internet at a particu-

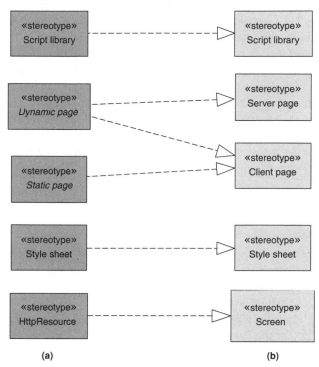

FIGURE A-2 Conceptual overview of component realizations of WAE stereotyped
classes: (a) component realizations; (b) class stereotypes

lar location and is the one used most frequently in Web applications. *Universal resource names* (URNs) are persistent, location-independent resource identifiers. So given a URN, a client will be able to retrieve it from any server that has the resource. The JavaScript protocol probably fits into this category, that is, javascript:parent.blank(). Because HTTP deals exclusively with URLs, we will consider making semantic interpretations only of URLs.

URL resolution begins with the «physical root» component package, which contains all the component files that can be directly requested by the client. If an additional layer of mapping is used to map HTTP resources to the physical files, a «virtual root» is needed with «HTTP Resource» elements underneath organized in a virtual URL hierarchy, and dependencies on the physical resources are needed.

The process for resolving a URL into the component that will service it begins by first looking at any «virtual root» package that has defined in its tag values the host and context that match the URL. If found, the package hierarchy under the virtual root is navigated, looking for an «HTTP Resource» element match. If the HTTP resource specifies a dependency on a «physical root» component, it is responsible for servicing the HTTP request. If the HTTP resource element realizes a logical-view class, that is, screen, the screen class is examined to determine which set of logical-view client and server pages created it. Following these relationships to their realizing components returns the total set of components that service the requested URL.

When looking at the sample code and models in this document, it is important to remember that when an href or a src HTML element attribute is specified, its value is not determined by the name of the class but rather by the component and the URL resolution process as a whole. In many cases, the class name and the component name are the same; therefore, at times it may appear that the value used for the href or the src is taken directly from the logical-view class.

Elements

<HTML> and <BODY> Elements

Every valid HTML page should contain a single HTML element with closing tag. This element is the container element for the entire page's document. The <BODY> element is the container of the rendered content of the page. It is where window object event handlers are placed.

Each <HTML>/<BODY> combination maps to a single «client page» stereotyped class in the logical view. The name of the class should be a derivative of the page name. The page name maps to the name of the component that realizes this «client page». The name of the «client page» class does not map directly to any HTML element and should be considered strictly a modeling artifact.

The following attributes are captured as tagged values of the «client page». The values of the HTML attributes are captured in the tagged value exactly as they appear in the HTML code. For example, the following HTML document defines an id, class, and onload handler.

```
<HTML>
<HEAD><TITLE>My home page</TITLE></HEAD>
<BODY id="RID0A4F52E4" class="info" onload="alert('hi!')">
<H1>Welcome to my home page.</H1>
</BODY>
```

This HTML fragment maps to a single «client page» whose name is derived from the page component name (home.html).

Client Page Class

Tagged Value	Value
title	My home page
id	RID0A4F52E4
class	info
onload	alert('hi!')

The <BODY> element has the following attributes.

Attribute	Description	Tagged Value
onload	Occurs when the user agent finishes loading a window or all frames within a <FRAMESET>.	*onload*
onunload	Occurs when the user agent removes a document from a window or a frame.	*onunload*

The core HTML attributes follow.

Attribute	Description	Tagged Value
id	Assigns a name to an element. This name must be unique in a document.	*id*
class	Assigns a class to the body.	*class*

The following standard events are also captured as tagged values of the «client page».

Attribute	Description	Tagged Value
onclick	Occurs when the pointing device button is clicked over an element.	*onclick*
ondblclick	Occurs when the pointing device button is double clicked over an element.	*ondblclick*
onmousedown	Occurs when the pointing device button over an element is clicked.	*onmousedown*
onmouseup	Occurs when the pointing device button is released over an element.	*onmouseup*
onmouseover	Occurs when the pointing device is moved onto an element.	*onmouseover*
onmousemove	Occurs when the pointing device is moved while over an element.	*onmousemove*
onmouseout	Occurs when the pointing device is moved away from an element.	*onmouseout*
onkeypress	Occurs when a key is pressed and released over an element.	*onkeypress*
onkeydown	Occurs when a key is pressed over an element.	*onkeydown*
onkeyup	Occurs when a key is released over an element.	*onkeyup*

<TITLE> Element

See the <BODY> element description. The inner text of the <TITLE> element, located within the <HEAD> element, maps to the `title` tagged value of the «client page» class.

`<A>` **Element**

The anchor element (`<A>`) can be an anchor or a link to another URI. As an anchor, this element defines a named location in a document, typically done to allow other links to specify and to reference a specific location within a document. Anchors also define selections of text that can capture and handle events. In a sense, it is a way to name a text region for use by DHTML scripts. To be used as an anchor, the element must define the `name` and/or `id` attributes.

As a link,[1] the anchor element represents a navigational path to another URI. The anchor element functions as a link only when the `href` attribute is defined. The value of the `href` attribute is the URL that the browser will request when the user activates the anchor, or clicks it. If the `target` attribute is defined, the requested URL is directed to a specific frame or window. The value of the `target` indicates the window location to load the URL into.

Only anchor elements functioning as links are mapped to UML associations. Anchor-only `<A>` elements are generally not considered structural elements at the UML logical-view level; however, in some circumstances, they might be. For example, event handlers might be assigned by the element, and those scripts might be part of significant client-side logic. The use of `<A>` elements might also identify something within a document that may be of significance, that may be directly referenced by something outside the page. The modeling of anchor-only `<A>` elements should be an option. When turned on, an `<A>` element without an `href` attribute specified will map to a «client page» attribute whose data type is Anchor.

Anchor links—`<A>` elements with `href` attributes specified—map to directed associations, stereotyped «link» from «client page» classes to other classes in the logical view. The supplier class must be a «client page», «server page», «frameset», or «targeted link» stereotyped class.

The following HTML fragment is from a page whose URL is `http://www.myco.com/cart.asp`.

```
<a href="www.myco.com/policies/shipping.html">Shipping Policies</a>
...
<a href="checkout.jsp">Checkout current shopping cart</a>
...
<a name="shop" href="/catalog/cover.html"
  onmouseover="flipImage('product')">
  Shop for more</a>
```

This document is modeled with the UML elements shown in Figure A-3.

---

1. This is not to be confused with the `<LINK>` element, which is similar to but not the same as an anchor link.

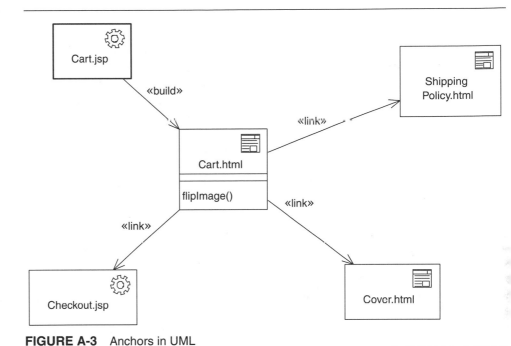

FIGURE A-3 Anchors in UML

Element Attributes Anchor elements share the common HTML attributes, and the UML «link» association defines the same tagged values as in the core HTML attributes. Anchor elements also share the standard events in the common HTML event attributes. In addition to these events, the anchor link accepts the following events.

Attribute	Description	Tagged Value
onfocus	Occurs when an element receives focus either by the pointing device or by tabbing navigation.	*onfocus*
onblur	Occurs when an element loses focus either by the pointing device or by tabbing navigation.	*onblur*

The following anchor attributes are also captured and stored as tagged values.

Attribute	Description	Tagged Value
type	Gives an advisory hint as to the content type of the content available at the link target address. This attribute allows user agents to use a fallback mechanism rather than to fetch the content if they are advised that they will get content in a content type they do not support. Authors who use this attribute take responsibility for managing the risk	*type*

Attribute	Description	Tagged Value
	that it may become inconsistent with the content available at the link target address.	
rel	Describes the relationship from the current document to the anchor specified by the href attribute. The value of this attribute is a space-separated list of link types. Sanctioned valid values are alternate | appendix | bookmark | chapter | contents | copyright | glossary | help | index | next | prev | section | start | stylesheet | subsection.	rel
rev	Describes a reverse link from the anchor specified by the href attribute to the current document. The value of this attribute is a space-separated list of link types (see valid values for rel).	rev
	Although there is no formal attribute for the link type, the tagged value link type indicates whether this association was generated from the <LINK> element or from an <A> or an <AREA> element. <LINK> elements appear only in the <HEAD> element and represent document structural relationships that are not directly rendered in the main window. The three possible values for this tagged value are anchor | area | link (see the <link> and the <area> element descriptions for more information). Also note that this tagged value has no connection with the term *link type* used to define the rel and the rev attributes; it's another case of too many concepts and two few words to describe them.	link type
innerText	(Optional): The value of the anchor element. This text appears between the opening and closing <a> tags.	innerText

HTTP URL Parameters   The specification for the HTTP GET request method specifies how parameters can be included with the page request. The URL is appended with a question mark (?) followed by ampersand-separated key/value pairs. The key represents the parameter name, followed by an equal sign and the value. Spaces in the values must be converted to '%20' or '+' characters (see specific Web server documentation

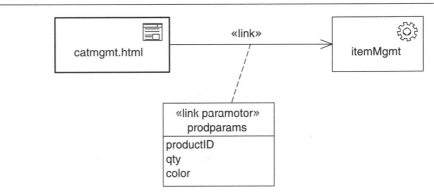

FIGURE A-4   Anchor link using link class

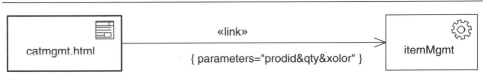

FIGURE A-5   Anchor link using tagged value

for allowable sets). Most Web servers allow parameters to be captured with the HTTP
POST request method as well.

The following example has an anchor link to the `additem.asp` page. The three
parameters are `prodid`, `qty`, and `color`. The value for `color` is `light blue`, and
because there is a space in it, a `%20` replaces it in the HTML URL.

```
<a href="additem.asp?prodid=3921&qty=1&color=light%20blue"
  Light Blue Cardigan</a>
```

There are two ways to model this anchor element. The parameters either map to a
«link parameter» stereotyped association class (Figure A-4) or are simply captured as
a single tagged value (Figure A-5). The link class should model as a nested class of
the «client page» that owns the «link» association, that is, the client class.

URL Uniqueness. The determination of the complete set of «link» associations directed
from a «client page» class is based on a combination of destination URL, parameter
content, and specified target.[2] For example, the following code fragment is modeled
with only two «link» associations, with one anchor's multiplicity set to `0..n`.

---

2. See the section `<FRAMESET>` Element later in this appendix for a description of targets and frames.

```
<a href="add.asp?prodid=3921">sweater</a>
<a href="add.asp?prodid=8327">shoes</a>
<a href="add.asp?prodid=3832">gloves</a>
<a href="add.asp?action=save">Complete transaction</a>
```

In this example (Figure A-6), two distinct «link» associations are made. Even though they reference the same page component, the combination of destination URL (add.asp) and parameter collection (prodid or action) is what defines unique «link» associations. When more than one anchor element maps to a class association, the multiplicity on the supplier role is set to 0..n.

In Figure A-7, the «link» elements are drawn from the client class («client page» cart html) to the supplier class («server page» add). It is important to point out that

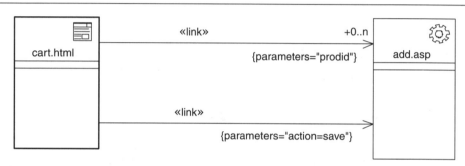

FIGURE A-6   Anchor elements

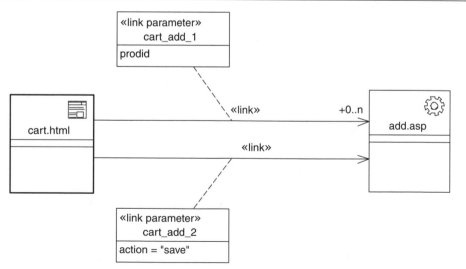

FIGURE A-7   Anchor elements using link classes

the URL `additem.asp` is constructed from the component that realizes the `add` «server page» class, not the class itself. This is how the class can be named `add` in the logical view yet be referenced by the URL `additem.asp`. The missing piece in this example is the component `additem.asp` in the component view that realizes the `add` class.

Targeted Links   See the section <FRAMESET> Element later in this appendix.

<AREA> Element

An <AREA> element is always a child element of a <MAP> element. The only job of the <MAP> element is to name and to contain a set of <AREA> elements. The <AREA> element identifies a region of main architectural significance in that it acts as a «link»; accordingly, it maps directly to a «link» stereotyped association. This association may, of course, be a targeted association. Some additional tagged values required for an <AREA> element follow.

Attribute	Description	Tagged Value
shape	Controls the interpretation of the coordinates. Acceptable values are `rect` | `circle` | `poly` | `default`.	*shape*
coords	A comma-separated list of lengths that define the limits of the bounds of the area region. Used in conjunction with the shape.	*coords*

Because it maps to a «link» association, the <AREA> element also captures the «link» events listed for anchor element event attributes in the section <BODY> Element Attributes earlier in this chapter. See Figure A-8.

```
<map name="navmap">
  <area coords="120, 20, 220, 70" href="northeast.html">
  <area coords="60, 210, 130, 180" href="southern.html">
  <area coords="10, 10, 120, 270" href="western.html">
</map>
```

<LINK> Element

The <LINK> element belongs in the <HEAD> element and is the place to establish links with external documents as style sheets and font definition files. The most common use of this tag is to reference an external style sheet definition. When the relationship is set to `stylesheet`, this element maps to a dependency relationship from the «client page» to the «style sheet» class. Otherwise, the <LINK> elements map to «link» stereotyped associations where the tagged value of *link type* is set to `link` instead of to the more common `anchor`. Additionally, the *rel* and the *rev* tagged values are typically also set.

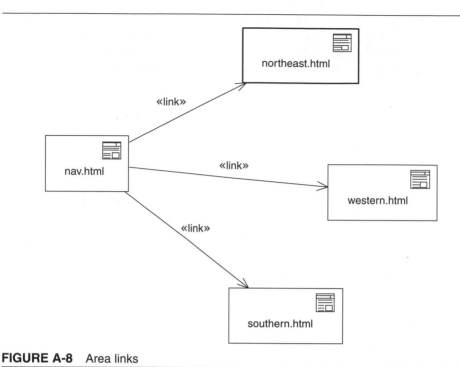

FIGURE A-8   Area links

The «link» association is created only when a valid URL is referenced by the href attribute. In this case, a «link» association is created to the page: «client page», «server page», «frameset», or «style sheet». If the relationship type is "style sheet" and the file that the URL resolves to is found on the file system, a «style sheet» component and class are added to the model.

When the rel attribute (relationship) is set to style sheet, the URL referenced by the href attribute represents a dependency on an included Cascading Style Sheet (CSS) file.

```
<head>
  <title>Section 3</title>
  <link rev="Prev" href="sect2.html">
  <link rel="Next" href="sect4.html">
  <link rel="stylesheet" type="text/css" href="stdStyle.css">
<head>
```

In this example, all the resulting «link» associations have their link type tagged value set to "link". The rev, rel, and type attributes are also captured as tagged values in the «link» associations. See Figure A-9.

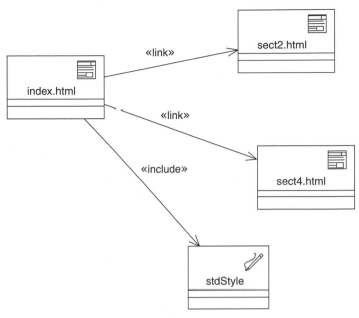

FIGURE A-9   Class diagram for <LINK> elements

<FORM> Element

A <FORM> defined in an HTML page maps directly to an «HTML form» stereotyped class. An aggregation relationship indicates that the form is completely contained by the HTML page. The component that realizes the «client page» must also realize the «HTML form». The name of the «HTML form» class comes from the name attribute of the <FORM> element.

The method attribute is captured as a tagged value. Its valid values are GET | POST. The default value is POST.[3]

When the action attribute contains a valid HTTP URL, the element maps to a «submit» stereotyped directed association. This directed association typically points to the «server page» that is realized by the component that the URL resolves to. It is still technically correct for the «submit» association to point to any stereotyped page that the component realizes: «server page», «client page», or «frameset». In the

---

3. In reality, most browsers default to GET, which is, however, deprecated owing to internationalization problems. Nonetheless, it is likely that GET will be around for a long time to come.

majority of situations, however, the relationship is most clearly indicated by a directed association to the «server page» class.

The attributes and tagged values associated with the «submit» association follow. See Figure A-10.

Attribute	Description	Tagged Value
action	In the case of non-HTTP URI references, this tagged value captures the URI as a string. For example, the action attribute might be a mailto reference: action="mailto:jconallen@ rational.com".	action
method	Indicates how the form's data should be sent to the server. The two valid values are POST | GET. POST is the default if none is specified.	method

The results of a submitted form can be directed to another frame or window. As with targeted link associations, a «targeted link» class and a «target» stereotyped class are defined in the model. See Figure A-11.

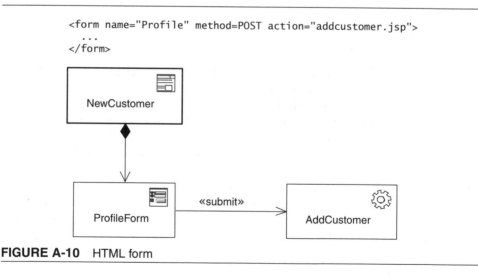

```
<form name="Profile" method=POST action="addcustomer.jsp">
   ...
</form>
```

FIGURE A-10   HTML form

```
<form name="Profile" method=POST action="addcust.asp" target="results">
  ...
</form>
```

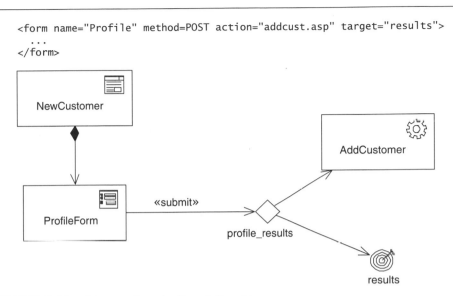

FIGURE A-11   A targeted «submit» relationship

<INPUT> Element

The <INPUT> element is an overloaded input field control that is placed in a <FORM> element. The <INPUT> element takes on many forms, depending on its type attribute, as follows.

Input Type	Description	Attribute Stereotype
text	A one-line field for typing text that gets submitted as the value of the element. For a multiple-line field, see the <TEXTAREA> element.	text
password	A text field that presents bullets or asterisks for each typed character to ensure over-the-shoulder privacy for the user. The plain-language text is submitted as the value for this element.	password
checkbox	A free-standing check box that provides two states: active and inactive. Its label is created by HTML text before or after the <INPUT> element tag. The value attribute value is submitted with a form, so multiple check boxes can have the same name but different values if the server script wants its data that way.	checkbox

Input Type	Description	Attribute Stereotype
radio	One of a related group of On/off buttons. Assigning the same value to the name attribute of multiple radio buttons assembles them in a related group. Clicking one button in the group activates it and unhighlights all others. The value attribute is submitted with a form.	radio
submit	The button for submitting the form. A custom label can be assigned by the value attribute. If name and value attributes are assigned for the element, their values are submitted with the form.	submit
reset	The button for reverting the form's elements to the values they had when the form initially loaded into the client. A custom label can be assigned via the value attribute.	reset
file	A button and a field that let the user select a local file for eventual uploading to the server. A click of the button generates a File dialog, and the name, or pathname, of the selected file appears in the field. The server must have a script running to accept the incoming file at submission time.	file
hidden	An invisible field often used to carry over database or state data from submission to submission without having to store the temporary data on the server. The name/value pair is submitted with the form.	hidden
image	A button that submits the form. The coordinate points x, y of the clicked image are submitted as two name/value pairs.	image
button	A clickable button whose action must be scripted. Its label is assigned by the value attribute. If you want to use HTML to format the label of a button, use the <BUTTON> element instead.	button

<INPUT> tags map to attributes of the «HTML form» stereotyped class. Each attribute of the class is itself stereotyped to indicate the input type. Each input attribute defined for the «HTML form» responds to the standard events listed in the section <BODY> Element Attributes and shares the same core tagged values described in that section.

The following attributes and tagged values are associated with <INPUT>-generated «HTML form» class attributes.

Attribute	Description	Tagged Value
checked	For check box and radio button input types, this Boolean value indicates whether the button is turned on when first rendered. Scripts can modify this value.	*checked*
disabled	A Boolean value that if true, disables—or makes inactive yet viewable—and is therefore unable to respond to user events.	*disabled*
maxlength	Defines the maximum number of characters that may be typed into a text field. Typically, the browser beeps when this limit is exceeded. This should not be confused with the size attribute.	*maxlength*
readonly	A Boolean value indicating that the control cannot be changed by the user.	*readonly*
size	Sets the character width of text input types.	*size*
src	A URL reference to image data to be rendered in an image-type input control.	*src*
tabindex	A number that indicates the sequence of this element within the tabbing order of all focusable elements in the document.	*tabindex*

The type attribute maps directly to the data type of the «HTML form» class attribute. The value attribute maps to the class attribute's initial value. If the name attribute is not specified, one is derived from the name of the form, or client page, name and the input data type.

<INPUT> elements also respond to the following events.

Attribute	Description	Tagged Value
onfocus	Occurs when an element receives focus either by the pointing device or by tabbing navigation.	*onfocus*
onblur	Occurs when an element loses focus either by the pointing device or by tabbing navigation.	*onblur*
onselect	Occurs when a user selects some text in a text field.	*onselect*
onchange	Occurs when a control loses the input focus and its value has been modified since gaining focus.	*onchange*

The following HTML code is modeled by an «HTML form» class. HTML forms do not specify operations, only attributes, since any scripts defined in a form element are visible in page scope: global object scope. See Figure A-12.

```html
<form name="Profile" method=POST action="updatedata">
  <input type="button" value="Toggle Sound" onClick="toggleSnd()">
  <input type="checkbox" name="connections" value="ISDN">ISDN
  <input type="checkbox" name="connections" value="DSL">ADSL/DSL
  <input type="checkbox" name="connections" value="T1">T1 (fractional)
  <input type="file" name="uploadFile">
  <input type="hidden" name="prevState" value="modify">
  <input type="image" name="graphicSubmit" src="submit.jpg" height=40
         width=40>
  <input type="password" name="pwd" maxlength=12 size=20>
  <input type="radio" name="creditcard" value="Mastercard">Mastercard
  <input type="radio" name="creditcard" value="Visa">Visa
  <input type="reset">
  SSN: <input type="text" name="ssn" value="###-##-####"
             onclick="validateSSN(this)">
  <button name="Check" type="button" value="CheckMe">Check it</button>
  <select name="Role" MULTIPLE>
    <option value="0">Admin</option>
    <option value="1">Dev</option>
    <option value="2">Guest</option>
  </select>
  <input type="submit" value="Send Encrypted">
</form>
```

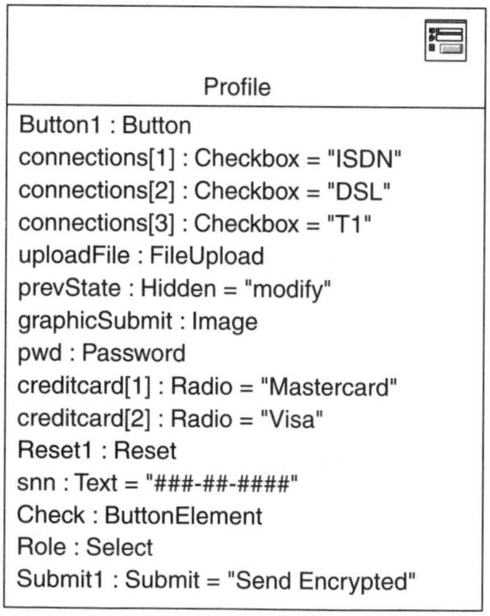

Profile
Button1 : Button
connections[1] : Checkbox = "ISDN"
connections[2] : Checkbox = "DSL"
connections[3] : Checkbox = "T1"
uploadFile : FileUpload
prevState : Hidden = "modify"
graphicSubmit : Image
pwd : Password
creditcard[1] : Radio = "Mastercard"
creditcard[2] : Radio = "Visa"
Reset1 : Reset
snn : Text = "###-##-####"
Check : ButtonElement
Role : Select
Submit1 : Submit = "Send Encrypted"

FIGURE A-12 HTML form

For the most part, the modeling rules are to use the element name attribute as the name of the class attribute and the value element attribute as the initial value of the class attribute. The type of the input element sets the type of the class attribute. When an element name attribute is not specified, one is derived from the stereotype and the number of occurrences in the form, to maintain uniqueness.

Unfortunately, HTML does not require uniqueness with field names in a <FORM>. This is typically the case with radio buttons. To define a radio group in an HTML form, the same name is used for the attribute of the input element. UML maintains a uniqueness constraint on attribute names; the use of array syntax can provide unique attribute names. The index of the array—brackets—is used to define an attribute's ordinal value.

Some browsers allow <INPUT> elements to be defined and used outside a <FORM>. In these cases, the element maps to a stereotyped attribute of the «client page».

<SELECT> Element

The <SELECT> element is an input control that allows the user to select from a list of options. Each option is identified by a string, which is displayed in either a scrolling list—list box—or a pop-up menu, or combo box.

This element maps directly to a class attribute whose data type is select. This attribute is typically an attribute of an «HTML form» class. Some browsers, such as Internet Explorer, however, allow <SELECT> elements to be defined outside the context of a form, in which case this element is an attribute of the «client page» class.

The individual <OPTION> elements typically found as children of a <SELECT> element are not considered architecturally significant. The reason is that they are often dynamically generated or constructed as a result of domain knowledge, not for structural reasons. See Figure A-13.

```
<form name="ColorSelect" method=POST action="setcolor.asp">
  <select name="FavoriteColor" MULTIPLE size=3 >
    <option value="blue">Blue
    <option value="green">Green
    <option value="yellow">Yellow
    <option value="red">Red
    <option value="orange">Orange
  </select>
  <input type="submit" value="Request Color">
</form>
```

```
                                                        [icon]
                        ColorSelect
            ─────────────────────────────────────────
            FavoriteColor : Select
            Submit1 : Submit = "Request Color"
```

FIGURE A-13 An HTML <FORM> modeled with a «form» stereotype

The <SELECT> element maps directly to an «HTML Form» class attribute with a data type of select. If the name attribute is not specified, one is derived from the stereotype name and the ordinal value of the number of select elements is specified in the form: Select1, Select2, and so on.

The <SELECT> element also uses the core HTML attributes and the standard HTML event attributes (see the section <BODY> Element Attributes). In addition to these attributes and tagged values, the <SELECT> element uses the following element attributes.

Attribute	Description	Tagged Value
disabled	Indicates that the control is initially rendered as disabled.	disabled
size	Specifies the number of rows the list box should display. The value 1 indicates that the selection is rendered as a pop-up menu, or combo box.	size
tabindex	A number indicating the sequence of this element within the tabbing order of all focusable elements in the document.	tabindex

The <SELECT> element also responds to the following events.

Attribute	Description	Tagged Value
onfocus	Occurs when an element receives focus either by the pointing device or by tabbing navigation.	onfocus
onblur	Occurs when an element loses focus either by the pointing device or by tabbing navigation.	onblur
onchange	Occurs when a control loses the input focus and its value has been modified since gaining focus.	onchange

<TEXTAREA> Element

The <TEXTAREA> element is a multiline text input control that captures from the user text input that spans multiple lines or that is of sufficient length to make single-line text inputs unusable. <TEXTAREA> elements require an end tag, and their field value is the inner HTML text.

The <TEXTAREA> element defines the attributes rows and cols to indicate the number of lines deep and the number of characters wide the text box should be. The <TEXTAREA> element maps directly to an «HTML form» class attribute with a data type of Textarea, or when not in the context of a form, as an attribute of the «client page». The <TEXTAREA element supports the core HTML attributes and the standard

HTML event attributes (see the section <BODY> Element Attributes). In addition to these events, the <TEXTAREA> element responds to the following events.

Attribute	Description	Tagged Value
onfocus	Occurs when an element receives focus either by the pointing device or by tabbing navigation.	*onfocus*
onblur	Occurs when an element loses focus either by the pointing device or by tabbing navigation.	*onblur*
onselect	Occurs when a user selects some text in a text field.	*onselect*
onchange	Occurs when a control loses the input focus and its value has been modified since gaining focus.	*onchange*

Additional <TEXTAREA> attributes and tagged values follow.

Attribute	Description	Tagged Value
disabled	Indicates that the control is initially rendered as disabled.	*disabled*
size	Specifies the number of rows the list box should display. The value 1 indicates that the selection is rendered as a pop-up menu, or combo box.	*size*
tabindex	A number indicating the sequence of this element within the tabbing order of all of the focusable elements in the document.	*tabindex*
readonly	A Boolean value indicating that the control cannot be changed by the user.	*readonly*

<BUTTON> Element

The <BUTTON> element is similar to the <INPUT> button but offers some additional control. This element maps directly to an «HTML form» attribute or, when not in the context of a form, the «client page». The data type of the «HTML Form» class attribute is "ButtonElement" to distinguish it from the <INPUT> element type "Button".

The name attribute of the element is used as the class attribute name. If no name is specified in HTML, one is derived from the stereotype and the ordinal value of the number of <BUTTON> elements defined in the context. The value attribute of the element is modeled as the attribute's initial value.

This element supports the core HTML events and the standard HTML attributes and tagged values (see the section <BODY> Element Attributes). <BUTTON> elements also support the following events.

```
<form name="ConnectionForm">
  <button name="connections" value="ISDN">ISDN</button>
</form>
```

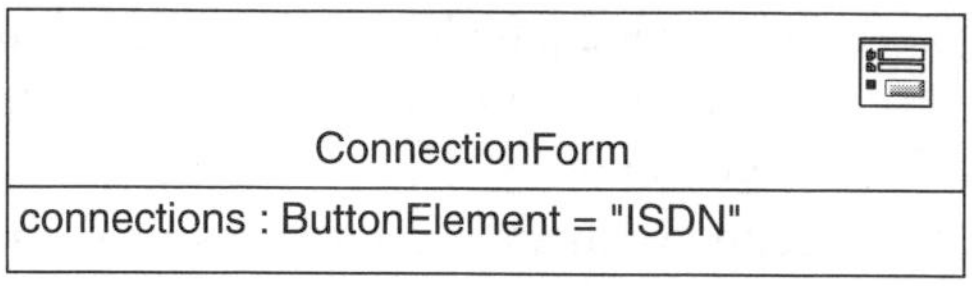

```
┌─────────────────────────────────────────────┐
│                                        ▤     │
│              ConnectionForm                  │
├─────────────────────────────────────────────┤
│ connections : ButtonElement = "ISDN"         │
└─────────────────────────────────────────────┘
```

FIGURE A-14   An HTML <BUTTON> modeled as an attribute of a «form» class

Attribute	Description	Tagged Value
onfocus	Occurs when an element receives focus either by the pointing device or by tabbing navigation.	*onfocus*
onblur	Occurs when an element loses focus either by the pointing device or by tabbing navigation.	*onblur*

This element supports the following additional element attributes. See Figure A-14.

Attribute	Description	Tagged Value
disabled	Indicates that the control is initially rendered as disabled.	*disabled*
type	Defines the internal style of browser button. The allowable set of values is button | reset | submit; default value is button.	*type*
tabindex	A number indicating the sequence of this element within the tabbing order of all focusable elements in the document.	*tabindex*
readonly	A Boolean value indicating that the control cannot changed by the user.	*readonly*

<OBJECT> Element

The <OBJECT> element supplies the browser with information to load and to render data types that are not natively supported by the browser. If the browser must load an external program, such as an applet or a plug-in, the information about the content that is to be rendered is contained by the object element, its attributes and, optionally, associated <PARAM> elements nested inside it. Note that the <APPLET> and the <EMBED> elements have been deprecated in favor of the <OBJECT> element.

The code attribute is used by IE to enable the <OBJECT> element to load applets. It is hoped that in the future, the classid attribute will be the single source for identifying an object resource. Today, however, the classid attribute, with a classid protocol

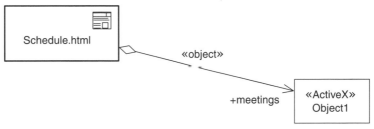

```
<object name="meetings" classid="clsid:83A38BF0-B33A-A4F2-C619A82E891D">
</object>
```

FIGURE A-15   <OBJECT> element specifying an ActiveX control

specified, typically indicates an ActiveX control resource. The code attribute typically specifies a Java class.

The <OBJECT> element is modeled as a stereotyped containment association from a «client page». The stereotype is «object». The element and the association support the core HTML attributes and the standard HTML event attributes (see the section <BODY> Element Attributes). If the element's name attribute is specified, it is used as the association name. If the classid attribute specifies a classid: protocol resource, it is modeled as a relationship to an ActiveX (or COM) object. See Figure A-15.

The clsid attribute is captured as a tagged value. This allows the developer to give a more meaningful name to the class after reverse engineering it, without losing important semantical information. The name attribute of the <OBJECT> element is used as the supplier role name. If the component's «coclass»[4] exists in the model with the «classid» specified, a directional containment association is drawn to the «coclass», instead of to the «ActiveX» stereotyped placeholder class.

The following element attributes are modeled as tagged values.

Attribute	Description	Tagged Value
classid	Specifies the location of an object's implementation via a URI. The attribute may be used with or as an alternative to the data attribute, depending on the type of object involved.	classid
data	Specifies the location of the object's data: for instance, image data for objects defining images or, more generally, a serialized form of an object that can be used to recreate it. If given as a relative URI, it should be interpreted relative to the codebase attribute.	data

---

4. This stereotype is part of Rational Rose's COM Profile.

Attribute	Description	Tagged Value
codebase	Specifies the base path used to resolve relative URIs specified by the classid, data, and archive attributes. When absent, its default value is the base URI of the current document.	*codebase*
type	Specifies the content type for the data specified by data. This attribute is optional but recommended when data is specified; it allows the user agent to avoid loading information for unsupported content types. If the value of this attribute differs from the HTTP content type returned by the server when the object is retrieved, the HTTP content type takes precedence.	*type*
codetype	Specifies the content type of data expected when downloading the object specified by classid. This attribute is optional but recommended when classid is specified because it allows the user agent to avoid loading information for unsupported content types. When absent, it defaults to the value of the type attribute.	*codetype*
archive	Used to specify a space-separated list of URIs for archives containing resources relevant to the object, which may include the resources specified by the classid and data attributes. Preloading archives will generally result in reduced load times for objects. Archives specified as relative URIs should be interpreted relative to the codebase attribute.	*archive*
tabindex	Specifies the position of the current element in the tabbing order for the current document. This value must be a number between 0 and 32,767. User agents should ignore leading zeros.	*tabindex*

`<PARAM>` **Element**

The `<PARAM>` element, always nested in either an `<OBJECT>` or an `<APPLET>` element, identifies a parameter and a value that should be passed through to the object as it is being loaded. Each `<PARAM>` element maps to an attribute of a special link class on the «object» association. This link class is stereotyped «object parameters». Each attribute of this class represents a `<PARAM>` element. The name attribute of the element is mapped to the name of the attribute of the link class. Its value attribute is mapped to the initial value of the class attribute. There is no WAE definition for the link class's operations. The object tag that is modeled is shown in Figure A-16.

```
<object name="calendar" code=ccalendar.class width=210 height=340>
  <param name="lst_img" value="brunfelsia.jpg;buddleia.jpg">
  <param name="color_fond" value="16761024">
  <param name="color_case" value="16765136">
  <param name="color_Comment" value="16711680">
  <param name="color_empty" value=" 16744576">
  <param name="field" value="DateField">
  <param name="form" value="DateForm">
</object>
```

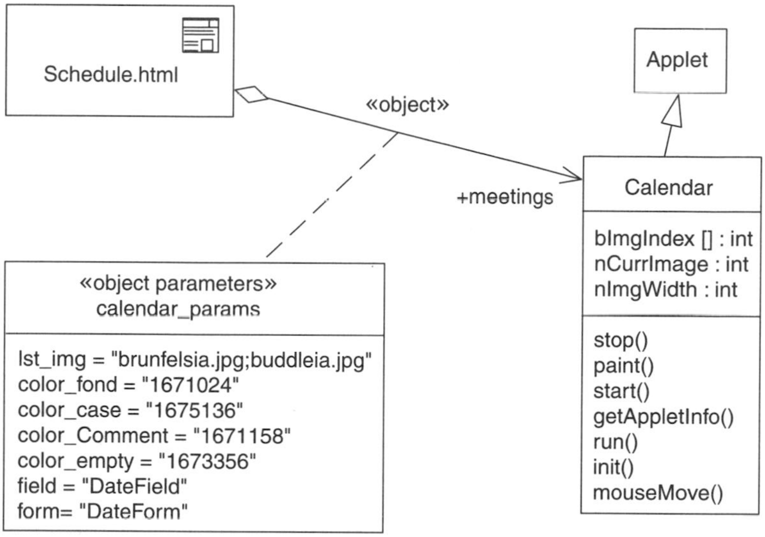

FIGURE A-16   An HTML <OBJECT> tag modeled as an association class

<APPLET> Element

Because the <APPLET> element is being deprecated and the <OBJECT> tag is now the preferred way to include an applet in a page, this element is modeled with the «object» association. See the preceding section, <OBJECT> Element, for details.

<SCRIPT> Element

This element is a container for lines of script code, typically written in JavaScript, although any scripting language can be defined. If another client-side scripting language is supported, the default scripting language should be a tagged value of the class. Additionally, the default scripting language should be a tagged value of all non-stereotyped attributes and operations of a «client page» and a «frameset» stereotyped class.

Because it is not HTML, the inner text in a <SCRIPT> element is parsed differently. The language of the script is identified by the language attribute of the <SCRIPT> element, JavaScript being the most common default.

The only portions of script modeled in UML are

- Variable declarations
- Function definitions

Variable declarations begin with the keyword var, followed by the variable name. Variables defined within the scope of the page—not within a function definition—are reverse engineered into an attribute of the «client page» class.

JavaScript variables are typeless, so no type information is reverse engineered into UML. If the variable is initialized with a primitive value, this is reverse engineered as the initial value of the attribute. Variables initialized with the results of a statement are not reverse engineered: for example, var foo = fcn();.

When a variable is initialized with a JavaScript or DOM object, however, useful type information can be identified for the class attribute. For example, Image is a standard object type available with most JavaScript implementations. The following statement should be reverse engineered into an attribute of type Image or as an association to an Image class with a role name of chart:

```
var chart = new Image();
```

The decision to reverse engineer into an attribute or an association should be a reverse-engineering option. For example, if the JavaScript framework library was loaded and the reverse-engineering option for reverse engineering known objects into associations, this statement would reverse engineer into an association with the role name of chart.

It is possible to declare a variable without the var statement by simply using it. However, this type of variable declaration should not be modeled as an attribute, by default.

A function is defined with the function statement. The function statement is followed by the name of the function and an optional list of comma-separated parameter names enclosed in parentheses. The body of function statements, enclosed in braces, follows.

Only functions defined in the scope of the page[5] need be modeled. In JavaScript 1.2, a function can be defined in the scope of another function. This embedded function is not usually modeled; nor are functions defined in the scope of an if/else statement block, do/while statement block, for statement block, while statement block, or switch statement block. The only functions modeled are those declared in the global object,[6] where the reference this resolves to the global object, or within a statement block or a compound statement—brace-enclosed collection of statements—of the global object. UML cannot model nested functions easily. All functions declared in this global object scope reverse engineer into an operation of the «client page».

---

5. JavaScript global object scope.

6. See Section 4.6.1 in David Flanagan, *JavaScript: The Definitive Reference* (Sebastopol, CA: O'Reilly & Assoociates, 1998).

The modeling of dynamically assigned event handlers is not appropriate for a structural model. For example, the following is *not* modeled in structural diagrams:

```
<script ... >
  function initialize() { /* do something */ }
  ..
  onload = initialize;
</script>
```

See the JavaScript reference document for a complete discussion of JavaScript syntax, the rules for comments, and string definition escape characters.

The following fragment reverse engineers into a single «client page» class with a single operation called imageChange. The operation also defines four typeless parameters (not seen in Figure A-17).

```
<SCRIPT LANGUAGE="JavaScript">
//Below is the code that pre-loads the graphics
{
//These are the large images
var alt0 = new Image();
alt0.src = "white.gif";

//These are the button images
var alt1 = new Image();
alt1.src = "hg_banner.gif";
var alt2 = new Image();
alt2.src = "jg_banner.gif";

//These are the first button graphics
var graphic1 = new Image();
graphic1.src = "but1.gif";
graphic1on = new Image();
graphic1on.src = "but1b.gif";

//These are the second button graphics

var graphic2 = new Image();
graphic2.src = "but2.gif";
graphic2on = new Image();
graphic2on.src = "but2b.gif";
}

//This is the function that calls for the change in the button's
function imageChange(imageID,imageName,imageID2,imageName2) {
  document.images[imageID].src = eval(imageName + ".src");
  document.images[imageID2].src = eval(imageName2 + ".src");
}

</SCRIPT>

...

<A HREF="http://www.htmlgoodies.com"
  onMouseOver="imageChange('global','alt1','one','graphic1on')"
```

```
onMouseOut="imageChange('global','alt0','one','graphic1')">
<IMG SRC="but1.gif" BORDER="0" NAME="one"></A>

<A HREF="http://www.javagoodies.com"
onMouseOver="imageChange('global','alt2','two','graphic2on')"
onMouseOut="imageChange('global','alt0','two','graphic2')">
<IMG SRC="but2.gif" BORDER="0" NAME="two"></A>

<IMG SRC="white.gif" WIDTH="130" HEIGHT="130" NAME="global">
```

JavaScript variables can be modeled as attributes or as associations. Semantically, the two are the same; however, diagrams modeled as attributes make the variables more compact, yet the connections to the common JavaScript framework are not immediately apparent. The preceding code modeled with associations is shown in Figure A-17. If the variables are modeled as attributes—treated as primitives—the class of Figure A-18 is drawn.

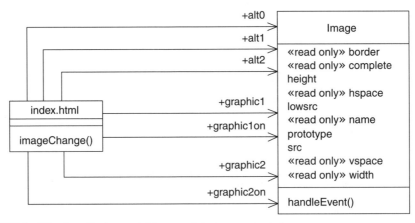

FIGURE A-17   JavaScript variables modeled as associations

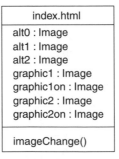

FIGURE A-18   JavaScript variables as attributes

```
<script language="JavaScript" src="stringParseLib.js"></script>
```

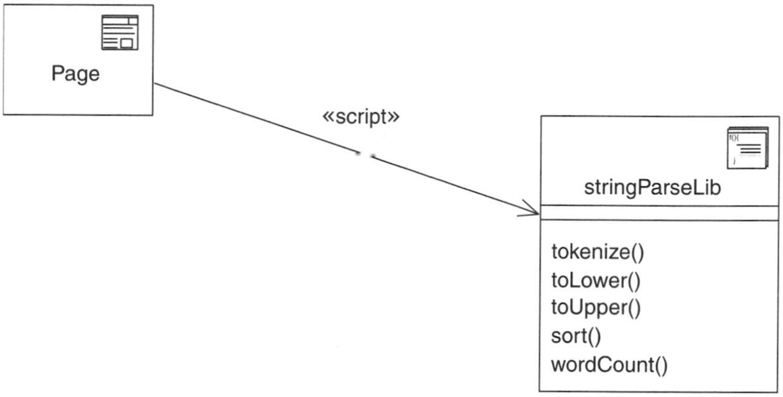

FIGURE A-19   Client-side JavaScript includes

Note that the Image class definition comes from the JavaScript Object Library Framework. The «read only» stereotype is used only by this framework and is not part of the WAE.

All reverse-engineered operations and attributes are by default public because the DOM does not support encapsulation.

A <SCRIPT> element may specify an src attribute. If this attribute is set, the URL resolves to a file with the .js extension, required in HTML 4. Then a «script library» component is expressed in the component view, and a «script library» stereotyped class is drawn in the logical view.

A «script» stereotyped association is created from the «client page» class and the «script library» class. All JavaScript var and function definitions are reverse engineered into the «script library» class, not the «client page». See Figure A-19.

<FRAMESET> Element

Setting the anchor element attribute target indicates that the results of the page request should be rendered in a specific browser frame or window. The frame or window is referenced by name, with the following names reserved.

Reserved Name	Description
_blank	The user agent should load the designated document in a new, unnamed window.
_sel	The user agent should load the document in the same frame as the element that refers to this target.
_parent	The user agent should load the document into the immediate <FRAMESET> parent of the current frame. This value is equivalent to _self if the current frame has no parent.

Reserved Name	Description
_top	The user agent should load the document into the full, original window, thereby canceling all other frames. This value is equivalent to _self if the current frame has no parent.

The target parameter is typically used in the context of a frameset. The only other use is when the target represents a separate window, or browser instance. In either case, an anchor link with a target attribute specified indicates a *targeted link*. In the case of a targeted link, the anchor element is modeled by a standard «link» association to a «targeted link» stereotyped *n*-ary association. The «targeted link» association connects a link request with a resource to a target. For example, a book.html fragment follows:

```
<frameset cols="150,*">
  <frame src="toc.html">
  <frame name="content" src="javascript:parent.blank()">
</frameset>
```

A toc.html fragment follows:

```
<a href="chap1.html" target="content">Chapter 1</a>
<a href="chap2.html" target="content">Chapter 2</a>
<a href="chap3.html" target="content">Chapter 3</a>
```

The resulting UML model is expressed in the class diagram of Figure A-20.

Modeling these HTML fragments creates a «frameset» stereotyped class named Book that maps directly to the <FRAMESET> element. The name of the «frameset» class is derived from the page name. The frameset contains two elements: a target named content and a «client page» named toc.html.

Because only the second <frame> defines a name, only one «target» stereotyped class is identified. This can be confusing since two frames are defined. The <FRAME> element maps to the containment relationship, not to any stereotyped class. Thus, if the frameset defines four frame elements, there should be four aggregations from the «frameset» class. This example also demonstrates how the src might be used to define a non-HTTP URI. The effective behavior is to ensure that the content frame is blank when loaded. In this situation, the src attribute reverse engineers into the src tagged value of the «target» class.

In general, if the <FRAME> defines a name, this containment relationship is to a «target» stereotyped class of that same name. If the frame defines only an src attribute, with a qualified HTTP URI, the containment relationship points directly to the page that the URL points to: «client page», «server page», or even another «frameset». If the <FRAME> defines both name and src attributes, this maps to a «target» stereotyped class with an additional «src» stereotyped directional association to the page: «client page», «server page», or «frameset». When the src attribute points to a non-HTTP

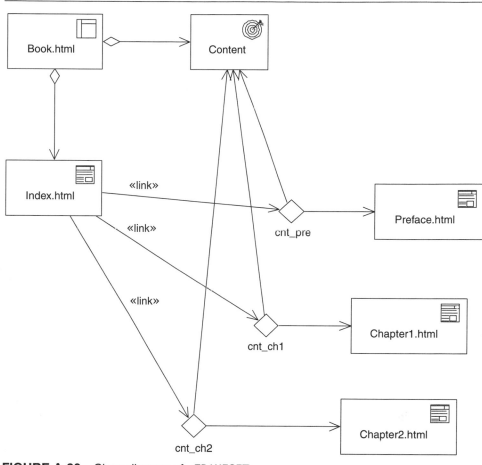

FIGURE A-20 Class diagram of <FRAMESET>

URI, no associations are created, and the value of the src is captured only in a tagged value.

Figure A-21 shows two code samples—for workspace.html and menu.html, respectively, and a diagram of the two framesets.

In this example, both frames define src attributes, one to a dynamic page that has a parameter defined. Only two unique «link» associations are detected in the menu «client page». Both are to the detail «server page». Because they reference different targets, however, they are modeled by two separate «link» associations.

<FRAME> Element

See the section <FRAMESET> Element.

```
<frameset cols="150,*">
  <frame name="itemmenu" src="menu.html">
  <frame name="WorkspaceContent" src="detail.asp?prodid=1">
</frameset>

<a href="detail.asp?prodid=1" target="WorkspaceContent">Sweaters</a>
<a href="detail.asp?prodid=2" target="WorkspaceContent">Shoes</a>
<a href="detail.asp?prodid=3" target="WorkspaceContent">Gloves</a>
<a href="detail.asp?prodid=4" target="WorkspaceContent">Sports cars</a>
<a href="detail.asp?prodid=0">Cover Menu</a>
```

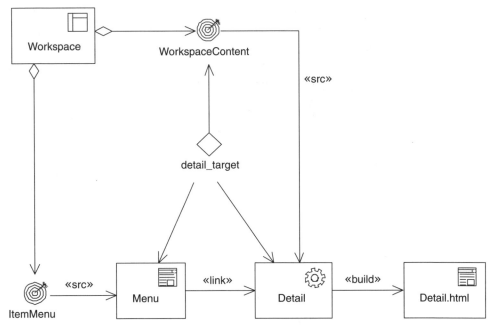

FIGURE A-21   Framesets with initial content specified

<IFRAME> Element

The <IFRAME> element creates an in-line frame within the natural flow of a document's content. This frame is a rectangular space in which another page is loaded.

An <IFRAME> element is reverse engineered into a containment relationship stereotyped «iframe». The width and height attributes are pretty much a presentation issue and can, optionally, be captured in tagged values.

Because a separate page occupies the contents of an <IFRAME>, the frame itself is not responsible for responding to any events. The only applicable element attributes

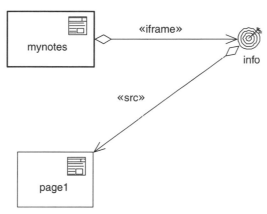

`<iframe src="quotes.html" width=150 height=90>`

FIGURE A-22   The `<IFRAME>` element

`<iframe name="info" src="page1.jsp" width=200 height=50></iframe>`

FIGURE A-23   An HTML `<IFRAME>` element modeled with a stereotyped containment
                   association

and associated tagged values are the `width` and `height` attributes and the core HTML attributes of the section `<BODY>` Element Attributes. See Figure A-22.

If the `name` attribute was specified in the `<IFRAME>` element, this represents a referenceable target that can be the result of a targeted link. In this situation, a «target» stereotyped class is reverse engineered, and an «src» association is created from the target and the intial page to load in the frame. See Figure A-23.

UML to HTML

This section describes the mapping of UML into HTML code in order to implement client page contributions to the code. The icon for each component package, component, and class is shown.

Component Packages

«physical root» Package

A physical root package contains components that map directly to HTTP responding resources: static or dynamic pages. These resources can be requested directly by client browsers or other dynamic pages. Not all components under the physical root package may be requested directly by clients; most can, however. The package structure under a physical root mirrors the file system directory structure of the resources as they are placed on the Web server.

A physical root may define the tagged value "server", which contains the domain name of the server to which this physical root acts as a virtual root. This value is used to resolve URLs' references to logical-view elements, when no «virtual root» package is present.

«virtual root» Package

A virtual root package represents a top-level URL server and path. All elements under this package represent valid URLs.

The virtual root is used to resolve URL references in the logical view. In the logical view, a «client page» class will have a «link» relationship to a class that is realized by an «HttpResource» component that resides under a «virtual root» package.

To resolve a URL, the client class first determines which HTTP resource component realizes the target class. The HTTP resource component is combined with the «virtual root» server tag value and any subpackages in the hierarchy that appear above the HTTP resource. They are all combined to produce a single URL that maps to the logical-view class and that provides a value for generating anchor <a> and form action tag parameters.

Components

«static page» Component

This component maps directly to an HTML, or any static file. This component does not undergo processing before being sent to the client. The file name of the component is the component name. A .html extension is applied by default to names without one.

The content of the HTML file depends on the classes that the component realizes. This component can realize at most one «client page» or «frameset» class but not a «server page» class.

«dynamic page» Component

A dynamic page component is an abstract stereotype indicating that the component requires processing on the server and that it produces dynamic content in the page. Language- and environment-specific profiles will define concrete instances of stereotypes.

«style sheet» Component

When a <LINK> element in the <HEAD> of an HTML document specifies a style sheet (rel = "stylesheet", type="text/css"), the href attribute of the <LINK> identifies a style sheet component. A «style sheet» class and a «style sheet» component are forward engineered into the model. The URL and the physical location of the file are determined by the component package hierarchy and the «virtual root».

«script library» Component

A «script library» stereotyped component maps directly to a file with the extension .js. This file contains JavaScript code that is included in an HTML page or document at the request of the browser. That is, a separate browser request is made to obtain the JavaScript file.

A «script library» component can realize only «script library» classes in the logical view. The file name for the component is determined in the same way as «HTML Page» components, using the «virtual root» package to define the root physical directory.

To implement a «script library» component, all the «script library» classes that it realizes are combined. The result is a set of JavaScript var and function declarations. See the section «Client Page» Class for a description of generating <SCRIPT> elements.

«HTTP Resource» Component

An HTTP resource component maps to a requestable URL in the web server. An HTTP resource component must be owned by a «virtual root» package or by a package under a «virtual root» package hierarchy.

An absolute URL identifier can be derived from the model by using the server name identified in the server tag value of the «virtual root» and using the package hierarchy as the path, with the HTTP resource component name as the final part of the URL.

Classes

«Server Page» Class

This class is the logical abstraction of a Web page as seen by the server. A server page, a Web page that undergoes processing by the Web application server, has relationships with server-side components: databases, middle-tier components, and so on. A server page can stream HTML output as a client page. This relationship is modeled with a «build» relationship to the «client page» class. Server pages can also be used to stream XML or WML (Wireless Markup Language) output. A detailed description of these specifications, however, is beyond the scope of this document.

The implementation and the interpretation of the attributes and operations defined in this class are dependent on the architecture and the technology. The implementation is typically a form of scripted page, such as JSP, ASPX, or PHP. In these technologies, «server page» attributes typically map to primitive variables that are accessible by operations or functions defined within the scope of the page. Operations defined in the page are typically implemented as functions.

«Client Page» Class

A «client page» class, logically, represents the <HTML> element, which has two principal child elements: <HEAD> and <BODY>. The <HEAD> element represents structural information about the HTML page, and the information in it is generally not rendered. The <BODY> element represents the majority of the displayed content.

- *Attributes:* All nonstereotyped attributes map to JavaScript var declarations. If an attribute has a type defined that matches the list of standard JavaScript objects, the variable declaration can be initialized with the new operator. See Figure A-24. In Figure A-25, an association is made to a JavaScript Library–supplied object.

```
<head>
<title>mypage</title>
<script language="JavaScript>
<!--
var browserVersion = new String();
var itemCount;

...

--></script>
</head>
```

mypage
browserVersion : String itemCount
detectVersion()

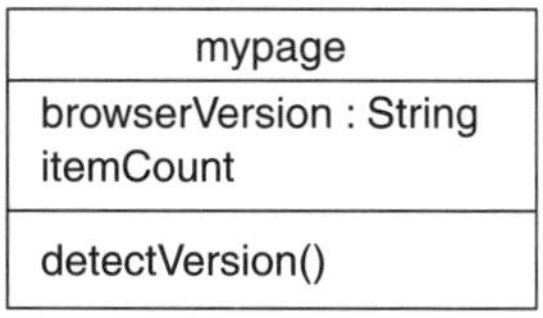

FIGURE A-24　Client page scripting variables as attributes

```
<head>
<title>mypage</title>
<script language="JavaScript>
<!--
var browserVersion = new String();
var itemCount;
var myImage = new Image();
...

--></script>
</head>
```

mypage
browserVersion : String itemCount
scrollBnr()

+myImage →

Image (from Document)

FIGURE A-25　Client page scripting variables as associations

- *Associations:* Code created from directed stereotyped associations from a «client page» depends on the specific association.
- *Operations:* Nonstereotyped operations specified in a «client page» map to JavaScript operations. The function bodies of these unstereotyped operations are derived from an examination of any sequence and activity diagrams associated with the class and its collaborations.

«HTML Form» Class

«HTML Form» stereotyped classes exist only in the context of a «client page» or, theoretically, «framesets». These classes map directly to a <FORM> element. The name of the form is used for the `name` attribute of the <FORM> element. The tagged value for `method` is used to set the `method` attribute; `POST` is the default.

One «submit» stereotyped association is allowed to a page stereotyped class, most likely a «server page». This association is used to determine the `action` attribute, which is set to the URL of the component that realizes the supplier class of the «submit» association (Figure A-26).

Attributes of the form map to form child elements. Only attributes that map to predefined form attribute types are forward engineered. See Figure A-27.

«HTML Form» Attribute Type	HTML Element
text	`<input type="text" ... >`
password	`<input type="password" ...>`
checkbox	`<input type="checkbox" ...>`
radio	`<input type="radio" ...>`

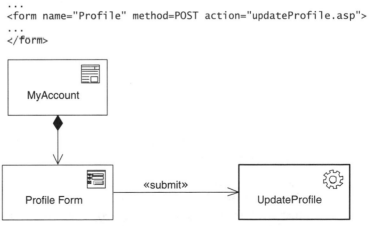

```
...
<form name="Profile" method=POST action="updateProfile.asp">
...
</form>
```

FIGURE A-26 An HTML <FORM> tag modeled as a stereotyped class

submit	`<input type="submit" ...>`
reset	`<input type="reset" ...>`
file	`<input type="file" ...>`
hidden	`<input type="hidden" ...>`
image	`<input type="image" ...>`
button	`<input type="button" ...>`
button element	`<button>`
textarea	`<textarea>`
select	`<select>`

All «HTML Form» attributes share the following tagged values and element attributes that are forward engineered.

Tagged Value	Element Attribute
id	Id
name	Name
disabled	Disabled
tabindex	Tabindex

For any attribute that specifies a single number in array syntax at the end of its name, such as [2], the array syntax is stripped from the name before it is used as an element name. Remember, this syntax was used to resolve the issue of attribute name uniqueness in UML, when it isn't required in HMTL.

If the attribute name is followed by "[0..n]", the attributes should have multiple instances in the form, probably to be determined at runtime.

```
...
<form name="stateoption" method=POST action="setstate">
  <% for(int i=0; i<states.count(); i++ ){
       String name = states.getName(i);
       String value = states.getValue(i);
  %>
     <input type="checkbox" name="state" value="<%=value%>"><%=name%><br>
  <% }
  %>
  <input type="submit" value="Set State">
</form>
```

A brief description of the forward-engineering actions for each value «HTML Form» attribute type follows.

- text: An <INPUT> element is created with the type attribute set to "text". If the class attribute has an initial value specified, it sets the element's value attribute. If the class attribute's tagged values for maxlength and size are specified, they are forward engineered as element attributes.

```
...
<form name="Profile" method=POST action="updatedata">
  <input type="button" value="Toggle Sound" onClick="toggleSnd()">
  <input type="checkbox" name="connections" value="ISDN">ISDN
  <input type="checkbox" name="connections" value="DSL">ADSL/DSL
  <input type="checkbox" name="connections" value="T1">T1 (fractional)
  <input type="file" name="uploadFile">
  <input type="hidden" name="prevState" value="modify">
  <input type="image" name="graphicSubmit" src="submit.jpg" height=40
         width=40>
  <input type="password" name="pwd" maxlength=12 size=20>
  <input type="radio" name="creditcard" value="Mastercard">Mastercard
  <input type="radio" name="creditcard" value="Visa">Visa
  <input type="reset">
  SSN: <input type="text" name="ssn" value="###-##-####"
         onclick="validateSSN(this)">
  <button name="Check" type="button" value="CheckMe">Check it</button>
  <select name="Role" MULTIPLE>
    <option value="0">Admin</option>
    <option value="1">Dev</option>
    <option value="2">Guest</option>
  </select>
  <input type="submit" value="Send Encrypted">
</form>
```

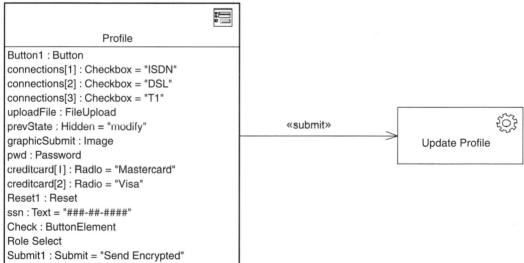

FIGURE A-27   HTML <FORM> fields modeled as attributes

- password: An <input> element is created with the type attribute set to "password". If the class attribute's tagged values for maxlength and size are specified, they are coded as element attributes.

- Checkbox: An <input> element is created with the type attribute set to "checkbox". If the class attribute's tagged value for readonly is set to true, it is coded as an element attribute, or one without a specified value. If the class attribute's tagged value `checked` is set to `true`, the attribute `CHECKED` is coded as a valueless element attribute.

- Radio: An `<input>` element is created with the `type` attribute set to `"radio"`. If the class attribute's tagged value for `readonly` is set to `true`, it is coded as an element attribute, or one without a specified value. *Optional feature:* The first time this is forward engineered, the attribute value appends the tag.

- Submit: An `<input>` element is created with the `type` attribute set to `"submit"`. If the class attribute's tagged value for `disabled` is specified, it is coded as an element attribute. If the class attribute has an initial value specified, it sets the element's `value` attribute.

- Reset: An `<input>` element is created with the `type` attribute set to `"reset"`. If the class attribute's tagged value for `disabled` is specified, it is coded as an element attribute. If the class attribute has an initial value specified, it sets the element's `value` attribute.

- FileUpload: An `<input>` element is created with the `type` attribute set to `"file"`. If the class attribute's tagged value for `disabled` is specified, it is coded as a valueless element attribute.

- Hidden: An `<input>` element is created with the `type` attribute set to `"hidden"`. If the class attribute has an initial value specified, it sets the element's `value` attribute.

- Image: An `<input>` element is created with the `type` attribute set to `"image"`. If the class attribute's tagged value for `disabled` is specified, it is coded as a valueless element attribute.

- Button: An `<input>` element is created with the `type` attribute set to `"button"`. If the class attribute's tagged value for `disabled` is specified, it is coded as a valueless element attribute.

- `<button>`: A `<button>` element is created. By default, a closing tag is created for this element, and the element's value is used as the inner text. If the class attribute's tagged value for `disabled` is specified, it is coded as a valueless element attribute. The tagged value for `type` sets the element's button type attribute. The default is `"button"`. The allowable values are `"button"`, `"submit"`, and `"reset"`.

- Textarea: A `<textarea>` element is created. A closing tag is required for this element, and the element's initial value is used as the initial inner text. This element is sensitive to white space in the inner text, so when forward engineering this element, do not add character returns or line feeds in the inner text. If the class attribute's tagged value for `disabled` is specified, it is coded as a valueless element attribute. The tagged values for `rows` and `cols` are generated as attributes in the element's opening tag.

- Select: A <select> element is created. A closing tag is required for this element. If the class attribute's tagged value for disabled is specified, it is forward engineered as a valueless element attribute. If the class attribute's tagged value for multiple is set to true, the valueless element attribute MULTIPLE is coded. The tagged value for size is coded as an attribute in the element's opening tag.

«Targeted Link» *n*-ary Association

A «targeted link» *n*-ary association acts as a ternary association that connects a requestable Web page—a «client page», a «server page», or a «frameset»—to a «target» class. All valid «targeted link» classes have two directional associations: one to the requestable page class—«client page», «server page» or «frameset»—and one to a «target» stereotyped class. The target class represents a named frame in a frameset or a separate browser window. The page class represents the content that is to be requested for the target.

This class does not directly map to an element of HTML code; rather, the «link» association that uses it does. A «link» association that points to a «targeted link» class uses the name of the target class as the value for the target attribute in the anchor element. The href is specified by the URL that realizes the page that the «targeted link» class points to. See Figure A-28.

«Target» Class

A target class represents a named window on the client and is either a frame in a frameset or a window in another browser instance. When contained by a «frameset» class, the target forward engineers into the name attribute of a <FRAME> element. The name attribute is set to the class name of the «target» class.

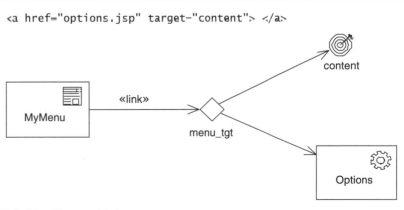

FIGURE A-28   Targeted link

If this class has an «src» stereotyped association to a page class—a «client page», a «server page», or a «frameset», this translates to the src attribute of the <FRAME> element. The value is set to the URL that the page class resolves to.

Target classes can be contained only by a «frameset» class. Therefore, the <FRAME> element is always a child element of a <FRAMESET>.

When not contained by a frameset, the target represents an independent window. In this case, it is used only by the «link» forward-engineering operation and does not contribute to a code itself.

See the sections «Frameset» Class and «Targeted Link» Class for examples.

«Frameset» Class

A frameset is a container of frames. The <FRAMESET> element defines a set of rectangular regions within a browser window. In the logical view, a «frameset» class is a specialization of a «client page» and therefore has the potential to have the same code that a «client page» does, although this is typically not the case. A «frameset» codes to a <FRAMESET> element just inside the opening <BODY> tag. In a frames-capable browser, the rendered page becomes a frameset. In a non-frames-capable browser, the rendered page is the rest of the content in the <BODY> element.

<FRAMESET> elements may be nested. Each <FRAMESET> element has a corresponding «frameset» stereotyped class.

Each nonstereotyped containment association that originates from a «frameset» class represents a frame. The noresize and the scrolling tagged values of the containment association are coded as <FRAME> element attributes. See Figure A-29.

«Script Library» Class

A «script library» class must be realized by a «script library» component that resides in or under a «physical root» package in the component view. All attributes and operations of the class are forward engineered into var and function declarations. Because the file is a .js file, <SCRIPT> elements do not need to be created in the file.

Any associations from the class are ignored; only attributes and operations of the class are used during implementation. See the section «Client Page» Class for a description of coding class attributes and operations.

«Screen» Class

A screen, an abstraction of a rendered Web page in a client browser, represents the final visualized user interface presented to the system user. A screen element is part of the UX model. Screen stereotyped classes are typically not realized by elements in the design or implementation models. However, in architectures in which the virtual URL and physical resource hierarchies are different, it can be useful to realize screens with «HTTP Resource» components.

```
<frameset rows="10%, *" cols="50%, 50%">
  <frame name="lbanner">
  <frame name="rbanner">
  <frame src="menu.html">
  <frame name="mainContent">
</frameset>
```

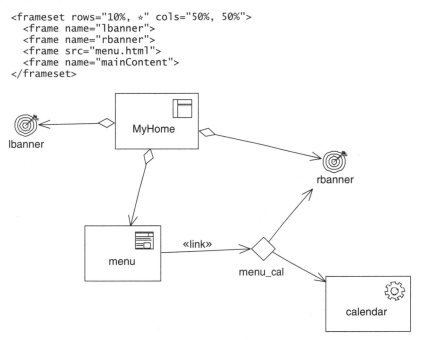

FIGURE A-29   An HTML <FRAMESET> modeled with a stereotyped class

«Screen Compartment» Class

A screen compartment is a well-defined screen region that is reused by multiple screens. A screen is an abstraction of a part of a rendered Web page in a client browser. A screen compartment element is part of the UX model and typically is not directly realized by a component. However, in certain architectures it is not unreasonable to have a «static page» or a «dynamic page» component realize screen compartments.

«Input Form» Class

An input form screen compartment is a well-defined screen region that is reused by multiple screens. It is an abstraction of a part of a rendered Web page in a client browser. A screen compartment element is part of the UX model. A screen compartment can be realized by a «static page» or a «dynamic page» component.

«Style Sheet» Class

See the section «link» Association later in this appendix for a description.

Association Class: «URL Parameters»

Using this association class is an optional way to model HTTP parameters. It is useful when the parameters are relatively complex or have special semantics and extra documentation is needed. For a description, see the section «link» Association.

Associations

«link» Association

A «link» association in the logical view is represented in code by one of two HTML elements: a <LINK> or an anchor <A>. If the association's supplier class is "stylesheet" or if the rel and rev tagged values are set, the association codes into a <LINK> element that is placed in the <HEAD> element. The rel and the rev tagged values set their corresponding element attribute values. If the supplier class is stereotyped «style sheet», the rel element attribute is set to "stylesheet" and the type element attribute is set to "text/css". If the supplier class is a normal page class—«client page», «server page», or «frameset»—the class association is coded as an anchor element. In either case, the URL that resolves to the supplier class is used as the href element attribute value. See Figure A-30.

The tagged value parameters lists in ampersand-separated form all the parameters that href URL uses. See Figure A-31

An equivalent way of expressing link parameters is with a link class stereotyped «link parameter». Figure A-32 shows an equivalent representation of this URL. Using

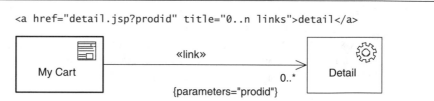

FIGURE A-30   An HTTP parameter modeled as constraints on the «link» association

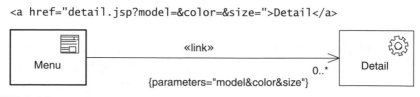

FIGURE A-31   Multiple HTTP parameters modeled with a single constraint but separated with ampersands

link associations offers the opportunity to specify attribute data types. These data types are not used for coding and are of use to the designer only in the context of the model. See Figure A-33.

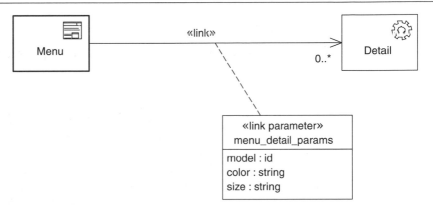

FIGURE A-32   Links using link classes

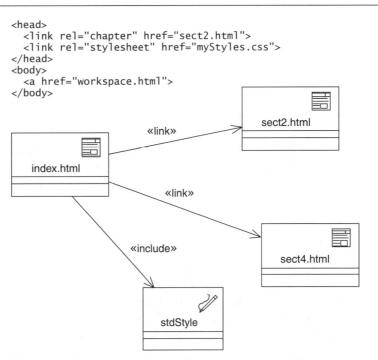

FIGURE A-33   Style sheet links modeled with «include» associations

```
<head>
 <meta http-equiv="refresh" content="2,http://www.newco.com/home.html">
</body>
```

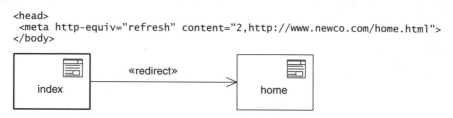

FIGURE A-34   Client-side redirection modeled as a stereotyped association

«redirect» Association

A redirection association indicates that the client page should be automatically replaced with another client page. This is typically done as a temporary measure as a site is redesigned or moves to a new domain.

This association codes into a <META> element with the http-equiv attribute set to "refresh". The content attribute contains the delay in seconds, followed by a comma and the URL of the page to redirect to. The delay is a tagged value of the «redirect» association. This element belongs in the <HEAD> element. See Figure A-34.

«submit» Association

Forms submit their data to other Web pages, although there are no restrictions on submitting themselves to other instances of their containing pages. This relationship codes into the action parameter of the <FORM> element. See the section «HTML Form» Class for more information.

«object» Association

The «object» containment association represents a contained data type or object in the context of an HTML page. This object is not necessarily visual, although it is usually rendered in the display. The «object» association can be used to specify many types of embedded objects, most commonly applets and ActiveX controls. See Figure A-35. In this example, the «object» association defines the id and classid tagged values, which are coded in the <OBJECT> element. The parameters for the object are specified by a link class.

«iframe» Association

The «iframe» stereotyped association represents an inset frame in an HTML page. This association forward engineers into a single <IFRAME> element. The src attribute of the element is the URL of the supplier class. An «iframe» association always originates from a «client page» or a «frameset» and is directed to another page class. The width and the height tagged values are generated into corresponding element

```
<OBJECT ID="RP1" CLASSID="clsid:CFCDAA03-8BE4-11cf-B84B-0020AFBBCCFA" WIDTH=176 HEIGHT=132>
<PARAM NAME="SRC" VALUE="/video/world/2000/04/24/rm.china.sect.affl.rm28.ram?embed=true">
<PARAM NAME="CONTROLS" VALUE="Imagewindow">
<PARAM NAME="AUTOSTART" VALUE="TRUE">
<PARAM NAME="NOLABELS" VALUE="TRUE">
<PARAM NAME="RESET" VALUE="FALSE">
<PARAM NAME="CONSOLE" VALUE="clip1">
</OBJECT>
```

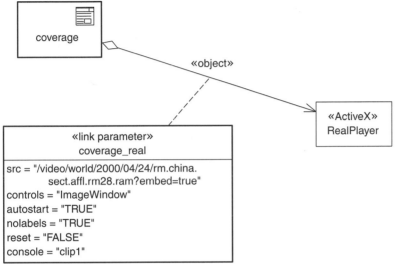

FIGURE A-35   Example of an ActiveX object

```
<iframe name="localquote" src="quotes.jsp"></iframe>
```

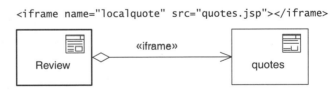

FIGURE A-36   An HTML <IFRAME> modeled with a containment association

attributes. See Figure A-36. Note that the end tag is required for the <IFRAME> element, although for the life of me, I don't know why. See Figure A-37.

«include» Dependency

Only dependencies stereotyped «include» are coded. The supplier class, a «script library» stereotyped class, must be realized by a valid «script library» stereotyped component in the model.

```
<iframe name="info" src="page1.jsp" width=200 height=50></iframe>
```

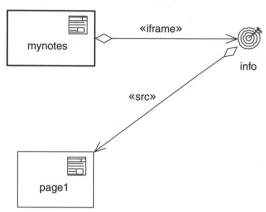

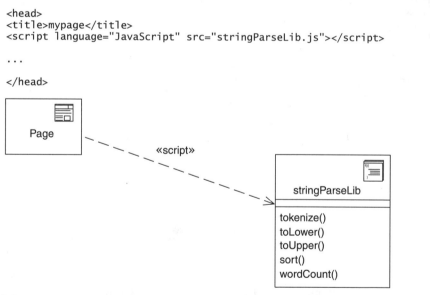

FIGURE A-37   `<IFRAME>` elements with an src parameter specified and modeled with an additional containment association

```
<head>
<title>mypage</title>
<script language="JavaScript" src="stringParseLib.js"></script>

...

</head>
```

FIGURE A-38   Example of an «include» dependency

Figure A-38 shows a dependency stereotyped «include» drawn from the «client page» page to the «script library» `stringParseLib`. This forward engineers into a `<SCRIPT>` element with the `language` and `src` attributes specified. The determination of the URL for the `src` is made by looking at the «clientscript» component that realizes the class `stringParseLib`. In this example, it happens to exist in the same virtual directory as the component that realizes the «client page» page.

Mapping Web Elements to UML, and Vice Versa

The core WAE profile is not vendor specific and can be applied to any scripted page-based Web application development such as JavaServer Pages, Active Server Pages, PHP: Hypertext Preprocessor, Cold Fusion Markup, and others. At the time of this writing, Microsoft's newest version of Active Server Pages (ASPX) has just been released and therefore a complete profile for this environment is not ready. Presently no concrete work has been made available for the other environments except for JavaServer Pages (JSP). JSP 1.1 has been available for some time, and a WAE-based profile is available and described in this and the following sections. The UML profile JSP is described, as the base WAE profile, from two viewpoints: mapping Web elements to UML, and the reverse, UML to Web elements.

JavaServer Page to UML

This section of the JSP profile describes the mapping of JSP-specific technology elements to UML elements. The JSP elements range from the XML-formatted Web application and tag library descriptors to JSP files. There is no 1:1 mapping of elements in either space, so careful attention must be paid when describing and understanding the transformation of the model.

Web Application

A Web application is a collection of servlets or JSPs that make up an application that delivers user functionality to client HTML browsers. In J2EE terms, an application is defined by the `web.xml` file. This configuration file contains a number of application definitions, including the servlet mapping, which is how the Web container resolves URLs into servlets or JSPs. This mapping is a key part of the «virtual root» and «physical root» component packages.

The following `web.xml` fragment specifies a servlet named `"searchServlet"` and also specifies a mapping to a URL. This is modeled with an «HTTP Resource» component directly under the «virtual root» package that represents the application's host and context. The resulting URL is relative to the host and application context, which are specified as tag values in the «virtual root» package that owns this HTTP resource. So if the name of the Web application were `glossary` and the `host` were `localhost`, the URL pointing to this servlet would be http://localhost/glossary/search.

```
<servlet>
  <servlet-name>search</servlet-name>
  <display-name>searchServlet</display-name>
```

```
    <description/>
    <servlet-class>app.glossary.Search</servlet-class>
</servlet>
...
<servlet-mapping>
    <servlet-name>search</servlet-name>
    <url-pattern>search</url-pattern>
</servlet-mapping>
```

Figure A-39 shows how this fragment would be modeled in the component view of the model. The «virtual root» has tag values specifying the host name { hostname = "localhost" } and the application context { context = "glossary" }.

JSPs that are not explicitly mapped in the web.xml file are structured under the «physical root» package in the component view of the model. The «physical root» maps to the root of the Web archive file. All JSPs that can be requested are located in a package hierarchy under the physical root that mirrors the file system. See Figure A-40.

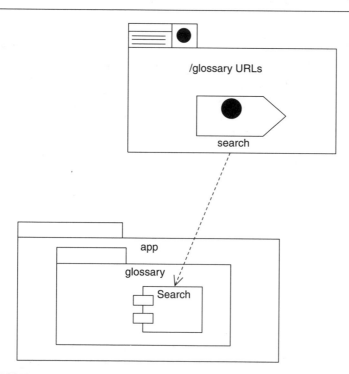

FIGURE A-39   Modeling a servlet mapping

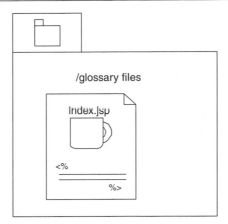

FIGURE A-40 Modeling JSPs in a «physical root» component package

JSP

A JSP file is modeled with a «JSP» stereotyped component or, optionally, a «dynamic page» component with a type tag value that indicates JSP. The contents of the JSP file are modeled in the logical view with «server page» stereotyped classes.

Operations and attributes defined in a <%! … %> block are mapped to «server page» static attributes and operations. Attributes defined in scriptlet blocks (<% … %>) are, optionally, mapped to «server page» attributes.

The following code fragment defines three operations and one static member variable. Four additional instance variables are defined. In this example, some of the page's code is executed in line, including the code that defines and assigns the instance variables for the page's scriptlets. The model for this code fragment is shown in Figure A-41.

```
<%!
  private int timesAccessed = 0;

  private void writeTable(SearchListing listing){
    ...
  }

  private void writeRow( Item item ){
    ...
  }

  private int getIndex( HttpRequest req ) {
    ...
  }

  private SearchListing search( SearchCriteria criteria, int startingIndex ){
    ...
  }
%>
```

```
<%
  // member variable definitions
  int index = 0;
  int totalPages = 0;
  SearchListing listing = null;

  // beginning of main page logic
  timesAccessed++;
  SearchCriteria criteria = (SearchCriteria) session.getAttribute("criteria");
  if( criteria != null ) {
    index = getIndex( request );
    if( index > 0 ) {
      listing = search( criteria, index );
    }
  }
%>
<html>

<head>
  <title>Library Listing</title>
</head>
<body>
...
</body>
```

<%jsp:usebean … %>   This tag maps directly to a «use bean» stereotyped association from a «server page» class to a JavaBean. The following use bean declaration is modeled in Figure A-41.

```
<jsp:useBean id="library" scope="page"
class="com.mycompany.catalog.Library"/>
```

<%jsp:include … %>   The JSP include element is modeled with a simple «include» relationship from a «server page» to another page class. This is modeled the same way as the JSP include directive. Because there are architectural differences in these two types of include, the tag value "type" is set to "{ tag | directive }" to indicate which type of include is required.

<%jsp:forward … %>   The JSP forward element is modeled with a simple «forward» relationship to the page class that will take over control of the page request.

<%jsp:plugin … %>   The JSP plug-in element is modeled with an <object> tag from the client page that is built from the server page.

<%@include file="…"%>   The include directive is modeled with a simple «include» relationship from a «server page» class to the page class that is to be included. This is modeled the same way as the JSP include element. Because there are architectural differences in these two types of include, the tag value "type" is set to "{ tag | directive }" to indicate which type of include is required.

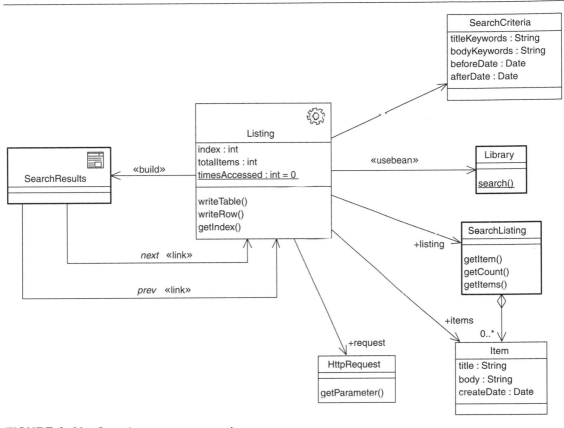

FIGURE A-41 Sample «server page» class

<%@taglib … %> A tag library itself is modeled with a «JSP tag library» stereotyped package. This package corresponds to a tag library descriptor file (.tld). The package contains a number of «JSP Tag» stereotyped classes, each representing one tag definition. Each tag has a dependency on a Java implementation class. This dependency is stereotyped «tag». An optional Tag Extra Info class may also be specified to define scripting variables that are available in the body of the tag. The Tag Extra Info class is identified by a «tei» dependency from the «JSP Tag» class to the class providing the extra information.

The following code is a tag definition in a descriptor file.

```
<tag>
<name>Entry</name>
<tagclass>app.glossary.taglib.EntryTag</tagclass>
<teiclass>app.glossary.taglib.EntryTEI</teiclass>
```

```
<bodycontent>JSP</bodycontent>
<attribute>
  <name>entryid</name>
  <required>true</required>
  <rtexprvalue>true</rtexprvalue>
</attribute>
<attribute>
  <name>convertLineBreaks</name>
  <required>false</required>
  <rtexprvalue>true</rtexprvalue>
</attribute>
</tag>
```

The body of the Tag Extra Info class follows.

```
public class EntryTEI extends TagExtraInfo {
public EntryTEI() { super(); }

public VariableInfo[] getVariableInfo(TagData data) {
  return new VariableInfo[]
  {
    new VariableInfo("id", "String", true, VariableInfo.NESTED),
    new VariableInfo("term", "String", true, VariableInfo.NESTED),
    new VariableInfo("acronym", "String", true, VariableInfo.NESTED),
    new VariableInfo("longTerm", "String", true, VariableInfo.NESTED),
    new VariableInfo("description", "String", true, VariableInfo.NESTED),
    new VariableInfo("includesHTML", "String", true, VariableInfo.NESTED),
    new VariableInfo("lastmodified", "String", true, VariableInfo.NESTED)
  };
}

}
```

The descriptor file specifies the tag attributes that it expects in the opening tag with «attribute» stereotyped attributes. Scripting variables available in the body of the tag are specified in the TagExtraInfo class. The tag described here is modeled in Figure A-42.

A tag library is referenced by a server page with the taglib directive.

```
<%@ taglib uri="/glytlb" prefix="gly" %>
```

In the model, it is drawn as «JSP Tag library» stereotyped relationship to the library package (Figure A-43). [7] The relationship is named gly, which is how the tags from this particular library are referenced in the JSP code.

---

7. In this diagram, a dependency is a limitation of the modeling tool I am using. A more proper relationship would be an association.

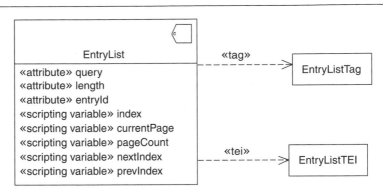

FIGURE A-42 Model of a JSP custom tag

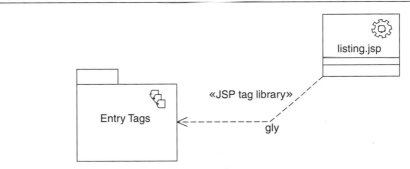

FIGURE A-43 Modeling server page use of tag libraries

response.sendRedirect(...) Method The method sendRedirect(...) is an architecturally significant call that can be made by server pages. When this behavior is a structural part of the design—is the normal flow of behavior—it can appear in the model as a «redirect» relationship from one server page class to another page class.

UML to JavaServer Page

This section of the JSP profile describes the mapping of UML elements into JSP-specific technology elements and components. All of the UML elements are stereotyped, and the range includes classes, packages, associations, attributes, and operations.

«JSP» Component

Each «JSP» component creates a single JSP file (.jsp) located in a subdirectory under the Web application root. The «physical root» package maps to the top-level directory in the Web archive file (.war). Each subpackage of the physical root is mirrored with a subdirectory in the Web archive folder. The following physical file, where

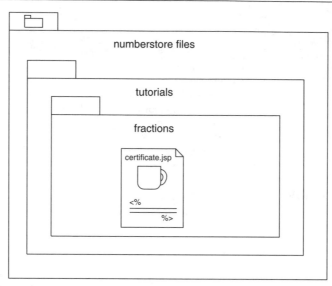

FIGURE A-44   Component mapping for JSP file

some Web root is located in the root of the Web context, results in the component mapping shown in Figure A-44.

```
/(some web root)/tutorials/fractions/certificate.jsp
```

«server page» Stereotyped Class

A «server page» stereotyped class is the logical abstraction of a JSP as it is executed on the server. The class's instance attributes correspond to instance variables used in the main body of the JSP code and that have pagewide scope.[8] Figure A-45 shows a class diagram with a server page defined. This class maintains two instance variables: to a `Product` and to a `ShopController`. The role names on these relationships are used as the variable names in the main body of JSP code.

This class diagram also defines a hyperlink from the client page class that it builds. This link is to a UX screen and as such requires a little bit of navigation and deeper understanding of the architecture to resolve. The architecture in this case maps the `product.scr` «HttpResource» component to the appropriate set of JSP pages.

```
<%@ page import="com.numberstore.catalog.*" %>
<%
  ShopController controller = (ShopController)
session.getAttribute("controller");
  Product special = controller.getProductSpecial();
```

---

8. Not declared inside a function declaration or a statement block { }.

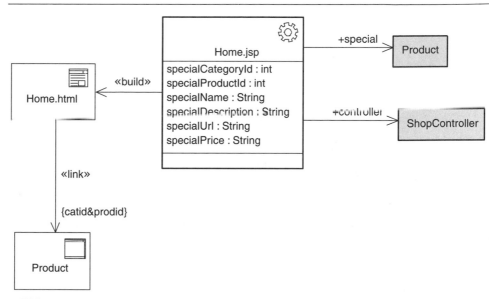

FIGURE A-45   Server page with object relations and a link

```
 int specialCategoryId = special.getCategoryId();
 int specialProductId = special.getId();
 String specialName = special.getName();
 String specialDescription = special.getDescription();
 String specialPrice = special.priceString();
 String specialUrl = response.encodeURL("product.scr?catid=" +
specialCategoryId
      + "&prodid=" + specialProductId );

%>
<html>
...
  <p> <a href="<%=specialUrl %>"> <%= specialName %> </a> </p>
  <p> <%= specialDescription %> </p>
...
</html>
```

The class diagram of Figure A-46 shows a server page with three defined operations and one static attribute, all coded in a JSP <%! ... %> block. The two instance variables are scriptlet variables used in the page and with page scope (see the following code).

```
<%!
  private int timesAccessed = 0;

  private void writeTable(SearchListing listing){
    ...
  }
```

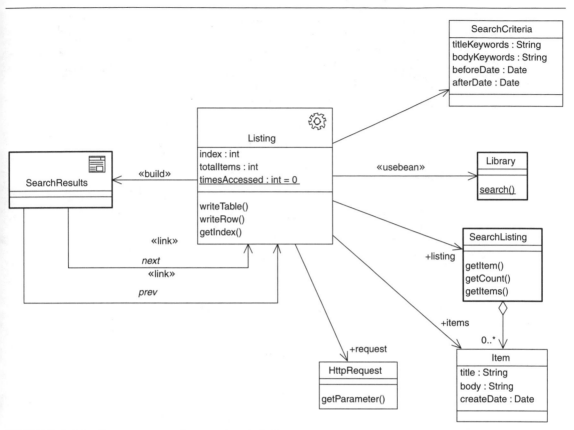

FIGURE A-46 Server page with operation definitions

```
private void writeRow( Item item ){
    ...
}

private int getIndex( HttpRequest req ) {
    ...
}

private SearchListing search( SearchCriteria criteria, int startingIndex ){
    ...
}
%>
<%
// member variable definitions
int index = 0;
int totalPages = 0;
SearchListing listing = null;
```

```
    // beginning of main page logic
    timesAccessed++;
    SearchCriteria criteria = (SearchCriteria) session.getAttribute("criteria");
    if( criteria != null ) {
      index = getIndex( request );
      if( index > 0 ) {
        listing = search( criteria, index );
      }
    }
%>
<html>

<head>
  <title>Library Listing</title>
</head>
<body>
...
</body>
```

«use bean» Association

The «use bean» association between a JSP and a Java class in the model is coded with a simple JSP use bean tag.

«include» Association

An «include» association from a server page class can be coded as either a JSP directive (`<%@ include file="..." %>`) or a JSP tag (`<jsp:include page="..." ... />`). The version of the include is dictated by the type tag value (`type = { tag | directive }`).

«forward» Association

A «forward» association is coded with the `<jsp:forward page="..."/>` tag.

«redirect» Association

A «redirect» association is implemented by the `sendRedirect(String location)` operation on the `HttpResponse` object, which is available in the context of a JSP by the `response` variable.

«JSP Tag» Class

A «JSP Tag» in the model corresponds to a JSP custom tag (Figure A-47). The class defines a number of tag attributes and scripting variables. Attributes of the «JSP Tag» that are stereotyped are element attributes that can be specified in the opening tag. These attributes are captured in the tag library descriptor file with the following XML fragment:

```
<tag>
  <name>Entry</name>
  <tagclass>app.glossary.taglib.EntryTag</tagclass>
  <teiclass>app.glossary.taglib.EntryTEI</teiclass>
  <bodycontent>JSP</bodycontent>
```

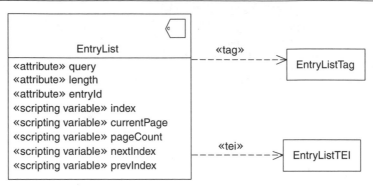

FIGURE A-47   Sample «JSP Tag» class

```
<attribute>
  <name>entryid</name>
  <required>true</required>
  <rtexprvalue>true</rtexprvalue>
</attribute>
<attribute>
  <name>convertLineBreaks</name>
  <required>false</required>
  <rtexprvalue>true</rtexprvalue>
</attribute>
</tag>
```

Tag values on the attributes indicate whether the attribute is required (required = { yes | no }).

Scripting variable stereotyped attributes must be defined in a TagExtraInfo class, which is identified by a «tei» stereotyped dependency from the «JSP Tag». The TagExtraInfo class for the example in Figure A-47 follows.

```
public class EntryTEI extends TagExtraInfo {
public EntryTEI() { super(); }

public VariableInfo[] getVariableInfo(TagData data) {
  return new VariableInfo[]
  {
    new VariableInfo("id", "String", true, VariableInfo.NESTED),
    new VariableInfo("term", "String", true, VariableInfo.NESTED),
    new VariableInfo("acronym", "String", true, VariableInfo.NESTED),
    new VariableInfo("longTerm", "String", true, VariableInfo.NESTED),
    new VariableInfo("description", "String", true, VariableInfo.NESTED),
    new VariableInfo("includesHTML", "String", true, VariableInfo.NESTED),
    new VariableInfo("lastmodified", "String", true, VariableInfo.NESTED)
  };
}

}
```

The «JSP Tag» implementing class is identified with a «tag» dependency. Its implementation must include certain operations (see the JSP specification for details). The class in this example follows, with operation bodies removed for clarity. Each specified attribute must provide a `get` and a `set` operation.

```
Public class EntryTag extends BodyTagSupport {
  public String getConvertLineBreaks(){  }

  public void setConvertLineBreaks(String _convertLineBreaks ){}

  public String getEntryid() {}

  public void setEntryid(String _id ){}

  public void doInitBody() throws JspException {}

  public int doStartTag() throws JspException {}


  public int doEndTag() throws JspTagException {}

  public void release() {}

}
```

«JSP Tag Library» Package

A JSP tag library (Figure A-48) maps to a `.tld` descriptor file. This file uses the «attribute» stereotyped attributes and the two dependency relationships to the implementing classes («tag» and «tei») to define most of the fields in this descriptor file.

```
<?xml version="1.0" encoding="ISO-8859-1"?>
<!DOCTYPE taglib PUBLIC "-//Sun Microsystems, Inc.//DTD JSP Tag Library 1.1//EN"
        "http://java.sun.com/j2ee/dtds/web-jsptaglibrary_1_1.dtd">
<taglib>
  <tlibversion>1.0</tlibversion>
  <jspversion>1.1</jspversion>
  <shortname/>
  <tag>
    <name>Entry</name>
    <tagclass>app.glossary.taglib.EntryTag</tagclass>
```

FIGURE A-48 Tag library package

```
          <teiclass>app.glossary.taglib.EntryTEI</teiclass>
          <bodycontent>JSP</bodycontent>
          <attribute>
            <name>entryid</name>
            <required>true</required>
            <rtexprvalue>true</rtexprvalue>
          </attribute>
          <attribute>
            <name>convertLineBreaks</name>
            <required>false</required>
            <rtexprvalue>true</rtexprvalue>
          </attribute>
      </tag>
</taglib>
```

Appendix B
The Number Store Reference Application

Vision

In most software development efforts, the vision document is created early to obtain funding. In this book, the need for this application was solely to provide a nontrivial example of the Web Application Extension (WAE) profile for UML for this second edition. The publisher and I are in essence the primary stakeholders, and it is to this audience that this document is oriented.

Because the publisher and I are the primary stakeholders and are undertaking this vision document solely to produce supplementary material for the book, the vision does not contain much market analysis or cost/value comparisons. Rather, it contains a lot of the mental discussions I've had with myself about what type of application would be a good exemplar of a J2EE application, one that would be good candidate to show the most important aspects of the WAE.

Background

Understanding and building sophisticated Web applications is difficult. One of the biggest overall issues facing development teams is managing complexity. With each succeeding generation, our applications are becoming increasingly large and complex. In addition, these applications are taking on more mission-critical roles. All this underscores the need for good tools and processes that will make our teams more efficient and result in a higher quality of work.

A primary goal of the book is to demonstrate how teams can effectively leverage UML as a development tool for building Web applications, which in this context are

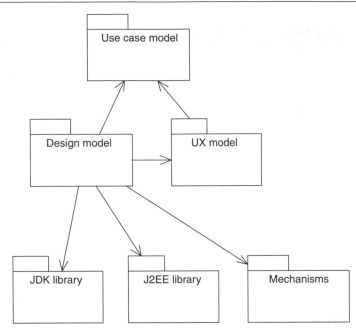

FIGURE B-1   Top-level model and package summary

software applications that manage business state and that have adopted a Web-centric presentation tier that relies heavily on standard Web technologies and standards, such as HTTP, HTML, Web browsers, and client-side scripting.

The WAE focused primarily on the presentation tier of modern Web applications. As a result, most of the discussions center on the shape and the nature of this tier, leaving detailed discussions of other tiers—business logic, entity, data—to other books.

All the UML elements are managed in one Rational Rose 2002 model file. The top-level package diagram is shown in Figure B-1. The full UML model is not included in this appendix but can be downloaded, along with all the source code for the application, from the Addison-Wesley Web site at www.awl.com/cseng. The model is available in Rational Rose 2002 format (.md1 file).

Requirements and Features

For this application to be an effective tool for understanding the WAE and Web application architectures in general, the following architecturally significant design elements must be included:

- JSP and servlet classes
- Client-side scripting
- Specializations for certain browser versions
- JavaBean use in JSPs

To keep the focus on the modeling and architecture, a commonly understood domain, such as a retail applications, should be used. Having to explain both the domain problem and the architecture would distract from the goal of seeing the modeling technique in action. Well-documented code and simplicity and understandability are favored over efficiency and performance.

Software Architecture Document

The Number Store is a J2EE application that allows users to browse a catalog of numbers and select some for purchase. When a customer purchases a number, fictitious payment information is collected and processed. Real users are advised not to submit credit card information because anything that is provided will be accepted. In addition to browsing a catalog of numbers, a user can take a tutorial on adding fractions.

The principal goal of the Number Store application is not to give its users functionality of value but rather to provide a J2EE exemplar application for demonstrating the Web Application Extension for UML (WAE). The WAE is a formal Unified Modeling Language (UML) profile that allows Web application development teams to use UML to model design-level abstractions of their Web applications. The vision document for this application outlines the overall goal and context that this application is being developed in and is treated as the originating requirements source. The meat of this application, however, can be found in this document.

This abbreviated architecture document describes the underlying architecture of this application and relies on the use of the WAE. The intent is that this document, combined with the entire UML model, will serve as a sufficient example of the use and benefits of UML modeling.

The architecture is expressed in terms of multiple views of the system. Each view represents certain aspects of the system under construction. This document contains the most architecturally significant elements across all development artifacts. As a result, the document may appear to be a summary of the entire collection of software development processes' artifacts.

Requirements View

The requirements for the Number Store application are drawn from the vision document. The vision document, of course, cannot contain all the application's requirements, which are contained in a full-size requirements document/database. In this section of the architecture document, only the significant architectural requirements (SARs) are expressed. These requirements directly lead to design decisions in the architecture.

The nonfunctional requirements are not conveniently expressed in terms of dialogue scenarios between the system's users and the system. This simple application has few of these requirements.

1. Fundamental Architectural and Design Elements
    1.1. Use both JSP and servlets to accept and build page requests.
    1.2. The application will use servlets to accept incoming HTTP requests and JSPs to build outgoing HTML pages.
    1.3. The JSPs will include other JSPs, as well as reference and use beans.
    1.4. If possible, JSPs will use custom tag libraries.
    1.5. The application will have at least one instance in which a targeted link is used.
    1.6. The application will use common Web application design patterns.
        1.6.1. Model View Controller pattern: Separate, discrete elements for managing the business state, building and presenting the user interface, and coordinating and controlling their activities.
        1.6.2. Controlled Controllers pattern: Allowance for use and definition of multiple concurrent controllers in the application.
        1.6.3. Paged List pattern: A way to present large lists of data to the user one page at a time. The user will scroll through pages of data one at a time to examine the list. This keeps the maximum page size and response time to a manageable level.
        1.6.4. Shopping Cart pattern: A mechanism for application users to maintain references to items in the application throughout a session or a scenario. The items are selected for further processing, that is, purchase.
2. Domain
    2.1. The application should mimic a common e-retail application. Its interface should be simple and not contain many specializations. In effect, the problem domain should almost be commonplace and invisible to the architecture.
    2.2. The problem domain shall be a store that sells numbers. The products of this store are therefore numbers: integers, primes, squares, and so on. Using numbers as products should simplify the process of creating a sample inventory.
    2.3. The product catalog should be divided into category groups. The initial release will contain categories for integers, primes, perfect squares, and miscellaneous.

2.3.1. The integer category will have products ranging from 1 to 499.

2.3.2. The primes category will contain the first 1,000 prime numbers.

2.3.3. The squares category will contain the first 20 perfect squares.

2.3.4. The special category will contain three values—PI, the natural log root, and the number 42, the ultimate answer to the universal question, whatever that might be. (This is a nod to the *Hitchhiker's Guide to the Galaxy* trilogy.)

2.4. Each product will be able to produce a value for its name, that is, a numerical value, a brief description, and a price.

2.5. Shopping

2.5.1. Users should be able to select and to purchase numbers.

2.5.2. The shopping cart should be accessible at all times and exhibit the standard behaviors for shopping carts.

2.5.3. The checkout process shall accept fictitious payment information and appear to process it.

2.5.4. Orders are to be confirmed to the user with an invoice.

2.6. Tutorials

2.6.1. A tutorial controller shall be added to the application, after the shopping and ordering functionality is completed, to demonstrate how controllers can be added without affecting (too much) the rest of the application design.

2.6.2. The tutorial will present a lesson on adding simple fractions.

2.6.3. The tutorial will leverage DHTML and will present a separate user interface to leverage the capabilities of one specific browser version. The browser version will be IE 3.0 or greater. This browser has a straightforward interface for doing dynamic text replacement in a Web page on the client. Other browser versions will see a non-DHTML-enabled page.

3. Runtime Environment

3.1. The application should be capable of running both the client and the server tiers on the same machine to facilitate examination and experimentation. The application can also be deployed on a separate node without design change.

3.2. The use of a formal entity and data tier should be minimized and eliminated, if possible. The focus of the modeling technique is on the presentation tier. The other tiers should be stubbed out when possible.

4. Performance

4.1. Page response times should be under 5 seconds for all pages during normal operation.

5. Security

5.1. There are no special security requirements or policies for this application.

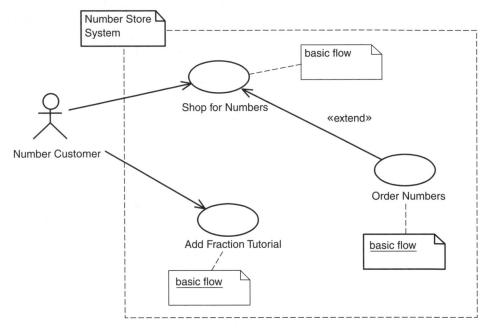

FIGURE B-2   Use case model top-level diagram

Use Case View

The Number Store has only three use cases, so all three are architecturally significant. Figure B-2 shows the top-level use case view diagram for the application.

This application has a single actor: Number Customer. The customer is an anonymous Internet user who will browse the catalog and purchase items. Figures B-3 through B-6 outline the basic flows of the scenarios.

User Experience View

The user experience (UX) model expresses the application from the viewpoint of screens of information and is very much a user interface model. The two class stereotypes for elements in the logical view are screen and form. A screen is a complete user interface presented to the user. A form is a user input element that accompanies requests to the server.

In this model, the convention of using a dollar sign ($) indicates that the screen is accessible from most screens in the system: The screen is in a global scope. The plus sign (+) is appended to screen names that implement the paged list mechanism. These screens display a large list of items one "page" at a time. The dollar sign and the plus sign are simply notational conventions used in the context of this application and do not represent a defined modeling convention in the WAE or any other UML profile.

The customer uses a standard Web browser and navigates to the Number Store home page.

The system displays the home page and lists product specicals for the day.

Select product special

The customer decides to examine the store's special product of the day.

The system displays the details of the product special.

Add to cart

The customer decides to add the selected product to the shopping cart.

The system displays the current status of the cart.

Update line item quantity

The customer changes the quantity of one or more of the line items in the cart.

The system updates the cart and redisplays the current cart.

Browse catalog

The customer decides to browse the catalog.

The system displays a list of all the product categories in the catalog. Each category identifies its name and has a brief description.

The customer selects one of the categories.

The first page of the list of category products is displayed.

The customer browses the entire list one page at a time. The maximum number of items in a page is a configurable system setting. The user can view the next, previous, first, and last pages of products in the list.

Each list identifies a product with a name and a short description. The customer can select any of the products for further examination.

The system returns with a page that has the product mentioned, and displays its price.

The customer can add the product to the cart (see Add to cart).

Extension points: order numbers

At any time the cart is displayed, the customer can decide to check out and purchase the items. See Order Numbers use case.

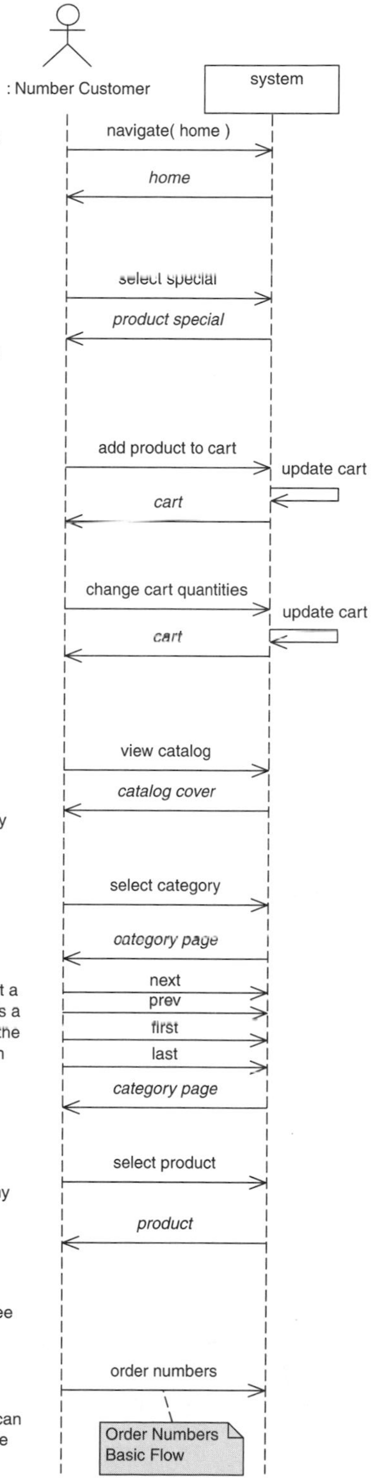

FIGURE B-3 Shop for Numbers: basic flow

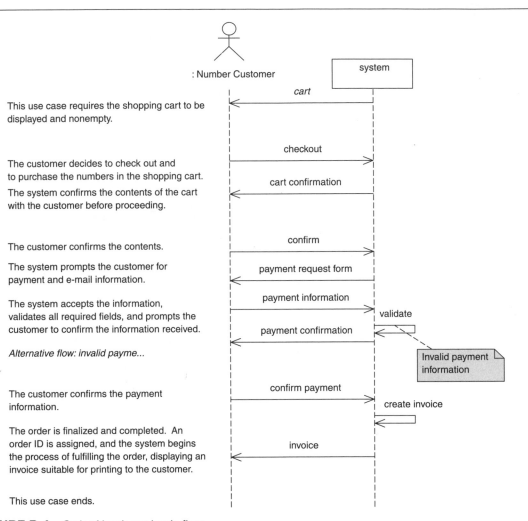

This use case requires the shopping cart to be displayed and nonempty.

The customer decides to check out and to purchase the numbers in the shopping cart.

The system confirms the contents of the cart with the customer before proceeding.

The customer confirms the contents.

The system prompts the customer for payment and e-mail information.

The system accepts the information, validates all required fields, and prompts the customer to confirm the information received.

Alternative flow: invalid payme...

The customer confirms the payment information.

The order is finalized and completed. An order ID is assigned, and the system begins the process of fulfilling the order, displaying an invoice suitable for printing to the customer.

This use case ends.

FIGURE B-4   Order Numbers: basic flow

Figure B-7 shows the top-level UX model expressed as a class diagram and using the WAE stereotypes for screens and forms. In this diagram, the principal navigational routes through the system are expressed as associations between the screens. When form input is used—the user supplies data, not just hyperlink selection—the form is expressed as a stereotyped association class.

Figure B-8 shows the same navigation map but with its details exposed. In this diagram, all the dynamic content is exposed.

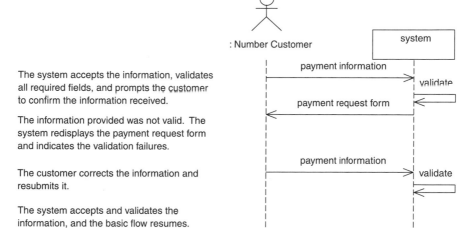

The system accepts the information, validates all required fields, and prompts the customer to confirm the information received.

The information provided was not valid. The system redisplays the payment request form and indicates the validation failures.

The customer corrects the information and resubmits it.

The system accepts and validates the information, and the basic flow resumes.

FIGURE B-5   Invalid Payment Information: alternative flow

Figure B-9 shows the main compartments defined in this application. Nearly every screen in the application uses these compartments.

The UX model has additional elements and diagrams that are not shown here. For the most part, these additional elements do not, from a UX design point of view, represent anything architecturally significant that cannot be understood from the figures shown already.

Figure B-10 shows a top-level summary of the storyboards defined in the application. Each storyboard, or UX realization, realizes a use case defined in the use case model. The sequence diagram for the Shop for Numbers storyboard is shown in Figures B-11 and B-12. The remaining storyboards can be found in the UML model.

Design

The top-level package diagram is shown in Figure B-13. This is a small application, one that is focused almost exclusively on the client and presentation tiers, so the model was not organized along tier boundaries but includes the elements for all tiers in the same packages.[1]

The Number Store recognizes four major architectural tiers: client, presentation, entity, and data. Only the client and the presentation tiers are implemented.

---

1. This is a departure from the recommended way to partition a design model according to the Rational Unified Process and Rational's general design guidelines.

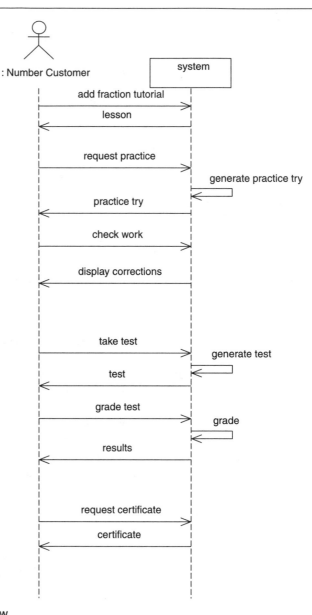

The customer or student requests the tutorial on adding fractions.

The system presents the lesson.

The student requests a practice try.

The system generates a new pair of fractions, and prompts the student to fill in each step required to add the fractions.

The student fills in the values and asks the system to check the work.

The system checks the work and reports the results to the student.

The student can either try a practice session again or request to take the test.

The student requests the test.

The system generates a new test and presents it to the student.

The student completes the test and submits the results to the system for grading.

The system grades the test and reports the score and any corrections to the student.

The student can take another test, go back to the lesson, or try the practice lesson again.

If the score was 70% or greater, the student can request a certificate of achievement to be displayed.

This use case ends.

FIGURE B-6 Add Fraction Tutorial: basic flow

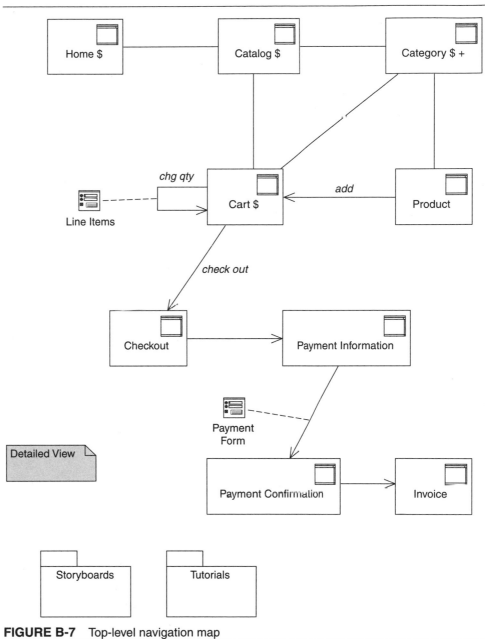

FIGURE B-7   Top-level navigation map

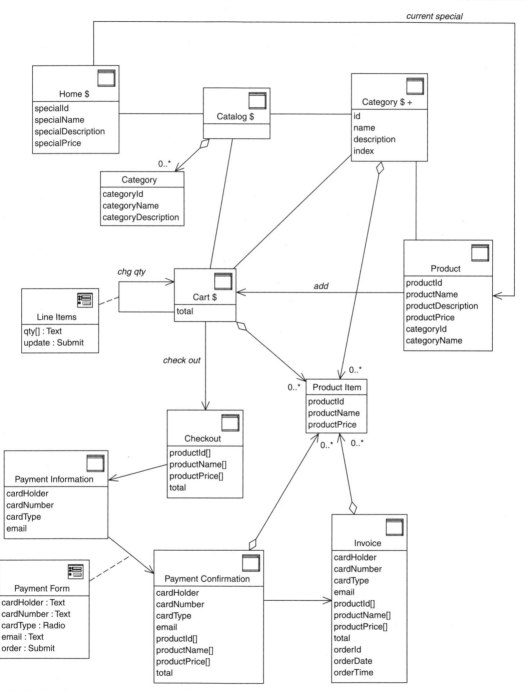

FIGURE B-8   Detailed view of navigation map

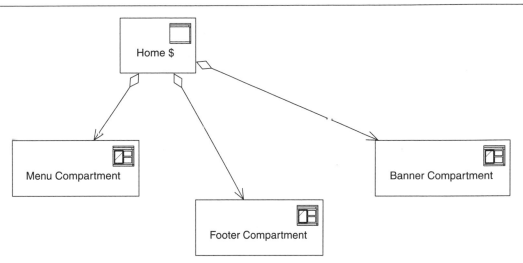

FIGURE B-9   Common compartments

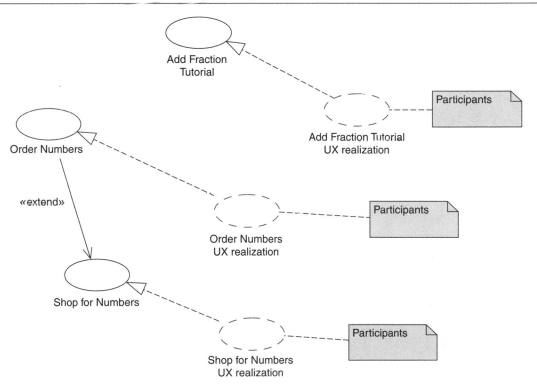

FIGURE B-10   Storyboards

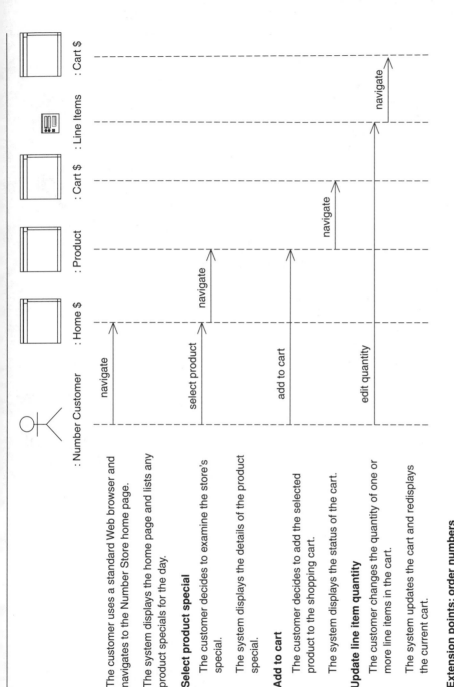

navigate · select product · add to cart · edit quantity

: Number Customer : Home $: Product : Cart $: Line Items : Cart $

navigate · navigate · navigate · navigate

The customer uses a standard Web browser and navigates to the Number Store home page.

The system displays the home page and lists any product specials for the day.

Select product special

The customer decides to examine the store's special.

The system displays the details of the product special.

Add to cart

The customer decides to add the selected product to the shopping cart.

The system displays the status of the cart.

Update line item quantity

The customer changes the quantity of one or more line items in the cart.

The system updates the cart and redisplays the current cart.

Extension points: order numbers

At any time the cart is displayed the customer can decided to check out and purchase the items. See Order Numbers use case.

Browse catalog

FIGURE B-11 Shop for Numbers storyboard

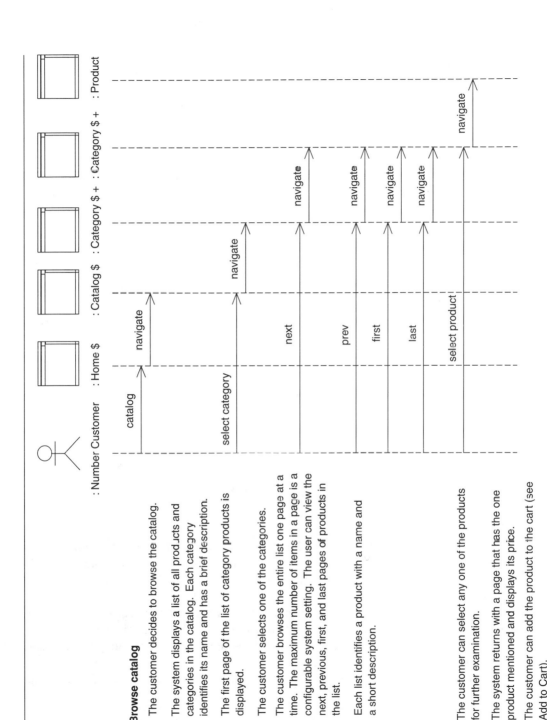

Browse catalog

The customer decides to browse the catalog.

The system displays a list of all products and categories in the catalog. Each category identifies its name and has a brief description.

The first page of the list of category products is displayed.

The customer selects one of the categories.

The customer browses the entire list one page at a time. The maximum number of items in a page is a configurable system setting. The user can view the next, previous, first, and last pages of products in the list.

Each list identifies a product with a name and a short description.

The customer can select any one of the products for further examination.

The system returns with a page that has the one product mentioned and displays its price.

The customer can add the product to the cart (see Add to Cart).

FIGURE B-12   Part 2 of the Shop for Numbers storyboard

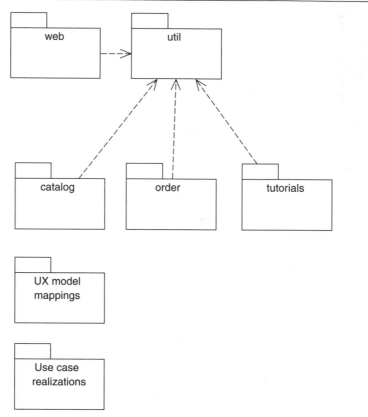

FIGURE B-13   Top-level design model packages

Client Tier

Most of the implementation in the client tier has already been accomplished with the use of standard Web browsers. The only custom client-tier code in this application is the JavaScript scripting in the fraction tutorial practice (Try It) page and the polynomial tutorial applet. Figure B-14 shows the Web page classes that implement the fraction tutorial client scripts. In this diagram, the `TryItIE.html` page is included only when an Internet Explorer browser is detected, because this particular set of scripting does not work in other browsers. For other browsers, no client scripting is used, and the `TryItOther.jsp` is used to build the page.

Figures B-13 and B-14 show the polynomial tutorial applet and the client page interactions.

Presentation Tier

The vast majority of the design and code in this application is in the presentation tier. This tier is responsible for responding to client requests and preparing suitable HTML

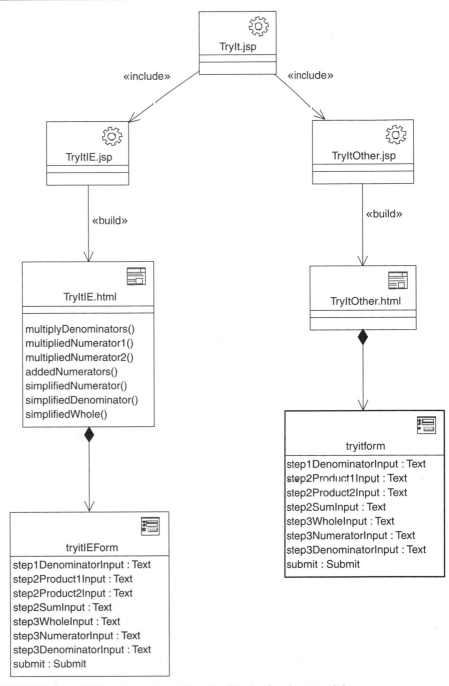

FIGURE B-14   Web page elements involved in the fraction tutorial

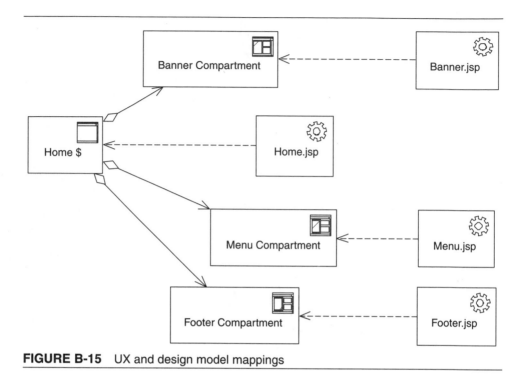

FIGURE B-15   UX and design model mappings

responses. The principal components in this tier are the Web server and the JSP engine. In this implementation, Tomcat 3.2.3 is used. Tomcat is a reference implementation for the Java servlet 2.2 and JavaServer Page technologies.

Each page request in this application is a request for a named screen. The screens are defined in the UX model. Figure B-15 shows the mappings from the Home screen and its compartments to the JSPs that are used to build that screen. The suffix .jsp is only a naming convention, used here to help distinguish between client and server pages, which often have similar names. Each screen in this application has mappings to the JSPs, or HTML pages, that are used to build it. The dependency from the screen to the server page uses the name to indicate which template parameter the JSP fulfills. In this figure, the home page is made up of a banner, a footer, and a content page. The JSPs that make up this screen are the dependent classes.

A fundamental part of this system's architecture is the mechanism it uses for accepting and processing incoming requests. This mechanism is derived from two common Web application architectural patterns: Controlled Controllers and Master Template, which are described in Appendixes C and D.

Page Request Handling

The overall architecture for handling page requests in this application begins with a mapping in the web.xml file that redirects all incoming requests for pages with the .scr extension to an instance in the `RequestProcessor` class. The request processor is a servlet and, technically, a «server page» stereotyped class, although in this particular model, it is stereotyped «HttpServlet» as a result of the UML tool's code engineering engine.

The request processor accepts all incoming requests and then instructs the appropriate controller to update the state of the business with the request, which contains not only the requested URL but also all incoming parameters and form input. Once the state has been updated, the processor checks to see whether another controller has been requested: a parameter on the URL. If a new controller has been requested, the processor checks with the active controller to see whether it requires exclusive control. If it doesn't, the new controller is made active, given the incoming request to update with, and placed on top of the active controller stack. A `UseCaseCoordinator` class is responsible for managing this stack. As a last step, the request processor asks the active controller for the next screen ID to redirect to. With this ID, control is passed, via a request dispatcher forward, to the `ControlTemplate`.

The `ControlTemplate`, a JSP that provides a utility method for defining screen definitions, is responsible for setting in context any scriptlet values useful in the `PresentationTemplate`. The `PresentationTemplate` is the JSP that is the main template of the Master Template pattern. This JSP is responsible for formatting all outgoing pages consistently. It accesses the screen definition attributes and uses them as the template's parameters. Most of these parameters point to JSPs that are aggregated to produce one output screen. The `PresentationTemplate` uses five parameters: a header, a footer, content and menu JSPs, and one string value for the page name, used in the title element of the head element. Figure B-16 shows principal classes and JSPs involved in processing all page requests.

The design model use case realizations show how each page request updates the active controller and then redirects the output page, building to a set of server page classes. The basic scenario for handling page requests is shown in the sequence diagram in Figure B-17.

Figure B-18 shows some of the utility classes that participate in the page request scenarios. The `RequestProcessor` servlet is the main point of entry for all HTTP requests. It uses the `UseCaseCoordinator` object, held in the user's `HttpSession` object, to coordinate the controllers. The `ScreenDefinition` class is a small wrapper around definitions for screens, that is, composition of individual JSP pages.

Defining Controllers

The Number Store application is heavily dependent on discrete controllers for managing navigational flow and coordinating business logic execution. Figure B-19 shows the page classes that support shopping functionality. Figure B-20 shows the main Java classes that provide access to the business logic in the page, along with the `ShopController` class.

The `ShopController` is a special controller; it is the default controller for all users of the application and never expires, so it can always be found on the controller

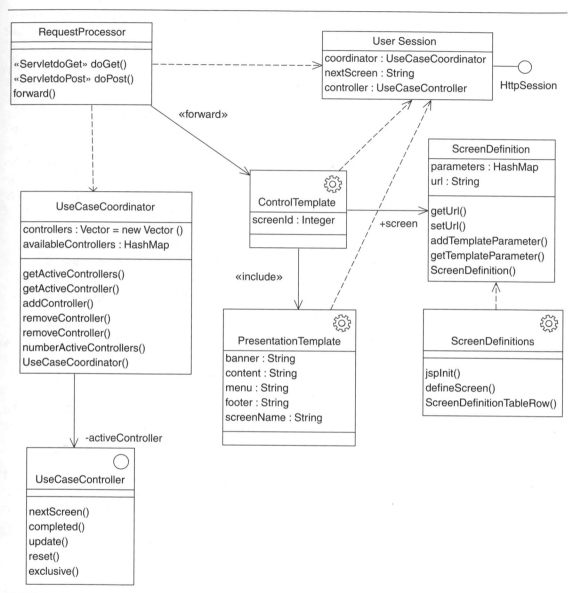

FIGURE B-16   Overview of page request class

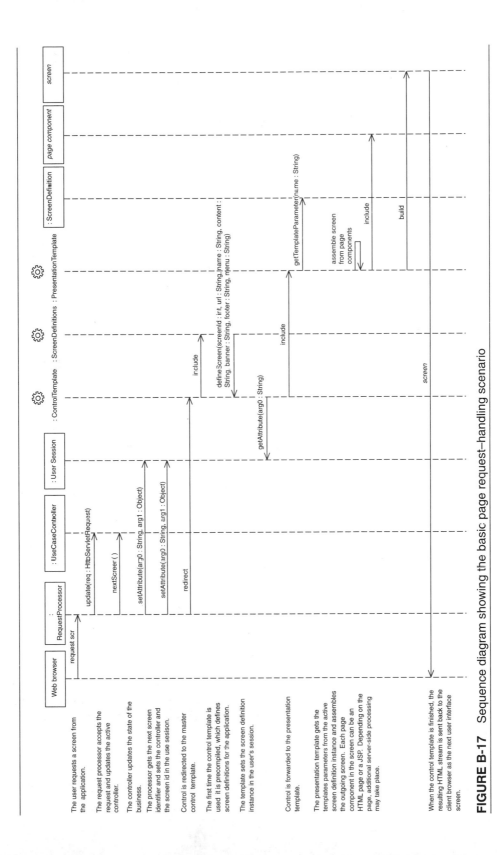

FIGURE B-17 Sequence diagram showing the basic page request-handling scenario

The user requests a screen from the application.

The request processor accepts the request and updates the active controller.

The controller updates the state of the business.

The processor gets the next screen identifier and sets the controller and the screen id in the use sesison.

Control is redirected to the master control template.

The first time the control template is used it is precompiled, which defines screen definitions for the application.

The template sets the screen definition instance in the user's session.

Control is forwarded to the presentation template.

The presentation template gets the templates parameters from the active screen definition instance and assembles the outgoing screen. Each page component in the screen can be an HTML page or a JSP. Depending on the page, additional server-side processing may take place.

When the control template is finished, the resulting HTML stream is sent back to the client browser as the next user interface screen.

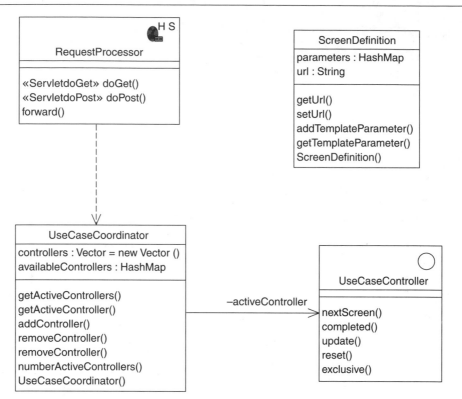

FIGURE B-18 Utility classes involved in page request handling

stack. All controllers in this application define a state machine.[2] The state machine for the shopping controller is shown in Figure B-21. The state machine can easily be seen reflected in the `determineNextScreen()` operations in each of the controllers.

UX Mapping

An example of the UX and design model mapping diagrams is shown for the Fraction Tutorial section of the application (Figure B-22).

Entity Tier

In a real Web application, business state is changed. This state usually corresponds to elements in a database. The entity tier is the layer on top of the database, responsible for all the business rules and logic in the system. This tier is in a J2EE application and

---

2. It was the only way I could keep my sanity when developing the application. Until I started defining state machines for each controller, I found myself continually trying to correct boundary conditions in behavior.

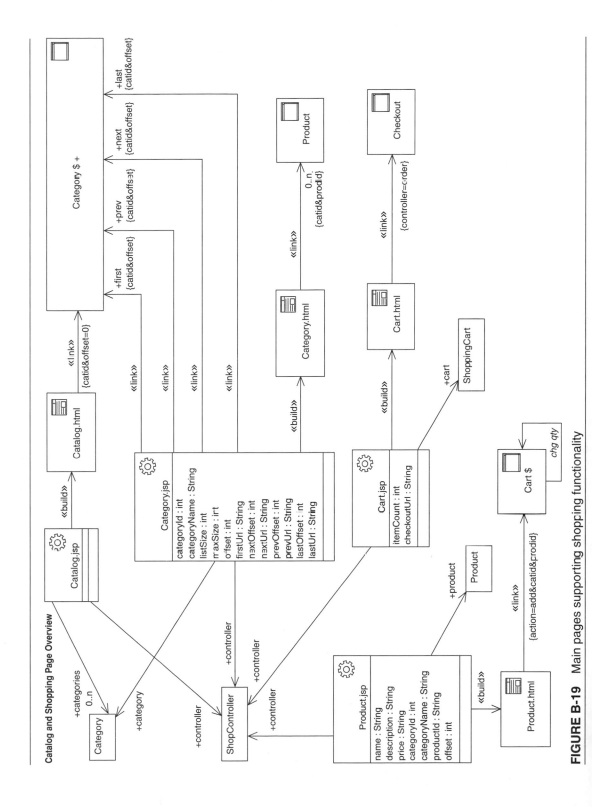

FIGURE B-19 Main pages supporting shopping functionality

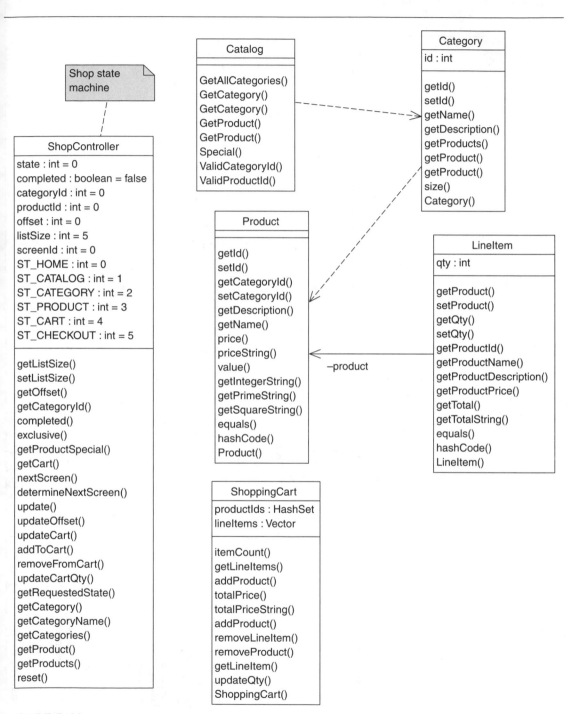

FIGURE B-20   Main Java classes supporting shopping functions

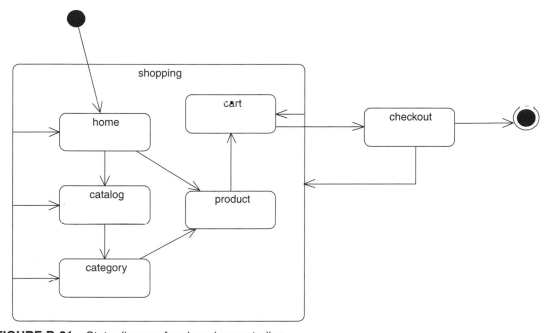

FIGURE B-21   State diagram for shopping controller

is implemented with Enterprise JavaBeans (EJB). The EJB container(s) manage all the transactional logic in the system. For this reference application, however, EJBs are not used, since the purpose of this application is to show how to model presentation-tier components. For details on how to model EJBs, refer to the official Java specification for modeling Enterprise JavaBeans with UML (Java Specification Request, or JSR, 26). Instead, this application uses standard Java classes to implement the entity tier. Figure B-23 shows some of the entity classes that make up the catalog.

Data Tier

The persistence part of the application is the data tier. In this application, all persistence is mimicked by classes in the presentation tier. The data tier provides persistence services to the entity tier. In some architectures, this tier might implement business logic—stored procedures—whereas in others, only integrity constraints are implemented. In this application, the data tier doesn't exist.

Component View

To accurately model the component view of this application, two separate but connected hierarchies in the model, identified by the package stereotypes «virtual root» and «physical root». The «virtual root» contains component elements that map

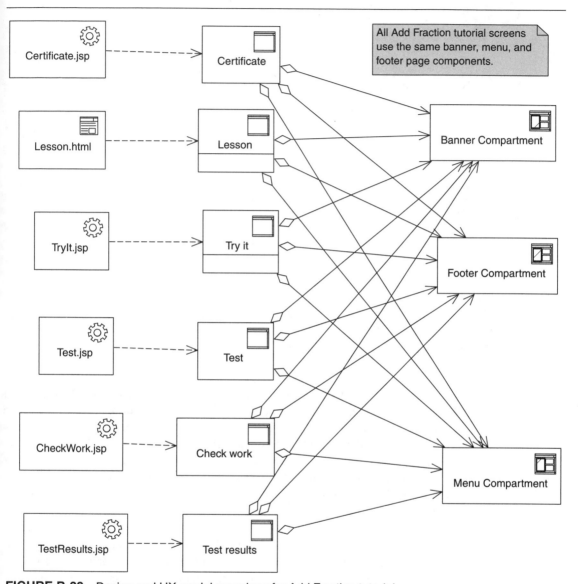

FIGURE B-22   Design and UX model mappings for Add Fraction tutorial

directly to valid URLs that the system will respond to. Each component is stereotyped «HttpResource» and realizes the screen elements in the UX model. The «physical root» contains JSP and HTML stereotyped elements that map directly to JSP and HTML files in the development file system and, presumably, the relative runtime file system. Figure B-24 shows the top-level component view.

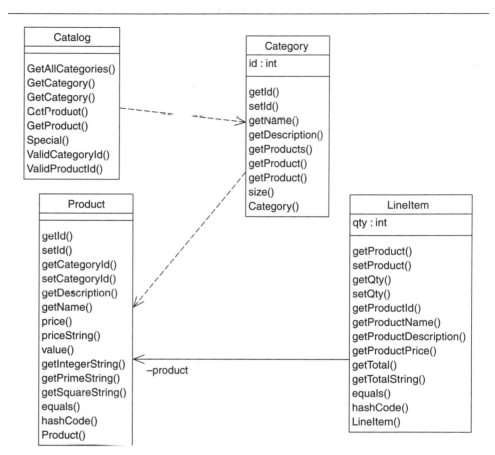

FIGURE B-23   Entity-tier classes, implemented as standard Java classes

Under the «virtual root» package, NumberStore Web, are components stereotyped «HttpResource». Each of these components represents a valid URL in the system that a client browser can request. All the components have a .scr extension, which is identified by the Web server container. All HTTP requests made for resources with this extension are forwarded to the RequestProcessor servlet. Figure B-25 shows the contents of the «virtual root» package in a hierarchy tree. Next to this tree are some contents of the «physical root» package. In this component package are «static page» and «dynamic page» stereotyped components—in this case, the JSP components are stereotyped «JSP». Also under this hierarchy is a component for the web.xml configuration file and some key image files.

Figure B-26 shows a component diagram in the «virtual root». In this diagram, all the screen definitions are organized by use cases.

Component realizations begin with «HTTPResource» components that realize screens in the UX model. «JSP» components in the «physical root» package realize

NumberStore Web

Application Web resource components hierarchy (referenceable URLs)

Web

Application Web components physical package hierarchy (JSP, HTML implementations)

com

Application Java class packages

java

javax

JDK 1.3 and J2EE class packages

FIGURE B-24   Top-level component diagram

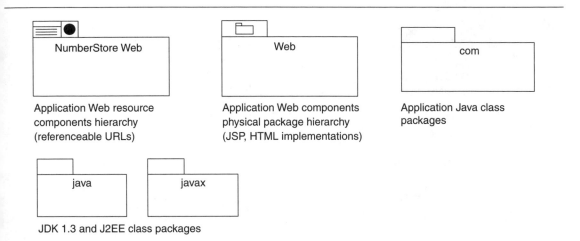

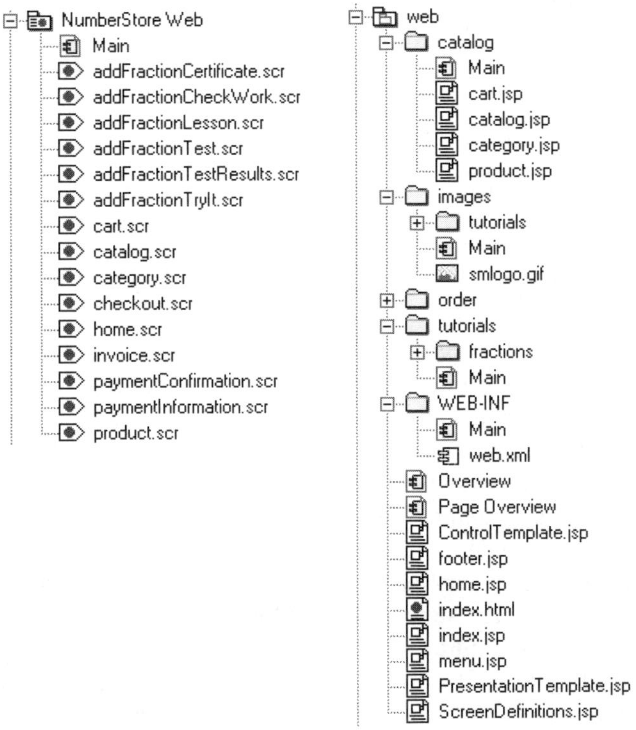

FIGURE B-25   Component hierarchies of the packages «virtual root» and «physical root»

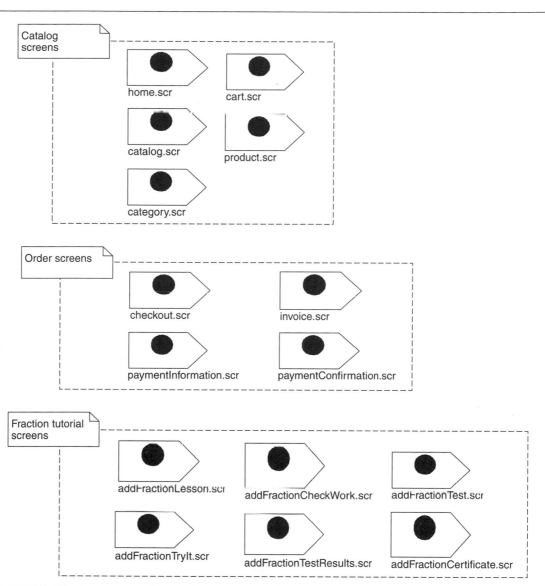

FIGURE B-26 Component diagram for the «virtual root» containing «HTTPResource» stereotyped component elements

«server page» and «client page» classes in the design model. The connection between which HTTP resources (URLs) are handled by which «JSP» components can be determined only by the UX and design model mappings. Using the mapping between the UX screen and the «server page» or «client page» logical class and then following the realization to the component will identify which JSP pages are used to respond to which requested URLs (Figure B-27).

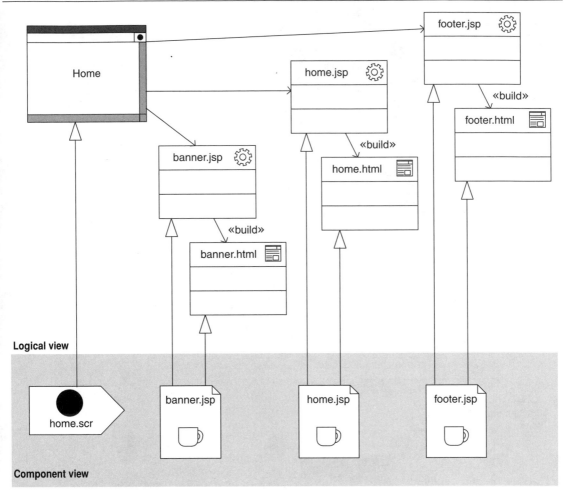

FIGURE B-27   Realizing components

This may seem overly complex—and in my opinion it is. However, this architecture does have advantages for extensibility and maintainability. The architecture imposes certain rules and regulations for expanding the application with new pages and controllers. Adhering to the rules will make application maintenance much easier than what might happen in an application without a formal control-driven architecture.

Sample Screen Shots

Figures B-28 through B-33 are screen shots that show the kinds of things the user would view at some point in the Number Store application.

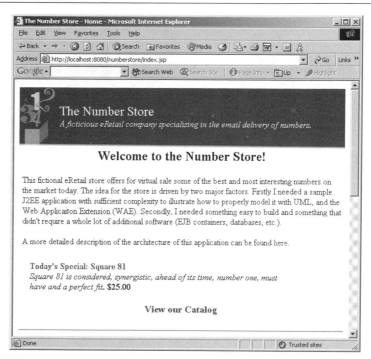

FIGURE B-28 The house page for the Number Store application

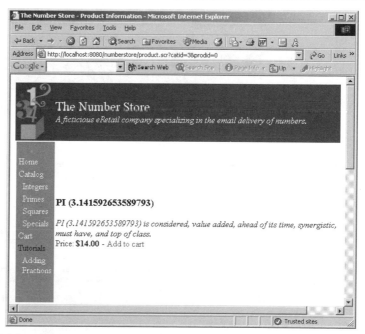

FIGURE B-29 The product details screen for the number PI

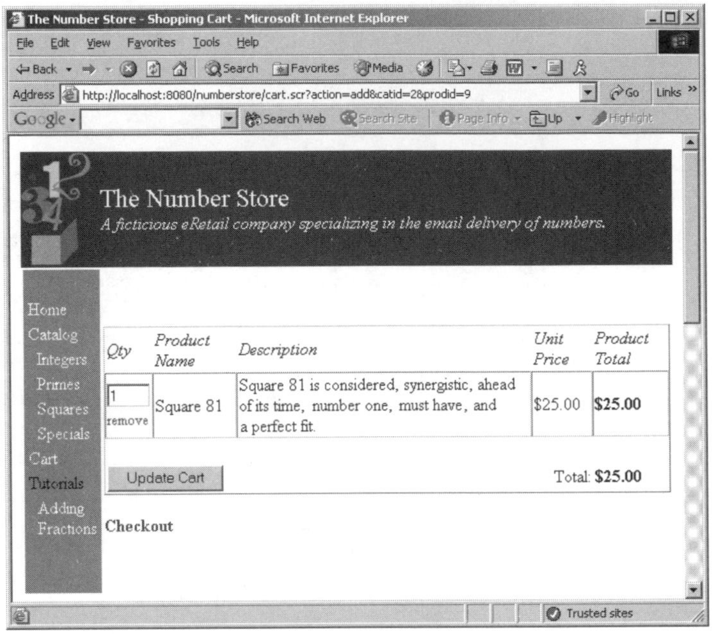

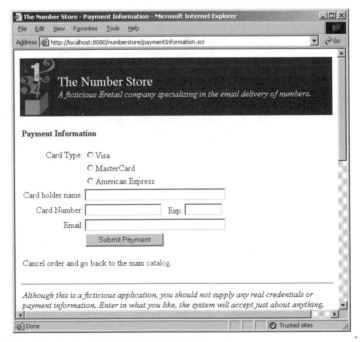

FIGURE B-30　The shopping cart screen

FIGURE B-31　The payment information screen

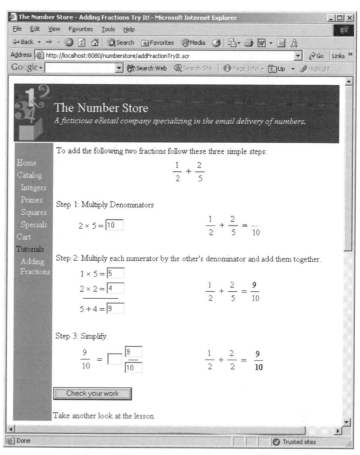

FIGURE B-32   The fraction tutorial's try it screen

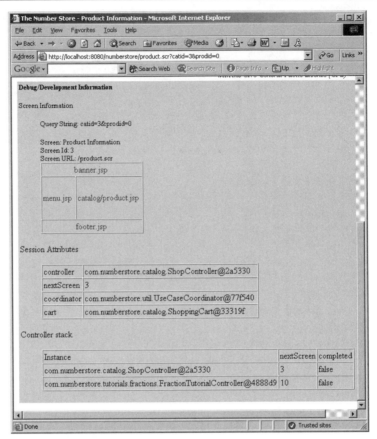

FIGURE B-33   Debug information appears at the bottom of every screen of the application

Appendix C
Controlled Controllers Pattern

Use Case View

The controlled controllers mechanism allows the application to be designed around multiple discrete presentation-tier controllers. Related to the Model View Controller (MVC) pattern, the controlled controllers mechanism is a manager of individual MVC controllers. Each controller represents a separate use case and is responsible for managing the dialogue between the user, or actor, and the system for all supported scenarios. The top-level use case model is shown in Figure C-1. The basic flow for accepting and

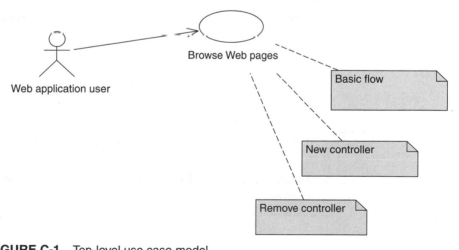

FIGURE C-1 Top-level use case model

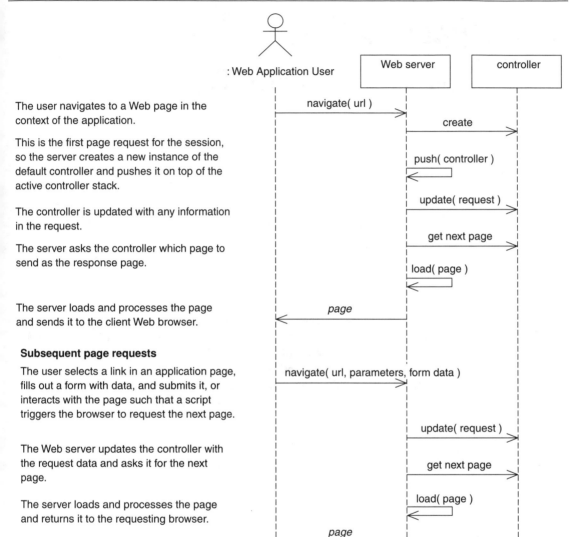

The user navigates to a Web page in the context of the application.

This is the first page request for the session, so the server creates a new instance of the default controller and pushes it on top of the active controller stack.

The controller is updated with any information in the request.

The server asks the controller which page to send as the response page.

The server loads and processes the page and sends it to the client Web browser.

Subsequent page requests

The user selects a link in an application page, fills out a form with data, and submits it, or interacts with the page such that a script triggers the browser to request the next page.

The Web server updates the controller with the request data and asks it for the next page.

The server loads and processes the page and returns it to the requesting browser.

FIGURE C-2   Basic flow scenario

managing a user page request is documented in the sequence diagram of Figure C-2. The sequence diagram for adding controllers to the stack is shown in Figure C-3. Figure C-4 shows how controllers are removed.

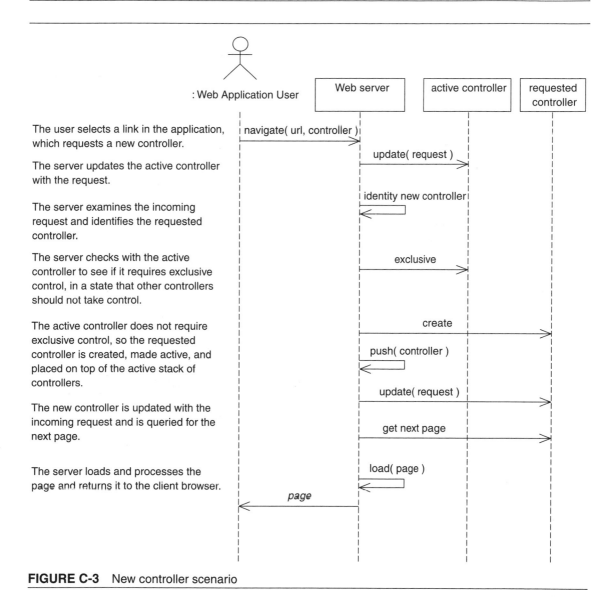

The user selects a link in the application, which requests a new controller.

The server updates the active controller with the request.

The server examines the incoming request and identifies the requested controller.

The server checks with the active controller to see if it requires exclusive control, in a state that other controllers should not take control.

The active controller does not require exclusive control, so the requested controller is created, made active, and placed on top of the active stack of controllers.

The new controller is updated with the incoming request and is queried for the next page.

The server loads and processes the page and returns it to the client browser.

FIGURE C-3 New controller scenario

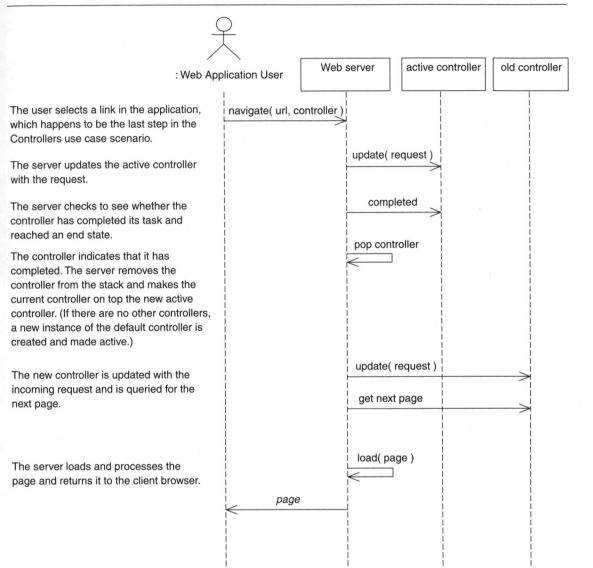

The user selects a link in the application, which happens to be the last step in the Controllers use case scenario.

The server updates the active controller with the request.

The server checks to see whether the controller has completed its task and reached an end state.

The controller indicates that it has completed. The server removes the controller from the stack and makes the current controller on top the new active controller. (If there are no other controllers, a new instance of the default controller is created and made active.)

The new controller is updated with the incoming request and is queried for the next page.

The server loads and processes the page and returns it to the client browser.

FIGURE C-4   Remove Controller

Analysis Model Classes

Each controller is a single object—which may have many helper objects, if necessary—but all support a common interface. A key element in this mechanism is that the Web application server is configured to route all incoming requests through a single class: one object instance for each user session. This object is the RequestProcessor.

At the heart of this mechanism is the coordinator, an object that manages all the active controller instances for a particular user. When a user begins using the application, the default controller is pressed into service and manages all the user page resource requests. A different controller can be requested to take control of the user session, by specifying it as a parameter in a URL hyperlink. This implies that at least some hyperlinks in the application will have knowledge of the other controllers that can be activated and used by the user. (A good example of this is a common menu HTML component whereby each hyperlink in it specifies the controller that manages that activity.)

When it sees a request for a new controller, the coordinator first checks with the active controller to ensure that it doesn't require exclusive control—for example, in the middle of an important scenario that cannot be postponed. If it doesn't, the current controller is placed on a stack, and the new controller is made the current one. All subsequent page resource requests are managed by this controller until it is completed.

When a controller is completed, the coordinator removes it from the active stack, and the next controller on the top is made the current active controller. (If there are none on the stack, a new instance of the default controller is created.) Figure C-5 shows an analysis-level diagram of the coordinator and its relations to the individual controllers.

Each controller must be able to accept an incoming HTTP request for a page resource, process any parameters or field data, update the state of the business, and identify the next page resource to send to the requester. In some situations, the requested page resource cannot be returned to the user, and a different one is sent. For example, the user might submit payment information, and normal flow would be to the page that redisplays this information and prompts for confirmation. If the data was invalid, the requested page—payment confirmation—shouldn't be returned; rather, the payment information request page should be, with an informational message indicating the invalid information. The controller is responsible for processing the payment information and determining which of the two response pages should be sent back.

Each response page may interact with the state of the business in order to get and to assemble the dynamic content in each page. It is also expected that each "page builder" can easily get a reference to the current active controller, which provides a convenient access point to the business state. Figure C-6 shows an analysis diagram of the controller and its relationship to the individual page builders and page user interfaces.

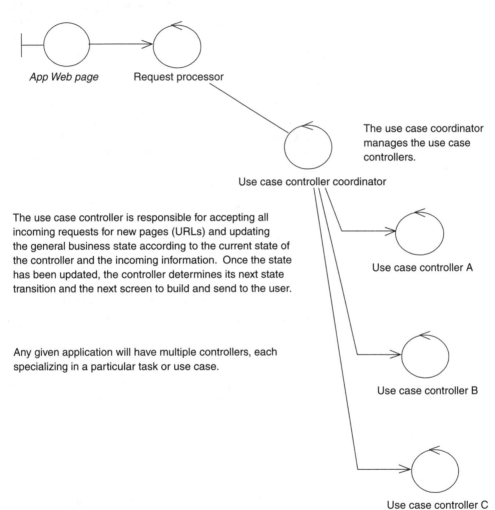

The request processor accepts the incoming request, identifying new controller requests and then delegating the processing of the request to the active use case controller. It uses the coordinator to manage the controller stack.

App Web page   Request processor

The use case coordinator manages the use case controllers.

Use case controller coordinator

The use case controller is responsible for accepting all incoming requests for new pages (URLs) and updating the general business state according to the current state of the controller and the incoming information. Once the state has been updated, the controller determines its next state transition and the next screen to build and send to the user.

Use case controller A

Any given application will have multiple controllers, each specializing in a particular task or use case.

Use case controller B

Use case controller C

FIGURE C-5   Main analysis-level class diagram for mechanism

The use case coordinator manages the use case controllers and is responsible for accepting all incoming requests, identifying new controller requests, and then delegating the processing of the request to the active use case controller.

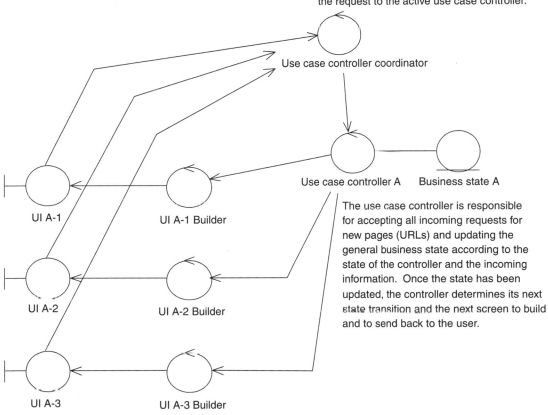

Use case controller coordinator

Use case controller A   Business state A

UI A-1   UI A-1 Builder

UI A-2   UI A-2 Builder

UI A-3   UI A-3 Builder

The use case controller is responsible for accepting all incoming requests for new pages (URLs) and updating the general business state according to the state of the controller and the incoming information. Once the state has been updated, the controller determines its next state transition and the next screen to build and to send back to the user.

Depending on the tasks of the use case, the set of user interfaces and builders vary. In general, each user interface has a builder, and every user interface submits its requests for new pages to the single use case controller instance (one per user session) for processing.

FIGURE C-6 *Sample set of controllers*

Analysis Model Collaborations

The basic dynamic behavior of this mechanism is shown in Figure C-7. In this sequence diagram, the client browser requests a page resource. The RequestProcessor handles this request and delegates the processing of any input data—URL parameters or form data—to the current active controller. If this is the first page request, a new instance of the default controller is created and made currently active. The processor then requests the next page resource to load, execute, and send back to the client browser.

The Figure C-8 sequence diagram shows how the request processor and the coordinator add a controller to the active stack. In this scenario, the request processor examines the incoming request for a parameter that indicates a new controller request. Before invoking the new controller, the request processor makes sure that the current controller doesn't require exclusive control. If it doesn't, the new controller is made current and active and given the input request for processing. The new controller now is the current active controller.

In Figure C-9, the current controller indicates that it is finished and that the coordinator can remove it from being active. The next controller in the stack is now returned to active and current status and is given the input request, which it most likely will ignore, and asked which page to load and send to the client. The overall flow of this mechanism is shown in Figure C-10.

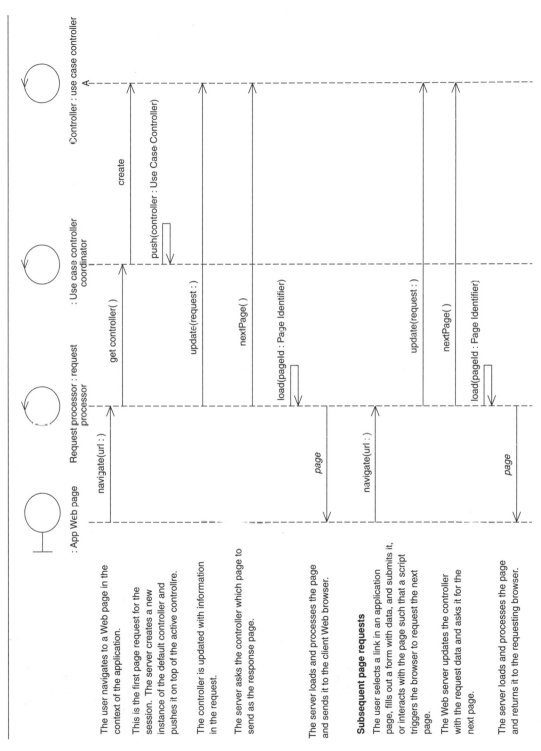

The user navigates to a Web page in the context of the application.

This is the first page request for the session. The server creates a new instance of the default controller and pushes it on top of the active controlire.

The controller is updated with information in the request.

The server asks the controller which page to send as the response page.

The server loads and processes the page and sends it to the client Web browser.

Subsequent page requests

The user selects a link in an application page, fills out a form with data, and submits it, or interacts with the page such that a script triggers the browser to request the next page.

The Web server updates the controller with the request data and asks it for the next page.

The server loads and processes the page and returns it to the requesting browser.

FIGURE C-7   Basic flow use case realization

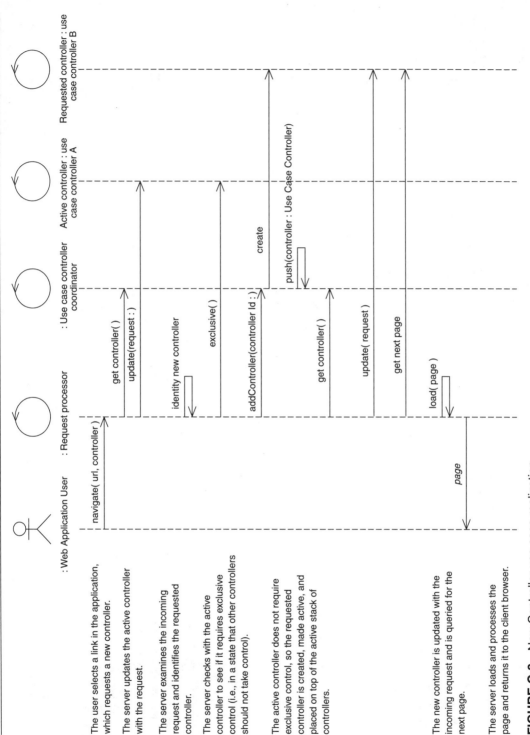

The user selects a link in the application, which requests a new controller.

The server updates the active controller with the request.

The server examines the incoming request and identifies the requested controller.

The server checks with the active controller to see if it requires exclusive control (i.e., in a state that other controllers should not take control).

The active controller does not require exclusive control, so the requested controller is created, made active, and placed on top of the active stack of controllers.

The new controller is updated with the incoming request and is queried for the next page.

The server loads and processes the page and returns it to the client browser.

FIGURE C-8 New Controller use case realization

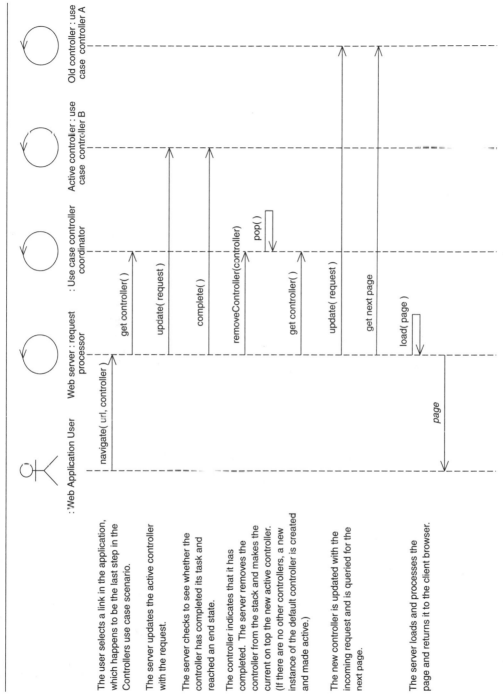

The user selects a link in the application, which happens to be the last step in the Controllers use case scenario.

The server updates the active controller with the request.

The server checks to see whether the controller has completed its task and reached an end state.

The controller indicates that it has completed. The server removes the controller from the stack and makes the current on top the new active controller. (If there are no other controllers, a new instance of the default controller is created and made active.)

The new controller is updated with the incoming request and is queried for the next page.

The server loads and processes the page and returns it to the client browser.

FIGURE C-9   Remove Controller use case realization

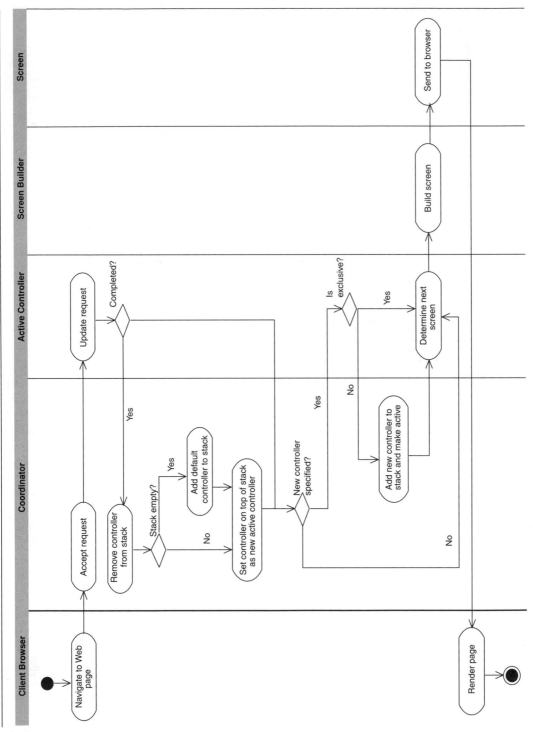

FIGURE C-10 Activity diagram summarizing mechanism

Appendix D
Master Template Pattern

Overview

The master template mechanism was influenced by the Java Pet Store 1.0.1 example documented in the Java BluePrints. In this mechanism, one page template (JSP) is used for all outgoing pages, thereby helping enforce a consistent user interface look-and-feel and providing a single source for updates. This mechanism is most useful for applications that can benefit from an explicitly controlled user interface template, one in which pages are expected to be added to the application. This mechanism does carry some performance penalties, so it should be examined in detail before being used in applications that are expected to scale quickly.

Use Case View

The basic use case for page requests has only one scenario flow. Figure D-1 shows the top-level use case diagram for this mechanism. The basic flow scenario is shown in Figure D-2.

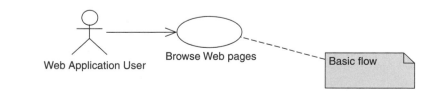

FIGURE D-1   Use case diagram

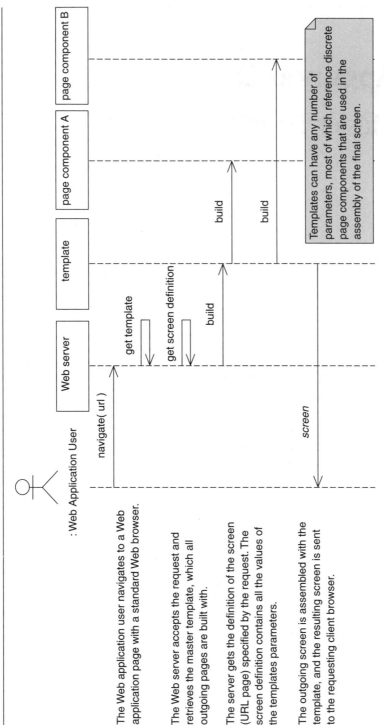

The Web application user navigates to a Web application page with a standard Web browser.

The Web server accepts the request and retrieves the master template, which all outgoing pages are built with.

The server gets the definition of the screen (URL page) specified by the request. The screen definition contains all the values of the templates parameters.

The outgoing screen is assembled with the template, and the resulting screen is sent to the requesting client browser.

FIGURE D-2 Basic flow scenario

Logical View

The class diagram in Figure D-3 shows the principal participants in this mechanism. The user screen represents any Web page rendered on the client. Each screen could be assembled from the output of many Web server "pages," or JSPs. Each page component may contain dynamic content and so may interact with the application server or middle-tier components of the application. The Web server is the main controller for this mechanism and the single point of entry for page requests. The Web server is most likely a commodity component, such as Tomcat, WebSphere, Web Logic, and IIS.

The screen template is the single template used to assemble and to format all outgoing screens, or pages. Depending on which URL was requested, the template uses the URL as a key to the screen's dictionary. The screen definitions are a dictionary, or map, of possible screens. Each entry has a set of parameter values that are used by the template when assembling the outgoing screen. A screen component is one part of an outgoing page and is implemented by either a static HTML fragment file or a dynamic page—JSP, PHP, ASP—which produces HTML fragments with dynamic content.

The parameters of the template are string identifiers of the individual page components. Typically, they point to files to include and contain HTML fragments or, in the case of dynamic components, contain JSP, PHP, or ASP code, which is processed before it returns the HTML fragments. Each parameter is named; this name is used by

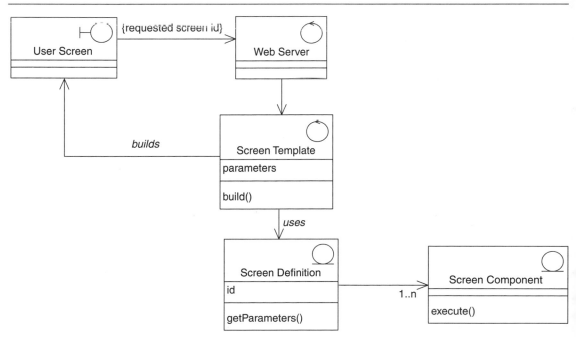

FIGURE D-3   Main analysis class diagram

the template as a key to get the parameter value. For example, a template that defines a header, a footer, and the main body would have three defined parameters. The header and footer values might reference a standard HTML document that is intended to be used in every outgoing page, whereas the main body parameter would most likely reference a dynamic page that assembles the bulk of the application's presentation.

For each incoming screen request, the Web server delegates the request to the single "master" template, which examines the request and uses it to determine which screen definition to use for the outgoing page. With the next screen identified, the template gets its parameters and uses them to load and to process the page components individually. The result is sent to the requesting client browser. Figure D-4 shows the sequence diagram of this basic flow.

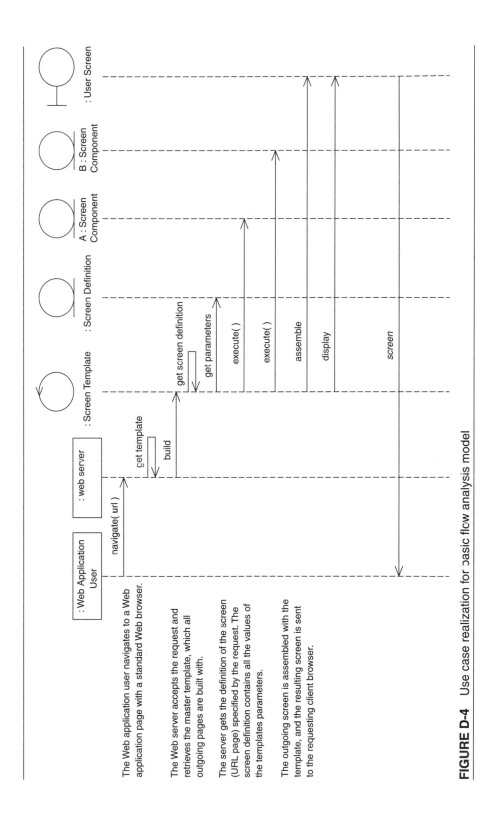

FIGURE D-4 Use case realization for basic flow analysis model

The Web application user navigates to a Web application page with a standard Web browser.

The Web server accepts the request and retrieves the master template, which all outgoing pages are built with.

The server gets the definition of the screen (URL page) specified by the request. The screen definition contains all the values of the templates parameters.

The outgoing screen is assembled with the template, and the resulting screen is sent to the requesting client browser.

Appendix E

Glossary Application

Introduction

In the first edition of this book, a simple Active Server Page sample application was created to demonstrate the UML artifacts that were created. This is the second, J2EE version of that application. For the most part, the functionality of the application remains the same; however, one new feature was added: versioning. This feature allows users to examine the history of changes to any glossary entry.

Requirements and Use Case Model

The overall goal and vision for this application is to demonstrate, in the context of a simple and functional application, a technique for modeling Web applications with UML. Because the WAE is applicable for only client- and presentation-tier elements, most of the effort in this application can be found in these two tiers. The entity and data tiers, although functional, are not the focus of the development efforts and are not very interesting.

A new requirement for this second version of the Glossary application is to include an example of a «client script object». An excellent example of a well-engineered JavaScript object is the Menu object designed by Gary Smith of Netscape. This object was included in this application without modification and shows how you can build objects in JavaScript.

Another requirement is to allow HTML formatting in entry definitions. The application, however, must not require users to know or to understand HTML, so the use of HTML-encoded descriptions should be optional.

This application has only two simple use cases: Browse Entries and Edit Entry. The top-level model is shown in Figure E-1. The Edit Entry use case extends the normal browsing of the Glossary application by allowing an entry to be edited only in context, which, of course, means that it must be browsed to first.

The basic flow scenarios for the two use cases are shown in Figures E-2 and E-3.

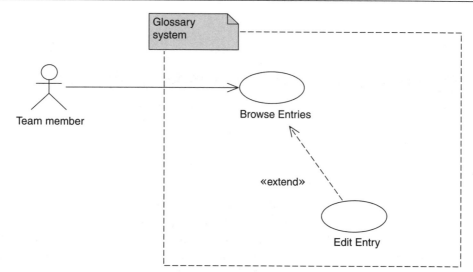

FIGURE E-1   Glossary use cases

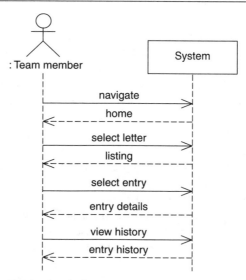

FIGURE E-2   Browse Entries basic flow

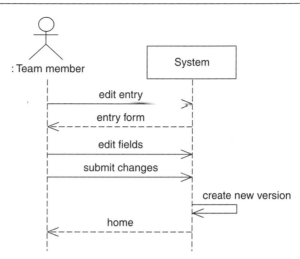

FIGURE E-3 Edit Entry basic flow

User Experience Model

The top-level diagram of the UX model for the Glossary application is shown in Figure E-4, which shows definitions for five screens. Two of the screens contain input forms. One complex-content-type class, Entry, is identified in this diagram. Entry is the key entity in the system; indeed, Entry is the only entity of this application.

The two storyboards for this application are expressed in the sequence diagrams of Figures E-5 and E-6.

Design Model

The design model contains an expression of the logical structure and behavior of the application's main objects. At the highest level, the design model is partitioned into architectural tiers (i.e., client, presentation, business, and data).

Client Tier

The client tier is limited to the objects and collaborations that execute in the client browser. Each Web page in this application contains a pop-up menu implemented with JavaScript. The menu is modeled by the «client script object» menu. Most pages define two instances of the menu: one main menu (actionMenu) and one submenu (browseMenu).

The Menu class contains member variables of type Array, shown in Figure E-7 as associations to the JavaScript Array object. The complete JavaScript 1.3 object model is included in this application's model as a reference.

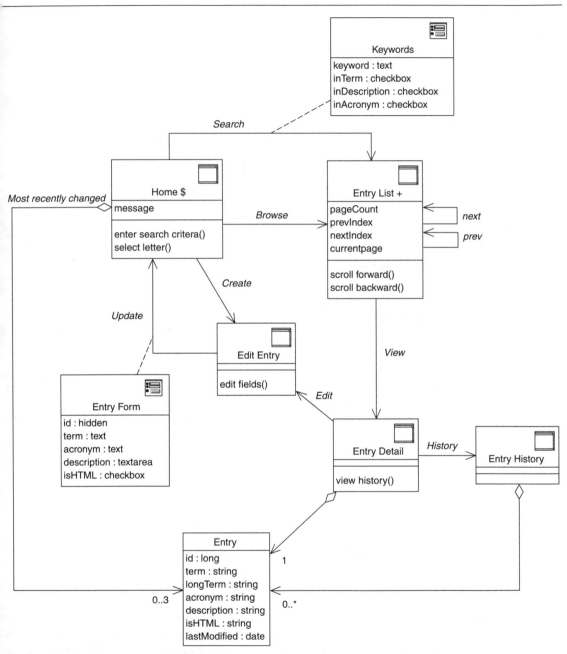

FIGURE E-4   Top-level navigation map

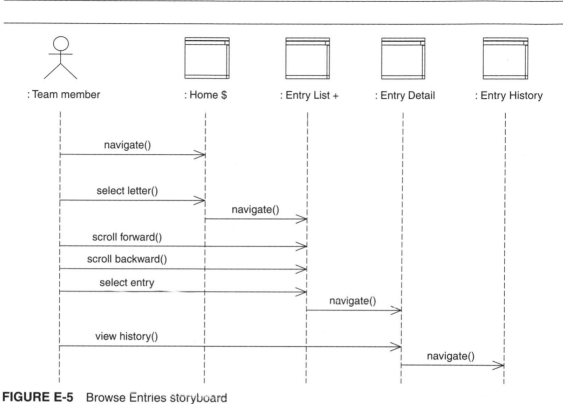

FIGURE E-5   Browse Entries storyboard

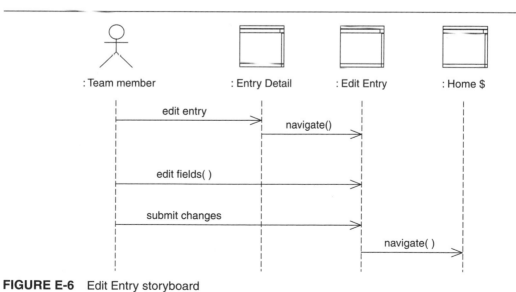

FIGURE E-6   Edit Entry storyboard

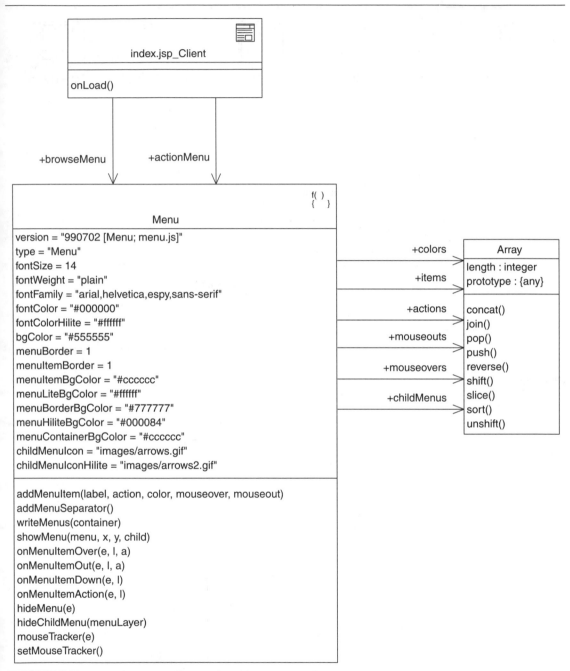

FIGURE E-7   Use of menu «client script object» Menu class

Presentation Tier

The majority of the work in this application is in the presentation tier. In this application, the navigational control is left to the individual pages; there is no single controller, as might be found in MVC-based applications. This application uses custom JSP tags extensively. The tag library is modeled as a «tag library» stereotyped subsystem and is seen in Figure E-8 modeled by the Entry Tags subsystem. In this diagram, the server pages index.jsp and listing.jsp both use the library.

The Entry Tags library contains three tag definitions: EntryList, EntryLoop, and Entry. Figure E-9 shows the «JSPTag» stereotyped elements with stereotyped dependencies to their implementation classes. Each tag defined here also defines several scripting variables that can be used in the tag body. These variables are modeled as «scripting variable» stereotyped attributes. The other attributes of the «JSPTag» elements are the tag attributes, the legal attributes that can be specified when using a JSP custom tag. For example, in the following code fragment, the Entry tag specifies the entryid and convertLineBreaks tag attributes and uses the term and description scripting variables in the body's tag. A detailed view of the classes that make up the tag implementation classes is shown in Figure E-10. The TEI classes are required for all tags that define scripting variables.

The JSP interacts with the entity tier through the tag implementation classes. All communication to the entity-tier components is via the custom tags (Figure E-11). This allows the JSP source to have a minimal amount of Java code and instead contain mostly HTML or HTML-like code.

The EntryList tag is required in every JSP that uses the tags and must be a parent tag to the other two tags: EntryLoop and Entry. The EntryList tag is responsible for connecting to the Glossary entries, which are then made available by the other two tags. The EntryLoop tag is used to get entry values that are part of a list, as would be the case when browsing. The Entry tag is used when only one entry is required, as is the case in the entry view and editing pages.

The tags are also responsible for ensuring that the encodings of the entity values are appropriate for HTML. This means that string values in entry attributes should convert less-than and greater-than characters to the appropriate HTML: < and >.

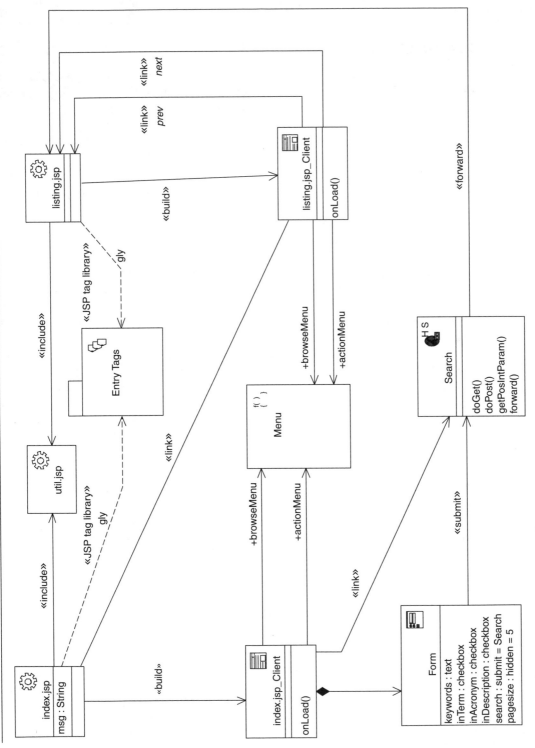

FIGURE E-8 Web pages involved in Browse use case

```
<gly:Entry entryid="5" convertLineBreaks="yes">
  Entry: <%=term%>
   <p><%=description%></p>
</gly:Entry>
```

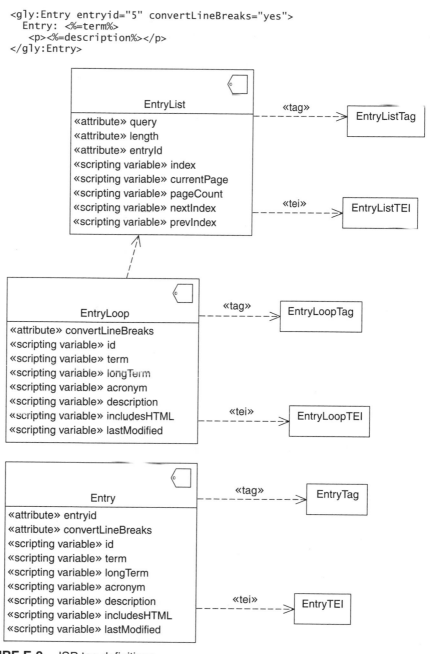

FIGURE E-9   JSP tag definitions

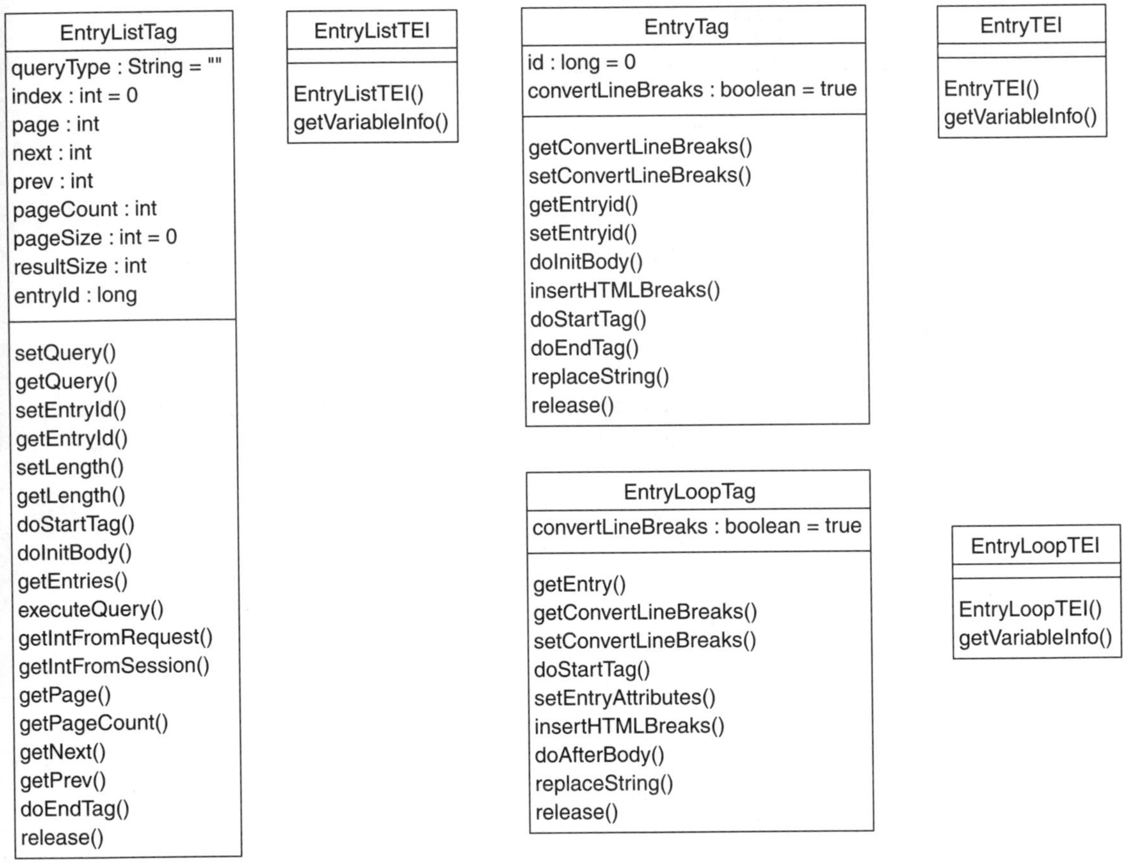

EntryListTag
queryType : String = ""
index : int = 0
page : int
next : int
prev : int
pageCount : int
pageSize : int = 0
resultSize : int
entryId : long
setQuery()
getQuery()
setEntryId()
getEntryId()
setLength()
getLength()
doStartTag()
doInitBody()
getEntries()
executeQuery()
getIntFromRequest()
getIntFromSession()
getPage()
getPageCount()
getNext()
getPrev()
doEndTag()
release()

EntryListTEI
EntryListTEI()
getVariableInfo()

EntryTag
id : long = 0
convertLineBreaks : boolean = true
getConvertLineBreaks()
setConvertLineBreaks()
getEntryid()
setEntryid()
doInitBody()
insertHTMLBreaks()
doStartTag()
doEndTag()
replaceString()
release()

EntryTEI
EntryTEI()
getVariableInfo()

EntryLoopTag
convertLineBreaks : boolean = true
getEntry()
getConvertLineBreaks()
setConvertLineBreaks()
doStartTag()
setEntryAttributes()
insertHTMLBreaks()
doAfterBody()
replaceString()
release()

EntryLoopTEI
EntryLoopTEI()
getVariableInfo()

FIGURE E-10   Entry Tag's implementing classes

Entity Tier

The entity tier in this application has only one true entity—Entry—and one entity manager—Glossary. An additional class acts as a wrapper for an entry query. This class combines all the search criteria information and makes it easier to cache and to pass along to the Glossary. An instance of this class is cached in the user's session (HttpSession) in the presentation tier. The interfaces for the main entity-tier classes are shown in Figure E-12, and the classes that implement them are shown in Figure E-13.

Data Tier

The logical data model is very simple and was intended to use only a minimal number of database features, in order to be portable across many relational databases. In this reference application, the mySQL database was used, but this application has also

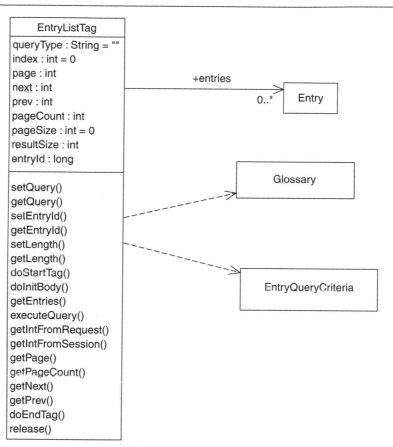

FIGURE E-11 `EntryListTag` interacting with entity-tier objects

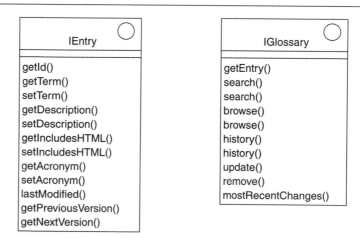

FIGURE E-12   Key entity-tier interfaces

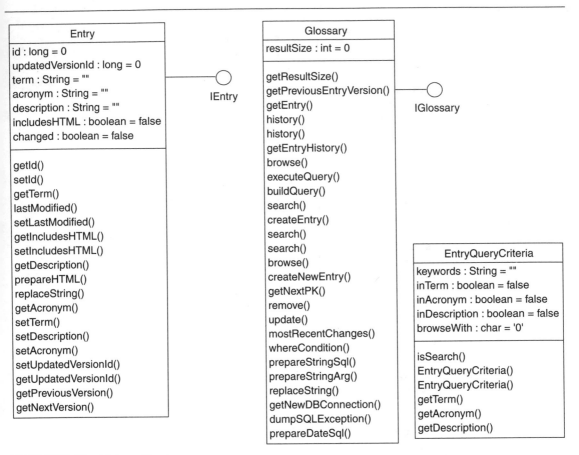

FIGURE E-13 Main entity classes

been successfully used with SQL Server, Oracle 8, and even MS Access. The only real requirement is to support standard SQL and to have a JDBC (Java Database Connectivity)-compliant driver.

Figure E-14 shows the database diagram, which contains two tables: PK and Entry. The PK table is simple and is used for primary key creation. One column in this table contains the name of another database table—in this case, there is only one row for the Entry table. The other column is an integer-type column that keeps the value of the next primary key for the table. To get a new primary key, the application must lock the row, get its value, increment it by 1, and then unlock the row.

The Entry table contains all the attributes of the glossary entry. Versions are managed by a self-referential foreign key (FK). When this FK is null, the entry row is considered to be the current version. When this row is updated, the columns in the row are not updated; rather, another row is inserted into the database, and the FK of the original

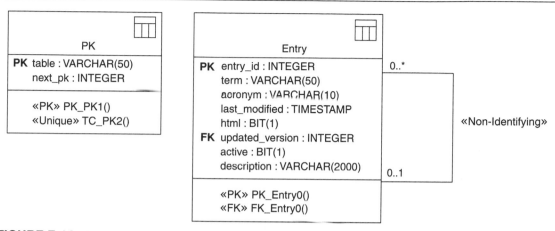

FIGURE E-14   Logical data model diagram

row is set to the new row. This simple mechanism for versioning database rows works well enough for an application like this, with an expected low volume of use.

Component View

The top-level package view of the application's component is shown in Figure E-15. In this diagram, the «virtual root»/glossary defines the application's URL hierarchy, and the «physical root» Glossary defines the physical location of all JSP files that are requestable by the browsers. This diagram shows the component package hierarchy for the additional Java classes (`app.glossary.taglib`) and two reference Java packages that are part of the JDK and J2EE specifications.

Some of the requestable URLs are implemented with servlets instead of JSPs. Because the physical location of servlets is bound to their package hierarchies in the component view, «HTTPResource» elements are created to map these servlets into the URL space under the virtual root (Figure E-16).

The components under the physical root (Figure E-17) make up the rest of the requestable HTTP resources. These components are modeled with «JSP» components, with one «static page» and one «script library» component.

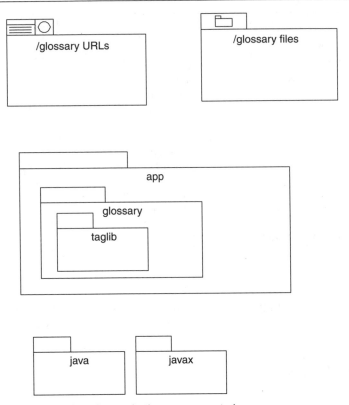

FIGURE E-15   Top-level packages in the component view

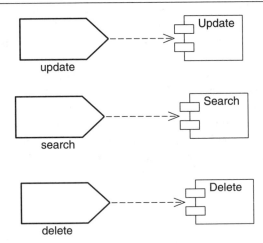

FIGURE E-16   «HTTPResources» elements mapped to the system's servlets

FIGURE E-17   «JSP» components in the «physical root»

Sample Screen Shots

Figures E-18 through E-22 are screen shots the user would view at different points in the Glossary application.

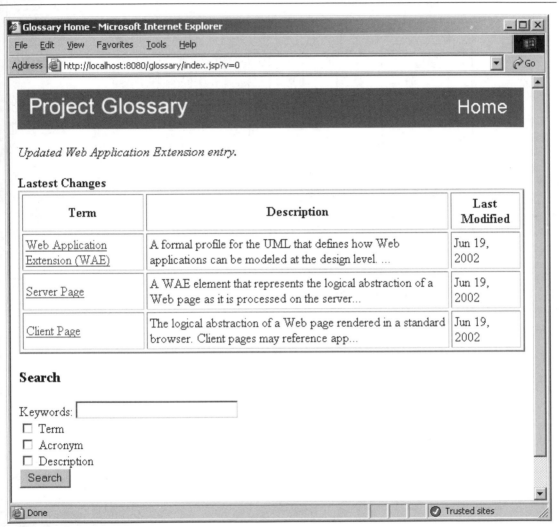

FIGURE E-18   The Glossary home page, showing a message of the most recent user activity and the most recent definition changes

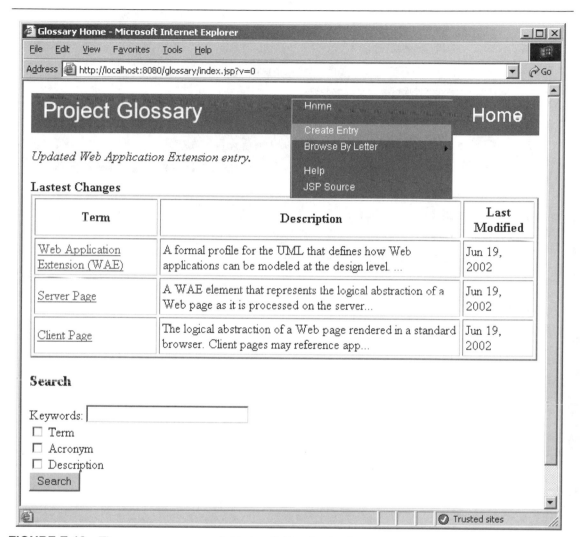

FIGURE E-19   The pop-up menu, available by clicking the top banner

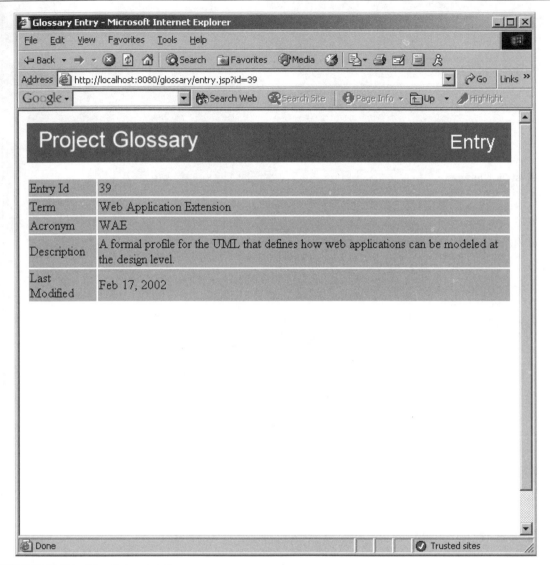

FIGURE E-20   The Entry details screen

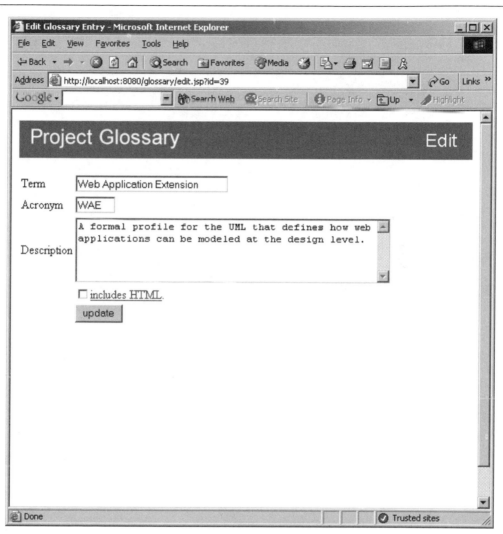

FIGURE E-21   Edit Entry screen

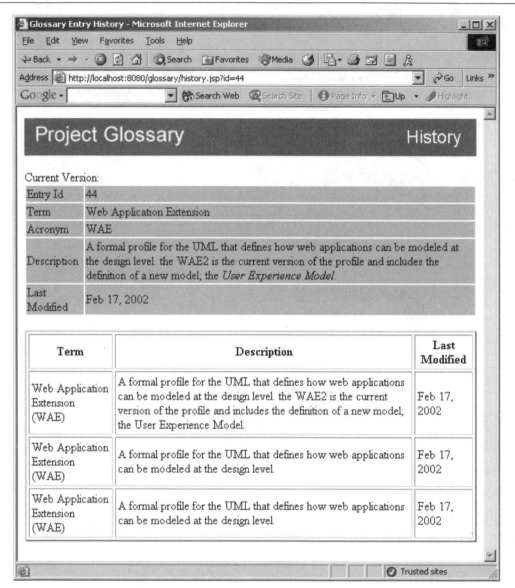

FIGURE E-22   An Entry History screen, showing version history

Index

Rational Minds and Addison-Wesley Authors—
What a Combination!

DEVELOPING ENTERPRISE JAVA APPLICATIONS WITH J2EE™ AND UML
KHAWAR ZAMAN AHMED
CARY E. UMRYSH
Foreword by Grady Booch

0-201-73829-5

USE CASE MODELING
KURT BITTNER
IAN SPENCE
Foreword by Ivar Jacobson

0-201-70913-9

OBJECT-ORIENTED ANALYSIS AND DESIGN WITH APPLICATIONS
GRADY BOOCH
SECOND EDITION

0-8053-5340-2

OBJECT SOLUTIONS
MANAGING THE OBJECT-ORIENTED PROJECT
GRADY BOOCH

0-8053-0594-7

THE UNIFIED MODELING LANGUAGE USER GUIDE
GRADY BOOCH
JAMES RUMBAUGH
IVAR JACOBSON
The ultimate tutorial to the UML from the original designers

0-201-57168-4

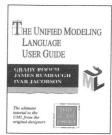

Software Leadership
A Guide to Successful Software Development
Murray Cantor

0-201-70044-1

BUILDING WEB APPLICATIONS WITH UML SECOND EDITION
JIM CONALLEN
Foreword by Grady Booch

0-201-73038-3

DRAFT COVER AS OF 4/02
BUILDING J2EE APPLICATIONS WITH THE RATIONAL UNIFIED PROCESS
PETER EELES
KELLI HOUSTON
WOJTEK KOZACZYNSKI
Foreword by Philippe Kruchten

0-201-79166-8

IVAR JACOBSON
THE OBJECT ADVANTAGE
BUSINESS PROCESS REENGINEERING WITH OBJECT TECHNOLOGY

0-201-42289-1

Ivar Jacobson
COMPUTER LANGUAGE Productivity Award Winner 1992
Object-Oriented Software Engineering
A Use Case Driven Approach

0-201-54435-0

SOFTWARE REUSE
Architecture, Process and Organization for Business Success
Ivar Jacobson • Martin Griss • Patrik Jonsson

0-201-92476-5

THE UNIFIED SOFTWARE DEVELOPMENT PROCESS
IVAR JACOBSON
GRADY BOOCH
JAMES RUMBAUGH
The complete guide to the Unified Process from the original designers

0-201-57169-2

THE RATIONAL UNIFIED PROCESS AN INTRODUCTION SECOND EDITION
PHILIPPE KRUCHTEN

0-201-70710-1

MANAGING SOFTWARE REQUIREMENTS
A UNIFIED APPROACH
DEAN LEFFINGWELL
DON WIDRIG
Foreword by Ed Yourdon
"The most practical book ever written on requirements. The authors have obviously 'been there.' A must read for every practitioner."
—Al Davis, Omni-Vista, Inc.

0-201-61593-2

UML FOR DATABASE DESIGN
ERIC J. NAIBURG
ROBERT A. MAKSIMCHUK
Foreword by Grady Booch

0-201-72163-5

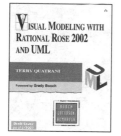
VISUAL MODELING WITH RATIONAL ROSE 2002 AND UML
TERRY QUATRANI
Foreword by Grady Booch
Draft Cover as of 4/02

0-201-72932-6

SOFTWARE PROJECT MANAGEMENT
A UNIFIED FRAMEWORK
WALKER ROYCE
Foreword by Barry Boehm

0-201-30958-0

THE UNIFIED MODELING LANGUAGE REFERENCE MANUAL
JAMES RUMBAUGH
IVAR JACOBSON
GRADY BOOCH
The definitive reference to the UML from the original designers
CD-ROM included

0-201-30998-X

SOFTWARE CONFIGURATION MANAGEMENT STRATEGIES AND RATIONAL CLEARCASE®
A PRACTICAL INTRODUCTION
BRIAN A. WHITE
Foreword by Geoffrey M. Clemm

0-201-60478-7

For more information on these books by Rational Software Corporation employees, please go to **www.awprofessional.com**

Wouldn't it be great

if the world's leading technical publishers joined forces to deliver their best tech books in a common digital reference platform?

They have. Introducing
InformIT Online Books
powered by Safari.

■ **Specific answers to specific questions.**
mIT Online Books' powerful search engine gives you relevance-
ed results in a matter of seconds.

■ **Immediate results.**
h InformIT Online Books, you can select the book you want
view the chapter or section you need immediately.

■ **Cut, paste and annotate.**
te code to save time and eliminate typographical errors.
ke notes on the material you find useful and choose whether
ot to share them with your work group.

■ **Customized for your enterprise.**
stomize a library for you, your department or your entire
anization. You only pay for what you need.

et your first 14 days **FREE!**
a limited time, InformIT Online Books is offering its
bers a 10 book subscription risk-free for 14 days. Visit
//www.informit.com/onlinebooks for details.